EARLY IRISH GOLF

The First Courses, Clubs and Pioneers

JUN 1990

WILLIAM H. GIBSON

OAKLEAF PUBLICATIONS

796.352/315005

Published by Oakleaf Publications,
Two-Mile-House, Naas, Co. Kildare.

Hardback ISBN   0 9513724 0 8
Paperback ISBN   0 9513724 1 6

First edition: 1988

Cover: The background is the Eglinton (Montgomery) Tartan, worn by a competitors in the first British Open (*see also p. 37*).

Cover design and colour separations by Masterphoto, Dublin.
Typeset in CG Times by Omega Typesetting Ltd., Newbridge, Co. Kildare
Printed by the Leinster Leader Ltd., Naas, Co. Kildare.

For Mary, Mary-Clare, Deirdre
Robert and William.

i

Early Irish Golf

CONTENTS

Early Irish Golf

SOURCES OF ILLUSTRATIONS

The author wishes to acknowledge, with thanks, permission received from the following sources for reproduction of photographs and prints:

BBC Hulton Library, 37.
Miss Susan Balfour, 41(c).
Bord Fáilte, vii(t), viii(t), viii(b), ix(t), ix(b), x(t), rear cover.
George M. Colville D.C.M., 30(b).
Golf Illustrated, 46, 49, 53, 110(t).
Martyn Turner, xix, xx, xxi, xxii, 18, 66, 80.
Northern Ireland Tourist Board, vii(b), x(t).
Ordnance Survey Ireland, 36.
Portmarnock G.C., 226.
Prestwick G.C., 23(l), 28.
Ransomes, Sims and Jefferies P.L.C., 96, 97.
Royal Belfast G.C., 40(r), 40(l), 56, 119.
Royal Musselburgh G.C., 29.
Royal Portrush G.C., 110.
The Argyll & Sutherland Highlanders, 35.
The Blackwatch Regiment, 63.
The British Museum Library, 2(t), 6(b).
The Golfing Union of Ireland, 52.
The Irish Field, 48, 84(t).
The Illustrated London News Picture Library, 22, 30(t), 34.
The Irish Golfer, 50, 61, 68(b), 73.
The Irish Ladies Golf Union, 116.
The Kings Own Scottish Borderers, 43.
The National Library of Ireland, 68(t), 81, 117, 123, 137, 174, 176, 192, 195, 204, 207, 220, 235, 239, 244.
The Queens Bays Regiment, 23(r).
The Royal Highland Fusiliers, 41(l), 41(r).

Early Irish Golf

INTRODUCTION

A London taxi driver who recognised his fare as Bertrand Russell seized the opportunity of a lifetime and asked the philosopher: "What's it all about, then?" Recounting the story afterwards, the cabbie added in a tone of indignation mixed with sarcasm and contempt: "Do you know — he couldn't tell me!" The taxi driver should have asked a journalist. We newspapermen are trained to produce the instant reaction and a basic question about the nature of the universe and the meaning of life would be a doddle, turning on a flow of plausible, amusing and slightly cynical wine-bar wisdom.

In my own field of golf writing the tyrannical deadline admits of no second thoughts, no reflection in tranquility and, if the major excitement occurs late in the day, as it mostly does, not even time to commit one's thoughts to paper before reaching for the telephone. One of my colleagues, to be identified only by the name of Jack, once received a return call from the sports editor shortly after dictating his report. "Great stuff," said the sports editor, "but we must have some quotes from the player." "Certainly," said Jack, "put me over to the copy-takers." He then proceeded to dictate a series of cogent, pithy and witty remarks with which to embellish his previous report. Hearing this exchange, I taxed him with having invented every word on the spot. "Of course," he said with as much dignity as he could muster, "but I am a professional and when I make up quotes I always say what the player would have said if he had been bright enough to think of it."

This discourse is not a bid for sympathy nor even a plea for understanding of the appalling problems which golf writers have to face every day. Rather it is a background briefing to explain my envy of scholars and historians. William Gibson wrote to me some years ago when he embarked on the task of setting the record straight about early Irish golf in general and the origins of the Curragh Golf Club in particular. Our correspondence was more useful to me than to him, I fear, and at the time I mused on the difference in our situations. If I had been commissioned to write a piece on early Irish golf I would have had to make a quick sweep through my library, sit down at the typewriter and finish by lunchtime. How satisfying it must be, I thought, to have the time to follow up every lead, to browse among the records, to pursue the faintest of clues and to accumulate the proof which separated fact from mythology. And not just time, for such work also requires deep commitment, patience, organisation and a profound knowledge of the subject. At this point I abruptly terminated my contemplation of the comparative greenness of the other man's grass because I realised that I had conjured up a false vision. I was comparing my lot with that of a professional historian enjoying a fat endowment from a scholarly foundation for a research project. But William Gibson is a serving officer in the Irish Army, latterly occupied with keeping the peace in the Lebanon. He had to make the time for this extra work which was clearly a labour of love. The wonder is not that he did it so well as that he managed to do it at all. We should all be grateful because this book fills an important gap in the history of golf and in the social history of Ireland.

I am particularly pleased at the publication of a definitive and readable book about my favourite golfing country but there is another selfish, professional reason why I shall read it over and over again. My kind of writing, which is supposed to be informed and of necessity must be done on the instant, often in airport lounges and hotel bedrooms, is known in the trade as "sucking it out of your thumb". A book such as this provides the juice of truth and a distinctive flavour for thumb-sucking.

15th September 1987   PETER DOBEREINER

Chelsfield Hill House,
Chelsfield Hill,
Platts Bottom,
Nr. Orpington, Kent.

NORTHWEST GOLF CLUB, LISFANNON, CO. DONEGAL (1891)
(Courtesy Bord Failte)

ROYAL PORTRUSH GOLF CLUB, CO. ANTRIM (1888)
(Courtesy Northern Ireland Tourist Board)

LAHINCH GOLF CLUB, CO. CLARE (1892)

(Courtesy Bord Failte)

BALLYBUNION GOLF CLUB, CO. KERRY (1896)

(Courtesy Bord Failte)

ROSAPENNA GOLF CLUB, CO. DONEGAL (1895)

(Courtesy Bord Failte)

PORTMARNOCK GOLF CLUB, CO. DUBLIN (1894)

(Courtesy Bord Failte)

ROYAL CO. DOWN GOLF CLUB, CO. DOWN (1889)
(Courtesy Northern Ireland Tourist Board)

CURRAGH GOLF CLUB, CO. KILDARE (1883)

(Author)

MRS. CHRISTINA ADAMS, GRAND-DAUGHTER OF DAVID RITCHIE.
Photographed on 13th July 1982 holding the Curragh G.C. Commemorative Trophy, which had been instituted in honour of her grandfather's game at the Curragh on 15th July 1857.
(*See pages 17, 18 and 19*)

Early Irish Golf

LIST OF MAPS

The Author gratefully acknowledges the assistance given by Bord Failte in preparation of maps on pages xvii and xviii.

Early Irish Golf

LIST OF ILLUSTRATIONS

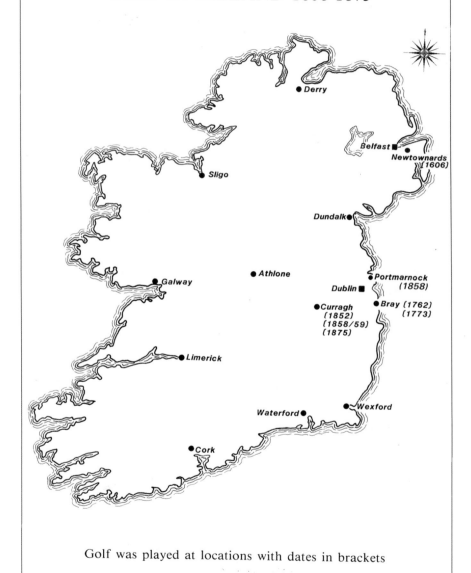

GOLF IN IRELAND 1606-1875

Golf was played at locations with dates in brackets

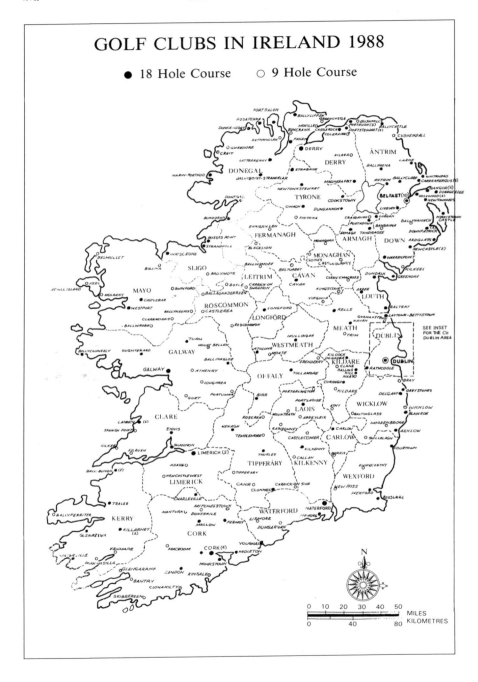

GOLF CLUBS IN IRELAND 1988

● 18 Hole Course   ○ 9 Hole Course

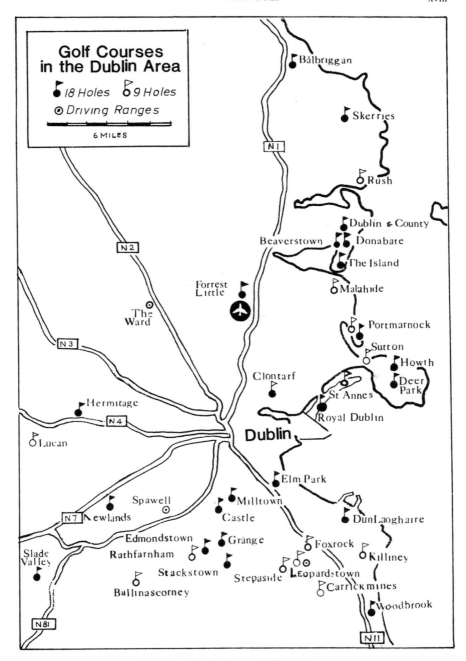

Golf Courses in the Dublin Area

● 18 Holes ⚐ 9 Holes
◉ Driving Ranges

6 MILES

Bálbriggan

Skerries

N1

Rush

Dublin & County

Beaverstown
Donabate

The Island

Forrest Little

Malahide

The Ward

N2

Portmarnock

N3

Sutton

Howth

Clontarf

Deer Park

St Annes

Hermitage

Royal Dublin

N4

Dublin

Lucan

Elm Park

Spawell

Milltown

Newlands

Castle

DunLaoghaire

N7

Edmondstown

Grange

Rathfarnham

Foxrock

Killiney

Slade Valley

Stackstown

Leopardstown

Stepaside

Carrickmines

Ballinascorney

Woodbrook

N81

N11

IRISH GOLF COURSES 1988

c1500 Early Dutch Golf (page 1)

1762:

1606: Students at Goff, Football and Archery (page 5)

Golfing and Dining at Bray (page 9)

1900: Galway golf duel (page 170)

1881: "The Tearing of the Green"
(page 76)

1888: Portrush's Early Golfers (page 50)

1917: The Tillage Act (page 91)

Early Irish Golf

PREFACE

From the first mention of the game of "goff" in the era of the Hamilton and Montgomery plantation of Ulster in 1606 there has been a lamentable lack of documentation of this favourite Irish sport. Many Irish clubs have lost their earliest records and their "founding fathers" are unknown in many cases. There is controversy regarding exact dates of institution of some of these clubs which are now beginning to celebrate their centenaries and, in many cases, the locations of their earliest courses are unknown. The present writer has spent six years researching in Ireland, Scotland and England; as far is possible, this book is the most complete account of the early evolvement of the game in this country.

Ireland's oldest club celebrated its centenary in 1981. Royal Belfast was not the first club in this country, as will be seen; however, when the Captain of the Curragh Golf Club returned from the celebrations he asked the present writer to carry out research on this Co. Kildare club, whose early records were missing. Visits to the National Library of Ireland and Trinity College, Dublin, revealed that no definitive account of the origins of the game in Ireland existed. One or two early golf guide books carried conflicting material on the Curragh club itself and the daunting task of researching back through the early newspapers and magazines was undertaken with reluctance, initially, but with growing enthusiasm for the project when one gleaming nugget after another, of early Irish golf history, was unearthed. Much crucial information was only available from sources in Scotland and England. The major Irish libraries do not possess many of the early golf publications which were published between 1883 and 1923. Throughout the pages of this book the newspapers, books and magazines of the period are allowed to speak for themselves. In this way the style and opinions of the early commentators are allowed to tell the story in their own words.

With so many Irish clubs due to celebrate their centenaries over the next twenty years it became clear that a framework on which their histories could be based was required. There were many early sponsors for the development of the game in Ireland, especially the Scottish Regiments and expatriates from the land of the thistle, who carried their love of the game here. There were many initial difficulties for these early golfers in the political, social and economic climate of the period. A debt of gratitude is owed to the early Scots and Irish pioneers who persisted with the propagation of the game.

It is not intended to document the histories of the Golfing Union of Ireland or the Irish Ladies Golf Union, only insofar as these two bodies fostered the early development of the game. In due course the history of these two Unions will be published, which will chart the history of competitive golf in this country. This book documents the rise of Ireland's earliest golf champions but it is not proposed to compile the statistical lists; these are already available in several recent publications.

In many cases Irish clubs will find definitive material on their origins which has not been available to them before now. The reader will find much material on the early influences which led to the rapid expansion of golf in the Ireland of the 1890s. From an early date, a healthy sense of humour was associated with the playing of the game in this country and the reader will find many instances of this in the impish contributions of Lionel Hewson. This man was an outstanding chronicler of the game in this country for over fifty years, from 1905.

Only clubs founded prior to 1923 are documented in this book; the present research has been limited to this period. In 1922 the new Irish State came into existence; it was a period of great social tension which culminated in the withdrawal of the British Army from the greatest part of the country. Irish golf had passed through its most testing years and great maturity was displayed by the Golfing Union of Ireland and the Irish Ladies Golf Union at that time. The administrators of the game in Ireland continue to exercise the undivided attention of all Irish golfers. Long may it continue so.

As a major sponsor of championship golfing events in the Irish golfing calendar, we are pleased to be associated with the publication of this remarkable book on early Irish golf — the culmination of over seven years research and writing by Comdt. Gibson. It is a truly outstanding contribution to our knowledge of the origins of the game in Ireland.

Manager Ireland,

Thomas Cook Travellers Cheques.

Early Irish Golf

FOREWORD

The formation of the character of a golf club develops naturally upon its traditions and, as the years race by, pride of achievement gives rise to reflections of the past and to a desire to confirm those traditions by historical facts.

It is unfortunate that, very often, a sense of history matures only when those who initiated that history are no longer with us to recall the facts. It is therefore very fortunate that someone with commitment, tenacity and patience was prepared to dedicate so much time researching and writing about the foundations of Golf in Ireland. The Author, Commandant William Gibson, has surely displayed these qualities.

What started out some years ago as a quest to trace the origin of the Curragh Golf Club — the History of which he had been requested to write — developed into a crusade to assist other Irish Clubs in ascertaining their roots.

Like the Curragh, many of our courses were laid out for the recreation of the members of Scottish and English Regiments stationed here up to 1922. Commandant Gibson deserves the highest commendation for his single-minded dedication to discover the locations and authentic origin not only of those with a military association but of every other course over which golf was played in Ireland up to that time.

Already a small number of our affiliated clubs have attained their Centenary. Soon, many more will join this exclusive group and any historian faced with the task of writing the history of his club will welcome the information contained in "Early Irish Golf".

On behalf of the Golfing Union of Ireland, and on my own behalf, I compliment the Author on producing a really valuable and interesting reference book.

—DESMOND REA O'KELLY,
Honorary Secretary,
Golfing Union of Ireland.

Introduction of Golf to Ireland — 1606

It is near Prestwick, on the west coast of Scotland, that the story of golf in Ireland began nearly four hundred years ago when a Scottish adventurer, from that area, set his heart on an area of Ulster. The repercussions of the fulfilment of his desires are with us to this day.

James VI of Scotland had succeeded to the English throne, on the death of Elizabeth I in 1603, at a time when Ireland was recovering from the defeat at Kinsale. Around this time Hugh Montgomery, Laird of Braidstane, near Ayr, had become interested in acquiring some land in Ireland. There are many accounts of how he actually achieved his aim but there is no doubt that Montgomery and another Scottish adventurer, James Hamilton, had managed to acquire the greater portion of the Ards Peninsula for themselves from the luckless Con O'Neill by 1606.

Hugh Montgomery was born circa 1560 of a very ancient Scottish family which traced its ancestry back to Normandy. Some of the family must have been with William The Conqueror when he invaded England in 1066 and they settled in south-west Scotland. One branch of the family became the Earls of Eglinton and another became the Lairds of Braidstane. Hugh Montgomery was the sixth Laird and was well educated, having been a graduate of Glasgow University. It is of some interest to note that he had served in the Scottish Regiment in Holland as a captain under Philip, Prince of Orange, the great-grandfather of King William III.[1] At that time a form of golf was very common in Holland and Montgomery may have been exposed to the game of "colf", as it was known there.

DUTCH COLF

Over the past century controversy has continued when the origins of golf are discussed, any suggestion that the game began anywhere other than in Scotland was strongly opposed by many learned commentators. However, Mr. Steven J. Henger Van Hengel's book *Early Golf*, published in 1982, is a major work of historical research into golf in the Low Countries which leaves little doubt that the origins of the modern game had Dutch roots. In his book Van Hengel shows that a game called Colf was played around the village of Loenen, in Holland, in 1296, by eight players with wooden clubs. There were four players on each side who struck a wooden ball in turn for the minimum of strokes for each "hole". The course measured 4500 metres for the four holes. This game continued to be played for 550 years until 1831 when part of the course was demolished.

DUTCH COLFERS C. 1500

Colf was played in other areas of Holland as is evidenced by the many references to the game in old charters and maps. One of the many illustrations of this game is to be seen in a picture from a *Flemish Book of Hours* in the British Library, London, of the period c. 1500-1510. Here one can see a fourball playing golf in the countryside, with a clubhouse (?) in the background. One of the players has adopted an unorthodox stance to putt the ball into the hole.

Many of the great Dutch and Flemish artists painted their countrymen playing the game, especially in winter scenes, where they can be seen playing golf on ice.

SCOTTISH GOLF — 17th CENTURY

Prior to 1650 golf had been played in many areas of Scotland. On the 6th March 1457 King James II had to issue an Act of Parliament by which he decreed that ". . . the fute-bal and golfe be utterly cryed down, and not to be used . . ."[2] The Scotsmen had become so devoted to football and golf at this time that the skills of archery were becoming forgotten. This of course could not be allowed to continue and the act provided for the setting up of archery butts beside every parish church in order to keep up the training of men who would be mobilised in time of war. Ardent Scots golf enthusiasts will argue that their "golfe" predates this famous sporting prohibition but Scottish records of the game do not exist prior to this date.

In *Inveresk Parish Lore From Pagan Times*, published in 1894, Mr. R. M. D. Stirling writes: "It is to be remembered that intercourse between Holland and Scotland came at that period (15th century) to be very friendly. The herring shoals had deserted their old haunts and had found their way to the British coasts. The maritime instincts of the Dutch, and the improvements they had introduced into the process of curing naturally sent them in pursuit of the harvest of the sea and it became their interest to keep in the good graces of those upon the shores where they plied their calling. The prosperity of Holland owes not a little to its trade in salt herrings, at a time when cured fish were in universal request as food upon the fast days enjoined by the church. To the Firth of Forth Dutch luggers accordingly came and a brisk trade sprang up with Musselburgh. Evidence of it is still patent to everybody in the 'knockhouse' and clock of the 'honest town'."[3]

In his book, Van Hengel points out many other early connections between the two countries, including the fact that between 1574 and 1826 Scottish mercenaries served in the forces of the States General in great numbers. Many of those Scotsmen married Dutch women and marriage registers in the Netherlands between 1574 and 1665 record 4,800 of these.[4] As early as 1486 Dutch ball makers were exporting balls to Scotland, when a "Ritsaert Clays" paid 6 groats toll at the toll station at Bergen-op-Zoom for the export of one barrel of balls in the ship captained by Per Bolle.[5]

These Dutch balls would have been either wooden or of white sheepskin leather, filled with cows hair. By 1618 the import of Dutch balls had obviously become a drain on the reserves of the Scottish Bourse for on the 5th August that year a royal decree was issued[6] ". . . no small quantity of gold and silver is transported yeirly out of his Hienes' Kingdom of Scotland for buying of golf balls". James Melville was granted, with some others, the right of making balls within the Kingdom and all others were prohibited from making or selling them for the space of twenty-one years.

The King in question here was James VI of Scotland (1567-1625) who had succeeded to the English throne in 1603 on the death of Queen Elizabeth I and thus became James I of England, of which more will be heard later. One of his favourite pastimes was playing golf and in a letter dated 14th April 1603 he appointed ". . . William Mayne, during all the days of his lyftyme . . . clubmaker to his Hienes".[7] James' mother, Mary Stuart (Mary Queen of Scots) had also been a golfer and it is recorded in the lore of Scotland that "in the fields beside Seton"[8] she played at golf and Pall Mall with Bothwell after the murder of her husband Darnley on 10th February 1567.[9] Mary Stuart is the earliest recorded lady golfer.

In their excellently researched book, *Golf In The Making*, Henderson and Stirk make the point that golf "remained confined to the East Coast of Scotland until the nineteenth century".[10] Van Hengel also states "in fact it never reached the West Coast of Scotland before 1850".[11].

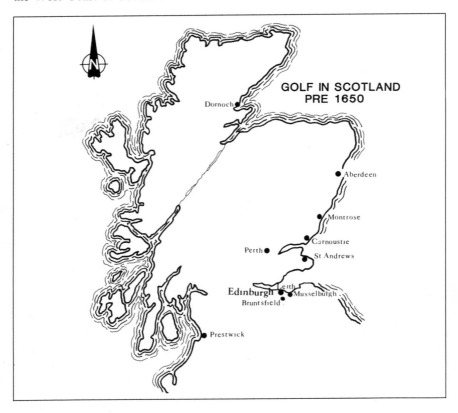

The map above shows the areas of Scotland where golf was played prior to 1650, all locations except one are on the East Coast and they include Musselburgh, Bruntsfield,[12] Leith,[13], St. Andrews and Carnoustie.

Van Hengel also points out that "all the places where golf was played in (at that time) are on the side facing the low countries . . . and were ports which traded across the sea with the low countries.[14]

However, away on the west coast of Scotland, in the vicinity of Prestwick there has always been the tradition of a famous game of golf played many centuries ago . . . "there is the well known match for his nose between a monk of Crossraguel and a Lord of Culzean. The match was played at Prestwick. The monk lost. He may have been a Cardinal because they were much more common in Scotland than they are now. The story accordingly must be true because there the Cardinal's Nob exists to this day as a lasting monument to the poor monk's nose".[15]

PLANTATION OF ULSTER 1606

By 1606 James Hamilton and Hugh Montgomery had acquired the greater portion of the Ards peninsula for themselves. Both men had been close to the new King James I and he gave the royal sanction for the adventure. Hamilton settled in the area of Bangor where he built ". . . a fayre stone house . . . about 60 foote long and 22 foote broad . . .".

The Montgomery clan's traditional base was in the present county of Ayrshire in Scotland. It is quite likely that Hugh Montgomery had been exposed to golf in his home environment, which was close to the links where the monk had lost the match for his nose. The acknowledged head of the clan was the Earl of Eglinton and Hugh had pledged himself and his successors "to present to the head of the house of Eglinton a horse, worth £30, in testimony of the feudal superiority of the latter".[16] The Earl of Eglinton of a later era had a major role to play in the history of golf, as will be outlined in future chapters.

Montgomery's colonisation of his newly acquired lands is clearly documented in *The Montgomery Manuscripts* ". . . First of all he sent over to Donaghadee before him some hewn freestone, timber and iron etc. of which he caused to be built a low stone walled house for his reception and lodging when he came from or went to Scotland. Mariners, tradesmen and others had made shelter for themselves before this time but the Viscount's was the first stone dwelling in all the parish . . . The said first Viscount Montgomery[17] also wholley repaired the church of Greyabbey . . . His Lordship also built the quay or harbour at Donaghadee a great and profitable work, both for public and private benefit, and built a great school at Newtown, endowing it, as I am credibly told, with twenty pounds yearly salary, for a Master of Arts, to teach Latin, Greek and Logycks, allowing the scholars a green for recreation at goff, football and archery . . ."[18]

Here we can see the first recorded mention of "goff", or golf, in Ireland. Montgomery was a keen sportsman himself as his chronicler recounts ". . . but he delighted little in soft easy recreations (fit only, he said, for ladies and boys), from his youth taking most pleasure in the active sports which the tennis court, the foyles, the horse, the dogs or fowling piece gave him . . ." [19] That "goff" is specifically mentioned in Montgomery's plans for the school at Newtownards certainly indicates his appreciation of the sport. He must surely have played the game himself and the legends of ancient golf in the Prestwick area [20] bear testimony to mediaeval golf in Ayrshire.

The Plantation of Ulster was commenced by James I in a systematic way in 1609, when he saw the success of the Montgomery and Hamilton estates. Over 40,000 settlers were attracted to the Province between 1610 and 1630. A diligent, hardworking and mainly Scotch Presbyterian group, they soon transformed the land of Ulster. It is not beyond the bounds of credibility that among these newcomers there were other keen "goffers" and possibly lying somewhere in an old family chest in Ulster there are other memoirs of early golf in Ireland.

Nothing more is recorded of golf in the Newtownards area until late in the nineteenth century, with the modern golf boom. The locality of the Montgomery plantation was devastated in the rebellion of 1641 and the school would appear to have been a victim of that period. One of the legends of that time is the manner in which Charles I (1600-1649) learned of the Irish rebellion. John Gilbert depicted this Stuart king (son and successor to James I) receiving the news while playing golf on Leith links near Edinburgh. [21]

CHARLES I, WHILE PLAYING GOLF ON LEITH LINKS, RECEIVES NEWS
OF THE BREAKING OUT OF THE IRISH REBELLION

FOOTNOTES

1. *A Genealogical History of the Family of Montgomery*, page 38.
2. *The Golf Book of East Lothian*, page 26.
3. "Honestas" is the motto of the town of Musselburgh.
4. *Early Golf*, page 3.
5. *Early Golf*, page 51.
6. *Golf Book of East Lothian*, page 39.
7. *Ibid.*, page 39.
8. East of Edinburgh close to Musselburgh.
9. *Golf Book of East Lothian*, page 35.
10. *Golf in the Making*, page 20.
11. *Early Golf*, page 33.
12. Probably the earliest painting of Scottish golf depicts golfers on Bruntsfield links near Edinburgh, in 1746, by Paul Sandby R.A., *Golf in the Making*, page 14.
13. Considered by many to have been the earliest Scottish links, it ceased to exist in the nineteenth century.
14. *Early Golf*, page 2.
15. *Prestwick Golf Club, A History and Some Records*, page 2. Robert Browning also relates this story in his *A History of Golf*. In addition he relates how Kennedy of Bargany had a "laigh", i.e. a flat or broken nose due to "one straik of ane goiff ball on the hills of Air in recklesnes".
16. *Montgomery Manuscripts*, page 111.
17. *Complete Peerage*, pages 138-139. Montgomery was knighted on 15 May 1605 at Richmond and created Viscount Montgomery of the Great Ardes on 3 May 1622.
18. *Montgomery Manuscripts*, pages 119-129. A very comprehensive account of the Montgomery plantation, which was compiled by William Montgomery of Rosemount Co. Down circa 1696-1706.
19. *Ibid*, pages 119-120.
20. *Prestwick Golf Club, A History and Some Records*, page 2.
21. The interest in golf continued through the Stuart family down to Bonny Prince Charlie who was born in Rome in 1720. In 1738 Lord Elcho encountered the Prince and his brother Henry playing golf at the Borghese gardens in Rome. (*The History of the R&A*, page 17).

Golf in the 18th century — Scotland, Ireland and United States of America

Although golf had been played from at least the 15th century in Scotland, there is no evidence of the existence of "Club" or "Society" golf there or elsewhere prior to the 18th century. It was in Scotland that the first golf clubs as we know them, with records, came into being. Royal Blackheath, near London, claims 1608 as its foundation date. However, in the *Irish Golfer* of 4th April 1900 the Editor has this to say — "Blackheathens must pardon me if I cavil at their ancient and honourable traditions. I am very far from wishing to do so. But since it seems to be generally accepted as a fact that the club dates from 1608, it is surely not unreasonable to ask for proof. Golf is, of all things, an accurate game. If we accept unsupported traditions we shall be no better than the angler who swears by the big pike or monster salmon — which escaped him."[1]

Here we can see the dilemma for the golf historian who is confronted with the claims of ancient folklore. Tangible proof of antiquity is required by the sceptic and in the realms of claims to seniority and standing of a club, surely the Editor of the *Irish Golfer* was correct. The controversy still continues, however, and in Scotland the age of certain clubs has been challenged due to lack of documentation or other supporting evidence. At present the following are the generally accepted institution dates of the oldest Scottish Golf Clubs.[2]

Edinburgh Burgess	1735
Honourable Company of Edinburgh Golfers	1744
Royal and Ancient Golf Club of St. Andrews	1754
Bruntsfield Links Golf Club	1761
Royal Musselburgh Golf Club	1774
Royal Aberdeen Golf Club	1780
Glasgow Golf Club	1787

The Royal Musselburgh Golf Club does not have its earliest minute books, but does have independent evidence of existence from, at least, the claimed date. Each year members of the club continue to compete for the old Club Cup which dates from 1774 and to which is attached a medal by the winner every year since first competed for. (In itself the existence of a cup from 1774 would indicate the foundation of a club prior to that date, but no claim is made for an earlier institution date). The earliest minute books of the club date from 1784.

IRELAND'S FIRST GOLF CLUB — 1762

The reader might ask why a discussion on the relative age of Scottish clubs is relevant to golf in Ireland in the 18th century. Modern golf records show that the oldest golf club in Ireland is the Royal Belfast Golf Club which came into existence in 1881. There is little doubt, now, that it certainly was not the first Irish golf club! *Faulkners Dublin Journal* No. 3704 of 23rd October 1762 carries the following intriguing notice:

> "The Goff Club meet to dine at the house of Mr. Charles Moran at Bray on Thursday the 28th October, at half an hour after three o'clock.
>
> ELIAS DE BUTTS, Esq. in the Chair."

Here then is the first known mention of the existence of a "goff" or golf club in Ireland. The date 1762 is also quite significant, as the club (which may have had an earlier foundation date) would be at least fifth in the seniority of Scottish golf clubs. We may never know who Mr. Charles Moran was or the location of his house, but Elias De Butts was the only son of Rev. Elias De Butts of Castlemaine, Co. Kerry, descendant of a Huguenot family.[3] He had been born in 1726, educated at Trinity College and three times married. There were no children of the first marriage, five sons resulted from the second marriage to Ann Cromie and there was one daughter from the third marriage to Martha Bennet. Sadly no other record of his golfing days were left but he is the first known and named golf club member in Ireland. (The De Butts name will be mentioned again later in chronicling the development of Irish golf in the 1880s — see Chapter 5).

The location of the actual golfing terrain at Bray is no longer a mystery due to the availability of some further evidence. In *Saunders News Letter* of 3rd May 1773 the letting of a house at SEAFIELD BRAY is advertised. Among the many virtues of the property is that it is "bounded on the East by a Common, famous for that manly exercise called Goff".

SEAFIELD, near BRAY.

TO be Tet for a Term of Years, and entered upon immediately, being a genteel Country Seat in complete Repair, within nine Miles of Dublin; the House is convenient for a large Family, and hath Locks, Grates, with all necessary Fixtures in every Room, beside the Kitchen; one of the Parlours is large, with a Bow Window to the Sea; there are 31 Acres of choice Land well divided and quicked, with a large Garden walled round, and planted with Fruit Trees, Offices of all Kinds strongly built and slated; it is near the Church, Market, and two yearly Fairs at BRAY, well situated for the Goats Whey, for Bathing, Boating, and Fishing, bounded on the East by a Common, famous for that manly Exercise called GOFF. Inquire of Mr. Thomas Cusack, Auctioneer, in Montague-street, Kevin's-port, who can shew a Map of the Premises.

Here we can see that the Bray golfers were playing on a "Common"[4] which, sadly, no longer exists in its original form. From a second documentary source the location of this area can be pinpointed as being the present seafront promenade area of Bray.

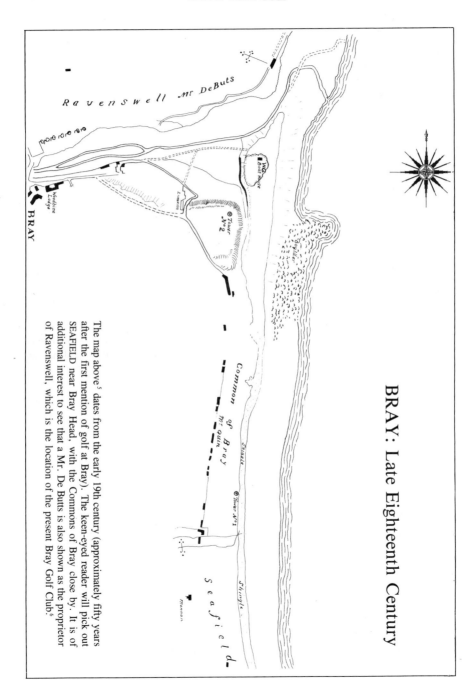

BRAY: Late Eighteenth Century

The map above[5] dates from the early 19th century (approximately fifty years after the first mention of golf at Bray). The keen-eyed reader will pick out SEAFIELD near Bray Head, with the Commons of Bray close by. It is of additional interest to see that a Mr. De Butts is also shown as the proprietor of Ravenswell, which is the location of the present Bray Golf Club.[6]

From the above we can see that in the relatively peaceful conditions prevailing in Ireland in the mid 18th century a colony of golfers had established themselves in Bray. The auctioneer dutifully extols the fine property of Seafield as being "well situated for the goats' whey for Bathing, Boating and fishing, bounded on the East by a Common famous for that that manly exercise called 'goff'" certainly descriptive of a settled seaside resort. Many questions arise on reading these newspaper accounts — where had the inspiration come from to establish golf at this location? Was there a Scottish influence? What happened to the club and its golfers? How many holes did they play over? Quite possibly the agrarian and political struggles leading up to the rebellion of 1798 ended the idyllic existence of Elias De Butts and his companions. He died in 1800 and it has not been possible to trace any further documentation of this pioneer, the first known club member in Ireland.

PRE-19th CENTURY GOLF IN THE U.S.A.

Henderson and Stirk in their excellent book, *Golf in the Making*, devote a section to the arrival of golf in the U.S.A. These writers state ". . . It has generally been accepted that the first organised golf of the new era was played by what became the St. Andrew's Club at Yonkers in 1888, organized by John Reid, often regarded as the father of U.S. golf. There is old documentary evidence of the Dutch playing golf in New York when it was a Dutch Colony . . . Recent research into the Port of Leith (Edinburgh) records has disclosed a large shipment of 96 clubs and 432 balls to Charleston, South Carolina, in 1743. This was a time when the first Societies or Clubs were being formed in Scotland. In due course the South Carolina Golf Club was formed (in 1786), followed by the Savannah Golf Club in 1795 — the only surviving evidence of which is the invitation to a Miss Eliza Johnston to a ball given by the members of the Club on 20th Dec. 1811."[7]

Here we can see a situation in the United States which parallels the Bray background, with clubs being founded there in the 18th century, but little tangible evidence remaining.

FREEMASONRY AND EARLY GOLF CLUBS

Henderson and Stirk in their *Royal Blackheath*[8] maintain that Freemasonry had much to do with the formation of the early Scottish golf clubs and Royal Blackheath itself. By its very nature Freemasonry is secretive, with great importance being attached to the maintenance of confidentiality concerning the rites and secrets. (From very early times the Royal Family has had close ties with the Freemason movement and this was true of the Stuart period).[9]

It is possible that golf in the Southern U.S. States and Bray may have had a Masonic connection, whereby the records would have been deliberately destroyed on the break-up of the clubs in order to preserve the code of Freemasonry. It can be said here that the present research into golf in Ireland has not revealed any direct connection with Freemasonry.[10]

FORMATION OF EARLY CLUBS

Mr. J. Cameron Robbie, the historian of the Royal Burgess Golf Society of Edinburgh, gives a credible account of how the first golf clubs came into existence. In the context of a golf club in Bray in the mid 18th century, the theory certainly seems to match the few known facts . . . "In Scotland by the end of the seventeenth century, the inhabitants of many places had a prescriptive right of playing golf on certain areas usually termed 'commonities'. Already possessing this right, there was no need of a club to provide it, and of that the early golfers took advantage and exercised their rights. But obviously, congenial society and private matches at specified times were essential for complete enjoyment. The players would dine together at a convenient inn, where as regular clients they would be regarded as a society of golfers and given the personal attention usually accorded to consistent customers . . . of course no one had need for rules except as to regulating the payment of the dinner bill and perhaps bets. This may have been the beginning of some of our prominent clubs . . ."[11]

The historian of the Royal Musselburgh Golf Club had this to say of the 18th century activities of his club. ". . . The Society, Company or Club (all of these terms were used in the early records) met in the local inns and taverns in the afternoon for Dinner,[12] − preceded by the matches entered in the Club Match Book at the previous meeting, usually foursomes arranged for 12 noon; these were played for 'neither more nor less than 6d each hole . . . and no wager above Ten Shillings and Six pence shall be laid upon any match that shall be entered in the books' . . . it could have been said that the Company of Golfers was rather a Dining Club, which held monthly meetings. The dinner which was timed for about 3.30 p.m. to 4.00 p.m. being preceded by the playing of matches arranged at the previous meeting. . . . Dining, wining and fining formed the greater part of the Club regulations and Laws . . ."[13]

The story is told of a group of golfers of a famous Scottish club of that period who were dining after their game of "gouff". Too much claret had been drunk by all and an unfortunate servant received the unwelcome attentions of the gentlemen by being ejected from an upstairs window. The very worried proprietor went to one of the party and enquired as to what he was to do with the waiter who had been injured. To which he received the immortal reply "Put him on the bill".

In this way we can imagine the golfers of Bray at their play, followed by dinner at the house (tavern?) of Mr. Charles Moran − a very pleasant way of passing the time with friends.

FOOTNOTES

1. *The Irish Golfer*, edited by J. W. Percy — a wonderful organ of early Irish golf journalism.
2. Source of these dates — *Golf in the Making*, pages 41 and 42.
3. *The Landed Gentry of Ireland* — Burke, page 223.
4. The playing of golf on commons land in 18th century Scotland was a notable "common" factor, e.g. Aberdeen, St. Andrew's, North Berwick, Musselburgh.
5. N.L.I. Call No. 16 J 17 (2).
6. Founded in 1897.
7. *Golf in the Making*, pages 34 and 35. The *Irish Field* of 7th March 1914 carried an interview with Mr. A. H. Findlater on early golf in America: ". . . the game was a public nuisance in the open spaces of Fort Orange (which is in Albany N.Y.) in 1659'. Van Hengel records the following: "The 'Small Bench of Justice' of Fort Orange and the village of Beverwyck (now Albany N.Y.) saw fit to issue an ordinance in 1659 for that area, forbidding golf along the roads at a fine of 25 guilders. The reasons — you could guess them by now! — were, damage to window panes in houses, the chance of hurting passers by and the blocking of streets." (*Early Golf*, page 31).
8. *Royal Blackheath*, pages 7 to 16.
9. The *Cork Examiner* 22nd February 1883 reported: "The Press Association is informed that the Prince of Wales (later Edward VII) will again be proposed for re-election as Grand Master of the English Freemasons on March 17th". The Royal Family's ties with Freemasonry are outlined in *The Brotherhood*, pages 211 to 215, by Stephen Knight (1983).
10. The only indirect evidence will be found in a newspaper article of 1865, see footnote 20 to Chapter 4.
11. *The Chronicle of the Royal Burgess Golf Society of Edinburgh 1735-1835*, pages 5 and 6.
12. The Bray Club obviously met in the house of Mr. Charles Moran in similar manner.
13. Privately printed *History of Royal Musselburgh Golf Club*, prepared by Mr. Robert Ironside for his bi-centenary year of captaincy (1974).

CHAPTER 3

Golf in Ireland − 1852 to 1857

THE BEGINNING OF THE NEW ERA

Between 1800 and 1852 a total of 16 golf clubs were founded of which all but two were Scottish (the others were Manchester 1817 and Royal Calcutta 1829). [1] When it is considered that in 1800 the number of clubs already in existence was 7, [2] it can be seen that the pace of golf development was relatively slow. The main cause of the sudden surge of interest in the game from the mid 1800s was the discovery of the "gutty" golf ball and an improvement in living standards due to the industrial revolution, with more time for personal recreation. Prior to this period, from at least 1743, [3] the Scots had mainly used the "feathery" type of ball. Elias De Butts and his friends would have played "featheries" at Bray in 1762.

The making of a feathery ball was a difficult time-consuming process. Tom Dunn, who married the daughter of one of the most famous feathery ball makers − John Gourlay of Musselburgh (of whom much more will be written in this chapter) − stated "It was considered good work if a man could turn out three feather balls in a day. The case was of cowhide and a high hat full of feathers, in their loose and dry state, was needed for the stuffing. These were dumped and crammed into the three parts finished case and sewn up". [4]

The major feather ball makers were Allan Robertson and Tom Morris at St Andrews, the McEwans of Musselburgh, the Gourlays also of Musselburgh and Johnny Jackson of Perth. [5] By all accounts they made a reasonable living but in 1848 a revolutionary discovery was made when it was found that the milky juice of the gutta percha tree in Malaya was suitable for fashioning into a golf ball. [6] The substance hardened on exposure to air and was already in use in Malaya for making the handles of knives, whips and hoes. [7] It was noticed that the gutta percha could be softened and refashioned by immersion in hot water.

It is generally accepted that the gutta percha ball made its first appearance at Blackheath Golf Club (London) in 1848 [8] and was brought to the premier Scottish golf clubs in that year. The new discovery had a dramatic effect, for the old featheries had cost up to 2/6d (12½p) each (Gourlays were the premier balls) whilst the new balls cost only one shilling (5p); furthermore the gutta could be softened and hammered back into shape when badly worn. In fact it was found that the gutta flew better when it had been cut from play and players deliberately scored the balls' surface to assist it. Everybody in Scotland was delighted with the new discovery, except the "feathery" ball makers. James Balfour in his *Reminiscences of Golf* states "We at once wrote off to London some of these balls and went to Musselburgh to try them. Gourlay the ball maker had heard of them and followed us on round. . . . He was alarmed." Gourlay

did not hesitate, as we learn. . . . "It has often been related that the first thing
he did after seeing the gutty fly was to fulfill a standing order from Sir David
Baird (founder Captain of North Berwick) for featheries, sending him nine
dozen. Sir David as a result was playing the feather ball long after his partners
had moved onto the new ball."[10]

This new invention reduced the cost of playing golf and many new recruits
took to the game. One of the most famous golfing songs was written at this time
in celebration of the new ball, some of the more pertinent verses are herewith
reproduced from Robert Clark's classic book, *Golf: A Royal and Ancient Game*
(1893).

IN PRAISE OF GUTTA PERCHA

*Sung at the Meeting of The Innerleven
Club – 1st September 1848.*

Of a'the changes that of late
Have shaken Europe's social state
Let wondering politicians prate
And 'bout them mak a work a'
A subject mair congenial here
And dearer to a golfer ear
I sing the change brought round this year
By balls of Gutta Percha.

Though Gouf be of our games most rare,
Yet truth to speak, the tear and wear
O'balls was felt to be severe,
And source of great vexation,
When Gourlays balls cost half a crown
And Allans not a farthing down
The feack o'wad been harried soon,
In this era of taxation.

They say it comes frae yont the sea
The concrete juice o'some rare tree[11]
And hard and bonny though it be,
Just steep it in hot water –
As soft as potty soon twill grow
Then 'tween your loofs a portion row –
When cool a ba' ye'll get, I trow
That ye for years may batter.

EVOLUTION OF THE GOLF BALL FROM FEATHERY TO GUTTA
(Note Gourlay balls)

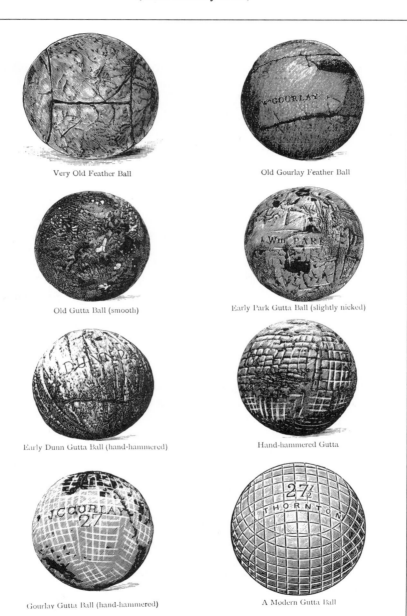

Very Old Feather Ball

Old Gourlay Feather Ball

Old Gutta Ball (smooth)

Early Park Gutta Ball (slightly nicked)

Early Dunn Gutta Ball (hand-hammered)

Hand-hammered Gutta

Gourlay Gutta Ball (hand-hammered)

A Modern Gutta Ball

GOLF ON THE CURRAGH 1852 – DAVID RITCHIE

The story of the discovery of golfing activity on the Curragh in the 1850s began with a gutta percha ball. In a letter to *The Irish Field* of 3rd October 1908 Mr. E. I. Gray* stated . . .

> It may interest you and "L. L. H.," to know, that I have authentic proof of their being a golf course on the Curragh, near the famous Donnelly's Hollow, in the year 1857, and that I have a ball that was used at the time, given my by the player who is to-day hale and hearty. This same old gentleman, I may state, was a member of the Musselburgh Club, Edinburgh, in 1845, so he can claim to be one of the oldest, if not the oldest golfer in Ireland. Apologising for trespassing so much on your valuable space.—I remain, yours faithfully,
> E. I. GRAY.
> Naas, September 25th, 1908.

The Irish Field 3rd October 1908.

. . . "It may interest you and LLH[12] to know that I have authentic proof of there being a golf course on the Curragh, near the famous Donnelly's Hollow, in the year 1857, and that I have a ball that was used at the time given me by the player who today is hale and hearty. The same old gentleman, I may state, was a member of the Musselburgh Club, Edinburgh in 1845, so he can claim to be one of the oldest, if not the oldest golfer in Ireland . . ."

This intriguing letter is a key item of documentary evidence for the next phase of Irish golf which had all but been forgotten until research began in 1981. The story of this old gutta[13] ball had been carried in subsequent newspaper articles including in *The Irish Field* of 14th November 1942 when J. P. Rooney wrote a piece on the occasion of the destruction by fire of the Curragh Clubhouse. In the article Rooney states: ". . . As a matter of fact, four years prior to the formation of the Curragh (Camp) there existed a course near Donnelly's Hollow not far from the Kildare plain; but, unfortunately, an historic document revealing that fact is no longer available.

"Some years ago I came across this document and, naturally, handed it over to Royal Dublin. It was in the shape of an old gutty ball, with label attached, on which was written 'STRAFFAN, Co Kildare. THIS BALL WAS PLAYED BY ME IN A MATCH WITH THE LATE ALEXANDER LOVE ON THE LINKS NEAR DONNELLY'S HOLLOW,[14] Curragh on July 15th 1852 Signed: DAVID RITCHIE".

Rooney continued later in the article to relate what happened to this priceless relic ". . . The gutty ball and the label attached to it disappeared from the mantelpiece at Dollymount, and with them the only existing evidence that golf was played in the Hollow in those days".

At this point it is important to review some of the above matters.

    1. In 1908 an old man, a former member of Musselburgh Golf Club (near

*Editor and proprietor of the *Kildare Observer*, Naas.

Edinburgh) had given Mr. E. I. Gray of Naas an old gutta ball dated 1857 which had been played on a golf course at the Curragh in that year.

2. In 1942 J. P. Rooney, golf writer of *The Irish Times*, and of the *Irish Field*, stated that he had come into possession of important documentary evidence relating to golf on the Curragh in the form of an old "gutty" ball with a certificate dated 15th July 1852 signed by a David Ritchie.
3. Rooney stated that the ball had disappeared from a mantelpiece in Royal Dublin Golf Club.[15]

MARTYN TURNER'S CARTOON FOR CURRAGH COMPETITION 15th JULY 1982
125th anniversary of David Ritchie's golf match.

It will be noted that there was a difference in dates mentioned (1852-1857) but in July 1982 the committee of the Curragh Golf Club decided to mark the 125th anniversary of the 1857 date with a commemorative competition. Dermot Gilleece, the golf correspondent of *The Irish Times*, carried the story in his column on the 13th July and that evening a phone call to the Curragh Golf Club transformed the event into a major celebration. Mrs. Christina Adams had been an avid reader of *The Irish Times* for most of her 89 years and had read in amazement that morning of the competition to be held on the Curragh. Her grandfather had been the said David Ritchie and she, being seventeen years old when he died in 1910, had known him well.

The present writer had a memorable meeting with her the following morning and, among other items, he was given the picture of David Ritchie which now hangs in a place of honour in the Curragh Golf Club. Mrs. Adams also had a scrapbook belonging to her mother Christina which contained several old cuttings from newspapers of the 1920s and 1930s. [16] Also included was David's death notice in the *Kildare Observer* of 17th September 1910 which stated ''He claimed, and we believe rightly, so to be the oldest golfer in Ireland, as he had ample proof of playing with the late Mr. Alexander Love on links he organised at Donnelly's Hollow, Curragh, in the early fifties of the last century''. Another unreferenced newspaper article in the scrapbook was even more specific as J. P. Rooney had been contradicted by Tom Ritchie (David's son) who had told him ''. . . that the ball must be one of a few his father brought from Edinburgh in 1851. He added that in 1853 his father laid out a course at the Curragh, in the vicinity of the 'Slaughter House'. There was no 'camp' there at the time, the troops being under canvas. . . . Mr. David Ritchie, however, found it difficult to induce the officers to play the game; as a matter of fact although there were two Scottish Regiments stationed there, he could get only a few to go a round.''

DAVID RITCHIE (1824-1910)
Founder of first golf course at the Curragh
in 1852.

Here one can see that David Ritchie, at last, had been revealed as the originator of the first course on the Curragh in the early 1850s. (It will be shown that the son, Tom, erred by one year in the date of the first course). Other verifiable facts reflect the accuracy of the above articles. The Curragh Camp was not built until 1855, as a result of the need for extra accommodation for troops being trained for the Crimean War (1853-56). Any troops using the Curragh plains prior to that would have been under canvas. [17] The slaughter house mentioned was the Commissariat Butchery (now Military Abattoir) constructed in 1855. This was within 300 yards of Donnelly's Hollow and has given its name to the 15th hole of the present Curragh course. [18] Why the game did not continue to be played is not revealed in the scrapbook articles, nor could Mrs. Adams throw any light on the matter. However, further evidence was to reveal much more concerning the game on the Curragh in the 1850s!

DONNELLY'S HOLLOW, CURRAGH
Site of David Ritchie's course 1852. Note present 15th tee in background.

FIELD ARTICLE 1875

The librarian of the R&A, Mr. R. A. L. Burnett, was able to produce the next key to unravelling the story of this forgotten era. This article from *The Field* of 11th September 1875 is the first printed account on the new era of Irish golf to have appeared and contains much invaluable information. It had been written by Major Alexander Cunningham Bruce of the 91st (Argyll) Highanders who had been sent to his regiment then stationed in Ireland, when commissioned in June 1852.[19]. As a consequence he was able to write . . .

CURRAGH CAMP GOLF LINKS.

Many years have passed since the national Scottish game of golf has been played on the beautiful plain of the Curragh of Kildare. Memory carries us back to the days of yore, when his excellency the Earl of Eglinton used to come from Dublin Castle to play a round of the links with his friend and professional compatriot Col. Campbell, Queen's Bays, and many a hard fight these two golfers—now, alas! byegones—had to win their last hole for the game. Since those days this fine pastime has been forgotten, until chance placed on the roster for duty on the Curragh the gallant 91st Highlanders, among whom are many good players. It is now hoped that the golfers of this regiment have inaugurated a permanent stand for the game, and each succeeding season may see a renewal of golf on the Curragh by the regiments stationed there during the summer manœuvres. The links, as now laid out, are very judiciously chosen, following the run of the plain to advantage. A few more bunkers and dangers might be encompassed by extending the links to include furze breaks—a gravel pit being the only obstacle that requires "getting well over." The links number twelve holes, and the distance round nearly two miles, passing over the ground lying to the front or north of the camp, near the head quarter hut, and bearing to the left, by the cricket ground, to the grave but, and returning with a slight detour.

Some matches have lately been played, with the following results: Mr Colin Campbell and Mr Middlemas against Mr Craufurd and Major Borrowes, the latter couple won three games in succession, through the forward play of the former partner, and the fourth game was even all at the eleventh hole, when a Tom Morris tee shot of Mr Colin Campbell placed the ball so favourably that victory fell to that side without much difficulty. Major Bruce and Major Borrowes lost a match of two rounds (twenty-four holes) by one hole to Mr Crawfurd and Mr Middlemas. Mr Craufurd and Mr Collings gained a match, one round, from Capt St. Clair and Major Borrowes, five to the good.   THE CADDY IN SCARLET.

Extract from *The Field* 11th September 1875.

"Many years have passed since the National Scottish game of golf has been played on the beautiful plain of the Curragh of Kildare. Memory carries us back to the days of yore, when his excellency the Earl of Eglinton used to come from Dublin Castle to play a round of this links with his friend and professional compatriot Col. Campbell Queens Bays, and many a hard fight these two golfers − now, alas, byegones − had to win their last hole for the game. Since those days this fine pastime has been forgotten, until chances placed on the roster for duty on the Curragh the gallant 91st Highlanders, among whom are many good golfers . . ."

THE LINK TO 1852

Without question the above information was of vital importance, Major Bruce had been a witness and probably a participant to a forgotten era of Irish golf. The Earl of Eglinton had been twice Lord Lieutenant of Ireland, from March to December 1852 and again from 13th March 1858 to 4th July 1859. It was a question of determining in which of these two periods of office he had played on the Curragh. This was easily resolved because the service records of the Queens Boys Regiment[20] showed that they had arrived in Ireland on 14th July 1852 and had been posted to Newbridge. The commanding officer was Lt. Col. William Campbell and the entire regiment had been posted to India in July 1857 on the outbreak of the Indian Mutiny.[21] There is no doubt that it was through the summer and autumn of 1852 that these two Scottish friends had played golf together on the Curragh.[22] This in turn was an independent source of evidence for the claim in David Ritchie's obituary and also in his son Tom's claim that his father had laid out a course on the Curragh in the 1850s. That he had erred by one year (1852 *not* 1853) is evident but understandable.

THE EARL OF EGLINTON

Who was the Earl of Eglinton? If the reader casts his mind back he will see the historical connection to 1606. Archibald William Montgomerie (1812-1861) was the 13th Earl of Eglinton whose family home was at Eglinton Castle in Ayrshire. He was one of the keenest golfers in Scotland of that era, having been founder Captain of Prestwick Golf Club in 1851, Captain of North Berwick in 1838 and, in the year following his first visit to Ireland, in 1853, would become Captain of the Royal and Ancient Golf Club of St. Andrews.

The Illustrated London News
19th October 1861.

Eglinton mentioned a recent visit to the races at the Curragh in a letter he wrote to Lord Naas on 22nd April 1852 (NLI MS 11031). This is the only evidence in his own hand of a visit to the area, regrettably there is no mention of golf in any of his diaries. Further details on the subsequent golfing activities of the Earl will be seen in Chapter 4.

LT. COL. WILLIAM CAMPBELL

Lt. Col. William Campbell (c. 1815-1858) was from Craigie[23] in Ayrshire and had been commissioned in 1832. Information on him is very scanty and his regiment does not have any details concerning his golfing activities. The picture in their records is herewith reproduced as is the photograph of a Col. Campbell which hangs among the Captains portraits in Prestwick Golf Club. The latter picture[24] when compared with the former is clearly the same person — the Captain of Prestwick Golf Club of 1854, Lt. Col. William Campbell of the Queens Bays Regiment and listed as a founder member of that club.[25] He is also recorded in the minute books of the R&A on 18th October 1848 — "The Captain proposed Lt. Col. Campbell, younger of Craigie (as a member), seconded by Sir J. McKenzie".[26] The Captain of the R&A in 1848 was James Wolfe Murray of Cringletie, a name which will be heard of in a later chapter.

COLONEL CAMPBELL
Captain Prestwick Golf.
Club 1854.

LT. COL. WILLIAM CAMPBELL
Commanding Officer Queen Bays
Regiment, Newbridge, 1852.

1850s – SCOTTISH IMMIGRATION

David Ritchie certainly had illustrious companions for his inaugural year of playing golf on the Curragh, he had come to Ireland in 1851 and his grand-daughter stated that at least one brother had accompanied him.[27] Arising from this research the fact that a sizeable Scottish immigration into Ireland in the 1850s had occurred became evident.

In a pamphlet printed by Thoms in 1858 entitled *The Social State of Ireland 1858*[28] Mr. Thomas Miller related his success in settling 660 natives of Scotland and 96 English within the previous ten years and stated ''. . . it is in the County of Kildare where they are located in the largest groupings and more especially in the vicinity of Athy, in the neighbourhood of which place about forty of them are settled . . .''. It is clear that David Ritchie had not come alone to Ireland. It is not inconceivable that at least some of these Scotch immigrants were also golfers who would have used the course near Donnelly's Hollow.

THE SHORTGRASS COUNTY[29]

One of the major factors which would have inspired David Ritchie and his Scotch contemporaries to play golf on the Curragh would have been the advantage of all-the-year-round short grass. Another factor of course would have been that the plains are a ''common'' and in 1852 the Crown's rights to the Curragh had not yet been finally established and this would not be so until the Curragh of Kildare Act was passed in 1868. The perennial problem of long grass in Summer, without the means to keep it under control had militated against the spread of golf and this was the reason why most of the golf "links" at that time were located in close proximity to the sea on the links land, with its associated sanddunes and sandtraps.

To find a large common, well grazed by sheep, with a wide variety of terrain and hazards in the form of gorse, old quarries and areas of casual water, all in the area of Donnelly's Hollow, must have been a heartwarming discovery. The sheep themselves would have been a hazard to be taken account of and one wonders if any local rules were introduced on this account.

SIGNIFICANCE OF THE DATE OF DAVID RITCHIE'S GOLF BALL

The date which David Ritchie recorded on his famous gutta ball, namely 15th July 1857, has certain significance when a variety of facts are analysed:

1. Lt. Col. William Campbell had been one of the first 1852 golfers as has been seen. He and his regiment had a variety of postings in Ireland viz. to Dublin in April 1853, to Dundalk in April 1854, back to Dublin in September 1855 and from there to Liverpool en route to India on 11th July 1857.[30] Campbell obviously retained close connections with the County Kildare area for he is pictured in the famous painting of the Corinthian Cup at Punchestown in 1854 by Michael Angelo Hayes R.H.A.

2. The Curragh Camp was built in 1855 and strength returns of the period of 1855 to 1858[31] show up to 10,000 troops there. The presence of so many troops, among them cavalry, caused friction in the area among the local farmers and sheepmen until eventually The Curragh of Kildare Act 1868 was passed which laid down the Crown's rights and privileges, whereby the presence of the military camp was legalised.

3. Lt. Col Campbell was a very active golfer as it is clear that his military service in Ireland had not prevented his being Captain of Prestwick in 1854. The question arises as to how he could have travelled to the Curragh for golf at this time (while stationed in Dublin and Dundalk). There is no doubt that he would have travelled by railway, as the Dublin to Cork railway (with a siding at the Curragh) was opened in 1849 and the trip to the Curragh was less than an hour.[32]

It is this writer's opinion that in recording the date of 15th July 1857, on his gutta ball, David Ritchie was hanging up his golf accoutrements, having found that the military presence in the Donnelly's Hollow area inhibited the playing of golf. His influential military acquaintance Lt. Col. William Campbell had departed Ireland, with his regiment, for service in India only four days beforehand. With his departure David Ritchie must have felt isolated and would not appear to have played golf on the Curragh after that date. However golf *did* continue on the Curragh in the 1850s as is clear from the next crucial item of evidence which will be seen in the following chapter. That the Scottish influence had resulted in the making of at least one other Irish golfing location in the 1850s will also be revealed.

FOOTNOTES
1. *Golf in the Making,* 41-42.
2. *Ibid.*
3. Prior to this date wooden balls were also in use in both Scotland and Holland, however, it is generally accepted that by 1743, when Thomas Mathison had written his poem "The Goff" and therein described the making of the feathery ball, that the demise of the wooden ball had occurred.
4. *The Life of Tom Morris*, page 61.
5. *Ibid.*, page 60.
6. There is controversy over who first introduced the gutta percha golf ball. *Golf in the Making* covers this matter in great detail.
7. *Golf in the Making*, page 48.
8. *Reminiscences of Golf at St. Andrews Links*, page 17.
9. *Ibid.*, page 17.
10. *In The Winds Eye* (History of North Berwick Golf Club), page 25.
11. *The Illustrated London News* of 9th April 1853 reported that it took 10 trees to yield one picul i.e. 135½ lb. of solid gutta and that the destruction of trees between January 1845 and the middle of 1847, when no fewer than 6.918 piculs were sent from Singapore to Europe, must have resulted in the vast number of 69,180 trees being sacrificed. It was only later that the colonists found they did not have to cut down the tree to get the precious liquid but could "tap" the tree and thereby drain off the liquid gutta as required.
12. Lionel Hewson, a famous golf writer for *The Irish Times* and *The Irish Field* in early 1900s – editor of *Irish Life*, editor of *Irish Golf.*
13. Prior to 1880 the ball was composed of mainly gutta percha and consequently the name "gutta". After 1880 different types of compounds were mixed into the gutta percha and were called "gutty" balls to distinguish them. With the passage of time the two terms have become synonymous.
14. A well-known landmark close to the 15th (Abattoir) hole in the present Curragh Golf Club.
15. Writing in his *Irish Golfers Blue Book* published in 1939 Rooney states that the ball was picked to bits by penknives in Royal Dublin "as they were 'curious' to see what it was made of"!
16. Unfortunately most of the Ritchie scrapbook cuttings were undated, nor was the name of the relevant newspaper recorded.
17. The Curragh had been used as a military camping area on many occasions over the centuries, especially during the Napoleonic era.
18. See note 14 above.
19. *Army Lists 1852* and letter from Lt. Col. P. G. Wood, regimental secretary The Argyll and Sutherland Highlanders dated 24th August 1982. The 91st Highlanders were in Dublin from March 1853 to September 1854 having been in Enniskillen, Cavan and Charlemont before that. They departed from Cork in December 1854 for service in Malta.
20. The Queens Bays Regiment (2nd Dragoon Guards) were amalgamated with the 1st Kings Dragoon Guards on 1st January 1959 to form The 1st The Queens Dragoon Guards. Information supplied by Mr. B. Thirkhall, Regimental Curator.
21. *A History of the Queens Bays*, page 125.

22. *Ibid.*, page 151. Lt. Col. Campbell died in India on 10th July 1858 near Cawnpore and was certainly not in Ireland for Eglinton's second tour.
23. *Burkes The Landed Gentry*, page 285.
24. Received by courtesy of Mr. R. A. Clement, Captain Prestwick Golf Club 1983.
25. *Prestwick Golf Club, A History*, page 73.
26. Letter from librarian R&A H 13/2 dated 17th January 1983.
27. Parish records of the Church of Ireland, Kill, Co. Kildare document the baptisms of several children born to Thomas and Alice Ritchie of Newtown, Kill in the 1890s. This would not have been David Ritchie's son Tom, as his wife's name was Mary. The flyleaf of the Ritchie scrapbook, now in the writer's possession, is inscribed "TO INA RITCHIE (MRS. ADAMS MOTHER) FROM HER COUSIN TOM, NEWTOWN 26 OCTOBER 1871."
28. NLI, P770(16).
29. County Kildare is known as the "shortgrass county" because of the Curragh with its short grass.
30. *A History of the Queens Bays*.
31. W O 17/1120, 1121, 1122.
32. It is evident that the Earl of Eglinton also travelled to the Curragh by train for in a letter dated 22nd April 1852 to Lord Naas (NLI MSS 11031) he states . . . "I was well received at the Curragh, but I was much annoyed at being escorted by a body of mounted police, with drawn swords, from the Station to the Stand . . .". In this case Eglinton was attending the Curragh races as he was a keen racing fan. See Chapter 4 footnote 9.

CHAPTER 4

Golf in Ireland — 1858 to 1875

In Chapter 3 the golfing activities on the "links"[1] near Donnelly's Hollow were outlined and it can be seen that there was no evidence of the formation of a club at that time, unlike the Bray evidence of 1762. In this chapter the reader will not find a claim for the foundation of a club but will see very clear indications of the existence of organised golf on the Curragh in the period 1858 and 1859.

THE INTRODUCTION OF THE GAME INTO IRELAND

Correspondence.

THE INTRODUCTION OF THE GAME INTO IRELAND.

TO THE EDITOR OF THE IRISH GOLFER.

SIR.—During the course of a recent holiday amongst the Cheviot Hills, and by

"Tweed's fair river, broad and deep."

I spent some time near the historic village of Norham, which takes its name from the adjoining "castled steep" so well described by Scott in his ode, "Marmion, a Tale of Flodden Field."

One evening, with my host, I called to see a friend there—Mr. Andrew Smith-Maxwell, who has passed the allotted span, and, although approaching four score years, has not found life to consist of labour and sorrow, but is still bright and chirpy, able to enjoy a good game of golf. Speaking on that interesting topic, Mr. Smith-Maxwell, who had known many of the past masters of the Ancient and Royal game, said that he believed he was the first to introduce it into Ireland. It appears that when Lord Eglinton was Lord Lieutenant here, between March, 1858, and June, 1859, he missed the pleasures of Prestwick Links, where he had been in the habit of playing.

Mr. Andrew Smith, who afterwards took the name of Maxwell, as his mother was heiress to the estate of Sir John Maxwell, was then stationed at the Curragh with the 2nd Royal Lanarkshire Militia. A Major Harrington, of that regiment, was acquainted with Colonel Hamilton, of the Viceregal Staff, and it was conveyed to Mr. Smith that His Excellency was anxious to have a links laid out. Accordingly, Mr. Smith arranged with Gourlay, a golf ball maker, of Musselburgh, to come over, and between them the first links were laid out at the Curragh. When ready for play, Lord Eglinton came down with members of his staff, and after a round had luncheon, which

was provided at the grand stand on the racecourse. After justice had been done to the good things provided, Lord Eglinton turned to Mr. Smith and asked did he know what a golfer's luncheon consisted of. He was promptly answered yes – bread, cheese, and a bottle of stout. "Well," said His Excellency, "that's what I want when I come again. I have plenty of this– pointing to the champagne, etc.—at the Castle."

For some time Lord Eglinton came down once a week, and, as he wished to have perfect retirement, his only companions were usually Colonel Hamilton, Major Harrington, and Mr. Smith, but as Major Harrington was an indifferent player, the professional Gourlay sometimes took his place in the foursomes. Mr. Smith-Maxwell very kindly presented me with two iron clubs, one of which was used on these occasions. It was made by Hutchison, N. Berwick, and does not differ very much from those now made, except that the shank is somewhat long.

It would be interesting to know whether there

is any record of the game having been regularly played in Ireland prior to 1858.—Yours, etc.,

ARTHUR W. BEATTY,
Portmarnock Golf Club.
54 Grosvenor-square, Rathmines, Dublin,
3rd September, 1903.

[Mr. John Jameson, father of the present Mr. John Jameson, of St. Marnock's, Portmarnock, had a private links of 9 holes extending from St. Marnock's to the red tiled boathouse near the fifteenth hole of the Portmarnock links some 45 years ago, which would be about the time golf was played at the Curragh.—Ed. I.G.]

Confirmation of revival of golf on the Curragh in 1858.

A letter from Mr. Arthur W. Beatty of Portmarnock Golf Club which was published in the *Irish Golfer* of 9th September 1903, provides clear documentary evidence of a major development of the game of golf in Ireland. The Earl of Eglinton's previous golfing activities in Ireland were outlined in Chapter 3 and therefore the claim by Mr. Smith Maxwell to have been the first to introduce the game into Ireland would not be correct. However, all of the other information in the article is verifiable and is of paramount importance in documenting an otherwise forgotten era of Irish golf.

The Earl of Eglinton had come back to Ireland in early March 1858 during his second term as Lord Lieutenant. The 2nd Royal Lanarkshire Militia had arrived on the Curragh on 6th April 1858[2] and Lt. Smith Maxwell with Major Harrington were officers of this Scottish Regiment.

MAJOR WALTER FERRIER HAMILTON

Major Walter Ferrier Hamilton of the Royal Ayrshire Rifles, mentioned in the article, was an aide de camp[3] to the Earl of Eglinton and there is no doubt that he too was a keen golfer. In 1851 he had been a founder member of Prestwick Golf Club with the privilege of being Captain of that club in 1855.[4] In 1856, when Prestwick Golf Club proposed the establishment of a golf tournament for Scotland he was one of three members (Major Fergusson and Capt. Fairlie were the others) appointed to look after the organisation of it.[5] His grandniece, Mrs. J. B. Findlay, states that his mother was a daughter of Lord Gort which gives an Irish connection; in addition, he was "a racy speaker and perhaps, like so many, he drank a bit too much".[6] Surely a strong Irish element in his character. Unfortunately he did not leave any papers or diaries.

MAJOR W. F. HAMILTON
Golfer on Curragh 1858
Captain Prestwick Golf Club 1855.

JOHN GOURLAY 1815-1869

Without doubt the discovery that one of the top professionals of that era had come over to the Curragh, in 1858, to lay a course is of extreme importance. John Gourlay's name had already been mentioned as being a premier feather ball maker of the pre-1850 period. He followed in his father William's footsteps in the family ball making business at Musselburgh. Douglas Gourlay, his grandfather, had been ballmaker at Bruntsfield, Edinburgh, in

JOHN GOURLAY
Musselburgh professional.
Resident at the Curragh 1858.

1780.[7] Rev. John Kerr has this to say about John Gourlay: "He was invited down to North Berwick year after year by the old club to superintend the arrangements for their meeting, for John was a perfect master of ceremonies at gatherings of the kind. . . . He was very handsome in appearance – well built, well proportioned, and over six feet in height. He had as a golfer a perfect style of play, every action in his swing being easy and graceful. In his day he was the greatest authority on the rules and regulations of the Royal and Ancient game and this, combined with the fact that he was a thorough gentleman in manner and tastes, and the soul of honour in all his actions, made him popular with the gentleman players of the period . . . altogether he was a man of genius and his name is of outstanding eminence in golfing annals. His sudden death in 1869 from heart disease may be said to have eclipsed the gaiety of the golf world. From the time of his death till his funeral was over, the Honourable Company (now at Muirfield) suspended play and over two hundred golfers followed his remains to his last resting place in Inveresk Churchyard."[8].

Feathery balls made by John Gourlay or his brother William fetch up to £1,500 sterling in the premier London auction rooms. Illustrations of early feathery balls, including several "Gourlays" are to be seen on page 16.

THE STANDHOUSE AT THE CURRAGH

In the 1903 *Irish Golfer* article Mr. Smith Maxwell states ". . . and after a round had luncheon, which was provided at the grandstand on the racecourse". This of course was the standhouse of the local Curragh racecourse which had been erected in the 18th century and had been much improved in 1853. This information would appear to be quite relative to the 1852 golfing activities, because of Eglinton's strong racing associations,[9] the standhouse may have have been used as a "golf house" at that time also.

THE STANDHOUSE AT THE CURRAGH
Clubhouse for the Curragh golfers 1858.

THE STANDHOUSE, MUSSELBURGH LINKS
Residence of John Gourlay until 1869.

John Gourlay was no stranger to standhouses for it was in the standhouse at Musselburgh that he carried on his trade! In the history of *The Honourable Company* it is recounted that after the move of that famous club (now located in Muirfield) in 1836 to Musselburgh. [10] ". . . At first the club had no premises of their own, part of the grandstand of the racecourse being used . . . The course was shared with the Royal Musselburgh Golf Club . . . In 1850 the indefatigable John Gourlay from the famous family of ball makers receive £10 'for making the new course' and afterwards an annual fee of £5 for his attention to the interests of the club . . . He was also the tenant of the Grandstand and, as such, supervised the races." [11]

Unfortunately, the minute books of the Turf Club, Curragh, for the 1858 period have been mislaid and it has not been possible to ascertain any further detail on the use of the standhouse for golfing activities at that time. The use of the standhouse, rather than one of the officers messes in the camp, would indicate an attempt to re-create the Musselburgh "atmosphere", with John Gourlay more than likely being in residence there during his Irish stay. There is further evidence that the standhouse continued in use as a sports centre at least until 1861. The *Express* of 16th July 1861 reported on a meeting of the Curragh Archery Society . . . .

"To relieve in some degree the tediousness of military life at the camp, the members of this society consisting of the most part of officers of the garrison, and ladies resident in this locality, held an archery meeting at the standhouse of the Curragh racecourse today and gave a ball in the evening for the ladies and gentlemen who assembled to witness the archery fete . . .".

The standhouse, of course, was in close proximity to the railway by which the Earl of Eglinton would have travelled, with his companions, from Dublin. We will never know whether David Ritchie participated in this revival of the game on the Curragh with any of his friends. It would seem that he did not do so for his gutta ball dated 1857 would appear to have been his golfing epitaph.

The question regarding the possible foundation of a club on the Curragh during the period 1858-1859 must remain unresolved until positive evidence is discovered. Certainly the ingredients existed, with the past Captains and founder members of Prestwick Golf Club playing there in company with one of the top professionals in Scotland. Some Irish clubs have claimed foundation dates on much flimsier evidence but the present Curragh Club does not claim an earlier foundation date than 1883.

PORTMARNOCK 1858

In a postscript to Mr. Beatty's letter in the *Irish Golfer* of 9th September 1903 the editor J. W. Percy states: "Mr. John Jameson, father of the present Mr. John Jameson of St. Marnocks Portmarnock had a private links of nine holes extending from St. Marnocks to the red tile boathouse near the 15th hole of the

Portmarnock links some 45 years ago, which would be about the time golf was played at the Curragh.''

This certainly is an intriguing entry, however no further information is available as the present Jameson family have no recollection of this early course. The Portmarnock club was founded in 1894, material on which may be found under the club's entry in Appendix 1. Mr. Jameson was the father of the Mr. John Jameson who granted permission to use the ground to the early Portmarnock golfers. *The Irish Field* of 23rd May 1908 stated "Mr. W. Pickeman and deputation went to Mr. Jameson D.L. . . . who had seen golf played there as a boy, and assisted in every way". John Jameson's father had leased the land at Portmarnock in 1847 after his arrival in Ireland and built a house there on the land which comprised 580 acres. The lease was for 999 years. However the story of how the Jameson family came close to losing this property will be related in a later chapter.

GOLF IN THE PHOENIX PARK PARK 1850s

Several recent Irish publications have reported that Scottish regiments played golf in the Phoenix Park in the 1850s, however no evidence appears to exist to support this claim. One early mention was given in *The Irish Field* of 7th March 1908 when an article on early Irish Golf was reprinted from *The Scotsman* and which states in part "Golf was first played in Ireland at the Curragh, Kildare, and in the Phoenix Park, Dublin, probably by the officers of the Scottish regiments". Nothing further is given to indicate which regiments were involved or the source of the information.

The reader can see that *The Scotsman* was wrong on several points as golf was not first played in Ireland at the Curragh; there had been golf at Bray in 1762. It had not been first played by Scottish regiments on the Curragh because a civilian, David Ritchie, had laid out the first course there. However one must allow that golf may have been played at the Phoenix Park, as elsewhere in Ireland, in the 1850s as undoubtedly there must have been many golfing Highlanders in Ireland at that time. The story of golf in the Phoenix Park is related in Appendix 1.

GOLF AT LAYTOWN IN THE 1850s

Robert Browning in his *A History of Golf* (page 157) states: "There is also a tradition of golf being played early in the nineteenth century at Laytown in County Meath''. There is no doubt that these memories would have been related to the golfing exploits of Mr. Tom Gilroy and his family of the 1880s which are documented in Chapter 5. Present research has revealed no evidence of pre-1880s golf in this area.

ROYALTY ON THE CURRAGH IN 1861

On 29th June 1861 the future King Edward VII of England arrived at the

Curragh Camp to undergo a period of ten weeks of training with the Grenadier Guards "under the strictest discipline that could be devised . . . and learn the duties of every grade from ensign upwards." [12] This was part of the continuing education for the Prince, his university education had begun in 1859 with preliminary lectures at Edinburgh University.

None of the books written about the life of "Bertie" give any account of his early golfing career. Prior to entering Oxford as an undergraduate in October 1859 Edward attended lectures at Edinburgh University for a short time. [13]. *The Scotsman* reported in 1901 [14] " . . . he was initiated to golf . . . while attending classes at the High School and University of Edinburgh forty two years ago (i.e. 1859), he went down with some of his friends to golf at Musselburgh and would have gone oftener had the crowds, who passed to watch his game, not been so troublesome . . ."

The Prince therefore had been initiated into the game two years before his arrival at the camp, at a time when the Musselburgh professional had recently been at the Curragh. Apparently the Prince did not find that the local caddies at Musselburgh treated royalty with any great reverance as was recounted in *The Irish Golfer* of 22nd January 1902.

"The late Sir James Gardiner Baird Bart, of Edmonstone, was King Edwards first partner; and Tom Brown was his first caddie. When the Royal player was getting his first lesson he gave the ball a push at the last hole instead of the orthodox hit, on which he was reproved by the faithful 'coach'. Sir James reprimanded Tom for this whereupon the caddie, to the amusement of his Royal Master remarked that 'His Royal Highness maun learn, for if he dune that in a match he would hae lost the hole' . . ." [15].

Another clue to Edward's interest in golf at this early date is told in *The Story of the R&A*: " . . . and on the occasion of the marriage of the Prince of Wales and Princess Alexandra in 1863 the members (of the R&A) sent royal addresses to the Royalties. In the address to the Prince of Wales occurs this paragraph 'Understanding that your Royal Highness has some knowlege of, and considerable proficiency in the Ancient and noble game of golf, we humbly crave your patronage to our Royal and Ancient Club' . . . [16] In 1863 Edward became Captain of the Royal and Ancient Club of St. Andrews, a fact which is not recorded by any of his biographers.

A TRAGIC LINK 1861-1875

Unfortunately there are no accounts of Edward playing golf on the Curragh in 1861. However there was to be one link with his story and the revival of 1875. An engraving in *The Illustrated London News* 13th July 1861 depicted the scene of his residence in the Camp. It was here that an indiscretion on his part was to become a major scandal, which had a long-term effect on the Royal Family and in his relations with his mother, Queen Victoria.

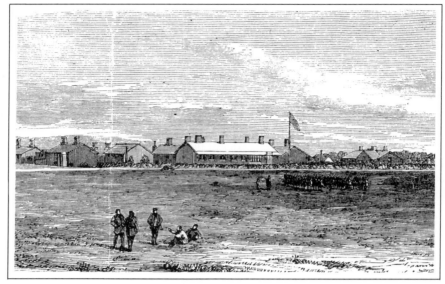

Residence of future King Edward VII at the Curragh in 1861.

This same spot was to be the starting point of the 1875 Curragh golf links and is within 100 yards of the present 17th green.

An account of Edward's escapade is given by Giles St. Aubyn: " . . . the Prince formed a most disreputable liaison with a vivacious young actress named Nellie Clifden. She was already a favourite at the Curragh and knew her way round the camp in the dark. Some of the Prince's fellow officers were intrigued by his sheltered life and saw the precautions designed to protect him as a challenge. Most of them thought nothing of keeping a mistress or two in their baggage, so it was not very surprising that after a wild evening in the mess, when General Bruce had retired for the night, Miss Clifden was shown into HRH's quarters. Admittedly, the Prince took the opportunity offered, that there is nothing to suggest it was a serious affair. The thing had been intended as a practical joke and he accepted it as such. But, when rumours of these happenings reached Windsor, Her Majesty was not amused, and what started in fun ended in tragedy." [17]

Albert, the Prince's father, was shattered by the news from the Curragh. Within weeks he was dead, ostensibly from an attack of typhoid fever. Queen Victoria thereafter blamed Edward's affair for the loss of her beloved husband. A matter which was to affect relations between the two of them until her death.

ANOTHER 1850s GOLFER

The reader will already have seen mention of golf's 1875 revival on the Curragh at page 21. Credit for this rests with the 91st Argyllshire Highlanders who had arrived in Ireland on 29th July 1874. The regiment moved to the Curragh from Newry (there were detachments at Armagh and Monaghan also) on 30th March 1875 and occupied "H" Lines, site of the present Military College.

A key figure in the revival was Major Aléxander Cunningham Bruce, who was the only officer of the regiment with previous Irish service in the 1850s.

MAJOR ALEXANDER CUNNINGHAM
BRUCE, Argyll Highlanders.
Reviver of golf on the Curragh 1875.

Bruce was the only one who would have known of the golfing exploits of the Earl of Eglinton in 1852. He must have known Lt. Col. Campbell of the Queens Bays Regiment, in Dublin, in the period April 1853 to April 1854[20] when both regiments were stationed in Dublin and possibly they travelled to the Curragh to play golf together on David Ritchie's course.

It is quite clear from his narrative that he was unaware of the golden days of golf at the Curragh in 1858 and 1859 as he states "since those days (Eglinton & Lt. Col. Campbell in 1852) this pastime had been forgotten". This is understandable as he had left Ireland himself in December 1854 when the 91st Highlanders departed for Malta. That he was a man with a deep love of the game is in no doubt as he had the foresight to document these historic Irish golfing entries in the main sports journal of the day.

THE CURRAGH COURSE OF 1875

Alexander Bruce gave a clear description of the course which therefore is the first such description in Irish golf history. He describes it thus . . . "The links number twelve holes and the distance round nearly two miles, passing over the ground lying to the front or north of the camp, near the headquarters hut and bearing to the left by the cricket ground to the gravel pit and returning with a slight detour".

These landmarks can be seen on the map below which was printed in 1873. The headquarters hut mentioned was the residence of the Prince of Wales in 1861 during his eventful period of service in the camp. The cricket pitch is the present Curragh RFC grounds and the gravel pit would probably have been the

one in the region of Donnelly's Hollow. The 12 holes may have been an echo
of the old course at Prestwick which up to 1883 had consisted of 12 holes. When
the first British Open had been held there in 1860 the competition, won by Willie
Park of Musselburgh, had been over three rounds of twelve holes. [21]

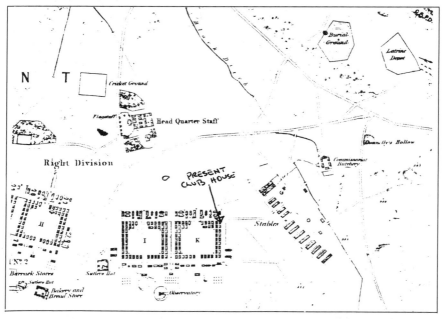

MAP OF AREA OF CURRAGH CAMP'S GOLF LINKS 1875.

DEATH OF TOM MORRIS JUN. – Dec. 1875

There were Prestwick golfers among the 1875 Curragh golfers, one of them
was Lt. William R. Houison-Crauford whose son Brigadier J. A. Houison-
Crauford became Captain of Prestwick Golf Club in 1926. It was in Prestwick
that the great Tom Morris Junior won his hat-trick of victories in the British
Open, for the "Challenge Belt", thereby winning it outright. However on the
27th December 1875 *The Field* recorded a tragic story by their St. Andrews
correspondent: "Golfers generally will learn with regret of the death of Tom
Morris Junior . . . at a very early age he won laurels on the green, and before
his teens in 1869 he scored his successive victory at the Champion contest on
the Prestwick links and secured for his absolute property the 'Belt' the gift of
the late Earl of Eglinton. . . . the deceased was in his 25th year". [22]

Here we can see the last recorded mention of the Earl of Eglinton's golfing
activities for it was he who had given the first British Open trophy in 1860 (won
by Willie Park of Musselburgh). All of the professionals wore jackets of

BBC Hulton Picture Library

TOM MORRIS JUNIOR
Wearing the British Open
Championship Belt which he
won outright in 1870.

THE FIRST BRITISH OPEN 1860
Tom Morris Sen. (with club) in Eglinton Tartan.

Eglinton tartan on that inaugural occasion. Eglinton had died on 4th October 1861 after playing a game of golf at St. Andrews. In *The Story of the R&A* a strange account is given concerning death warnings by the Bodach Glas, or dark-grey man:

"The Earl of Eglinton a nobleman alike beloved and respected in Scotland, and whose death was truly felt as a national loss, was playing on the day of his decease on the links of St. Andrews at the national game of golf. Suddenly he stopped in the middle of a game saying 'I can play no longer, there is the Bodach Glas. I have seen it for the third time; something fearful is going to befall me.' He died that night at . . ., as he was handing a candlestick to a lady who was retiring to her room. The clergyman from who I received this story endorses it as authentic and names the gentleman to who Lord Eglinton spoke".[23]

The 91st Highlanders left the Curragh on 23rd June 1876 for Enniskillen (with a detachment at Londonderry). In May 1877 they were in Belfast (with a detachment at Carrickfergus) being moved to Dublin on the 15th April 1878 for service in the Royal (now Collins) Barracks where they stayed until their move to Aldershot in January 1879. It is quite likely that this regiment played golf in some of their other Irish stations but no documentary evidence of this has come to light. It would be six years later before documented golf is again heard of in Ireland with the beginning of the modern era of Irish golf history.

FOOTNOTES

1. David Ritchie's mention of "links" on the ball certificate and also in *The Field* article of 1875 (see page 24) indicates that both writers were "links" players. Ritchie had played the famous old links at Musselburgh and although Major Bruce's home club has not been discovered he may have been a member of the R&A because of reference to Tom Morris in the article. Morris in 1875 was professional to the R&A. Links courses now, of course, are those located on "links land" close to the sea.

2. The Lanarkshire Militia had been embodied (i.e. mobilised) because of the Indian Mutiny where so many of the native regiments there had mutinied. These militia regiments would have been officered by the "landed gentry" of the various counties and there would have been golfers among these similar to Lieutenant Smith Maxwell.

3. *Thoms Directory* 1859, page 633.

4. Major Hamilton's photograph , which hangs in Prestwick Golf Club, was provided by Mr. R. A. Clement, Captain of that club in 1983.

5. *Prestwick Golf Club, A History and Some Records*, page 5.

6. Letter from Mrs. J. B. Findlay dated 2nd November 1984.

7. *Golf in the Making*, page 47. John Gourlay had two brothers, William (1813-1844) and Douglas (1816-1839). As both of them had died prior to 1858, the Gourlay referred to could only have been John who was born in 1815 and died in 1869.

8. *The Golf Book of East Lothian*, page 322.

9. The Earl was one of the leading horse owners in the United Kingdom at the time, having won the St. Leger with Blue Bonnet in 1842, with Van Tromp in 1847 and the Derby and St. Leger with The Flying Dutchman in 1849. (DNB, page 751).

10. *Muirfield and The Honourable Company* by George Pottinger, page 31.

11. The old course at Musselburgh, on which golf had been played from the earliest times, was situated within the confines of the racecourse there. The Royal Musselburgh Golf Club played there from at least 1774 until 1925 when they moved to Muirfield. Two other famous Scottish clubs also used the Musselburgh course for periods of their existence: Edinburgh Burgess Golf Society (1874-1895) and Bruntsfield Links Golf Club (1818-1895). Reference: *Five Open Champions* by George Colville, pages 59, 60 and 61.

12. *King Edward The Seventh* by Philip Magnus, page 43.

13. *Encylopaedia Brittanica*.

14. Reprinted in the *Irish Golfer*, 1901, page 455.

15. Reprinted from *The Ascendancy of Golf* by Dr. J. G. McPherson.

16. *The Story of the R&A*, page 121.

17. *Edward VII Prince and King*, pages 50 and 51.

18. The smaller garrison towns of Ireland would normally have been occupied by company-sized (100 all ranks) elements.

19. WO 76/457 Records of Service. His marriage to Constance Marianne Wyllie is also recorded and their fourth daughter, Marion, is documented as being born in Tramore on 19th November 1874.

20. WO 17/1119 (1852-53)/1120 (1854-55).

21. *Prestwick Golf Club, A History And Some Records*, page 30.

22. In 1839 the Earl of Eglinton had held his famous Eglinton Tournament, which was a lavishly re-enacted medieval jousting tournament. Unfortunately, the event was completely disrupted by torrential rain (a full account is documented in *The Knight And The Umbrella* by Ian Anstruther). It would appear that the presentation of a "Champion Belt" was a continuation of Eglinton's interest in the medieval contests; such a belt was the prize for the successful knight of old.

23. *The Story of the R&A*, pages 106 and 107, retold from page 344 of *Notes on the Folklore of the Northern Counties of England and The Borders 1879*. The Earl of Eglinton died in the home of his good friend John Whyte Melville at Mount Melville. It would appear that the Earl had been a freemason for in the *Mail* of 24th October 1865 there is an article on the unveiling of a statue to the late Earl "erected in Ayr . . . with full Masonic honours by the Right Worshipful Grand Master of Ayrshire assisted by members of the Provincial Grand Lodge . . ." A statue of the Earl in Stephens Green, Dublin, was blown up on 26th August 1958.

Scotland's Gift To Ireland

Part 1: THE EARLY CLUBS AND COURSES 1881 TO 1885

IRELAND'S OLDEST CLUB – ROYAL BELFAST 1881

Prior to 1881 the playing of golf in Ireland had not been organised in the accepted sense. The one exception had been the club at Bray as outlined in Chapter 2, unfortunately the circumstances surrounding that club's foundation and demise may never be discovered.

BELFAST GOLF CLUB.—To the already numerous and fast increasing list of golfing societies throughout the United Kingdom has now to be added the one bearing this title. At a meeting held in the Chamber of Commerce on Wednesday last, under the presidency of the Mayor (Mr Edward Porter Cowan), the club was formally constituted, and if local influence, unanimity, and enthusiasm avail anything, Belfast Golf Club ought to have a successful career. The Kinnegar at Hollywood, permission having been kindly granted by Capt. Harrison, J.P., will be headquarters, and from personal knowledge of the spot we can vouch for its capability of being easily converted into a first-class golfing arena.

FOUNDATION OF THE BELFAST CLUB
The Field 19th November 1881.

The institution of Ireland's oldest golf club was documented in *The Field* 19th November 1881 which stated . . . "at a meeting held in the Chamber of Commerce on Wednesday last, under the presidency of the Mayor (Mr. Edward Porter Cowan), the club was formally constituted and, if local influence, unanimity and enthusiasm avail anything, Belfast Golf Club ought to have a successful career. The Kinnegar at Hollywood, permission having been kindly granted by Capt. Harrison J.P., will be headquarters . . ."

In a letter to the magazine *Golf Illustrated* 9th January 1903, one of the club's founders, Dr. William F. Collier, gave a detailed account of the club's foundation: "The germ from which the tree has sprung was planted one October morning in 1881 when Mr. – now the Right Honourable – Thomas Sinclair called on Dr. William F. Collier at the Belfast Royal Academy to ask for an introduction to a member of the staff, who was known to be a skilled golfer. Mr. Sinclair had lately come from a summer holiday at St. Andrews and when Mr. G. Baillie, a native of Musselburgh, where he had grown up with a golf club in his hand, appeared on the scene, Mr. Sinclair suggested that an attempt should

THOS. SINCLAIR
Co-founder Belfast G.C.

G. L. BAILLIE
Co-founder Belfast G.C.
Ireland's oldest club.

be made to form a club in Belfast for the pursuit of the royal and ancient game.
. . . Matters were now ripe for an initial meeting, which was called by a circular dated November 5th 1881 and signed by the following seven: Clement K. Cordiner, John Findlater, Thomas Sinclair, W. F. Collier, W. Murphy Grimshaw, John O. Brown, Geo. L. Baillie . . . This meeting proving highly successful, the club was launched with Captain Harrison as President, Mr. Sinclair, Captain, Mr. Brown, Hon. Treas. and Mr. Baillie, Hon. Sec. . . .''

Some of the early Belfast members had not previously played golf and it is recorded that Dr. Collier took a nett 200 to ''go around'' in the first competition held on 26th December 1881.[1] Later a newspaper reported in 1886 that the fifth annual competition for The Murphy-Grimshaw Vase had been won for the first time by an Irishman, George M. Shaw.[2] This would indicate that most of the early members were expatriate Scots, like their founding fathers. It would also appear that this vase was the first such Irish perpetual club trophy.[3]

IRELAND'S SECOND OLDEST CLUB — THE CURRAGH 1883

On 16th November 1882 The Highland Light Infantry (71st Regiment) arrived in the Curragh Camp, Co. Kildare, from Edinburgh.[4] There were several keen golfers with the Regiment, one of whose proudest possessions was its golf medal which had been instituted in 1880. It is interesting to note that this medal was first competed for at Musselburgh when it was won by Lieut. J. Mitchell-Innes.

The Irish Times 12th March 1883 carried the following announcement in its column of Army News from the Curragh: "Maj. Gen. Fraser, V.C., C.B., Commanding the Curragh Brigade, has sanctioned the formation a garrison golf club in connection with the officers recreation club. Lieutenant A. G. Balfour of the 71st Battalion H.L.I. stationed in the camp has been appointed Secretary. The Rules of the Club will be the same as those of the Royal and Ancient Golf Club of St. Andrews."

The only surviving document of this period in the possession of the Curragh Golf Club is a small bound copy of these rules. In it the rules of golf, as then played at St. Andrews, are reprinted; which reveals a close connection between the two clubs. This not surprising as the first Honorary Secretary's father, John Balfour of Balbirnie, had been Captain of R&A In 1842. [5] In due course Lt. A. G. Balfour was also to become the first known captain of the club in 1887. [6]

LT. A. G. BALFOUR
First Hon. Secretary
Curragh Golf Club 1883.

← H.L.I. Golf Medal

→ H.L.I./93rd Regt. Inter Regiment Golf Medal

Played for
on Curragh
1883 and 1889.

Played for
on Curragh
1888, 1889, 1890.

News of the club's foundation was carried to Scotland very quickly and the following details are documented in *The Golfers Handbook 1883*, edited by Robert Forgan Jnr. of St. Andrews: "Est. 1883. Patron Maj. Gen. C. C. Fraser, V.C., C.B.; Secretary, Lieutenant A. G. Balfour, 71st Highland Light Infantry. The Round is about 1¾ miles and there are 16 holes . . ."[7] This entry was the first listing of an Irish club in any foreign golf publication. (Although the Belfast Golf Club had been founded 16 months earlier, there is no mention of that club in *The Golfers Handbook 1883*).

Lt. A. A. Wolfe Murray of the Highland Light Infantry is recorded as course record holder in *The Golfing Annual 1888/89*, with an 86 (the course at this time had 18 holes). His father had been Captain of the R&A in 1848 and this provided a link to the 1852 Curragh golfers as James Wolfe Murray had proposed Lt. Col. William Campbell as a military member of that illustrious club in his year of Captaincy.[8]

SCENE AT GINGER BEER HOLE, ST. ANDREWS
The Earl of Eglinton, John Balfour and J. Wolfe Murray are among the spectators.

It is also of historical interest to find that the Earl of Eglinton, John Balfour of Balbirnie and James Wolfe Murray of Cringletie are each depicted in the famous painting, "The Golfers". This picture, which has been sold widely as a print, depicts a scene at the famous Ginger Beer hole at St. Andrews.

GOLF AT KINSALE — 1883

In common with many other Scottish regiments, the Kings Own Borderers (later, The Kings Own Scottish Borderers) had several golfers in its ranks. In April 1883 the regiment arrived at Kinsale from Fermoy and *The Field* 16th June 1883 carried a lengthy report on their golfing activities at their new station: "The Kings Own Borderers have resuscitated their old golf club and under very favourable auspices. The links, which are of a very sporting character, are situated at the Musketry Camp, about four miles from Kinsale, where a considerable stretch of ground is available. There are eight holes and the course is fairly good . . . [it] will become a very good one after a few months play and at present a most enjoyable game may be obtained . . . There are caddies in plenty to be had, as may be expected in a Scotch Regiment in which so many of the men know the links of St. Andrews, Musselburgh, etc. . . . ." The report also carries an account of matches recently played, naming several officers of the regiment.

KINGS OWN BORDERERS — GOLFERS AT KINSALE 1884

The Kings Own Borderers departed Kinsale in late 1884 and some of the officers are named in contemporary newspaper accounts of early Dublin Golf Club competitions, in 1885. The Regimental Golf Club would appear to have been active in 1884 golf in the Phoenix Park (See details on pages 45 and 46).

GOLF AT CORK — 1883

An intriguing entry in *The Belfast Newsletter* 1st November 1886 gives a fragmentary clue to the existence of another golf course in Cork in 1883 . . . "Since November 1881 when the Belfast Golf Club was instituted . . . no less than three additional courses have been laid down in different parts of the country. The second was at Fota Island . . . one of our contemporaries noticing an opening game there in 1883".

Confirmation of early golf in Cork is given in a *Field* article relating to the setting up of Royal Malta Golf Club: "almost immediately after his arrival in the Autumn of 1888, the present Governor (Sir Henry Torrens) announced his intention of introducing the game by hook or by crook. He had, he said, set it going at Cork when commanding there; in South Africa, when duty called him to the Cape; and why not Malta?" [9]

LT. GEN. SIR HENRY D'OYLEY TORRENS, C.B.

This officer was born on 24th February 1833 at Meerut, India, the son of H. W. Torrens of Bengal Civil Service. He was commissioned into the Royal Welch Fusiliers on 18th September 1849 [10] and had a very distinguished military career prior to his appointment as Officer Commanding the Belfast District on 10th November 1879. [11] On 1st October 1881 Torrens was transferred to command the Cork District, an appointment he held until 13th January 1884 when he was appointed to Command the troops in South Africa. His final post was Governor and Commander-in-Chief, Malta, which he held from September 1888 until his death on 1st December 1889. [12]

Torrens' grandfather had been a Major General and was from an old Londonderry family. When or where he acquired his passionate interest in golf is unknown; it would appear that he had departed Belfast prior to the institution of the golf club there. It is possible that he was influenced by the golfers of the Kings Own Borderers at Kinsale. In addition, the 2nd Battalion Royal Scots were in Fermoy from December 1881 until March 1883 when they moved to the Curragh. [13] The conjunction of the two Scottish regiments may have led to golf being played in the Cork area at this time, however there is no evidence for this in the regimental archives.

There is no question concerning Torrens' international efforts to spread the game. He is acknowledged as the founder of the Royal Cape Golf Club, having called the first meeting to form the club on 14th November 1885.[14] The previously mentioned *Field* article relating to golf at Malta acknowledges Torrens as the prime motivator there. Without doubt he must be considered one of the key figures in spreading the game outside the British Isles.

TORRENS LINK TO BRAY IN 1762

An amazing link to the early golf club in Bray is revealed in the biographical detail relating to Sir Henry's wife. The evidence for a golf club in the Co. Wicklow town, in 1762, is related in Chapter 2. Elias De Butts had a prominent position in the Bray club and a study of the subsequent lineage of his family reveals that in 1876 General Torrens married Georgina Francis De Butts, daughter of Col. Francis De Butts of the Madras Engineers. The latter was eldest son of General Sir Augustus De Butts, K.C.H., who in turn was the fourth son (born in 1766) of the aforementioned Elias.[15]

It is unfortunate that Torrens did not publish any material on his golfing exploits as his efforts in Cork, although unfruitful at the time, are part of the story of early Irish golf.

A MILITARY GOLF CLUB IN DUBLIN – 1884

MAJOR DAVID KINLOCH
Founder of Military Golf Club,
Phoenix Park, 1884.

Robert Browning relates the next development in his famous book, *A History Of Golf.* . . "The man who introduced the game to Dublin was a young subaltern in the Grenadier Guards, who later became Brig. Gen. Sir David Kinloch of Gilmerton . . . In the Autumn of 1884, when he was quartered with his regiment in Richmond Barracks, Dublin, he and Mr. John Oswald, of Dunnikier, who was at that time one of the Viceroy's staff, laid out a few holes in the Phoenix Park. The idea caught on and a small club was formed . . ."[16]

An article in *The Irish Field* 2nd January 1926, on the history of the Royal Dublin club recorded details of the founding meeting of that club on 15th May 1885: ". . . and now came the remarkable fact that prior to the meeting there existed in Dublin a Military Club which played regularly in the Phoenix Park".

The existence of this earlier Military Club has been ignored in subsequent accounts of the origins of golf in Dublin. There may have been an element of antipathy involved in the setting up of a purely Military Club in 1884. At that time there were three Scottish regiments stationed in Dublin[17] and they probably felt that they had enough experienced golfers in their ranks without involving a civilian membership.

The transition to a fully integrated club would appear to have occurred quickly. A match between the militiary and civilian members of the Dublin club is recorded in November 1885, which was won handsomely by the soldiers. The same account told of a return match "to be shortly played".[18] (Further details of golf in the Phoenix Park are given in Appendix 1.)

FOUNDATION OF THE DUBLIN GOLF CLUB – 1885

On 15th May 1885 a group of expatriate Scotsmen gathered at number 19 Grafton Street in response to a circular from Mr. John Lumsden, a native of Banffshire. Lumsden had come to Ireland in 1867, when 27 years of age, from India where he had been employed in the banking business. Initially he worked in Kilkenny and then was transferred to the Provincial Bank in Drogheda where he remained for thirteen years. He was then transferred to Dublin where he became manager of the Provincial Bank's branch in College Street.

An account of John Lumsden's decision to commence a golf course in the Phoenix park is given in *The Irish Times* 29th July 1922. In writing up his interview with the old man, J. P. Rooney helped spread the myth that

JOHN LUMSDEN
Founder of the Dublin Golf Club
in 1885

the thought had struck John Lumsden as he strolled through the Park with his two sons, as if there had been no previous existence of the game in the metropolis. . . . "The thought struck him that it was an ideal place to play a game. A game of what? Any game would do, so long as it was a game. Golf! It was an inspiration. That decided it."

That the members of the new Dublin Golf Club were cogniscent of the prior existence of the Military Club is clear in the letter written by Mr. R. M. Charles, Hon. Secretary, to the Board of Public Works on 30th May 1885[19] . . . "A meeting of gentlemen interested in the game of 'Golf' was recently held for the purpose of forming a club to promote the growth of the game in Dublin. A Military Club had been playing for about a year on a portion of the Phoenix Park which is considered the only ground in the district suitable for the purpose. This club has been merged into the new one, which already numbers about 80 members . . ." The Hon. Secretary then requested permission to erect a house or hut for the members.

Why the "new" Dublin Golf Club did not take its date of foundation from that of the Military Club is not documented, however the experience of the members of the Royal Wimbledon Golf Club may have been uppermost in John Lumsden's mind at the time. In 1881 the London Scottish Golf Club was riven with dissension culminating in a split between the military and civilian members. All of this was widely publicised in the golf columns of *The Field*[20] and eventually a new club (Wimbledon) was formed. The lessons learned from the Wimbledon debacle may have inspired the canny Scots to avoid such trouble. Further evidence for this Wimbledon connection is given in the abovementioned *Irish Times* account: ". . . a friend in Wimbledon provided a book on golf, a bag of clubs and some old balls, and with these . . . Mr. Lumsden set out on Easter Monday 1885 for the Phoenix Park, accompanied by his sons and brother-in-law. They laid out their 18-hole course without as much as a 'by your leave', cut the holes, planted the red flags and played their first game opposite the Viceregal lodge, the first tee being 'built' some distance beyond the Phoenix cricket ground. There and then was laid by Mr. Lumsden the foundation stone of the Royal Dublin Golf Club." It is clear that the honour of having the first eighteen-hole course in Ireland rests with the Royal Dublin Club from its foundation in 1885.

Another "first" for the club was the appointment of the first club professional in Ireland, W. Thompson, shortly after the foundation of the club. John Gourlay's short stay at the Curragh in 1858 may have been a short-term engagement by a club of sorts, no evidence has been found for this.

The new club and the four-year-old Royal Belfast Golf Club played the first Irish inter-club match, 10-a-side, in the Phoenix Park on 30th October 1885. An entry in *The Field* one week later[21] recorded a win for the home team by 70 holes to 58: "Both before and after the match, the strangers were entertained in the tasteful little clubhouse, which, by permission of the Board of Works, has been erected in the Park."

On the Dublin team was another pioneer of Irish golf who had arrived from Scotland earlier in the year and settled at Mornington, near Drogheda. From an early date in 1885 he became an active member of the Dublin Golf Club and was captain in 1888, 1889 and 1894. Tom Gilroy was to play a significant part in the early development of the game in Ireland, which will be told in later chapters. An account of the club's subsequent moves to Cush Point, Sutton and finally, Dollymount, are given later in this chapter and in Appendix 1.

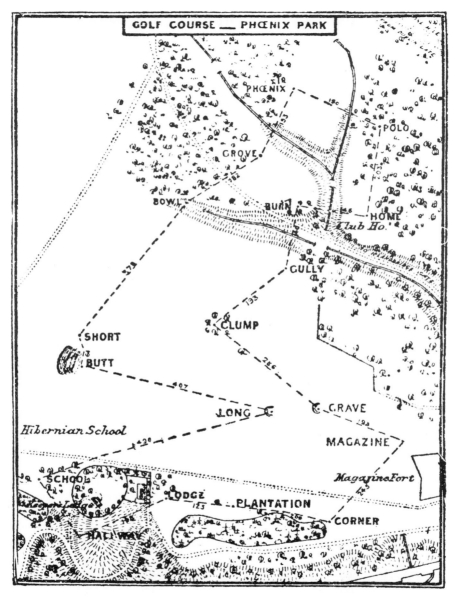

THE DUBLIN GOLF CLUB'S COURSE IN THE PHOENIX PARK
1885 to 1889.

Part 2: CONSOLIDATION 1886–1889

TOM GILROY AND MORNINGTON GOLF COURSE – 1886

From the moment of his arrival, in 1885, it is clear that Tom Gilroy set out to foster the game of golf in Ireland. A comprehensive article on him appeared in *Golf Magazine* in 1893.[22] He had been born in Dundee on 2nd October 1852 and from the age of six or seven had played golf at Carnoustie. It was obvious

that he had talent at that early age and Jack Butchart (whose son would later become professional at Newcastle) took him in hand, coaching him together with George Morris (a brother of old Tom). Gilroy was educated at St. Andrews where he often played with young Tom Morris.[23]

By 1893 his handicap at Royal Dublin was plus 4 and he was widely acknowledged as the best golfer in Ireland. In a later chapter it will be seen that he was used as the "template" on which the earlier Irish handicapping system was based.

TOM GILROY
Ireland's premier golfer 1885 to 1895.

In the newspaper *Sport* 6th November 1886, under the title Dublin v. Belfast, the following entry occurs: "The return match . . . came off on Saturday last at Mornington, a small fishing village, situated at the mouth of the Boyne's ill-fated river and close to the residence of Mr. T. Gilroy of the Dublin Club . . . through the courtesy of Mr. Owen Reynolds . . . Mr. Gilroy was enabled to make some splendid golf links, which were simply perfect. The hazards gave general satisfaction . . . there are eleven holes in the round of the course at Mornington and the match on Saturday was of two rounds of 22 holes."

Robert Browning's source of information for the following entry in his *A History Of Golf* that ". . . there is also a tradition of golf being played early in the nineteenth century at Laytown in County Meath"[24] was clearly inaccurate. Gilroy was to play a leading role in the setting up of the Co. Louth Golf Club in 1892, becoming its first Captain. His sons, Aldie and Norman, were fine golfers also.[25] The subsequent history of this course is given in Appendix 1 (there is no evidence that a club was ever established here).

PORTRUSH – MAY 1888

An entry in the minutes of The Royal Belfast Golf Club for 3rd May 1888 recorded: "The Secretary announced that the Portrush links would be opened on 12th May and that the Northern Counties Railway Company had kindly offered a free pass to all the members of Royal Belfast Golf Club for that day." It is obvious that the railway company envisaged a substantial increase in business from the golfers of Belfast.

A detailed account of the club's origins are given in Appendix 1; however,

THE FIRST CLUBHOUSE AT PORTRUSH 1888

a description of the opening of the course as retold in *The Irish Times* 13th February 1903 is well worth retelling. It gives an insight into the awe inspired in the local population at the sight of these new fanatics: "Eh mon, it's a queer game this. D'ye see yon mon wi the red coat. They tell me h'is yin o'them Colonels. He tuk a lang stick an gied the ball a crack, an' it gied awa an awa, till the sicht o't left ma eyes. An' then he went to look for it, an' when he fund it he stoopit down and lookit at it for a wee an' then he walkit roond and roond it, and then he turned his back and walkit awa' frae it, an' then he came back an' tuck anither stick an' gied it a bigger whack. But it did'na go, it just stuck in the sand an' he said d---." Surely modern golfers can recognise the symptoms and would sympathise with the Colonel!

The club had a modest clubhouse to commence with as can be seen in the sketch which appeared in the *The Irish Golfer* 1st November 1899. Their first abode was a little shed hidden among the sand dunes. The inaugural meeting had been held on 21st April 1888 in the Northern Counties Hotel, presided over by H. H. McNeile, D.L. It is of interest that the first Honorary Secretary was G. L. Baillie, the co-founder of the Belfast Club. From an early date the club considered itself as the St. Andrews of Ireland. *The Irish Times* 17th September 1889 reported the imminent opening of the new clubhouse ". . . on which occasion the magnificent challenge cup presented by Mr. J. S. Alexander, D.L., ex-Captain and open to all Irish clubs will be played for the first time".

That the club council were not satisfied with the institution of an open cup is evident from an entry in *The Field* 19th April 1890: "The County (Antrim) GC is in the van of the movement with its unrivalled links at Portrush and with an enterprising council, it is not difficult to surmise where the future St. Andrews of Ireland is destined to be . . . not yet quite two years old . . . its members numbering 200 are now, however, the happy possessors of a four-mile course of 18 holes, laid out under the supervision of the veteran Tom Morris . . . The council for the County Club are now taking the preliminary step towards the foundation of an Amateur Championship of Ireland open to the world."

The County Club, later renamed Royal Portrush, were set to become the leading disciples in the setting up of the Golfing Union of Ireland in the following year.

CUSH POINT, SUTTON – OCTOBER 1888

Following a particularly heavy growth of grass in the Summer of 1888 the members of the Dublin Golf Club were not very happy with the state of their course. In a detailed account carried in *The Irish Field* 2nd January 1926, J. P. Rooney reported that at ". . . a committee meeting of October 1888 . . . the President (John Lumsden) made a statement to the meeting explaining his action regarding a course at Sutton on the property of Lord Howth and that permission had been received to play over the ground at a nominal rent of one shilling per month, three months rent in advance being paid by him".[26]

The committee approved the President's actions but they also decided to retain the course of Phoenix Park for another twelve months. Very soon afterwards, at the committee meeting of 19th January 1889, a discussion took place ". . . for the purpose of considering the advisability of changing the course from Sutton permanently to the Bull". Once again the President explained that he had approached Col. Vernon of Clontarf and the Port and Docks Board and he was able to announce that permission had been granted.

It can be seen that the Dublin Golf Club only occupied Cush Point course at Sutton for three months or so over the Winter 1888/89. Rooney's account of 1926 reported the reason for the sudden change as ". . . it was out of reach of the majority of the playing members . . .".

AUGHNACLOY – DECEMBER 1888

The next Irish club formed was Aughnacloy, Co. Tyrone, which was founded on 23rd December 1888 with Mr. W. H. Mann as the first Captain and Mr. James Pringle as President. An entry in *The Irish Times* 29th March 1889 documented a visit by a famous golfer: ''Mr. Thomas Gilroy, Captain of the Dublin Golf Club, visited the links and played over the course of nine holes and notwithstanding the many difficulties of the ground completed the round in the score of 51.'' It can be seen that the first course was a nine-hole one, extended to eighteen afterwards.[27] In many subsequent golfing publications the club is credited with having the first eighteen-hole course in Ireland, which is not correct.

The magazine *Irish Golf* May 1950 documented the amazing rediscovery of the old Aughnacloy Putter, a highly decorated trophy which had been long forgotten following the demise of the club after the First World War. It had been

THE AUGHNACLOY PUTTER
First played for in 1889.

found in the attic of Dr. G. M. Pringle's house at Aughnacloy where it had lain for over thirty years. The trophy had first been competed for in May 1889, open to all Irish clubs, and an account of the competition was carried in *The Field* 18th May 1889. There had been over forty entries, the winner being Hugh Shaw of Royal Belfast, with a score of 79 off scratch.[28] An account of the club is given in Appendix 1.

NEWCASTLE, CO. DOWN – 23rd MARCH 1889

The origins of golf at Newcastle are very closely linked with the Royal Belfast Golf Club. At a meeting of the latter on 25th January 1889 the following entry clearly documents the beginning of the world-famous golf links: ''The Treasurer was authorised to advance Mr. Baillie a sum not exceeding £5 for preliminary expenses in connection with the establishment of links at Newcastle – to be repaid by the club when constituted.'' At a further meeting on 1st March 1889 it was recorded: ''Mr. Baillie also submitted a letter from Mr. Moore-Garrett, agent of the Annesley estate, intimating that Lord Annesley would be willing to become President of the proposed Co. Down Golf Club at Newcastle and would give ground to the links there at a yearly rent of £5 . . . Mr. Baillie mentioned that he hoped to arrange for an opening day there before the end of the month and it was proposed by Mr. Wheeler that the Treasurer be authorised to advance Mr. Baillie a further £5 for expenses . . ."

It is interesting to note the date of the latter meeting, above, for on that day Baillie had been playing golf at Newcastle.

On that morning the first professional of the Royal Belfast Golf Club, Alex G. Day,[29] had arrived by boat and ". . . He found Mr. Baillie waiting at the quay . . . proceeding by train to Newcastle, owing to the fact that Mr. Baillie was engaged at that time laying out a nine hole course for the new County Club, they found the links covered with snow. Nothwithstanding this drawback they arranged to play a four ball. Day had brought over with him a supply of red painted balls, as it was customary in Scotland to provide red balls for Winter play. Wooden pegs simply denoted the location of the holes, and strange to relate these remained for two years of the new club's existence . . ."[30]

The first Hon. Secretary of the club was G. L. Baillie who was appointed at the first meeting of the club, held on 23rd March 1889. The chair was occupied by the Earl of Annesley who owned most of the land in the Newcastle area. It was not until the council meeting of 11th March 1890 that the first Captain, Mr. Armar Lowry-Corry, was named. It is of interest to note that the 5th Earl of Annesley, first President of the club, had been Aide-de-Camp for the Earl of Eglinton in 1858/59, while the latter was Lord Lieutenant of Ireland.[31] The 5th Earl was then a Captain in the Scots Fusilier Guards and because of Eglinton's golf outings to the Curragh at that time (see Chapter 4) must surely have become acquainted with the game there.

When the Golfing Union of Ireland was inaugurated, in November 1891, the club sent three delegates. George Combe was elected Honorary Secretary at the first meeting, an office he filled with great distinction until 1899. A very pragmatic individual, he inaugurated the first handicapping scheme in Ireland. Combe also introduced George Fernie as a travelling professional to visit the various clubs in Ireland, in order to improve the standard of Irish golf.[32] He was captain of the club in 1895, 1896 and 1904.

GEORGE COMBE
First Hon. Secretary of the
Golfing Union of Ireland 1891.

QUEENS COUNTY HEATH G.C. – NOVEMBER 1889

Present golfers at this midlands course are modest when they claim 1930 as the institution date of their club. There is no doubt that the first golf club on the Heath at "Maryboro" was instituted in November 1889. *The Irish Times* 21st July 1891 carried a report on The Queens County Heath Club: "This club, formed during the Winter of 1889, gives every promise of being a great success, certainly the members may congratulate themselves upon having links which, old golfers say, are second to none, embracing as they do a variety of holes over modulating ground, with hazards and bunkers . . . the members meet for play every Friday, and the 'Stand House' fitted up luxuriously by the officers of the 4th Leinster Regiment, has very kindly been placed at the disposal of the members."

This club is listed in *The Golfing Annual 1893/94* with T. Webber as Captain and an exact institution date of November 1889 is given. Subsequently this club is continuously listed in *The Golfing Annual* until 1910 and in *The Irish Golf Guide* between 1910 and 1916. (See Appendix 1 for further detail).

COOKSTOWN, TYRONE – 1889

The earliest mention of golf in the Cookstown area is given in *The Belfast Newsletter* 28th February 1889 when the "golfers" of the town are referred to in an article on Ulster golf. *The Golfing Annual 1888/89* recorded: ". . . Another prominent member of the Country (Portrush) Golf Club, Mr. H. Adair of Cookstown has laid out a nine hole course near the town . . ." This latter publication was issued in May 1889, however there is no listing of a Cookstown (or Killymoon) Club in the edition. Killymoon Golf Club, unfortunately, has no earlier records than 1922, a common situation for many Irish clubs. It has the distinction of being one of the founders of the Golfing Union of Ireland in November 1891.

A. J. BALFOUR – THE ESTABLISHMENT MESSIAH

Prior to his appointment as Chief Secretary of Ireland, in March 1887, Arthur James Balfour had been a member of the North Berwick Club in Scotland. It is not clear when he joined the Dublin Golf Club and the first mention of him playing golf in Dublin is given in the *Evening Mail* 19th January 1888. At that time the country was in a very agitated state, by August 1888 there were twenty-one Irish MPs in jail. The trouble had begun in 1886 with the Clanricarde evictions and finally as a result of three people being killed by police action at Mitchelstown the Chief Secretary acquired the title "Bloody Balfour".

In a letter to a friend in 1888 Balfour wrote: "I am taking great care of myself, golf or real tennis, 12 to 2, the Castle 2 to 7".[33] At that time he was accompanied by detectives wherever he went in Ireland and England and this fact is credited with drawing great attention among the public. In an article in *The*

Irish Field 29th July 1922 [34] it was recalled that ". . . [he] employed two caddies, one for carrying the clubs and the other to act as forecaddie, both being trusted (and fully armed) members of the famous 'G' Division of the D.M.P. . . ."

Following his period as Chief Secretary of Ireland, where he had gained great publicity for his political actions and public attention on the various golf courses, Balfour became one of the greatest proponents of the game. [35] He was widely sought to open new golf courses and became Captain of the R&A in 1894. Balfour was widely quoted in the golfing press and wrote of golf himself in some of the establishment magazines of the day. Typical of the tributes paid to him were the words of Lord Wemyss, then Captain of Luffness, when addressing the members of the London Scottish Club at a dinner in the 1890s. He attributed the rise in popularity of golf to three causes, the spread of education, the invention of the gutta percha golf ball and the well-publicised activities of Mr. A. J. Balfour. [36]

RIGHT HON. ARTHUR GOLFOUR, M.P.
As Irish Secretary known to fame,
Golfeur, links-eyed, pursues his favourite game.

ARTHUR J. BALFOUR
Premier golfer in Ireland and England
late 1880s to early 1900s

IRELAND'S FIRST OPEN GOLF COMPETITION − 1888

The first publicised open competition was the Henderson Cup of the Royal Belfast Golf Club which had been announced in November 1887. In donating the cup, Sir James Henderson, proprietor of the *Belfast Newsletter* and then Captain of the club, had stated that the competition would be ". . . competed for under handicap at Holywood (i.e. R.B.G.C.), Dublin, Mornington, Cork in rotation, the competition to be open to all members of recognised Irish clubs". [37]

The first winner of the Henderson Cup was Mr. J. H. Cameron with a 79 off 30 handicap, this result was announced in the *The Field* 16th May 1888. [38] Not to be outdone the new County Club at Portrush inaugurated a similar competition, through the generosity of their first Captain Mr. J. S. Alexander, and this was was played for at Portrush on the 5th October 1889, match play by heats of nine holes. *The Belfast Newsletter* 8th October 1889 carried the result, a win by one hole for Mr. Hugh Shaw of the Royal Belfast Club. It was announced that the Portglenone Cup would be played half yearly only on the links of the County Club. An earlier open competition was played at the Spring 1889 meeting of the new Aughnacloy Club, details are given in Appendix 1.

THE HENDERSON CUP, R.B.G.C.
Ireland's first open golf trophy
1887.

THE 1880s IN RETROSPECT

At the end of December 1889 there were seven golf clubs in Ireland, four in Ulster and three in Leinster. An attempt had been made in Munster but the Fota golf course would appear to have succumbed at a very early stage. Tom Gilroy's links at Mornington continued to be played over and the private links at Killymoon would soon become a club. There were several Scottish regiments serving in Ireland at this time including the Blackwatch, Highland Light Infantry, Gordon Highlanders and Sutherland Highlanders, amongst their ranks were some very active golfers who were sowing the seeds of the game in fertile ground.

The total number of golfers in the country would not have exceeded five hundred and there is little doubt that many of them were expatriate Scotsmen. None of the clubs actually owned their own course, three of them were on links land, two were on commons land and two on rented private property. There was no controlling body to give direction to the development of the game and the clubs acted in isolation from one another. The Portrush golfers were most ambitious and had taken upon themselves the mantle of the "Royal and Ancient of Ireland". Just three years after the foundation of their club they would give the impetus which would found the first golfing union in the world.

FOOTNOTES

1. *Centenary Brochure Royal Belfast G.C.*, page 29.
2. *Sport* 27th November 1886.
3. *Centenary Brochure Royal Belfast G.C.*, page 31.
4. Letter RHQ/G/14/1 dated 4th May 1982 Regimental Regimental Historian Royal Highland Fusiliers.
5. *The Story of the R&A* by J. B. Salmond, page 240.
6. Recorded in *The Golfing Annual 1887* (Vol. 1), page 143.
7. It will be noted that the 1875 course laid out by the 91st Highlanders had been of eleven holes (see Chapter 4).
8. Letter 4.13/2 from Historian R&A 17th January 1983: ". . . on 18th October 1848 the Captain proposed Lt. Col. Campbell, younger, of Craigie, seconded by Sir J. McKenzie . . .''.
9. *The Field* 4th April 1888.
10. P.R.O. W.O. 76/221.
11. Army Lists 1879.
12. Information kindly supplied by Norman Holme, Assistant Curator, Royal Welch Fusiliers Regimental Museum.
13. Army Lists 1881 and 1883.
14. *Royal Cape Golf Club Brochure, S.A. Championship 1985*, page 13.
15. Details from the *The Landed Gentry of Ireland (Burkes)*, pages 223/224; *Burkes Landed Gentry 1937*. *Modern English Biography (Boase)* 1892 confirms that Sir Augustus De Butts was ''son of Elias De Butts of Wicklow''.
16. In the introduction to his book, Browning refers to a mild controversy over the date of the start of golf in Ireland leading to an informative correspondence with Brigadier General Kinloch.
17. The Border Regiment, The Highland Light Infantry and the King's Own Borderers (Army Lists).
18. *The Field*, 21st November 1885.
19. *Centenary Brochure R.D.G.C. 1985*, page 13.
20. *The Field* 5th November 1881, 12th November 1881, Col. G. H. Moncrieff was Captain of the ''old'' London Scottish G.C. at this time. He would later become a member of the Curragh in 1890 and in 1891 he became a member of Royal Dublin. In 1893 he presented the Moncrieff Cup for competition at Dollymount and was President of the club in 1894/95.
21. *The Field* 7th November 1885.
22. *Golf* 17th February 1893, pages 395-6.
23. Winner of the Open Championship Belt 1868, '69, '70, thus becoming the outright owner. First winner of the Open Championship Vase at Prestwick in 1872. He died in 1875 at the young age of 24.
24. *A History Of Golf* by Robert Browning, page 157.
25. *The Irish Golfer* 21st February 1900 named the sons as Aldie and Norman. *The Irish Times* 6th June 1894 lists T. Gilroy, R. R. Gilroy and N. Gilroy on the Co. Louth team v. Royal Dublin.
26. It is clear from this account that Rooney had full access to the early minutes of the Royal Dublin Club. These were later lost in the 1943 fire.
27. *The Golfing Annual 1888/89*, published in May 1889, reported that the number of holes would ''shortly be increased''.
28. He would subsequently be a prime mover in forming Lisburn G.C.
29. Day's father was Walter D. Day, a famous old professional and clubmaker of Musselburgh.
30. *Irish Golf* April 1928, article by ''Pedes''.
31. *Thoms Directory* 1859.
32. *The Irish Golfer* 6th February 1901.
33. *Balfour* by Max Egremont, page 94.
34. An article on John Lumsden, who may have recalled this story for J. P. Rooney.
35. It is of interest to note that when the title Royal was granted to the Dublin Golf Club in May 1891 the letter was address to ''c/o Rt. Hon. A. J. Balfour M.P.'' (*The Irish Field* 2nd January 1926).
36. *Muirfield And The Honourable Company*, page 28.
37. *The Field* 19th November 1887. At that time Sir James believed that the Cork course was still functioning at Fota — See earlier entry re golf at Cork in 1883.
38. It was also announced that in 1889 the Dublin club would host the competition.

CHAPTER 6

The Boom Years — 1890 to 1899

Part 1: A UNION IS FORMED; MILITARY DISCIPLES

Of the seven clubs in existence in 1889, four were in Ulster; the three others were in Leinster. It was not until late in 1891 that the first Munster club was formed at Limerick and Scottish influence was much in evidence for that club's institution. The earliest club at Cork would appear to have been Rushbrooke (1892), Cork Golf Club's foundation date was given as 1st November 1894 in *The Golfing Annual 1895/96*. A Rathconey Golf Club, at Cork, was listed in the same publication for 1894/95, without date of foundation or membership details.

It would appear that much research is required still to uncover the early years of golf at Cork. Writing in his *Golf Addict Among The Irish*, George Houghton told of his visit to the club at Little Island: "There is a 'Captains' Board in the bar and the heading is lettered in gold:

THE CORK GOLF CLUB

Established 1820.

That '1820' staggered me. Could Little Island be older than Westward Ho!? This was mysterious. I would have guessed that the Cork Golf Club probably started in the golfing nineties or maybe later. I raised the point and this raised a laugh from Commander Crosbie . . . 'That's just a novelty' he said. 'The sign painter thought "Established something-or-other" would look good, so he asked the reigning Captain for a date. The Skipper said "just put 1820", so the sign painter did, and we all know it's wrong, but does it matter?' . . ."

Connacht's first club was Co. Sligo which was founded in October 1894 at Rosses Point. There is a tradition that officers of the Sligo Artillery (Militia) played golf at this location in 1890, however there is no evidence of foundation of a club at the time. Golf at Galway would appear to have been introduced by Lt. H. F. N. Jourdain of the Connaught Rangers. In his book, *Ranging Memories*, Jourdain wrote: "Golf at this time was just beginning to get a foothold in the West of Ireland I made a nine hole course with a famous young golfer of the 15th Regiment (East Yorkshire)." Jourdain had been commissioned in February 1893, however the East Yorkshire Regiment did not arrive in Ireland until the late Autumn of 1894 (Birr). At the earliest, the first course at Galway was laid out in late 1894! The Galway Golf Club was founded in 1895 with a retired army officer Capt. Joe Henley (ex 82nd Regiment) being the acknowledged founder. [2]

Scottish influence was evident in the reoccupation of Cush Point, Sutton, by the Dublin Scottish Club in June 1890. However, this club would not appear to have survived beyond April 1891. There was an ill-fated attempt to form a club at Leopardstown racecourse in July 1891, G. L. Baillie was also involved. Dublin's next club would appear to have been Island at Malahide in 1891. This club had its origins in the desire of some Royal Dublin members to play Sunday golf, which was forbidden at Dollymount at that time.

Despite some of the early setbacks, the 1890s were to witness the greatest boom in Irish golf which would not be equalled until the 1960s.

FOUNDATION OF THE GOLFING UNION OF IRELAND – 1891

Thirteen clubs were founded between 1890 and 1891, all but four were in Ulster (see Appendix 2). It is not surprising therefore that the movement to organise Irish golf began amongst the Northern clubs. A full account of the adjourned inaugural meeting, held on 13th November 1891, was carried in the magazine *Golf* 27th November 1891: "An adjourned meeting of the delegates of the Golfing Union of Ireland was held in the Royal Hotel Belfast on 13th Inst. Present: Mr. W. H. Mann (Captain County Club) in the chair; Mr. H. Herdman (Royal Belfast); Mr. George Combe, Dr. Magill and Mr. E. Young (County Down); Mr. H. Adair and Mr. A. N. Gaussen (Killymoon); Mr. R. Daniel, Mr. James Dickson and Rev. E. F. Campbell (Dungannon); Mr. R. A. Collingwood (Portsalon) and Mr. Hugh C. Kelly, Hon. Sec. Pro Tem. The following resolutions were passed:

1. That a Golfing Union be and is hereby established.
2. That the Union be managed by a council consisting of a President, three Vice Presidents, a Secretary, a Treasurer and delegates from different clubs of the union.
3. That Lord Ranfurly be President.
4. That Capt. McCalmont M.P. and Mr. J. S. Alexander be Vice Presidents and that the third Vice President be not appointed for the present.
5. That Mr. George Combe be Honorary Secretary.
6. That Mr. Hugh C. Kelly be appointed Honorary Treasurer.
7. That there be one delegate for each club and an extra delegate for each 150 members, always provided that there be not more than 3 delegates from any one club.
8. That the Subscription from each club to the Union be £1.1s per each delegate the club is entitled to have.
9. That the following clubs be the original clubs forming the GUI. The County, County Down, Royal Belfast, Killymoon, Dungannon, Aughnacloy, Ballycastle, Portsalon, Buncrana.
10. That any club wishing to join the Union shall be proposed by members of the Council and seconded by another and may be admitted on getting a majority of the votes of those members of the Council present at the next meeting.
11. That all clubs of the Union shall be entitled to have their fixtures published by the Union before 1st December and 2 Cards of such fixtures be sent to the Secretary of each club.
12. That the Union take steps to establish an Irish Championship open to

members of all recognized golf clubs, to be competed for on links appointed
by the Union.

13. That the discussion of the adoption of a uniform method of handicapping
    be postponed to a subsequent meeting of the Union.

14. That the Honorary Secretary be empowered to call a meeting of the Council
    at any time he may consider necessary and shall be required to do so on
    receiving a requisition signed by the delegates of any two clubs.

15. That Messrs. H. Herdman, G. Combe and H. C. Kelly be appointed a
    subcommittee to draw up rules both for the Union and Championship
    meetings and submit same to a subsequent meeting of the Union.''

One of the main motives in establishing the Union was the institution of an
Irish Championship. In a lengthy account of the Portrush Club Spring meeting
The Field 19th April 1890 had reported ''. . . the council of the County Club
are now taking the preliminary steps towards the foundation of an Amateur
Championship of Ireland, open to all the world''. It can be seen that, not
satisfied with the success of their previously established open competition (Portglenone Cup), this club had set its sights on a greater objective. No definitive
account of the origins of the Golfing Union of Ireland has yet been written,
however it is quite clear that the Portrush Club had partially achieved its aim
with the Union's establishment. The inaugural Chairman W. H. Mann and the
two Vice Presidents were all from the County Club. [3]

INSTITUTION OF THE IRISH OPEN AND CLOSE CHAMPIONSHIPS

The first competition for the Irish Amateur Open Golf Championship was held
at Portrush in September 1892 ''. . . designated the St. Andrews of the Emerald
Isle''. [4] Winner on this inaugural occasion was Mr. Alexander Stuart of the
Honourable Company of Edinburgh Golfers (then located at Musselburgh), he
gained victory over Mr. J. H. Andrew of the Prestwick Club by one hole in the
final.

In April 1893 the first Irish Close Championship was held, also at Portrush.
The Irish Times 27th April 1893 reported: ''. . . the competition under auspices
of the Golfing Union of Ireland . . . was open to all bonafide Irish born and
resident golfers, of whom there was a fairly good turn out''. After three days
of play the winner was Mr. T. Dickson of the Co. Down Club who was
victorious over his fellow club member George Combe, Hon. Secretary of the
Union.

THE FIRST INTERPROVINCIAL – 1896

The Irish Times 22nd January 1896 carried the first notice of an intended interprovincial match between Leinster and Ulster. Teams of 20 aside were to
compete prior to the Irish Born (Close) Championship at Portrush during Easter.
The outcome was to be traumatic for the Ulster golfers, who had considered

themselves masters of the game in Ireland heretofore.

Leinster were victorious by 37 holes to 34 and shock waves were felt all over Ulster. Further humiliation followed when Leinster were successful at Dollymount in 1897 (winning by 54 holes) and at Newcastle in 1898 also. Most of the Leinster players were members of the Royal Dublin Club, in itself this would become a "bone of contention" among the Dublin clubs. [5]

It will be remembered that one of the Union's objectives had been the adoption of a uniform method of handicapping. Arising from Leinster's resounding victory and because of the number of Royal Dublin members on the team, a meeting of affiliated club Secretaries decided to take drastic action (one could say "over reaction"). *The Irish Times* 19th December 1896 reported: ". . . the important question of handicapping was discussed. It was generally recognised that the handicapping in most of the Ulster Clubs had been too low, men being placed at scratch or even lower who would be no match for Scotch or English players with like handicaps. It was also pointed out that the interprovincial match, played at Portrush last Easter had shown the handicapping of the Royal Dublin Club to be about 4 strokes higher than that of Northern Clubs. Mr. George Combe proposed a resolution that was adopted unanimously to the effect that all the other clubs in Union should do what Royal Dublin [6] did two years ago — namely add 4 strokes to each member's handicap."

THE LEINSTER TEAM — WINNER OF THE FIRST INTERPROVINCIAL
VERSUS ULSTER 1896
Irish Golfer 1st November 1899.

In its own way the newly instituted interprovincial series had a stimulative effect on golf in Ireland. Ulster's dominance was broken and, coincidence or otherwise, 1896 was to see a record number of new clubs founded. Seventeen clubs commenced existence that year, eleven of them were non- Ulster clubs (see Appendix 2).

EXPANSION OF IRISH GOLF IN THE 1890s

In numbers of golf clubs founded, the decade from 1890 to 1899 would never be equalled in Irish golf history. This can be seen clearly in the table below:

Years	Clubs Founded	Remarks
1881/1889	8	
1890/1899	103	
1900/1909	68	
1910/1919	39	
1920/1929	51	Source of information
1930/1939	25	for years 1920 to 1985 —
1940/1949	21	GUI affiliation records.
1950/1959	6	
1960/1969	16	
1970/1979	20	
1980/1985	8	

Apart from these clubs there were a number of private courses which were documented in the golfing publications of the 1890s, these can be seen in Appendix 2. Why so many clubs were founded at that time may be attributed to a number of factors:

1. Following the agrarian troubles of the 1880s a more settled period followed in the 1890s.
2. Greater affluence among the middle classes caused them to look for outlets for their spare time.
3. Some of the leading landed gentry developed an interest in the game and in many instances gave the land free for the local club (see Co. Cavan, Massereene, Rostrevor).
4. Scottish and English Regiments stationed in a number of locations became involved with the local gentry in organising the game.
5. The independent railway companies saw golf as a means of improving traffic on their sections of railway. Allied to this a number of hotels organised golf courses as amenities for their clientele.
6. Experienced golfers among the religious, business and public service professions brought the game with them to their new postings in the provinces (see Banagher, Ballycastle, Lucan, Tramore as examples).

7. Golf in Dublin benefited from a great surge of interest amongst members of the Bar.
8. The founding of a golf club at Dublin University in 1894 introduced many provincial students to the game. The club became a major force in Irish golf shortly after its foundation.

THE MILITARY INFLUENCE

Regimental golfers had been among the leading pioneers of the game in Ireland, as outlined earlier. The Curragh, Kinsale, Dublin and Belfast had benefited from the presence of The Highland Light Infantry, The King's Own Borderers, The Blackwatch and The Gordon Highlanders.

The Blackwatch (42nd) Regiment: In 1891 the officers of the 2nd Battalion of this Regiment were actively involved in the founding of the Limerick Golf Club, one year later they helped organise Lahinch. The Regiment had come to Ireland in the Autumn of 1886 when they were first posted to the Curragh. In the following year they moved to Dublin and became actively involved with the Dublin Golf Club, presenting a medal which is still competed for. A move to Belfast took place in early 1889 where they remained until May 1891 when they moved to Limerick. The Regiment finally departed Ireland in January 1893.[7] The 1st Battalion of this Regiment were in Gibraltar in 1891 when the club was founded there in February of that year.

THE BLACKWATCH REGIMENT PHOTOGRAPHED AT THE CURRAGH 1886
Co-founders of Limerick and Lahinch Golf Clubs.

One of the key Blackwatch players, when they were in Ireland, was Lt. McFarlane and he is documented as playing in the opening game at Lahinch on Good Friday 1892.[8] McFarlane was killed at Modder River in December 1899 during the Boer war,[9] a fate which befell his best friend, Lt. F. G. Tait, only three months later.[10] Tait had been transferred into the Regiment from 2nd Battalion Leinster Regiment in June 1894 and when he won the British Amateur Championship in 1896 and 1898 he gave the Blackwatch G.C. as his club.[11]

Gordon Highlanders: When this Regiment was on the Curragh in July 1867 their unit history records: "Games of all sorts were played". Unfortunately, no details of the games being played were documented. On 30th August 1887 the 2nd Battalion Gordon Highlanders moved to Belfast from Guernsey and in October the wife of one of the officers of the Regiment became the first known lady golfer to play in Ireland (see Chapter 9). Lts. Aitken, Bethune, Urmstow and Lockhart were on the military teams which played matches against the Royal Belfast civilians in May and October 1889.[12] In the Spring of 1891 the Gordons moved to the Curragh and were actively involved with golf there, *The Field* 25th April 1891 documented a military v. civilian match at Royal Dublin. The match was 12-a-side and seven of the soldiers were from the Curragh, Lt. Lockhart and Lt. Aitken of the Gordons winning their matches by 12 holes and 4 holes respectively. A victory for the military men by 14 holes was largely contributed to by these two officers.

The Regiment departed Ireland in June 1894 for Glasgow, having spent their last eighteen months in Dublin. There is no other mention of their participation in Irish golf at that time.[13]

The Seaforth Highlanders: This Regiment's 1st Battalion arrived in Dublin on 14th March 1889 from Glasgow, there is no record of them playing golf there at that time. On 17th April 1891 the Regiment moved to the old barracks, Fermoy.[14] It is clear that the officers of the Seaforths were very active golfers. *The Irish Times* 11th May 1892 recorded a return golf match at Fermoy against Lismore Golf Club (see entry in Appendix 1). Officers named were Col. Garnett, Maj. Brooke Hunt, Lt. Broadford, Lt. Hopkinson and Lt. Lauder.

In the minutes of a Regimental Mess Meeting held in Fermoy on 3rd May 1893 the following entries occur:

> "10. Resolved that expenses connected with the boats and also the golf links, while the Regiment is at Fermoy, be defrayed out of the Baggage Fund.
>
> 12. A vote of thanks was unanimously accorded to Lieutenant and Quartermaster Lauder for the highly satisfactory way in which he had supervised the golf links during the past season . . ."[15]

In these same minutes subscriptions were set for the various Regimental Clubs but there is no mention of a golf club. However it would appear that the Seaforth

Highlanders formed a club at Fermoy prior to their departure for Tipperary on 20th October 1893. An Irish Regiment was stationed at Fermoy during the same period and the friendship established there is documented in the same Mess records of 1893: "The officers of the 1st Royal Irish Rifles having very handsomely presented a silver challenge cup to the officers of the 1st Seaforth Highlanders, to be competed for annually by the members of their golf club . . ." The conditions of competition were laid down and it is of interest that this cup is still in the possession of the renamed Queen's Own Highlanders (Seaforth and Camerons).

On 20th October 1893 the Seaforths moved to Tipperary and on 14th January 1894 they departed for Aldershot. It can be seen that the Royal Irish Rifles had presented a cup to the Regimental Golf Club, the only mention of such club is in the Mess records. There is no entry relating to golf at Tipperary, however it is evident that these active golfers would very quickly have organised a course for themselves there. *The Irish Golfer* 25th April 1900 reported that Col. H. D. Cutbill, Hon. Secretary of the Co. Down Club from 1897 to 1899 and Captain in 1900, had first played golf at Fermoy in 1892. He was the commanding officer of the 1st Battalion Royal Irish Rifles at the time they were in Fermoy.

13th Hussars: An article in *The Irish Field* 31st July 1909 recorded that this Cavalry Regiment had been involved in the founding of a golf club at Dundalk in 1896: "Golf was first played at Dundalk when the 13th Hussars were stationed there and the prime movers were Capt. MacLaren (of polo fame), Mr. P. L. McArdle, J. St. P. MacArdle and that well-known Co. Down sportsman Col. Wallace. This semi club died a natural death from want of support . . . it is wonderful to hear all the stories of the 13th Hussars when there and no wonder when such men as MacLaren, Wise, Tremayne etc. were in the Regiment . . ."

The 13th Hussars arrived at the Curragh in 1891, were in Ballincollig, Cork, in 1893/94, returned to the Curragh in 1894, to Dundalk 1895/96 and finally Dublin 1897/8 until their departure for Aldershot. [16] One of the most famous officers of the Regiment was Baden Powell of subsequent Boy Scout fame. He was with the Regiment in Ireland up to November 1895 and on his return from a trip to Africa rejoined his unit at Dundalk in March 1896. [17]

Athlone Garrison Golf Club: Unfortunately the earliest minute books of the Athlone Club are no longer available, however from its institution in 1892 until 1904 the club's name clearly identified its military origins. The only documented meeting of this club and the other military club at the Curragh is documented in *The Irish Times* 12th December 1896 when the visitors won by 18 holes to 12 holes. Until 1904 the committee was mainly composed of the local military garrison however, eventually, the civilian majority prevailed in that year.

Other Military Legacies: Several Irish clubs had mementoes to remember their departed military friends. Royal Dublin were major beneficiaries with the Coldstream Guards Cup and Moncrieff Cup in addition to the Blackwatch Medal. Tipperary received the East Yorkshire Regiment Cup in 1898.[18] The course at Newry had been laid out on military ground in 1892. Kinsale's course in 1897 was laid out around Charles Fort. Rosses Point's first golf had been played in the early 1890s by the Duke of Connaught's Sligo Own Artillery. A retired military officer had a key role in establishing Galway golf club in 1895. The Bantry course of 1897 had been laid out by officers of a local naval detachment. It is most likely that many of the major garrison towns would have received willing recruits for their golf clubs from the military stationed in their local barracks.

Portmarnock's narrow escape from military occupation in 1892 is documented in Appendix 1. Modern Irish golfers would consider it inconceivable that this area could be anything other than one of the premier courses in the country. However, if the British War Department had its way in June 1892 there would now be rifle ranges all over the famous links. It was for this reason that the Royal Belfast had to move from its original location at Kinnegar, which was a military range. Research in the provincial newspapers may reveal more on the local contributions of the garrisons all over Ireland.

Ladies Day at the Curragh

Prior to 1914 ladies were allowed to exercise their prowess at marksmanship on a rifle range near the Curragh Golf Club. Lionel Hewson told the following story . . . "Once with Col. St. Leger Moore I was on a green behind the musketry range. A bullet sang between us, we found out it was 'Ladies Day'."

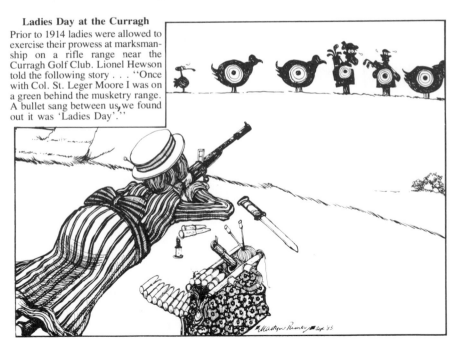

Part 2: EARLY SPONSORS, PIONEERS AND INTERCLUB ACTIVITY

RAILWAY COMPANIES BOOST THE GAME

It will be remembered that when the club was opened at Portrush in May 1888 the Northern Counties Railway Company had offered free tickets to the Royal Belfast Golfers. This early commercial interest was maintained throughout the 1890s. Uppermost in the minds of the golfing pioneers at this time was the proximity of a railway station, close to their intended golfing venture, and the railway companies were most willing to assist. Train timetables were altered to suit the golfing public, reduced fares were agreed with the golf clubs and in some instances the railway companies decided to build their own golf courses.

Great Northern Railways: In September 1891 when Royal Dublin held their first ever open competition, this company helped by giving reduced fares to the Ulster competitors.[19] Through its subsidiary, The Irish Highland Hotel Co., the first course was laid out around its hotel at Bundoran in 1894.[20] When the club at Warrenpoint was being revived in 1898, the GNR and Highland Hotel companies each gave £50.[21] The GNR also gave cups to the following clubs in the years as shown: Warrenpoint 1894, Rostrevor 1894, Bundoran 1896, Portmarnock 1897, Sutton 1897, Co. Louth 1898.

Great Southern & Western Railway: This company's hotel at Caragh Lakes, near Glenbeigh in Co. Kerry, built a nine-hole course for its guests in 1895. Anthony Brown of Royal Dublin was employed for this purpose.[22] In 1898 the company were offering cheap fares for golfers on their route to Lahinch via the famous West Clare Railway.[23]

London & North Western Railway: Greenore Golf Club owes its existence to this company and also to the keen eye of G. L. Baillie. The first 12-hole course, opened on 17th October 1896, and the clubhouse were constructed by the company.[24]

Lartigue Railway Co: This ill-fated company played a significant part in the foundation of the first course at Ballybunion. *The Irish Field* 26th December 1908 recorded that the company had defrayed the original costs of the course. A journey on this unique monorail system must have whetted the appetite of early Kerry golfers.

THE MONORAIL LARTIGUE RAILWAY AT BALLYBUNION C. 1900
(Courtesy of the National Library of Ireland)

Northern Counties Railway Committee: Greenisland Golf Club received a significant amount of help from Mr. B. D. Wise of this railway company. The sods for the greens were brought by rail, free of cost, from Magilligan in 1894.[25] In that same year the newly-founded Larne Club received from the company a grant in aid of £20 per year for five years to help boost its affairs.[26] *The Irish Field* 1st May 1909 reported that Portstewart Golf Club had received financial help from this company for their first clubhouse and also for

> **MIDLAND RAILWAY,**
> NORTHERN COUNTIES COMMITTEE,
>
> **SEASIDE GOLF LINKS at**
> **PORTRUSH** (near Giant's Causeway), **BALLY-CASTLE** (Antrim Coast), **LARNE** (Belfast Lough), **PORTSALON** (Lough Swilly), **ROSAPENNA** (North Donegal).
> Excellent Hotel Accommodation at each place.
> **HOTELS UNDER RAILWAY MANAGEMENT.**
> MIDLAND STATION HOTEL, BELFAST.—Most convenient for travellers to and from the North. The Hotel is elegantly furnished and lighted with electricity. Belfast Tram Cars start from Hotel door.
> NORTHERN COUNTIES RAILWAY HOTEL, PORTRUSH (near Giant's Causeway).—One of the most commodious and best appointed Hotels in Ireland. Splendidly situated. Two magnificent Suites of Sea and Fresh Water Baths. For terms, &c., apply to F. COX, Hotel Manager, Portrush.
> **NEW EXPRESS ROUTE BETWEEN IRELAND AND ENGLAND via BELFAST AND HEYSHAM.**
> **Magnificent Steamers. Luxurious Corridor Trains.**
> First and Third Class Breakfast, Luncheon, and Dining Cars. Trains run alongside steamers at Heysham.
> Luggage transferred at Belfast and Heysham free of charge. Passengers booked between the principal stations in Ireland and England at Through Fares.
> JAMES COWIE, Traffic Manager, Belfast.

Advertisement for golf holidays by Northern Counties Railway Group c. 1905.

changes to the course. The first links of the Royal Portrush Golf Club was originally leased by this company from Lord Antrim. This association continued until 1928.

Dublin Wicklow & Wexford Railway: When the shortlived Leopardstown course was opened, *The Irish Times* 16th July 1891 reported that this company had consented to give special fares to members of the Leopardstown fraternity who became "golf subscribers". In 1895 the company donated a cup for an open men's competition at Greystones.[27] A similar cup was competed for at Foxrock in July 1895.[28]

Dublin United Tramway Co: Royal Dublin received a cup from this company, reported by *The Irish Times* on 17th February 1896. Its value was £5, to be played for at the Spring meeting.

HOTELS

Several of the railway companies had associated hotels, as has been seen above. Both businesses complemented each other and with increasing numbers of people being able to take holidays it was a major growth area in the 1890s. Among the many localities which had hotels associated with the institution of a course were: Ardara (1898); Clonakilty (1895); Dunfanaghy (1897); Glenbeigh (1897); Portsalon (1891); Rosapenna (1893); Spanish Point (1896).

In addition, local hotels were keen to sponsor competitions, examples were the Grand Hotel Cup (1897) for the Malahide and Island clubs, [29] the Golf Club Hotel at Lahinch offered cups (1898) for both ladies and gentlemen. [30] When the Greystones Club was inaugurated in 1895 the local Grand Hotel presented a valuable cup for competition. [31] That some of the hotels profited from the golf boom is evident from the remarks of Lord Annesley who stated, in 1896, that a local Newcastle, Co. Down, hotel proprietor had reported additional income of £3,000 since the links had been laid out some years before. [32] A tidy sum in those days.

GOLF ADVOCATES AT THE BAR

From a very early date the legal fraternity became active disciples of the new game and there is much evidence to show that they were Dublin's most active pioneers in the early 1890s. *The Irish Times* 8th May 1891 documented a match at Dollymount between the Bar and the Curragh Brigade Club. The legal fraternity won by 12 holes to 3, their team consisting of F. E. Cuming, J. H. Pigot, D. M. Wilson, [33] J. H. Russell, G. C. May, D. Christie, M. O'C. Morris.

Three days later *The Irish Times* reported that ". . . those members of the Bar, who belong to the club, have presented a massive silver cup of beautiful design to be played for under handicap limited to 25 strokes twice a year in May and November". *The Irish Times* 29th June 1891 recorded the first winner as Geo C. May, who was a member of the Bar team himself. By 1896 the golf disease was rampant amongst the barristers at the Four Courts, *The Belfast Newsletter* 7th January 1896 reported: "There is a well known crier at the Four Courts who summons from the Library any Barrister who is fortunate enough to get a brief. If the Barrister is not in the Library the client asks where he had best search for him. The crier's stereotyped reply in these desperate golfing days is 'Try Dollymount'."

Portmarnock, too, had a strong legal membership, *The Irish Times* 1st July 1897 recorded the presentation of a Legal Cup to the club, to be played for over

36 holes, handicap limit 18. W. D. Meldon was the first winner two weeks later. The Bar team also engaged Portmarnock in matches and *The Irish Times* 6th May 1898 recorded a victory for the latter in a return match.

By the end of the 1890s, the legal profession were quite dominant in Royal Dublin affairs. *The Irish Golfer* 18th April 1900 carried an article on Mr. David Christie which reported that in 1890, when he joined Royal Dublin, there had been only two members of the Irish Bar on the rolls: "Mr. Christie played Circe so successfully that many more soon joined and at present some 70 barristers belong to and form a large part of the playing strength of the club."

Cecil Barcroft: A leading member of the Bar was Cecil Barcroft (1871-1924) who had joined Portrush in 1892 and came shortly afterwards to study at TCD when he joined Royal Dublin. He was Captain of Dublin University Club in 1897 and also Dungannon in the same year. In 1898 he was called to the Bar and in 1905 he was appointed Secretary of Royal Dublin, a post he would hold until just before his death in December 1924. Barcroft was one of the great pioneers, he wrote golf articles in *The Daily Express, The Evening Mail* and also contributed to *The Irish Golfer*. Tullamore, Naas and Carlow golf courses were laid out by him in 1922. *The Irish Times* 17th May 1922 reported that he had laid out about 20 courses and reconstructed about 30 others.

CECIL BARCROFT

Legal Language: That the elite of the Bar could swear with the best, at the time, is told in *The Irish Golfer* 23rd August 1899 —

Judge: (to small boy whose head only tops the front of witness box). "Do you know the nature of an oath lad?"

Boy: "Yes, Sir, sure I used to be your caddie."

THE UNIVERSITY INFLUENCE

One of the key elements in spreading the game throughout the country was the foundation of the Dublin University Golf Club in 1894. There were several experienced golfers in Trinity College at that time including the Provost, Dr. Traill, who became first President of the club. Cecil Barcroft was also a founder member.

An article on the club appeared in *The Belfast Newsletter* 16th November 1895 which stated: "For its membership, this new club, started a year ago, has probably the largest amount of golfing talent in the country". Because of the keen interest in golf amongst those early University golfers there is little doubt that other students from all over the country would have been exposed to the game. In due course, following graduation, they in turn would have brought this new sport back to their home towns.

GOLF PIONEERS OF THE 1890s

Tom Gilroy: Tom Gilroy, of Mornington fame, was a major pioneer of this period. He had helped lay out the original Phoenix Park course in 1885, he laid out his own course near Laytown in 1886 and assisted W. H. Mann in laying out the North West Club's course in 1891. Gilroy laid out the original nine holes at Baltray in 1892. An entry in the paper *Sport* 18th September 1886 documents his forthcoming entry for the British Amateur Championship at St. Andrews, the first such competitor from any Irish golf club. On three occasions he was Captain of Royal Dublin 1888, '89 and '94. He was Captain of Co. Louth in 1892/93. By all accounts Tom Gilroy was the most accomplished golfer in Ireland, his standard of play became the basis of the handicap system at Royal Dublin; eventually in 1896 the Golfing Union of Ireland accepted this standard for universal adoption, as mentioned earlier in this chapter. Many early newspapers carried results of his numerous wins and good scores in golf events at Portrush, Aughnacloy, Co. Down, Dollymount and Co. Louth. Mr. George Ross, first Captain of Portmarnock in 1894, and first Captain of Sutton in 1896, credited Gilroy with his introduction to the game. [35] Late in 1895 he accepted the post of Secretary of Seaford Golf Club in East Sussex and much to the regret of the Irish golfing fraternity he moved there with his family. [36]

G. L. Baillie: Many individuals contributed to the spread of late Victorian golf in Ireland, one man would appear to have made a profession of it. G. L. Baillie had been a key figure in the 1881 institution of Royal Belfast, he never became Captain of that club or Royal Co. Down which he helped found in 1889. From an early date he set out to sell "his courses" abroad as the advertisement from *The Golfing Annual* on page 72 shows. Over the next twenty years he laid out the following courses: Leopardstown (1891), Lisburn (1891), Bundoran (1894), Larne (1894), Knock (1895), Magilligan (1896), Greenore (1896), Castlerock (1900), Scrabo (1907), Omagh (1910). That he laid out many other courses is more than likely.

GOLFING TOUR in ULSTER,

EMBRACING

THREE GREENS—

Holywood and Newcastle, Co. Down,

AND

Portrush, Co. Antrim,

And affording an excellent opportunity of visiting the prosperous city of Belfast, the fine scenery of the Mourne Mountains, and the famed Giants' Causeway.

FARES,

Including Cabin Return to Belfast; First Class Return Rail Belfast and Holywood; First Class Return Rail Belfast and Newcastle, Co. Down; First Class Rail Belfast and Portrush; FOUR DAYS' Hotel Accommodation and free use of Golfing Greens.

From Liverpool,	£3	15	0
,, Barrow,	3	12	6
,, Glasgow,	3	17	6

Golfers will find this one of the cheapest and most enjoyable Tours ever arranged.

Full particulars on application to G. L. BAILLIE, 1, Brookhill Avenue, Belfast, Joint Secretary Co. Antrim and Co. Down Golf Clubs.

G. L. BAILLIE'S ADVERTISEMENT FOR ULSTER GOLF
One of the earliest promotions for golf in Ireland, in *The Golfing Annual* 1889/90.

Baillie was highly talented and the great Tom Morris made the following remark regarding his work at Co. Down: "I wonder why they send for me; this Mr. Baillie kens mair about laying golf links than I dae. They had nae need to send for me."[34] In many instances he is documented as acting Secretary of the new links (e.g. Leopardstown, Greenore and Co. Antrim) and may have been on a retainer from some of the railway companies for this purpose.

John Lumsden: From his first day with the Royal Dublin Club, Lumsden remained as patriarch of Dublin golf until his death in 1925. No full account has been written of his contribution to Irish golf and only occasional glimpses are to be found in newspapers of the day. He was listed amongst the committee of the ill-fated Stillorgan Club in 1891. Later *The Irish Golfer* 31st January 1900 recorded his contribution to the infant Rathfarnham Club: "Mr. John Lumsden, the Nestor of Dublin golf, may be said to have discovered the links . . ." He was listed amongst the attendance at Portmarnock's second annual general meeting in *The Irish Times* 24th January 1896, obviously he was a member of this club from an early stage. Lumsden was elected a Vice President of the Golfing Union of Ireland in 1892, when the Royal Dublin Club affiliated.

A. W. Shaw: When the Limerick Golf Club was founded in December 1891, Alexander Shaw became the first Captain and President. Shortly afterwards he was a key figure in setting up the links at Lahinch and he had a lengthy

ALEXANDER W. SHAW

association with this famous club, being Captain from 1893 to 1901 and President from 1893 to 1923. Shaw had a keen business mind, *The Sportsmans Holiday Guide 1897* recorded: ". . . a fine hotel has been built by a syndicate of gentlemen with Mr. Shaw at their head, in the Norwegian style and it serves the double purpose of hotel and clubhouse."

In 1895 the Lahinch Club had instituted the South of Ireland Championship. This would attract golfers from all over Ireland and mainland Britain, especially after Tom Morris had been brought over to pronounce blessings on the course. Shaw had founded the first club in Munster and in due course his position was recognised when he became Vice President of the Golfing Union of Ireland in 1902. He was knighted in November 1906.

INTERCLUB ACTIVITIES IN THE 1890s

From 1896 onwards the sports page of *The Irish Times* began to give details of numerous interclub matches, the Dublin and Belfast clubs, in particular, were most active. In the Provinces, Nenagh won by 22 holes against Limerick in January.[37] Killarney won by six holes against Cork at Killarney in April[38] and Tullamore gained a home victory by 8 holes over Mullingar in the same month.[39] Provincial clubs had been playing interclub matches before this date but 1896 was the first year in which a continuous reporting of results was given in *The Irish Times*.

The Belfast Newsletter had reported many Ulster interclub matches from 1894 onwards. Lurgan, at home, defeated Armagh by 34 holes in June.[40] Fortwilliam defeated Royal Belfast by nine holes at Carnalea in December.[41] Co. Down had a crushing victory by 40 holes over Royal County (Portrush) in the same month.[42] Beginning in 1895 reports of Leinster and Munster interclub matches and golf gossip regularly appeared. This newspaper, in particular, documented the beginnings of many Irish clubs, essential information for club historians who find themselves without early documentation. *The Irish Times* also documented the institution of many clubs in the 1890s as can be seen in Appendix 1.

At a meeting held on 15th March 1895 the Golfing Union of Ireland had divided the affiliated clubs into districts ". . . to arrange Inter-Club matches according to convenience of smaller clubs. Players to be selected as far as possible to ensure a good match but not necessarily victory for the large clubs . . ."[43] The following districts were set out:

Royal Co. (Portrush)	Royal Belfast	Co. Down	Royal Dublin
Shanes Park	Lurgan	Dungannon	Foxrock
Killymoon	Ormeau	Lisburn	Co. Louth
Ballycastle	Armagh	Belmont	Rostrevor
North West			Warrenpoint

FIXTURE PROBLEMS IN DUBLIN

From the date of its affiliation in 1892, Royal Dublin had become the voice of Southern Irish golf. The arrangements for holding the Irish Championship and interprovincial matches were made by the Royal Dublin Club when the Southern capital was the venue. It would appear that some of the Dublin clubs were unhappy with these arrangements and a lengthy letter from "a Bunker" published in *The Irish Times* 25th March 1898 criticised the choice of weekend for the forthcoming interprovincial fixture (arranged for Newcastle on 16th April). He pointed out that a meeting had been held in November 1897 at which secretaries of the Leinster clubs had agreed dates of open competitions and now twenty of Leinster's best players were affected.

"Bunker" criticised a particular Northern club for having too much influence in the selection of dates by the GUI. The selection of the Leinster team was dominated by Royal Dublin who arranged selection of same. Finally, "Bunker" suggested the getting together of captains and secretaries of Leinster clubs to fix each year the date of club competitions, make necessary arrangements for inter-provincial matches, championship meetings when held in Dublin and other matters of general interest.

The following day a letter appeared, signed by D. Christie Stephens, which pointed out that when the first interprovincial was proposed in 1896 it had been sent to Royal Dublin ". . . as the premier club . . . as almost the only club in Leinster . . .". He pointed out the dates did not suit Royal Dublin as they wished to hold the interprovincial in May when the Irish Close would be held at Dollymount. Swift action followed and *The Irish Times* 28th March 1898 reported that the Secretary of the Royal Belfast Golf Club had written that it had been found necessary to postpone the interprovincial.

The Secretaries of the Dublin clubs continued to meet annually to co-ordinate their fixtures, *The Irish Golfer* 13th December 1899 carries a notice regarding the meeting fixed for the Grosvenor Hotel, Westland Row, on the 14th. The seeds of the provincial branches of the Golfing Union of Ireland had been set.

IRISH GOLF IN THE 1890s: IN RETROSPECT
Numerous new golf clubs all over the country bore adequate testimony to the effects of the golf boom of the 1890s. Never again would so many clubs be formed in any ten-year period of Irish golf history. Scots assistance was evident

W. C. PICKEMAN
Founder of Portmarnock 1894.

in some cases, in particular the new club at Portmarnock which was the brainchild of W. C. Pickeman, a native of Edinburgh. He was particularly for-tunate in finding the Scottish family of Jameson equally enthusiastic in giving golfing privileges over their land at Portmarnock. However, many clubs founded during this decade owed their origin to Irishmen who had been exposed to the game during holidays, business travel or military service.

In some cases military personnel of the garrison towns had introduced the game, with the local gentry taking to the pastime so beloved of the widely reported Mr. A. J. Balfour. The gentry's sons, too, had been exposed to the game during their service with the colours. *Burke's Landed Gentry Of Ireland* lists all the prominent families of the period and the details of service of their numerous sons. Large families were quite common with the younger sons being required to "do their duty". In one way the presence of these middle and upper class gentlemen as members of the local club was a negative influence in giving mass popularity to the game. Class and social distinctions were quite marked at this time and the lower classes would have found difficulty in gaining membership of these clubs. Apart from the larger city clubs, *The Golfing Annuals* of this period reflect very low membership, from 20 to 60, in many clubs throughout the provinces. It would not be until the 1960s that greater affluence and a more enlightened attitude allowed for a dramatic rise in numbers of golf club members.

The foundation of the Golfing Union of Ireland in 1891 had been a major stepping stone in popularising the game on the island. Not all of the clubs in the country had been affiliated by 1899, of the 110 clubs founded only 51 had joined the Union.[44] Many clubs had found no good reason to join. With this in mind the Golfing Union of Ireland decided in May 1899 to organise senior and junior challenge competitions to be played for by teams from the affiliated clubs. This englightened decision would result in a doubling of the number of affiliated clubs over the next ten years.

The following poem by Dr. W. F. Collier, LL.D., a founder member of the Royal Belfast Club, conveys the flavour of Irish golf during the halcyon days of the "gay '90s".

GROANS OF AN IRISH CADDIE[45]

Air, "Wearin' of the Green"

Oh! Paddy dear, an' did ye hear
    The news that's in the pubs?
Them golfers is removin'
    All the shamrocks with their clubs.
The puttin' grass, so nately swep,
    Is nowhere to be seen,
For the mischief's in that mashie-club
    That's rippin' up the green.
I met with Arty Balfour,
    An' he tuk me by the hand,
An' sez he—"I've sliced the soil mysel'
    So, shure, I onderstand."
It's the most uprippit coun-thery
    That iver yit was seen:
From Dollymount to swate Portrush
    They're wearin' out the green.

Oh! some in coats o' cruel red,
    An' some in tartan knicks
An' some wid ties o' chaney blue,
    Bud all o' thim wid sticks.
An' they batthers at a weenie ball
    That's lyin' on the sod,
An' hits it—no! they hammers it,
    An' digs out pounds of clod.

If the ball wint wid the surface thin
    Them two'd complate the scene—
But no! it's sleepin' where it lay,
    Like a mishroon, white an' clean.
It's the most uprooted coun-thery
    That iver yit was seen:
From Aughnacloy to Kinnegar
    They're slicin' off the green.

They comes wid drivers, cleeks, an' spoons,
    An' clubs o' quarest name,
An' they calls a hape o' sand their tay,
    Bud it's whishky that they mane.
An' they calls the sods they're flitterin' out
    Big "divots" as they fly,
For they can't spake dacent English,
    Like yersilf, Paudeen an' I.
Oh! who's to save poor Oireland
    Whin they've sthript our Immirald Queen,
An' nothin's left bud bogs and rocks
    Contagious to be seen
In the most un-grass-ful coun-thery
    That iver yit has been—
Augh! divil take that mashie-stick,
    For it's KILLIN' out the green.

FOOTNOTES
1. Army Lists 1893 and 1894. Jourdain subsequently became the last commanding officer of the Connaught Rangers, disbanded in 1922.
2. *The Irish Golfer* 9th December 1903.
3. John Lumsden became the third Vice President in 1892.
4. *The Field* 17th September 1892.
5. *The Irish Times* 27th April 1897 listed that year's Leinster team. Royal Dublin had 11 players and 3 subs, Dublin University 3 players, Portmarnock 3 players, Foxrock 2 and Co. Louth 1.
6. The reference to Royal Dublin's action in 1894 related to that club's handicap scheme based on the play of Tom Gilroy. Further detail is given in Chapter 8.
7. Army Lists 1886 to 1893.
8. *The Irish Field* 29th May 1909.
9. *The Irish Golfer* 27th December 1899.
10. Tait's father, Professor P. G. Tait, had been Professor of Mathematics in Queen's College, Belfast, from 1854 to 1860 and his mother was daughter of Rev. James Porter of Drumlee, Co. Down.
11. *Guinness Book Of Golf Facts And Feats*, page 159.
12. *The Field* 11th May 1889 and *The Belfast Newsletter* 12th October 1889.
13. Information on movements of this Regiment supplied by Regimental Secretary, The Gordon Highlanders, also Army Lists 1887 to 1894.
14. Letter from Regimental Secretary Queen's Own Highlanders 5th August 1985.
15. *Rules & Records Of The Officers Mess 72nd Regiment*, pages 190-191.
16. Army Lists, 1891 to 1898.
17. *The Chief*, pages 62-73.
18. *The Golfing Annual* 1898/99.
19. *The Irish Times* 21st September 1891.
20. *The Belfast Newsletter* 21st May 1894.
21. *The Irish Times* 4th November 1898.
22. *The Irish Times* 18th December 1895.
23. *The Irish Times* 29th July 1898.
24. *The Irish Times* 27th October 1896.
25. *Irish Golf* April 1928.
26. *The Belfast Newsletter* 10th November 1894.
27. *The Irish Times* 13th March 1895.
28. *The Irish Times* 13th July 1895.
29. *The Irish Times* 31st July 1897.
30. *The Irish Times* 2nd May 1898.
31. *The Irish Times* 13th March 1895.
32. *The Belfast Newsletter* 2nd May 1896.
33. This man played a large part in the institution of The Island G.C.
34. *Irish Golf* April 1928 article by "Pedes".
35. *Irish Golfer* 15th November 1899.
36. *The Irish Times* 19th December 1895.
37. *The Irish Times* 17th January 1896.
38. *The Irish Times* 13th April 1896.
39. *The Irish Times* 27th April 1896.
40. *The Belfast Newsletter* 18th June 1894.
41. *The Belfast Newsletter* 11th December 1894.
42. *The Belfast Newsletter* 14th December 1894.
43. Letter from Secretary GUI to Greencastle G.C. 5th April 1973.
44. *The Golfing Annual* 1898/99, page 309. Each year this publication gave a complete list of all clubs affiliated to the GUI and ILGU.
45. Reprinted from *The Irish Golfer's Guide* 1910, page 100.

The Testing Years — 1900 to 1922

Part 1: THE PRE-WAR GOLDEN YEARS

THE SOUTH AFRICAN WAR 1899-1902

War was the main topic of conversation as the new century began, the South African War had erupted in October 1899 and led to a rapid redeployment of Imperial forces. Golf clubs in the garrison towns were beginning to feel the pinch with so many military members gone. *The Irish Golfer* 24th January 1900 stated: "The Hon. Secretary of Mallow writes to us that this season it is usual to have a good many interclub contests, but he adds 'so many of our good players have been called away to South Africa this year I am afraid we may not have any' . . ." Later, *The Irish Golfer* 21st March 1900 reported: "The Tipperary Club is so depleted through its members having gone to the front there is great difficulty in keeping up even the name. The Golfing Union of Ireland has made the club an Honorary member of the Union so long as its members are fighting for their country." At this time the Curragh Camp had been completely denuded of troops and the club was kept going by a small number of local people, Sir Henry Greer paying the ground staff out of his own pocket. [1]

The Boer War, as it was known, did not end until 1902. Many military golfers were killed on active service including Lt. Freddie Tait of the Blackwatch. Generally the population of the United Kingdom was unaffected by the fighting. The might of the British Army had been humbled by the novel tactics of the Boer farmers, especially during the battles of "Black Week" in December 1899. Fourteen years later it would be found that little had been learned from the failures in outdated tactics employed.

Apart from the absent soldiers, life continued normally on the home front. There were no food shortages although the price of gutta percha had gone up by 10 per cent. [2] A new ball developed by an American dentist was being tried out, which would eventually relegate the old gutty to the mantelpiece. The Haskell ball, as it was known, had a fluid centre and a wound rubber "innards". Its arrival was to have a major effect on golf course design (see Chapter 8).

THE GOLFING UNION OF IRELAND CUPS — 1900

Following its decision to institute senior and junior challenge cup competitions the Golfing Union of Ireland met in April 1900 to select the cups and badges required. *The Irish Golfer* 25th April 1900 reported that "it was agreed that a statue of Mr. F. G. Tait should stand on top of the senior cup as a tribute to his memory from the people of Ireland". [3] In this way a tangible reminder of a military golfer has been associated with the best in Irish golf to this day.

Portmarnock was the venue for the Irish championships of 1900, due recognition of its status as one of the premier links in the country. The senior and junior cup events were played for the first time, Dublin University being victorious in the senior event and the host club were the junior winners. A Munster[4] team was named to play an interprovincial match against Connaught, however the golf columns of the day do not document the outcome.

The host club also provided the winner of the Irish Amateur Close Championship,[5] R. G. N. Henry winning by 4 and 3 from J. McEvoy of Ormeau. Portmarnock, and Irish golf generally, were to be boosted over the following years by patronage of the highest in the land. Andra' Kirkaldy, a famous professional at St. Andrews, would call one of them the "King of Ireland" when trying to evade the due process of law.[6]

CENSUS OF IRISH GOLF 1901

On Thursday 29th November 1901 *The Irish Times* commenced its first weekly column on golf, "The Goff". Over the previous ten years the paper had carried intermittent articles on Irish golf. *The Belfast Newsletter*, through the Henderson family, had maintained a keen interest in golf-reporting in their paper, much more actively than their Dublin rival.

In *The Irish Times* 6th December 1901 the feature writer attempted a census of Irish golfers: "The Irish Golfing Union records cannot assist us for the Union includes less than one half of Irish clubs . . . from all statistics we have, however, compiled an approximate estimate . . . that there are 12,000 golfers in Ireland". Four weeks later the edition of 1st January 1902 reported: "Golf has not taken on in the South East of Ireland as it has in the North, owing to the great amount of time devoted to hunting and the numerous packs of hounds that there are to follow". The writer obviously presumed that the potential golfers of the area were the landed and professional gentry.

VICE REGAL AND ROYAL INTEREST IN IRISH GOLF

Commencing in 1852 with the Earl of Eglinton's golfing activities at the Curragh, several subsequent Lord Lieutenants took a keen interest in the game. When the Dublin Golf Club was founded in May 1885 the patron of the club was the Lord Lieutenant of Ireland, Lord Carnarvon.[7] Carnarvon was replaced in February 1886 by the Earl of Aberdeen, an active golfer who had been Captain of the Royal and Ancient the previous year. Aberdeen's term of office was shortlived, he was replaced in July 1886 by the Marquis of Londonderry.

Lord Cadogan: This man took office in August 1895 and he would appear to have been a keen golfer. *The Irish Golfer* 14th February 1900 reported that "George Sayers is at present at the Vice Regal lodge on his annual visit. He is engaged during the Spring season to give tuition in golf to the family and guests of the family''. Sayers was a professional from North Berwick in Scotland and he had clearly been coming over for some years. *The Irish Golfer* 5th February 1902 reported: ''The Duke and Duchess of Connaught and Lady Cadogan are amongst the regular attenders at the golf links in the Vice Regal Lodge, Phoenix Park''. It is clear that a golf course was in being at the Vice Regal Lodge during this Viceroy's tour and most probably Sayers had laid it out some time prior to 1900.

THE DUKE OF CONNAUGHT
VERSUS LIONEL HEWSON

Duke of Connaught: The Duke was the second youngest brother of King Edward VII and was Commander of the Forces in Ireland 1900-1904. He was a keen golfer and had been President of Royal Musselburgh since 1876. George Sayers laid out a course for him in the grounds of the Royal Hospital in late 1901 but it was not a success (see Appendix 1).

Lionel Hewson recalled an amusing incident relating to a game they had at the Curragh: ''In 1904 in South of Irish Horse I was told off to play the old Duke of Connaught. At first green I was 6 inches from hole and he was 10 yards. He remarked 'I always count 2 on greens and thus avoid putting'.''[8]

Lord Dudley: One of the Kingdom's wealthiest men succeeded Lord Cadogan as Lord Lieutenant in August 1902. Lord Dudley had no qualms of conscience when decisions had to be made about playing golf. Sunday golf was anathema to Christian folk in the 1890s, however *Golf* 2nd June 1899 recorded: ''. . . a considerable sensation was created at Gullane on a recent Sunday when a special train steamed into the station, there being no Sunday trains on the line. It appears that the Earl of Dudley and three friends, being desirous of having a fourball at Muirfield had chartered a special train to convey them to Gullane and back. The affair has led to a good deal of comment in the district . . .''

Lord Dudley had a private course of his own at Witley Court, Worcestershire, and he employed Andra' Kirkaldy as a professional and instructor.[9] Very quickly he took to the game in his usual fashion in Dublin and in October 1902 was playing Tom Hood the professional at Dollymount off level.[10] Money was no problem for Dudley, in his first year in Ireland he spent £80,000, his salary was £20,000. [11] Elizabeth Countess of Fingal told a number of stories relating to the extravagant effect of golf on him: "When his Excellency wanted his hair cut he would say: 'Telegraph to Charles to come across'. Charles would arrive, say, on Tuesday. Walter Callan would go into Lord Dudley with important letters, and when they were dealt with would say: 'When will you see Charles?' 'Oh, I can't now – I am going to golf at Portmarnock' . . . so it might go on for two or three days . . . in the end the Lord Lieutenant's hair cut might well cost him £20!" [12]

In another story . . . "Lord Dudley was the first Lord Lieutenant to use a motor car . . . (he) used to drive pretty often down to Portmarnock to play golf. It was nine miles or so from the Vice Regal Lodge. One day his Secretary was rung up by the Inspector General of the Police. 'Would you ask his Excellency to drive a little more slowly, as his bodyguard find it hard to keep up with him?'' . . . The Lord Lieutenant was filled with remorse when he realised that his guard had only push-bikes; and some motorcycles were provided". [13]

LORD DUDLEY IN HIS DAIMLER MOTOR CAR
(Courtesy of the National Library of Ireland)

The Irish Times 17th January 1903 reported that "as an ardent motorist he is able to move more easily than others to circumvent the 'inconstant' sea" (a reference to the boat journey from Sutton that Portmarnock golfers used to endure). "Before he left for Biarritz with Lady Dudley the Lord Lieutenant concluded arrangements with the Portmarnock club for the erection of a pavilion wherein to entertain his golfing guests during the coming season . . . the new departure will undoubtedly give a stimulus to Irish golf. Hitherto our golfing Viceroys have played the Royal and Ancient game in private and reserved their public patronage for other forms of sport.''

A major professional championship was held in April 1903 with the direct financial sponsorship of Dudley. The competition was played over Dollymount and Portmarnock and aroused immense interest in the newspapers of the day.[14] All of the top professionals competed including Braid, Taylor, Vardon, Kirkaldy and Sayers. Braid was the winner with 71 at Royal Dublin and 77 at Portmarnock.[15] Before departing Ireland in January 1906, Lord Dudley presented the St. Patrick's Cup[16] and a scratch cup to Portmarnock and Royal Dublin[17] respectively. Killarney golf club's ladies benefitted with a cup he presented for open competition.[18]

Lord Aberdeen: With the change of government in December 1905 a new Viceroy was appointed, he was no stranger to Dublin as he had served as Lord Lieutenant for a short term in 1886. As already mentioned, Lord Aberdeen had been Captain of the Royal and Ancient in 1885 and had a private course at his home at Haddo in Aberdeenshire.[19]

The Irish Field 14th July 1906 reported on his recent visit to Lahinch where he was entertained by A. W. Shaw and ''on the following day bestowed the Royal blessing on the youngest of Irish courses at sweet sounding, health giving Lisdoonvarna''. Later in May 1912 Lord Aberdeen struck the first ball on the new Clontarf Golf Club's course.[20] In February 1915 he departed Ireland for the last time.

THE MOTOR CAR

The publicity and prestige given to the game by the golfing Viceroys gave a major boost to the spread of the game in Ireland. Lord Dudley's activities were reported in the papers at the time and his use of a motor car to travel the country was a major selling point for the fledgling car industry. *The Irish Field* 20th February 1904 could state that with his motor car ''he is able, even during the busy Castle season, to sandwich a game 'twixt receiving a deputation in the forenoon and delivering a breezy and practical speech at a public meeting in the afternoon''.

Another major advertisement for the car industry at this time was the extravagantly publicised Gordon-Bennet race held in July 1903, on a course mostly laid out on the dusty roads of Co. Kildare. The newspapers and magazines of the period carried many articles and photographs of the event which was won by Gabriel Junatzy of Germany. Thousands of spectators lined the route and they must have been amazed at the power and speed of these new machines.

Prior to this the golfer had been tied to the local train timetable and the distance of the course from the station. The motor car opened new horizons for the golfer, especially in his new-found liberty of returning home at whatever time he pleased.

THE IRISH PROFESSIONAL CHAMPIONSHIP 1907

From as early as 1895 a professional championship had been held in conjunction with the Irish open amateur meeting.[21] *The Irish Golfer* 31st October 1900 carried a lengthy editorial bemoaning the cancellation of the annual professional competition . . . "dropped simply for the reason that the play of some of the professors (sic) detracted from the championship itself . . ." Some Irish clubs organised professional tournaments of their own, *The Irish Times* 2nd July 1902 reported on such a competition at Greystones, won by George Coburn of Portmarnock.

The professionals of Ireland had not "organised" themselves properly when in May 1906 they requested the Golfing Union of Ireland to "take their annual meeting into their charge". *Golf Illustrated* 25th January 1907 reported: "The President of the GUI, the Hon. Mr. Justice Barton has generously offered to give annually a large gold medal to the winner of the Irish Professional Championship". This new championship was first held at Portrush on 21st and 22nd May 1907. Twenty-two native Irish professionals competed, eight qualifying by eighteen holes stroke-play for the match-play section. J. Edmundson of Portrush was the victor over B. Snowball, the Portmarnock professional.

IRISH PROFESSIONALS DEFEAT SCOTS – 1907

An amazing victory for a team of native-born Irish professionals occurred on the 18th May 1907. Prior to this the standards of our professionals was not considered high and many Scottish professionals were chosen by Irish clubs in preference to the "native product". *The Belfast Newsletter* 20th May 1907 gave the full result:

H. Hamill (Ormeau)	3&1	B. Sayers (N. Berwick)	
B. Snowball (Portmarnock)	3&2	A. Simpson (Aberdeen)	
M. Moran (Dundalk)	5&4	J. Donaldson (Beldside)	
A. H. Toogood (Tramore)	6&5	W. Binnie (Kingshorn)	
H. McNeile (R. Portrush)	half	T. Watts (Ranfurly)	
J. Edmundson (R. Portrush)	6&5	B. Simpson (Carnoustie)	
H. Kidd (Malone)		C. Neaves (Lossiemouth)	4&3
T. J. McKenna (Malahide)		D. Watt (Portrush)	6&5
W. McNamara (Lahinch)	4&3	G. Gordon (C'cart Cas)	
Jas. McKenna (Carrickmines)	2&1	J. McAndrrew (Glasgow)	
A. Robertson (Co. Down)	4&3	A. Simpson (Cruden Bay)	
J. Barret (Hermitage)	3&1	T. Walker (Barry)	

By virtue of winning 9 to 2 in the singles the foursomes in the afternoon was a formality. Ireland were again successful by 4 matches to 2, giving an overall win of 13 matches to 4.

IRISH PROFESSIONALS IN THE "NEWS OF THE WORLD" COMPETITION AT THE CURRAGH 1909
Group includes: James McKenna, Willie McNamara, A. Robertson, Harry Kidd, J. Edmundson, H. Hamill, Tom Hood, J. Martin, M. Moran.

SIR D. PLUNKET BARTON

Sir. D. Plunkett Barton Bart: In 1906 Justice Plunkett Barton became President of the Golfing Union of Ireland. One of the great pioneers of Irish golf, he was President of Royal Dublin Golf Club from 1904 to 1924. In 1905 he had instituted the Barton Cup competition which is now the premier event in Leinster interclub golf.[22] He is also remembered in the Barton Shield All-Ireland competition, originally an inter-county championship. It was first played for in 1911, when Co. Donegal won.

THE IRISH PROFESSIONAL GOLFERS ASSOCIATION – 1912

Justice Barton had shown goodwill towards the professionals when they requested assistance from the Golfing Union of Ireland in 1906. When the professionals turned to the union in 1912 to help form an association, they were given every assistance. As a result, the Irish Professional Golfers Association was founded with a central council and two branch committees, one representing the Northern Branch (Ulster) and one representing the Southern Branch (Leinster, Munster and Connaught).

The Golfing Union of Ireland continued to oversee the Irish Professional Golfers Association until 1965.

MICHAEL MORAN

One of the professionals in the first Irish championships was a young man, Michael Moran, playing out of Dundalk Golf Club. By June 1907 he was

MICHAEL (DYKE) MORAN

employed as Tom Hood's assistant at Dollymount. [23] In *Golf Illustrated* 26th July 1907 their Irish correspondent could state: "I am convinced that Moran is one of the most consistently brilliant players I have seen on the Royal Dublin course". Moran was no stranger to Dollymount as *The Irish Field* 21st December 1918 pointed out: "For many generations his family resided in a house situated in the centre of the North Bull at Dolly-mount, close to 'Curley's Hole', his grandfather being a local celebrity named Patrick Curley. It was in this house that Moran was born thirty years ago. . . . a few years later found him roaming the links knocking a ball about with an old discarded iron . . ."

Moran won the Irish Professional Championship five times from 1909 to 1913. In 1914 he became professional to Seaham Harbour Golf Club but would appear to have been back to Ireland in August 1915 when he won a Red Cross competition at Rathfarnham. [24] Some time after this he went to France with the South of Irish Horse and returned to Ireland for the last time in August 1917 when he was pictured playing golf, in uniform, at Hermitage. [25]

Contrary to several recently published accounts of Moran's death he did not die after the War ended. *Irish Life* 20th December 1918 reported that his death "took place as long ago as 10th April at the War Hospital Le Cateau, which was at that time in the hands of the Germans . . ." *The Irish Field* confirmed the circumstances of his death and stated: "In France he transferred to the Royal Irish Regiment".

Michael Moran had died in the prime of his golfing life, in 1913 he had tied for third place in the British Open at Hoylake, with rounds of 76, 74, 89, 74 (313).[26] The event was won by J. H. Taylor with a total of 304, however Moran's disastrous third round must have been completely out of character. There is little doubt that this most presitigious championship would have been well within his grasp had he survived the war. His nickname "dyke" is used by Irish golfers to this day referring to birdies (one under par).[27]

THE END OF AN ERA — 1914

By all accounts the ten years prior to World War One were golden ones, with peace and prosperity the game of golf flourished all over Ireland. *The Irish Field* recorded the annual increase in affiliations to the Golfing Union of Ireland: in 1906 — 75; 1909 — 100; 1910 — 110; 1911 — 113; 1912 — 130.[28] In December 1909 the Union Secretary, Rev. J. L. Morrow, attended for the first time at a meeting of secretaries of 12 clubs from the Dublin area.[29] Finally in January 1913 the Leinster Branch was founded with George Price of Bray as Secretary; the Ulster Branch, with Mr. Davidson of Knock as Secretary, was instituted at the same time.[30] By January 1914 in the Dublin Metropolitan area alone there were 22 golf clubs. In the area between Skerries and Delgany there were seven 18-hole course, two with second nines under construction and thirteen nine-hole courses.[31]

Irish golf in 1914 was in a very healthy state, there was an approximate total of 190[32] golf clubs in existence, of which over 75 per cent were affiliated. However, there was some sadness at the beginning of the year when Thomas Sinclair died in February. The co-founder of Ireland's oldest golf club was followed shortly afterwards by one of his fellow founding members, Sir James Henderson. *The Irish Field* 28th February 1914 recorded: ". . . when the history of Irish golf comes to be written it will be difficult to obtain any authentic record of the infancy of the game . . . the pity is that the demands of commercial and public life prevented him (Sinclair) writing down a connected record of his reminiscences, as I begged him more than once to do. The regret of all golfers who knew him, is that the hand that could have written these is stilled."

Unfortunately, many other golfing hands would be stilled over the following four years.

*   *   *   *   *

Part 2: IRISH GOLF'S GREATEST CHALLENGE

WORLD WAR – AUGUST 1914

On 3rd August 1914 the "war to end all wars" began when German cavalry units led the invasion of Belgium. Newspapers and illustrated magazines of the period are filled with pictures of reservists mobilising and the regiments of the army in Ireland marching towards the docks. Once again the garrison towns of Ireland were being denuded, however the effects of this Great War were to be more keenly felt than any previous foreign war. The playing of golf was to become a shameful pastime for the duration.

In early September the Royal Dublin course at Dollymount was taken over for conversion to rifle ranges. *The Irish Field* 12th September 1914 reported that this Dublin club had lost 18 members so far dead, wounded or missing. The club employed forty persons at the time and their future was now most insecure. Shortly afterwards it was reported that ten of their caddies had enlisted.[33] The same tragic effects were being felt all over the country, once again the Curragh had been denuded as were all the garrison towns. Many of these club members who were regular soldiers would never return.

The Dublin clubs responded to Royal Dublin's plight with great generosity, offers of temporary membership were made by many.[34] Few of these clubs realised that their offers would have to be renewed for four years. In September 1914 a professional golfers corps was raised, fifty were enlisted in a body and drafted into the Kings Royal Rifle Corps.[35] It is not clear how many Irish professionals volunteered, the Curragh professional R. C. Lewis was recorded in 1916 as serving with this unit.[36] These men were subsequently known as the "Niblick Brigade".

Lionel Munn: One of the first casualties of the war had been Francis 6th Earl of Annesley, of Royal Co. Down, killed in action on a flying mission in early November 1914. Only three months before he had lost the final of the Irish Close Championship at Hermitage to Lionel Munn. Munn was Ireland's most gifted amateur at this time having won the "Close" in 1908, 1911, 1913, 1914 and the "Open Amateur" in 1909, 1910 and 1911. His performances until then had put him in the front rank of golfers in the British Isles, the war was to have a traumatic effect on his golf career. He enlisted and served as a lieutenant with the Royal Iniskilling Fusiliers.[37]

LIONEL MUNN

1915

By January 1915 it had become evident that the war was not going to be over quickly. Golf was not something to be spoken of when so many were dying on the Western Front. Many clubs were beginning to feel the pinch with decreased subscriptions caused by the enthusiastic rush to enlist. In many clubs, entrance fees were suspended in order to entice fresh members.[38] On March 19th 1915 *Irish Life* published a survey carried out of the effect on Irish clubs. A total of 180 clubs were circularised and 90 replied. Upwards of 1,250 Irish golfers were serving, a large number of whom were volunteers for Kitcheners Army. Ulster had the largest proportion, heading the list was Royal Co. Down with 110 serving.

Royal Dublin's Unique Honour: Prior to the war the Golfing Union of Ireland had been seeking entry in the rota for hosting the British Amateur Championship without success. Because of the war the Royal Dublin club had lost its links at Dollymount, however its annual general meeting was held in February 1915, at which time over 100 of the members were serving. Despite this the Royal and Ancient invited Royal Dublin to join the body governing the Amateur Championship.[39] This unique honour could not be availed of until December 1919, when the championship committee resumed business at St. Andrews.[40]

During 1915 many clubs organised entertainments for wounded soldiers, the Leinster Branch co-ordinated several meetings for this purpose. Over £9,000 was raised through collections and competitions.[41] Despite the military occupation of their course, some intrepid Royal Dubliners managed to play some golf during bank holidays when there was no firing on the course.[42] There was a rifle range on the Stillorgan Park golf course also at this time, as reported in *Irish Life* 20th August 1915, which also stated that all golf club members on active service could play free.

Ruhleben Prisoner Of War Camp: With the commencement of the war many civilians were unable to leave the belligerent countries, including Germany. *Irish Life* 27th August 1915 reported that C. S. Butchart, previously professional at Royal Co. Down, was now a prisoner in Ruhleben prisoner of war camp.[43] In a letter to the editor of *Golfing*, Butchart wrote: ''. . . the holes, five in number, are laid out on waste ground inside the racecourse . . . a club has been formed and there are 73 members . . . a number of firms have sent out clubs and balls so that the Ruhleben course is quite busy between the hours of eight and nine''. There was at least one Irishman incarcerated in this prison camp, R. M. Smyllie, editor of *The Irish Times* until 1954. He had been on the Continent as tutor to a well-to-do American in 1918.[44] The famous club maker Fred Smyth had learned his trade from Butchart at Newcastle.[45]

Finally, *Irish Life* 5th November 1915 recorded that Lt. Gerald Johnson of the

5th Battalion Connaught Rangers was the first Irish golfer (who had joined after August 1914) to receive a distinction for bravery. He was awarded the Military Cross for gallantry at Gallipoli . . . "a year ago he was off 16 or 18 handicap on the Dublin University team which created havoc amongst the golfers of Carlow in the Barton Cup".

1916

A reflection on the existing situation at the commencement of the New Year was given in *Irish Life* 28th January 1916: "No man feels exactly comfortable walking through the city with a big bag of clubs slung across his shoulder . . ."

A GUILTY CONSCIENCE DURING WORLD WAR I

Many clubs were maintaining a precarious existence by early 1916 and at Sutton a major change in club policy on Sunday golf was brought about at a general meeting of the club. Over the previous two years some far-sighted members had attempted to change club rules on this delicate subject, a similar motion in 1915 was lost by three votes and was widely reported in current newspapers. *Irish Life* 4th February 1916 reported that the Sunday play motion had been carried by 55 votes to 13, there had been a decrease of fifty members since the war started and the club's liabilities were now £325. In August, Portmarnock announced a reduction in their charge for green fees, in conformity with other Irish clubs. [46]

The Easter Rising of 1916 in Dublin caused the destruction of a large number of premises in Sackville (O'Connell) Street, one of them being No. 7, the premises of W. Lawrence. Lawrence had built up a considerable photographic business from the mid 1870s and his team of photographers had taken thousands of pictures, for the previous thirty years, all over Ireland. Many golf clubs were featured in the collection which is now in the National Library of Ireland (some of those photographs are documented in this publication). Lawrence also traded in golfing equipment as related by the ''Colonel'' in *Irish Life* 19th May 1916, he had witnessed the hail of golf balls coming from the shop's windows following an exchange of fire along Sackville Street.

Further golf clubs were taken over by the military authorities in 1916. Shanes Park (at Randalstown) and Tipperary were reported to have been taken over in *The Irish Golfing Guide* 1916.

One international win in golf is documented in *Irish Life* 25th August 1916. Lt. J. Fielding of the 9th Battalion Royal Dublin Fusiliers had won the Michelham Open Cup . . . ''a valuable silver gilt trophy offered by Lord Michelham, to British officers at the Michelham Convalescent Home at Cimiez, France . . .'' Fielding won off a 10 handicap and was a member of Clontarf.

1917

Golf news was sparse in the third year of the war. *The Irish Field* did not carry any Irish golf feature until September, when it reported the institution of a new club at New Ross.[47] Despite the war a number of clubs had been founded since the outbreak in 1914: Bessbrook, Cullybrackey and Inchydoney in 1915; Craig's Park and Rossmore in 1916; Claremorris and Woodville in 1918.

During the year the Leinster Branch had continued to organise entertainments by clubs for wounded soldiers. From the commencement of this programme in 1915 12,175 soldiers were entertained. Over half this total had benefitted in 1917.[48]

Tillage: Late in the year a major threat to golf arose with the passing of the Corn Production Act of 1917. *The Irish Field* 15th December 1917 carried a lengthy entry on the Tillage (Ireland) Racecourses And Golf Links Order 1918.

''1. The minimum tillage portion in the year 1918 of every holding to which this order applies shall be as follows:
   a. . . . . .
   b. If the holding is used as golf links, ten per cent of the area of the holding.

2. The holdings to which this order apply are as follows:
   a. . . . . .
   b. Any holding of not less than 10 Statute acres in extent, the whole or portion of which has been regularly used in the year 1917 as golf links and is so used in 1918.''

Many clubs now found that the government had, at last, decreed that the plough was mightier than the putter. The local populace were not too sympathetic and *Irish Life* 22nd February 1918 reported that several of the Ennis club's greens had been dug up; 3½ acres of their 35 acres had been tilled in 1917. By April 1918 Rev. J. L. Morrow had to enter a spirited defence of his club before an enquiry of Dublin Corporation . . . "regarding the desire of certain would be plotholders to seize some of the Dublin golf courses for the purpose of cultivation . . . the first of these courses for which application was made was Clontarf. . . ."[49] It is clear that the tillage order was complied with all over the country; Greencastle, Kingstown (Dun Laoghaire), Nenagh and Whitehead were also tilled.[50] The latter club closed for the duration of the war owing to the order. A poem in *Irish Life* 2nd November 1917 summed up the golfer's plight at this time:

"No longer on our course we blaze
  In staring scarlet coats,
Since to the sheep put out to graze
  They've added bulls and goats.

Our cup of sorrow now is full,
  We're cross-eyed, one and all;
With one eye fixed upon the bull
  The other on the ball."

1918

The new year opened with the news that Stillorgan had ceased to exist. *Irish Life* 4th January 1918 reported that the proprietorial course had "suffered from the disadvantage of being not very accessible". A defence of golf and golfers was carried in *Irish Life* 14th June 1918: "Many people are still disposed to carp and criticise golfers for playing their game at a time when others are fighting at the front . . . we might as well banish bridge from our houses, chess and billiards from our club . . ."

In August, Lahinch played a team from the Scottish Horse who were stationed in the neighbourhood . . . "their players included a plus 3, a plus 2 and 3 scratchmen . . . they did not know the course and had to borrow clubs . . ."[51] Lahinch won five of the eight matches, halving one.

Armistice: *The Irish Field* carried no golf material in 1918 until October and in the edition of 30th November Lionel Hewson wrote: ". . . it seems too wonderful to be true that once more we can, with a clear conscience, indulge in all the varied pleasures (and griefs) of the links. Thousands of golfers, who were not quite sure if they were doing all they could for the Empire, will now feel a light heart in their game".

With the end of the war, government finances had to be balanced and *The Irish Field* 7th December 1918 carried a report on the proposed Luxury Tax: "How then does the proposed Luxury Tax hit golf? It is comforting to discover that for ordinary golfers this tax will not, under its present schedules, intererefe unpleasantly with the game. Anything costing over £1 will be taxed. Now there is not much in the golfing rig out that costs over £1. A box of golf balls will cost in or about 30 shillings, but if one buys, say, a half a box at a time the tax will not be operative."

The writer of the piece, Lionel Hewson, displayed an impish sense of humour which was indicative of the relaxed attitude that golfers could now adopt. One sad postscript at the end of the year was the news of Michael Moran's death in the great German Spring offensive eight months previously. Irish golf was to sadly miss his undoubted talents in the post-war years.

A PEACEFUL INTERLUDE

In January 1919 the Co. Kildare (Naas) Golf Club held a victory ball as a method of raising funds for the club.[52] The Golfing Union of Ireland also recognised that golf could now be resumed as a normal pastime, at their meeting that same month they decided to revive "all of the Union's work".[53] Portmarnock was the venue for the Irish Close in May, and for the Professional Championship that same month. The ILGU were also coming out of hibernation and held their championship at Portmarnock in June 1919. *Irish Life* 20th June 1919 reported that at long last the military authorities were preparing to hand back Dollymount to its golfers.

Reviewing the war's effects on the game, Lionel Hewson wrote in *The Irish Field* 9th August 1919: "Broadly speaking, the war has added to the popularity of the game if also its expensiveness . . . naturally the greater cost of everything is a source of worry to golf club committees. Larger subscriptions must be expected . . ."

ANGLO-IRISH WAR 1919-1921

With the IRA attack at Soloheadbeg, Co. Tipperary, on 21st January 1919 the Anglo-Irish War began. By the end of the year the RIC had fourteen dead and twenty wounded. In 1920 the army lost 54 soldiers dead and 118 wounded, the RIC had 176 dead and 251 wounded.[54]

Against the background of increasingly bitter warfare in Ireland all sports activities were reported in contemporary newspapers in a detached manner. Occasionally golf clubs received belligerent attention, Skerries and Douglas clubhouses were burned and *The Irish Field* 25th June 1921 reported that Galway "had a lot of whiskey stolen recently". In April a major in the Auxiliary Division of the RIC was shot dead on Tralee golf course while playing golf, he would appear to have been the first and only such casualty.[55]

Following the signing of the Truce on 11th July 1921 an account in *The Irish Field* 30th July 1921 gave some idea of the conditions prevailing in some rural areas of Ireland: "An Honorary Officer of Tullamore Golf Club thought he would motor out the three miles to the course when the Truce was declared. Owing to trenched roads etc. the speedometer register twenty-three miles by the time the course was reached."

Relative peace returned for a period at this time and in December 1921 the

Anglo-Irish Treaty was signed which brought the Irish Free State into being. By June 1922 all British forces were to evacuate the Southern 26 counties and there is no doubt that it was a time of decision making for many of the gentry of Ireland. It was also a time for much soul-searching by the Golfing Union of Ireland.

A YEAR OF DECISION FOR IRISH GOLF — 1922

In September 1921 Rev. J. L. Morrow resigned as Honorary Secretary of the Golfing Union of Ireland having completed fifteen years in office. He had helped guide the Union through its most difficult years. Dr. George Price, LL.D., of Bray G.C., was immediately recommended to the Central Council as his replacement and this was duly accepted at the Union's meeting in November. [56] Through all this period Justice Barton remained as President and there is little doubt that he played a key role in guiding the Union through the turbulent years of the Anglo-Irish War. *Irish Life* 11th November 1921 reporting on the recent Central Council meeting stated: "It is good to see that the North and South are not divided in golf, at any rate, the one Union acting for both. Let us hope that it may be a happy augury of better things to come in the more serious side of life . . ."

The Civil War: During the gradual withdrawal of British forces in the Spring and early Summer of 1922 the daily newspapers carried increasingly ominous accounts of the split which was developing in the Republican groups. In April 1922 Anti-Treaty Republicans seized the Four Courts, and *The Irish Field* 15th April 1922 reported that the Royal Dublin course was to be taken over once again, as rifle ranges for the Provisional Government. The ranges were to be used two days a week but the clubhouse was not required.

On 2nd May *The Belfast Newsletter* reported the postponement of the Irish Open Amateur Championship due to be held at Dollymount, as Royal Dublin was unable to proceed with the arrangements. This was the first major test for the Golfing Union of Ireland, following the Treaty. At that time there were four clubs on the rota for the major championships: Royal Portrush, Royal Co. Down, Portmarnock and Royal Dublin. *The Irish Times* 12th May 1922 reported that Portmarnock was unable to host the postponed championship as the club was committed to another major event in August. The same newspaper account stated that the Open Championship would take place at Portrush in September.

Shortly afterwards *The Irish Times* 20th May 1922 reported: 'The Irish Army's 'occupation' of Dollymount has been comparatively brief. I learned this week that the riflemen had gone and that normal conditions prevail on the course . . .'' Unfortunately for Royal Dublin the return of their course was a fortnight too late.

On 21st June 1922 Sir Henry Wilson was assassinated in London and shortly afterwards full-scale Civil War commenced with the Provisional Army's attack on the Four Courts. Over the following months newspapers were filled with accounts of the military operations throughout the country. *The Irish Field* 2nd September 1922 reported the burning of Tullamore clubhouse as "another of those regrettable incidents which show that some Irishmen possess neither balance nor reasoning powers". At this time the newspapers were reporting, daily, the burning of large Anglo-Irish houses all over the country.

MATURITY

On 17th December 1922 the British Army finally departed Dublin, the Worcester Regiment being the last to leave. At no time during the year did the newspapers report any split in Irish golfing circles. With the political and economic division of the country the Golfing Union of Ireland continued to exercise undivided control of Irish golf. Similarly the Irish Ladies Golf Union received the loyal attention of its affiliated members.

There is no doubt that the maturity displayed by all levels of the body of golf sportsmen and women in Ireland, at that time, was most praiseworthy. In 1923 the Irish Close was held at Milltown for the first time and Royal Dublin, at long last, hosted the "Open" in 1924. The bonds of sportsmanship and friendly rivalry established over the previous forty years amongst the golfing fraternity of Ireland held firm, despite many tests. Modern Irish golfers have much to be grateful for the efforts of the administrators of Irish golf in the early 1920s.

FOOTNOTES

1. Greer had arrived to the Curragh in 1889 with the Highland Light Infantry, he had retired circa 1892 and purchased a local stable. He was first director of the Irish National Stud in 1915, and President Curragh G.C. 1922-1934.
2. *The Irish Golfer* 3rd January 1900.
3. John Ball Jun. was to be represented on the junior cup.
4. *The Irish Golfer* 16th May 1900 named the Munster team, there were seven Lahinch, two Cork, one Caragh and Dooks and one A. N. Other.
5. The Irish Native-born Championship was renamed thus in August 1899.
6. *Fifty Years Of Golf*, page 113. A reference to Lord Dudley.
7. *Sport*18th July 1885.
8. Letter dated 18th May 1952 to Hon. Sec. Curragh Golf Club. Hewson was one of the great Irish Golf writers. He was golf correspondent with *The Irish Times, Irish Field, Irish Life* and founded *Irish Golf* in 1928.
9. *Golf Illustrated* 22nd December 1899.
10. *The Irish Golfer* 29th October 1902.
11. *Seventy Years Young, Countess Fingal*, page 278.
12. *Ibid.* page 279.
13. *Ibid.* pages 279-280.
14. *The Irish Golfer* 8th April 1903 named the contest "the Lord Lieutenant's Carnival".
15. *The Irish Times* 10th and 11th April 1903.
    This cup was destroyed in Portmarnock's fire in January 1906 together with the Irish Open Championship Cup which had been won in 1905 by H. A. Boyd. Boyd was the first native Irishman to win this championship.
17. Royal Dublin also lost this trophy in their fire on 2nd August 1943.

18. *The Irish Field* 6th July 1907.
19. *Golf Illustrated* 10th January 1903.
20. *The Irish Field* 1st June 1912.
21. *The Irish Times* 14th September 1895 reported on a professional match held at Portrush in conjunction with the Irish Amateur Open Championship. Many of the top Scottish professionals participated in the event, the first in Irish golf history. Sandy Herd beat David Brown of Musselburgh in the final. *Golf* 10th July 1896 carried a notice for that year's open professional tournament, a sum of £100 in prizes was offered.
22. Won on the first occasion by Bray in 1905. *The Irish Times* 6th February 1903 carried a notice re this competition and requested entries by 16th March. It would appear that there were initial problems which delayed the event until 1905.
23. *Golf Illustrated* 21st June 1907.
24. *Irish Life* 3rd September 1915.
25. *Irish Life* 31st August 1917. He also played at Kingstown and Clontarf.
26. *Guinness Book Of Golf Facts And Feats*, page 67.
27. His nickname was associated by some with his athletic ability to jump the many dykes and drains on the course, others credited his ability to score one under pars as being the origin.
28. *The Irish Field* 10th November 1906, 3rd April 1909, 10 March 1910, 14th January 1911, 3rd February 1912.
29. *The Irish Field* 18th December 1909.
30. *The Irish Field* 18th January 1913.
31. *The Irish Field* 17th January 1914.
32. Appendix 2.
33. *Irish Life* 4th September 1914.
34. *Irish Life* 18th September 1914: Foxrock, Kingstown, Stillorgan Park, Clontarf, Killiney, Carrickmines, Milltown and Portmarnock, *Irish Life* 10th October 1914 gave the following additional clubs: Skerries, Delgany, Lucan, Rathfarnham, Island, Hermitage, Sutton, Castle, Greystones.
35. *Irish Life* 25th September 1914.
36. *The Irish Golfing Guide* 1916.
37. Munn survived the war and played on the Irish team in the Home Internationals of 1936 and 1937.
38. *Irish Life* 12th February 1915.
39. *Irish Life* 26th February 1915.
40. The first Irish club to host the British Amateur Championship was Portmarnock in 1949. Royal Portrush followed in 1960 and Royal Co. Down in 1970.
41. *The Irish Field* 19th June 1915.
42. *Irish Life* 23rd July 1915.
43. *Irish Life* 9th May 1919 reported he had been repatriated, having been professional at Berlin G.C. in 1914.
44. *The Irish Times* 11th November 1986.
45. *Golf Illustrated* 8th February 1907.
46. *Irish Life* 25th August 1916.
47. This was a revival, in fact, of the previously established club. See Appendix 1.
48. *The Irish Field* 24th November 1917.
49. *Irish Life* 5th April 1918.
50. Greencastle — information from Mr. G. Glover; Kingstown — *Irish Life* 12th March 1920; Nenagh — *Irish Life* 20th February 1920; Whitehead — *The Irish Field* 4th October 1919.
51. *Irish Life* 23rd August 1918.
52. *Irish Life* 17 January 1919.
53. *The Irish Field* 1st February 1919.
54. *The Troubles*, pages 84 and 85.
55. *The Irish Independent* 18th April 1921.
56. *The Irish Field* 19th November 1921.

CHAPTER 8

Golfiana Miscellanea[1]

COURSE CULTIVATION

When selecting ground for their course the Bray golfers would have had an easy task, a commons on links land was the ideal location. Likewise, David Ritchie's choice of ground would have been governed by similar factors, a commons with links-like grass.

The major factor militating against the spread of inland golf prior to 1900 was the perennial problem of nature's bounty, the evergrowing green sward of the

Introduced by Ransomes in 1905 the horse-drawn "Ideal" for cutting what were described as "rough golf courses".

Emerald Isle. Winter golf was the only hope for the inland golfer, at a time of the year when grass growth was not a problem. The *Golfing Annuals* of the period commonly reported "season October to May, Winter course only". The *Ransomes Lawn Mower Company 150th Anniversary Brochure (1982)* reported that mechanical grass-cutting was not generally accepted by golf courses until about 1890 when there was a rapid transformation. In 1899 there were over one hundred courses in the British Isles owning Ransomes mowers and, by 1911, of 255 clubs using Ransomes machines 22 were Irish.

Killarney was an early beneficiary of a generous landlord in 1896. ". . . Lord

Kenmare gave permission to have the grass cut right through the links and not only that but lent a large pair horse-mower for the purpose . . . the grass is now quite close except for the first 120 yards from each tee . . .''[2]

The golf magazines of the 1890s carry advertisements for these horse-drawn mowers. Special shoes were invented for the horse's feet to prevent him sinking into soft ground in the event of unseasonal Summer weather. During the Winter the poor old horse might not have too much work to do but, of course, he had to be fed and this caused a dilemma for more than one club. *The Irish Golfer* 24th January 1900 reported that Ormeau G.C. had tried an experiment with great success, the purchase of a horse for the grass mower in lieu of the almost daily hiring: "Our 5 guinea horse, under the capable management of Hugh Rusk, kept the grass over the whole course in excellent condition. The horse was sold at the end of the season at a loss of 7s. 6d."

It was because of the evergrowing grass that the Dublin G.C. was forced to seek new ground in 1888 and Lahinch would not have received such an early start in 1892 if the Limerick golfers had not suffered from the same problem at Ballinacurra.

Pictured in 1923 mowing a golf course fairway, a Ransomes horse-drawn triple gang mower, first made under licence in 1921.

Rabbits: There has been an intimate relationship between rabbits and golf from the earliest days in Ireland. When the Belfast club laid out its first course at the

Kinnegar in 1881 the old Gaelic placename carried the connection with it. "Coinín" is the Gaelic for rabbit and *The Saturday Review* 26th July 1890 reported: "Etymologists trace the name to 'coney-gar' or rabbit warren; but here the golfer has effectually displaced the rabbit".

When the new course was opened at Magilligan in 1896 the entire area was infested with rabbits. Eventually after about three years the rabbits won the uneven battle and the links became defunct. Ballycastle, also, was laid out in a former rabbit warren "but the troublesome bunny (was) sufficiently dealt with".[3]

Roscrea's course was also described in *The Sportsmans Holiday Guide* 1897 and . . . "the hazards are numerous and consist of trees and rabbit holes". The editor of the *Guide* was very concerned about Roscrea's plight and offered the following advice: "If the greenkeeper will fill in the burrows and then pour a little paraffin at the mouth of the hole, the troublesome bunny will be got rid of".

The Irish Golfer 23rd August 1899 reported on the same problem at Portmarnock: ". . . one drawback to the course is the number of rabbit scrapes and holes but the ravages of a 'bunny' on the line of play have now been well eradicated". *Irish Life* 25th February 1915 reported that permanent wire netting had been erected to prevent the inroads of the rabbit on to the course.

Other courses with rabbit problems in the early years were Lahinch,[4] Rosslare[5] and Kirkistown Castle. In the latter case, *The Golfing Annual* 1902/03 recorded that "the course of nine holes is laid out on the warren".

Sheep: As with rabbits, sheep and golf have had a close relationship from the earliest days. When David Ritchie laid out his 1852 course on the Curragh, there is no doubt that the close-cropped sward would have reminded him of his home links at Musselburgh. On many of the inland courses, which would have been leased or given rent free, sheep would have been among the natural hazards.

The Irish Golfer 20th September 1899 carried the following: "A member of Greystones was deploring to one of ours last week on the condition of the green this season, as he explained, upon the withdrawal of sheep from the course . . . this year the farmer evinced a decided reluctance to put sheep to graze in the vicinity of the golf links so that grass has grown and the golfer's heart is heavy within him at Greystones. The reason was the mortality in the sheep flock caused by the flight of the ball. This sounds rather startling but we are assured that there were three cases last year of sheep being killed by golf balls." Dead sheep would have been a cause of friction with landlords throughout the country, the minute books of Athlone Golf Club record a payment for a similar incident: "Kilroy, for lamb killed − 12/6".

Knock had a different problems as *The Irish Golfer* 27th December 1899 revealed: "Horse grazing has been done away with and sheep substituted . . .

(they) have proved most satisfactory''. Finally, just before World War One, *The Irish Field* 17th January 1914 documented a novel fund-raising project: "The Skerries club had a very successful year, having a profit over the years working of almost £100. The profit from the 'sheep farm' run by the club came to £48 which is eminently satisfactory and the club has 150 sheep in hand''.

The Haskell Ball: The development of the gutta percha ball in 1848, as outlined in Chapter 3, was a revolutionary step forward which caused consternation among the old "feathery" ball makers. Little change occurred in the ball-making trade over the next fifty years until Bertram G. Work and Coburn Haskell were granted a U.S. Patent for a rubber-cored ball surrounded with a wound elastic thread. A covering of gutta percha was then moulded on. These balls flew further than any existing gutty ball but had a nasty habit of suddenly "yawing" off line. Eventually, James Foulis, who was professional at the Chicago G.C., discovered that, when remoulding the gutta percha exterior of a used Haskell, a raised pebble-like finish (bramble pattern) gave a flawless flight to the new ball. The modern era of golf balls had arrived.

Within a short time the new rubber-cored ball was in great demand, even though its price was twice the price of the gutty. Golfers were hitting balls much farther and club committees found that their courses were now not long enough for the extra length ball. Courses had to be lengthened and, in many cases, extra land was leased or purchased. *The Belfast Newsletter* 13th May 1907 reported that Ardglass G.C. "had to extend its course due to the rubber-cored ball . . . accordingly Mr. and Mrs. McMaster of Ringford were approached with a view to ascertaining whether they would grant permission to the club to use a portion of a field at the extreme end of the links''.

NOVEL COMPETITIONS

Holes Match: When the match between the Military and Civilians of the Royal Belfast Club took place at Holywood on 4th May 1889, the soldiers lost by 12 holes to 14. *The Irish Field* 11th May 1889 gives a full account of the result and despite the fact that the military members won four of the six matches they lost the overall contest because Mr. H. Herdman trounced Capt. Cuthbertson (Blackwatch) by 13 holes! The match was played on the cumulative holes up result in each singles.

Against The Clock: A novel method of contesting an interclub match was the 1892 match between Lismore and the officers of the 1st Battalion Seaforth and Cameron Highlanders. It would appear that the game was played against the clock, counting strokes and *The Irish Times* 11th May 1892 reported: "Play at the end of the game (which lasted two hours), officers 507, Lismore Golf Club 572.

Colonel Bogey: "Bogey" competitions would appear to have become popular from 1896 onwards, in that year *The Irish Times* began to carry results of such competitions on a regular basis.[6] This form of competition originated in 1890 at Coventry Golf Club when some members decided to introduce a "ground score", which would be the number of strokes a top golfer would be expected to take at each hole. This form of competition became popular and at Great Yarmouth the ground score became known as "Bogey" because of a popular song being sung in the local music-hall, "Hush, Hush, Here Comes The Bogey Man".[7]

Early in 1892 when the Secretary of Great Yarmouth was playing at the United Services Club he introduced the idea of a Bogey competition there. The visitor (Dr. Thomas Brown R.N.) worked out a "Bogey" for the course and with Captain Vidal R.E. and Dr. Walter Reid R.N. he commenced to play a round against Bogey. When they were about to strike off Captain Vidal (Hon. Secretary of the United Services Club) said: "Stop! We must proceed in a proper Service manner. Every member of this club has a rank.[8] Our new invisible member who never plays a bad shot must surely be a Colonel. 'Colonel Bogey, Sir', he said, saluting, delighted to find you on the links' . . ."[9] In 1913 Colonel Bogey was immortalised when the Bandmaster of the 2nd Battalion Argyll and Sutherland Highlanders composed the ever-popular march tune.

Driving and Approach Competitions: The Greystones Club held a novel golf competition, as described in *The Irish Times* 28th September 1898: "31 competitors were watched by a large concourse of ladies and gentlemen. The drives were from the second tee to a post fixed at 150 yards distance, the balls having to pass between two posts 25 yards apart placed 100 yards from the tee . . . The approaching was to a hole on the green from a distance of 40 yards . . . W. D. Meldon won with an aggregate of 15ft. ¾ ins. from the post and 3ft. 2½ ins. from the hole . . ."

HANDICAPPING

One of the aims of the Golfing Union of Ireland from its foundation had been "the adoption of a uniform method of handicapping". Because of the varied degrees of skill attainable by golfers it was recognised that an equitable form of handicapping system would have to become standardised throughout the country. Prior to the formation of the Union, the various clubs had decided on their own handicapping system. Handicaps were allotted for the first competition at Belfast on 26th December 1881.[10] The competition was won with a nett of 121, two competitors finished with nett 200 and 228 respectively!

G.U.I. Handicapping Scheme: On 6th May 1893, the Hon. Secretary of the Union (Mr. G. Combe) was authorised to "prepare a scheme which was to comprise a list of handicaps (for use at open meetings only) for fifty golfers based on the handicap then allotted at St. Andrews to Mr. T. Gilroy, who was at that time the best golfer in Ireland''. [11] In April 1894 the Union decided ''that each affiliated club should select a 'green score' to which the members are handicapped. Any member returning a nett score lower than the 'green score' was to have his handicap reduced by as many strokes as his nett score was below the said 'green score' . . .'' [12]

Following the defeat of Ulster by Leinster in the interprovincial match of 1896 (see Chapter 6) much soul searching was carried out. At a meeting of the affiliated clubs on 11th December 1896 a radical change was agreed: ''It was generally recognised that the handicapping in most of the Ulster clubs had been too low . . . It was also pointed out that the interprovincial match, played at Portrush last Easter had shown the handicapping of the Royal Dublin Club to be about 4 strokes higher than that of the Northern clubs. Mr. George Combe proposed a resolution which was adopted unanimously to the effect that all the other clubs in the Union should do what Royal Dublin did two years ago — namely add 4 strokes to each member's handicap . . .'' [13]

The Ulster golfers all received increased handicaps, however the thorny handicap question was to raise its head again when the Golfing Union of Ireland instituted the senior and junior cups in 1900. In the senior cup final, Dublin University had a very easy win over Co. Down and an editorial in *The Irish Golfer* 13th June 1900 reported that ''the average Co. Down handicap was under 4, the average Dublin University handicap was 8 — in the interprovincial the Ulster handicaps were less than Leinster'' (the latter had won by 48 holes to 27).

Once again a dramatic revision of handicaps followed and *The Belfast Newsletter* 25th July 1900 reported: ''The decision of the Golfing Union of Ireland to reduce the handicaps in the clubs throughout the three Southern Provinces has been received on the whole favourably. . . . In Munster, Leinster and Connaught handicaps shall be reduced as follows: 5 or under by 2; 6 to 10 by 3: 11 to 18 by 4 and over 18 by 5''.

The development of the Irish handicapping system merits a chapter in itself. Much voluntary work was done by the early council members of the Union, the ''green score'' of all affiliated clubs had to be verified and *The Irish Times* 21st June 1897 noted a visit by George Combe to approve the ''par score'' (76) of the Co. Louth Club. Non-affiliated clubs had their own handicap system and *The Irish Golfer* 18th February 1902 recorded: ''The Co. Kildare (Naas) Club are not stingy in the allotment of handicaps to their members. Quite a number are on the 20 mark, a large number between that and 30, and between 30 and 40 about half the members of the club rank. The maximum handicap given is 80 and no less than three members are rated at minus 80''.

The unhappy plight of handicapping sub-committees all over is well recognised in the modern era of ''pothunters''. However *The Irish Times* 19th

March 1894 recorded a victory by Vernon Kyrke[14] at Royal Dublin when "he buried all his previous records in total eclipse and reduced the handicapping committee to tears".

SUNDAY GOLF

Throughout the early years of Irish golf the vexed question of golf on the Sabbath day was constantly mentioned in the golfing press. A lengthy article on the subject by W. Dalrymple informed the readers of *Golf Illustrated*[15] that Cromwell was responsible for the prohibition of the game on Sunday . . . "even Knox was reputed to have been seen playing on the Sabbath more than once at Leith".

The prohibition of golf on Sunday in the 1890s was widespread, *The Golfing Annuals* regularly testify that many Irish clubs had such a local rule. When John Jameson gave the extra nine holes to Portmarnock in 1896 he stipulated that there would be no Sunday play.[16] Royal Dublin was also one of the clubs with such a rule, and some of the members were forced to seek a quiet location for their Sunday fourball. As a consequence the Island golf course was formed in 1890.[17] Many Irish clubs found it profitable to advertise the fact that golf could be played seven days a week and *The Irish Golfer* 18th October 1899 reported: ". . . while the Queen's writ runs in Donegal, the Anathema Maranatha of the General Assembly does not and erring Scotchmen, having escaped from its jurisdiction, have more than once engaged on a Sunday with the profane native in a good tussle over 18 holes". A series of articles on Irish courses appeared in *Golf Illustrated* in the Autumn of 1899; Portsalon, Galway, Milltown Malbay, Lahinch, Rosapenna and Newcastle were documented. All of them were highlighted because Sunday golf could be played on them.[18]

The outbreak of World War One caused a number of clubs to abandon their Sunday golf rule for financial reasons, as was the case with Sutton (outlined in Chapter 7). After the war, the rule would appear to have prevailed mainly in the Province of Ulster. In 1919, Warrenpoint voted by a 2 to 1 margin in favour of Sunday golf.[19] Controversy raged at Royal Portrush in 1922 when a similar motion was proposed, *The Irish Times* 2nd August 1922 carried a lengthy letter from Mr. F. Audinwood, ex-Captain of the club, explaining the background to a forthcoming special meeting. Local clergymen were determined to prevent Sunday golf. (The matter finally went before the Northern High Court).[20] When Killiney purchased its own course *The Irish Field* 5th April 1924 could state: "This proceeding of course did away with the banning of Sunday golf".

The Irish Golfing Guides 1914 to 1916 reported a limited Sunday golf rule when play was "permitted without caddies". Obviously, the caddy was "working" while the golfer was relaxing.

RACECOURSES

The racing fraternity and golf have had a harmonious existence from the earliest days. When the Earl of Eglinton relaxed after his 1858 games of golf at the Curragh it was to the Standhouse at the racecourse that he retired with his companions. In 1889 the Queens Co. Heath G.C. used the Grandstand of the old racecourse as their clubhouse. The Limerick Golf Club made their first home within the racecourse near the city, in December 1891. Earlier that same year an ill-fated attempt was made within Leopardstown racecourse, G. L. Baillie would appear to have been a prime mover in that venture.

It may be of interest to Lahinch golfers to note that the area of their new eighteen-hole course is shown as a racecourse on the 1904 one-inch map. When the original course was laid out in 1892 the "back" nine were all to the East of the Liscannor Road, in this area.[21] *The Irish Times* 5th April 1895 reported the inaugural meeting of the Westmeath (Mullingar) Club at Newbrook racecourse: "Tea having been partaken in the Grandstand, an adjournment was made to the course . . ."

Tullamore had its course on the racecourse at Ballykilmurry circa 1896 and *The Sportsmans Holiday Guide* 1897 recorded that the Fermoy Golf Club "is situated on the Racecourse about a quarter of a mile from the station". In 1902 Tramore Golf Club was reconstructed beside the local racecourse, both were inundated by the sea in the Winter of 1912/13. When the Ballymena course was selected in 1904 it was announced . . . "The old racecourse at Baughshane has been secured . . ."[22]

Many of the old racecourses mentioned above no longer exist and are not documented in a recent history of Irish horse-racing.[23]

GIBRALTAR – AN IRISH GOLF CONNECTION

A letter to *The Field* 10th February 1876 sent in by "A Golfer" reported: "Sir, I send you a short account of an attempt to institute golf at Gibraltar by a few who thoroughly appreciate its charms. The North front is very well suited to form a links. A course of seven holes is at present laid out, salmon tins being used to keep the holes in shape, and the putting greens are decorated with the usual red flag. A keenly contested foursome was played on the 23rd ult. between Capts Cleland and Rogers of the 102nd Royal Madras Fusiliers, and Lieuts Lindsay and Blennerhasset of HMS Shah."

In 1873 the 102nd Royal Madras Fusiliers and the 103rd Royal Bombay Fusiliers were linked together and formed the 66th Sub District with a Brigade Depot in Naas (Co. Kildare). Following the Cardwell reforms, these two regiments became the 1st and 2nd Battalions of the Royal Dublin Fusiliers. Capt. Cleland, mentioned above, is shown as Commanding Officers of the 1st Battalion Royal Dublin Fusiliers in the Army Lists of 1882 (at which time they were in Ceylon). It is clear that among the officers of this Irish Regiment there were several keen golfers who carried their love of the game wherever the went.

EARLY IRISH GOLF FANATICS

The golf "bug" is by no means a modern phenomenon. In Scotland, Alexander McKellar (who died c. 1813) played every day of the week except Sunday at the Bruntsfield links at Edinburgh . . . "he was usually to be found playing at Bruntsfield most of the day and sometimes at the short holes by lamplight, even when the links was covered with snow . . ."[24]

An entry in *The Belfast Newsletter* 11th January 1892 proved that there were equally fanatical golfers in Portrush at that time . . . "Notwithstanding unfavourable weather, with two inches of snow on the links and a stiff Nor' Easter blowing, four couples ventured out for the monthly medal . . . Red balls had to be used and a good many of them were lost during the round. Putting on the greens from which the snow had not been cleared was the most difficult part of the game."

FOOTNOTES
1. *Golfiana Miscellanea* by J. L. Stewart (1887). This book carries an index of clubs in the British Isles. Only the Curragh G.C. is listed of the three Irish clubs then in existence.
2. *The Irish Times* 13th January 1896.
3. *The Sportsmans Holiday Guide* 1897.
4. *Golf Illustrated* 9th February 1900. An article by Rev. J. L. Morrow . . . "the rabbits and virgin roughness of the moss and bent were the chief difficulties . . .".
5. *Irish Golf* January 1944. Lionel Hewson stated: "My first visit to Rosslare saw a nine-hole course kept solely by rabbits, at least so it struck me".
6. *The Irish Times* 6th November 1896 reported a Colonel Bogey competition at Athlone. Earlier *The Belfast Newsletter* 7th January 1896 reported that the Shaw Cup at Lahinch had been won by Mr. W. McDonnell, 2 down to Bogey.
7. *Golf Illustrated* 17th November 1905 carries this story.
8. The United Services Club was a military club at that time.
9. Article in *Centenary Brochure Army Golf Club, Aldershot* by T. W. Jopling (Gosport & Stokes Pages).
10. *Centenary Brochure R.B.G.C.*, page 29.
11. Letter 10th April 1935 from Hon. Sec. G.U.I. to Royal and Ancient.
12. *Ibid*. The "green score" was the "par" of the course.
13. *The Irish Times* 19th December 1896.
14. Kyrke was a founder member of Royal Dublin and Hon. Treasurer of the club for many years.
15. *Golf Illustrated* 31st August 1900.
16. *The Irish Times* 24th January 1896.
17. *The Irish Field* 8th May 1926. Another club, Delgany, owes its existence to such a rule (see Appendix 1).
18. In *Golf Illustrated* 15th September 1899 the editor requested information from Hon. Secretaries of clubs which allowed Sunday golf.
19. *Irish Life* 19th December 1919.
20. *The Irish Field* 23rd September 1922.
21. *The Golfers Guide* 1897, page 395, map.
22. *The Irish Field* 10th September 1904.
23. *Irish Horse-Racing*, John Welcome (1982).
24. *The Chronicle of The Royal Burgess Golfing Society of Edinburgh*, vol. 1, page 79.

Early Irish Ladies Golf

THE FIRST LADY GOLFER IN IRELAND — 1887

When the "goffers" at Bray were playing their "manly game" it is unlikely that any ladies were involved. The game in the 18th Century was very much a man's game and the accounts of early golf in Scotland make little mention of lady golfers. Mary Queen of Scots was reputed to have played golf after the murder of her husband in 1567, as told in Chapter 1. She is widely acknowledged as being the earliest recorded lady golfer. [1]

Subsequently, the next mention of ladies golf is at Musselburgh when in 1810 "the club (later Royal Musselburgh) agreed to present by subscription a handsome new creel and skull to the best female golfer who plays on the annual occasion on the 1st January next old style (12th January new) to be intimated to the first ladies by Mr. Robertson the Officer of the Club. Two of the best Barcelona silk handkerchiefs to be added to the above premium of the creels." [2]

The first documented lady golfer in Ireland was Mrs. Wright, wife of an officer of the Gordon Highlanders then stationed in Belfast. An entry in *The Field* 1st October 1887 recorded the occasion for posterity when following a competition at Royal Belfast: "Mr. Gregg, Captain of the club, and Mrs. Wright, played in a foursome against Col. Lyon Campbell R.E. and Capt. Wright, Gordon Highlanders. The match attracted quite a turn-out of ladies. At the end of the first round the former were four up, the lady having played particularly well. In the second round, however, the Colonel and his partner pulled the game down to all even and one to play. The last hole was keenly contested and was won by a long and well laid put (sic) of Capt. Wright." (See Chapter 6 re details of service in Ireland of the Gordon Highlanders).

IRELAND'S FIRST LADIES CLUB — 1888

There is little doubt that Mrs. Wright was the inspiration behind the founding of the first ladies golf club in Ireland. Among the group of lady onlookers had been Miss C. E. McGee who was introduced to Mrs. Wright and "she inspired me with a wish to play the game". [3]

A full account of the founding of the Holywood Ladies Golf Club is given in Appendix 1, Miss McGee documented her memories in a letter to the club on the occasion of its 25th anniversary in November 1913. At the beginning there were fifteen members, only five of whom actually played golf. Miss McGee became the first Hon. Secretary with Mrs. R. Young Hillbrook as first Hon. Treasurer. The ladies had the use of the course at the Kinnegar and called themselves Holywood Ladies Golf Club until the old course was abandoned. When they moved to the new course at Carnalea they became the Royal Belfast Ladies Golf Club, with Mrs. G. M. Shaw as Captain, in 1892.

SOME OTHER EARLY IRISH LADIES CLUBS AND COURSES

An article on the inaugural competitions of the Aughnacloy Golf Club apppeared in *The Irish Times* 28th January 1889: "In the evening a ladies match was played and afforded much amusement and, at intervals, a considerable amount of instruction to the onlookers . . . So much progress had been made in their play that the ladies encouraged by their success have it in contemplation to form a ladies club, selecting a short course particularly suited for their play." Unfortunately for Aughnacloy there is no subsequent evidence in the *Golfing Annuals* to show the establishment of a ladies club or course.

The Irish Times 5th July 1890 documented a ladies handicap competition at the Curragh, won by Mrs. Norman Lee (wife of the Camp chaplain). The ladies played on a separate nine-hole course and there were seven competitors. Subsequently *The Sportsmans Holiday Guide* 1897 recorded the continued existence of this separate ladies course which would appear to have ceased to exist circa 1910. [4] Despite this interest in golf amongst the ladies of the garrison there would appear to be no evidence for the establishment of a ladies club. However, the nine-hole ladies course was the first such in Irish golf history.

It is not clear to whom the honour goes for establishing the second ladies club in Ireland. *The Belfast Newsletter* 26th February 1891 reported a ladies competition at Killymoon: ". . . there are two courses, the ladies on which the competition took place consisting of nine holes at shorter intervals and with less obstacles than the gentlemens . . ." An entry in *The Derry Journal* 25th February 1891 [5] documented the foundation of the North-West Club, shortly afterwards the same newspaper reported: ". . . the ladies have not been forgotten in the arrangements in connection with the club as immediately adjacent to the railway station at Buncrana an exceedingly good nine-hole course has been laid out and is rapidly being got into order." [6] The Queens County and Heath Club were very democratic from an early date, *The Irish Times* 21st August 1891 reported that Mrs. O'Hara had won the Emo Cup on its inaugural occasion. There were male competitors also and it would appear that ladies had equal rights in the club. It will be seen later that there were lady members of the Dungannon Club in 1891 also.

Despite the construction of separate ladies courses at Killymoon and Buncrana, there was no mention of the establishment of a ladies club at either location. It would seem that the ladies were members of the original club in both cases. The same conditions would appear to have applied to the first ladies at Portrush. An article in *The Field* 11th July 1891 recorded: ". . . on the 27th ult the first ladies competition took place over the new ladies course . . . which is marked by yellow boxes and flags, consists of nine holes . . . the ladies course may be said to embrace all the diversities of hill and dale, brook and bunker for which the Portrush links are famous." That these ladies organized the second Irish ladies club would appear proven by an entry in *The Golfing Annual*

1892/93 which gives an institution date of November 1891 for the Royal County Ladies Golf Club. In the same publication it is reported that the ladies now had an eighteen-hole course "as well as a separate clubhouse, handsomely furnished". The first lady Captain in 1892 was Mrs. Magill. [7]

Other ladies clubs followed, Belmont in 1892; Birr, Lurgan and Thomastown in 1893. This latter club is of interest as *The Golfing Annual* 1893/94 recorded this Co. Kilkenny club as Thomastown Ladies Golf Club . . . "no particulars forthcoming" . . . (1893 may not have been its year of institution). There were lady members at Fortwilliam in 1894 [8] and in May of that year the County Down Ladies Golf Club was instituted under the Presidency of the Countess of Annesley. [9] *The Golfing Annual* 1894/95 lists the ladies subscription at Foxrock as one guinea, the entrance fee was one guinea and the ladies had a separate pavilion for themselves. When the Co. Armagh Club was instituted in October 1894 ladies were able to join at half the men's subscription of one pound. [10] In the following year, 1895, there were ladies at Ormeau, Knock, Nenagh [11] and Malahide. [12]

The entries in the *Golfing Annuals* prior to 1895 show the establishment of separate ladies clubs only in the case of clubs already mentioned. It would appear that in all the other clubs, ladies were members of a branch of the men's club, paying in most instances a cheaper subscription than the men. In several cases ladies were amongst the "prime movers" behind the setting up of the original club itself. Portstewart in 1895 and Castlerock in 1900 are examples (see Appendix 1). Three Portstewart ladies led by Miss Lizzie Knox were prominent in organising that club. [13]

It was also not uncommon to see that ladies had a prominent part in the management of club affairs in the 1890s. Mrs. Ada Marshall was first Hon. Secretary of the Kings County and Ormond (Birr) Golf Club in 1893. [14] Mrs. Pearson was Hon. Secretary of the Athlone Garrison Golf Club in 1898. [15]

LADIES OPEN COMPETITIONS

In the absence of other proof it would appear that Killymoon had the honour of holding the first open ladies competition in Ireland. *The Belfast Newsletter* 14th May 1891 reported: "Yesterday the first competition for the Killymoon golf club's Ladies Scratch Medal took place, open to all Ireland . . . (there were) 14 entries from Dungannon, [16] Hollywood, Aughnacloy and Killymoon . . ." The account relates that the solid gold medal had been presented by the club Captain Mr. H. Adair and the winner was Miss Garratt of the Holywood (Belfast) club. *The Golfing Annual* 1891/92 reported that this competition "for ladies resident in Ireland (is) the only scratch prize, by the way, in the country".

It is quite probable that open competitions were held by other clubs in the early 1890s which this research has not uncovered. *The Irish Times* 14th June 1895 carried a notice re the forthcoming open competition for ladies for the Dublin, Wicklow and Wexford Railway Company prize, to take place at Foxrock on the

22nd inst. This would appear to have been the earliest sponsored open competition for ladies in Ireland. *The Belfast Newsletter* 5th May 1896 carried the result of a semi-open mixed foursomes at Foxrock, won by Miss Perry and Captain Hamilton. Lahinch held an open meeting in August 1896 and Mrs. Barrington won sixth nett in the competition open to men and ladies. [17] Malahide held an open ladies competition on Easter Monday 1897, which was won by Miss Florence Walker Leigh of Foxrock. [18]

Miss Leigh would subsequently become the first Southern golfer to win the Irish Women's Close Championship in 1907. The Malahide and Foxrock ladies were the leading metropolitan golfing pioneers of the 1890s, competition results appearing regularly in *The Irish Times*.

INSTITUTION OF THE IRISH LADIES GOLF UNION — 1893

On the 19th April 1893 the inaugural meeting to found the Ladies Golf Union was held, attended by thirty-two delegates. Subsequently the first Ladies British Open Amateur Championship was held at Lytham and St. Anne's Ladies Golf Club, won on the inaugural occasion by Lady Margaret Scott. Four male Vice Presidents were chosen at the inaugural meeting and it is of historical interest that Tom Gilroy was elected as the Irish Vice President. [19]

When the Irish ladies decided to form a Union in December 1893 they showed great independence and unlike their counterparts in England did not require any male assistance. The preliminary meeting to form the Union was held on December 15th 1893 in the G.F.G. Lodge, Belfast. There were eighteen ladies present, ten from the Royal Belfast Ladies Golf Club, three from Lisburn Golf Club, one from Dungannon Ladies Golf Club and four from the Royal County Golf Club (Portrush). The following resolutions were passed:

1. That in the interest of golf in Ireland it is desirable that a Union of the Irish Ladies Golf Clubs be, and is hereby formed and shall be called "The Irish Ladies Golf Union".
2. That the Union shall consist of a council which shall include a President, five Vice Presidents, Hon. Sec, Hon. Tres (sic) and representative members from the clubs comprising the Union.
3. That Miss Mulligan (Belfast) be Honorary Secretary.
4. That Mrs. G. H. Clarke (Lisburn) be Honorary Treasurer.
5. That the Countess of Annesley (Co. Down) be asked to be President.
6. That the council consist of delegates or representative members of each associated club. One delegate for every fifty members.
7. That an annual Championship meeting be held and that the first meeting be held at Carnalea in April 1894, at Portrush 1895, at Newcastle 1896.

Five Vice Presidents were then elected: Mrs. G. M. Shaw (Belfast), Mrs. Mann (Portrush), Miss Graham (Lisburn), Mrs. Stephen Maxwell (Co. Down) and Mrs. Moutray (Killymoon). [20] The chair at this inaugural meeting was taken by Mrs. Shaw and it is of interest to note that the minutes of the second meeting in February 1894 were signed by the "Chairwoman", a very modern euphemism.

THE FIRST IRISH LADIES CHAMPIONSHIP – 1894

There is little doubt that the Royal Belfast ladies had been prime movers in establishing the new Union and the choice of venue for the first Irish Ladies championship was their home course at Carnalea. The winner of this inaugural occasion was Miss Clara Mulligan, first Honorary Secretary of the I.L.G.U. She defeated Miss N. Graham of Lisburn by 2 and 1 in the final. *The Royal Belfast Centenary Brochure* records that in the months previous to the final Miss Mulligan had "played in the medal with scores ranging from 165 to 121. These are impressive scores when allowance is made for the primitive balls and clubs of the period, the flannel petticoats, the heavy ankle-length serge skirts (usually soaking wet), unsuitable galoshes, top heavy headgear and of course those whalebone corsets!" A photograph of the lady participants and officials appears on page 119, including, no doubt, many of the Union's founders.

MISS CLARA MULLIGAN
First Irish Ladies Champion 1894
and first Hon. Sec. I.L.G.U.

The entrance fee for this first championship was one shilling which was reasonable value. However, this sum only applied to members of the affiliated clubs and it was declared that "any lady wishing to play who is not a member of a club, or whose club has not joined the Union can do so by paying five shillings entrance fee".[21] This was a substantial sum in those days, the equivalent of a ladies subscription in many of the clubs. However, the Union were trying to indirectly recruit more clubs as affiliated members and a penal entry fee was seen as a method of gentle coercion on non-affiliated clubs.

THE L.G.U. CHAMPIONSHIP AT PORTRUSH – 1895

That the committee of the Ladies Golf Union decided to hold their third championship at Portrush was a major triumph for Irish ladies golf. The championship was held at Portrush in 1895 and the winner was Lady Margaret

LADIES BRITISH OPEN AMATEUR CHAMPIONSHIP AT PORTRUSH 1896
A group of the lady competitors (there were eighty entrants) pictured outside the former men's clubhouse. It is thought that May Hezlet is sixth from the left in the front row and Rhona Adair is second from the right on the balcony.

Scott, for the second of her three consecutive wins. Photographs of her swinging reveal a most graceful action, and it is clear that she was far ahead of her rivals. In the Portrush final she defeated Miss E. Lythgoe of Lytham and St. Annes by 3 and 2.

It is obvious that the visiting golfers and the L.G.U. committee enjoyed their first Irish visit; from 1895 to 1969 the championship has been played 15 times in Ireland. Portrush was the venue on seven occasions between 1895 and 1969, Newcastle also hosted the event on seven occasions between 1899 and 1963. Portmarnock was chosen in 1931. More will be written later of the early Irish champions in this event.

LADY MARGARET SCOTT'S
CLASSICAL SWING

INSTITUTION OF I.L.G.U. SENIOR CUP – 1897

At the annual general meeting held on 4th December 1896 a proposal to have a Challenge Cup for interclub competition was discussed for the first time. Full discussion on the proposal took place at the council meeting on the 28th January 1897 and, finally, at the council's meeting on 5th May a set of rules governing the competition were agreed to. "The Irish Ladies Golf Union League" had a total of seventeen rules. Matches were to be played on a home and away basis with every other club in the league. This competition was a landmark in the history of the I.L.G.U., however the format would appear to have been over ambitious and certainly the number of matches to be played was a costly exercise on the part of most clubs.

The Irish Field 3rd November 1923 carried a reprint of an article, on this competition, from *The Belfast Newsletter*: "The competition was inaugurated in the year 1897, the first winners being Royal Belfast. Since then the successful clubs have been Royal Belfast 1898; Killymoon 1898/99; Royal Portrush 1899/1900, 1900/01, 1902, 1906; North West 1907; Royal Portrush 1910; Fortwilliam 1920; Royal Co. Down 1920; Royal Belfast 1921; Armagh 1921; Royal Belfast 1922, 1923; Hermitage 1923. The apparent inconstancy of results and overlapping of dates will be explained later. In the early days of the competition there were no Southern clubs affiliated to the I.L.G.U. and each club entering for the event had to play a match with every other club during the year, the cup to be held by the club having the greatest number of wins. A memento prize in the shape of a silver club was given to the winning team. These conditions were altered in 1901, when it was decided that the holders might be challenged by any of the other affiliated clubs. The teams were seven a side and the holders were to have the choice of ground . . . the holders need not accept more than one challenge in three months, precedence to be given to the first challenge received . . . there has been a fairly lively amount of challenging during the past three years . . . after their first unsuccessful challenge (in 1922) when they travelled one short, Hermitage sent word along that they were willing to be up and doing . . . on the 18th inst (October 1923) they duly appeared at Carnalea with a strong side and won by the odd match . . . I (James Henderson) think we may say that the Dublin ladies thoroughly deserve their success which no doubt will give an impetus to the game in their province . . ."

That the I.L.G.U. were ahead of the G.U.I. in organising interclub events is clear. At the special council meeting of the I.L.G.U. on 8th June 1898 it was decided to hold a Junior League, similar to the Senior competition, for handicaps 14 and over. However, the early Senior events had been dominated by the Northern clubs as the Southern ladies were slow to affiliate to the Union.

GROWTH OF THE I.L.G.U. – 1894 to 1910

Despite Foxrock's affiliation in 1897, other Southern clubs were slow to affiliate and the records of affiliation given in the *Golfing Annuals* show that

Cork was the second Southern club to seek admission, in 1900. The same publications carry details of lady membership in many clubs prior to 1910, however it would appear that only in a few instances the ladies bothered to form ladies clubs of their own. The following table shows the sequence of affiliations as listed in the *Golfing Annuals* until 1910:

Edition	Number of Clubs	Names	Remarks
1894/95	9	Royal Belfast, Royal Portrush, Co. Down, Lisburn, Belmont, North West, Dungannon, Armagh, Killymoon.	
1895/96	12	*add:* Ormeau, Malone, Lurgan	
1896/97	13	*add:* Foxrock	
1898/99	13	*add:* Ballycastle, Helen's Bay	Belmont and Lisburn not listed
1900/01	16	*add:* Greenisland, Massereene, Cork	
1901/02	17	*add:* Greenore	
1903/04	19	*add:* Bangor, Lahinch	
1905/06	25	*add:* Fortwilliam, Whitehead, Greystones, Carrickmines, Killiney, Sutton	
1906/07	33	*add:* Holywood, Island, Ardglass, Knock, Dunmurry, Malahide, Bray, Castlerock	
1907/08	34	*add:* Rathfarnham, Lisburn	Killymoon not listed
1908/09	35	*add:* Co. Sligo	
1909/10	42	*add:* Killarney, Tramore, Tralee, Limerick, Greencastle, Hermitage, Milltown.	Final edition of *The Golfing Annual*

It can be seen from the table that the main growth of the Union began in 1905 and this followed a decision by the council to hold the championship meeting of 1904 at Lahinch. A lengthy letter from C. L. McNeile, Hon. Secretary of the I.L.G.U. appeared in *The Irish Golfer* 20th January 1904: ''The Union was first started in Belfast ten years ago and the first rule runs thus — 'Any ladies golf club in Ireland, having a designation and golfing green, shall be admissable into the Golf Union'. In December 1902, it was decided: 'That recognised golf clubs, having lady members or associates who have not a separate club of their own can join the Union on their behalf and shall also be eligible to elect delegates to send to the meetings'. There are now eighteen clubs in the Union, the only ones outside Ulster being Greenore, Foxrock and Cork. . . . as this year's Championship is to be held at Lahinch where we hope for a large entry from clubs that have not yet joined the Union . . .''

This appeal was clearly successful with an increase in excess of one hundred per cent in affiliation over the following six years, the majority of new applicants being Southern clubs. One of the non-affiliated clubs was Gorey G.C., which no longer exists. *The Irish Field* 7th February 1914 reported that the annual general meeting of the club was quite unique with the appointment of a lady as Captain of the club: ''. . . the lady having this distinction being Mrs. E. A. L. Turner . . .''

AFFILIATION OF FOXROCK — 1897

Foxrock Ladies Golf Club were the first Southern Club to affiliate to the I.L.G.U., in 1897. It is clear that a warm welcome was extended to this first Southern club as Miss Florence Walker Leigh was elected as a Vice President of the Union at the annual general meeting in December 1897. Miss Leigh had figured prominently in ladies golf events in Dublin from 1895 onwards. In 1901 and 1904 she was runner-up in the Irish Women's Championship finals. She became the first Southern lady golfer to win the event in 1907 and in 1911 was a losing finalist once again. Her major achievement would have been her losing appearance in the 1903 Ladies British Amateur Championship at Portrush (see footnote 23).

The year 1897 was also the first year in which the I.L.G.U. held their championship meeting outside Ulster. Royal Dublin was the venue and the Union's records reveal that the host club offered prizes value £5 for a competition in conjunction with the meeting.

FLORENCE WALKER LEIGH
Irish Lady Champion 1907.

I.L.G.U. HANDICAPPING SCHEME

At the Union's first annual general meeting in December 1894, a general discussion took place on handicapping. [22] It was decided to defer any decision until the following meeting when more information would be available. When the Council met on 6th February 1895 there would appear to have been general agreement on the scheme and the Honorary Secretary was instructed to circulate the new handicapping scheme to each affiliated club. That "Murphy's Law" was allowed for can be seen in the following details: "The scratch score of any links should be fixed by taking the lowest number of strokes required for a first class player to reach the green plus 2 for puts (sic). Two or three strokes should be added to each 9 holes for mistakes, these strokes might be increased or decreased according to the number of hazards or difficulties of each course.

Having found the scratch score a players best gross return should be deducted (or vice versa) and the difference would be her handicap. (Example: scratch = 74, player's best score 80. Handicap 6)."

The scheme was the essence of simplicity and at the council meeting of 24th April 1895 a maximum handicap of 36 was agreed. This limit has not changed although the handicapping scheme itself has been modified over the years.

EARLY SHOWERS AT LAHINCH

The early enthusiasm for golf at Lahinch was outlined in Chapter 6 and from an early stage lady golfers were encouraged to stay and play over the embryonic links. An amusing account of one lady's experience of "wash day" at the Clare resort was carried in *The Irish Golfer* 8th August 1900: "Visitors to Lahinch in former days wishing *to wash*, had no choice but a plunge in the briny, or the village bathhouse, a somewhat old world structure, where the common or garden shower bath was administered *through a hole in the roof* by an attendant with a watering can. There is a story of a lady getting into her bath being unpleasantly surprised by a *manly* voice suggesting she should 'move a little more to the *wesht*' to have the full benefit of the shower."

EARLY IRISH LADY CHAMPIONS

A glorious golden age of Irish ladies golf began in 1899, when a 17-year-old girl won the Ladies British Amateur Championship at Newcastle, Co. Down. Over the following twelve years this prestigious tournament was to be dominated by Irish players in a sequence of victories and near victories which may never be equalled. There was an Irish interest in nine finals, with five victories. [23]. May Hezlet, a member of Portrush, won just one week after her seventeenth birthday, the youngest player ever to win this championship. Her sisters Florence and Violet were also to reach the final on three other occasions. Rhona Adair from the Killymoon club was the second young Irish star to win in the 1905 final.

May Hezlet: This young girl first came into prominence in 1898 when she reached the final of the Irish Ladies Championship. After a tremendous contest she was defeated on the 18th by Miss Magill (R.B.L.G.C.). In the following year's 36-hole final she gained a 5 and 4 victory over Rhona Adair at Newcastle. The same venue was the scene of the Ladies British Amateur contest one week later and May Hezlet disposed of one contestant after another with ease until she reached the final. Her opponent was Miss Magill, her opponent in the previous year's Irish Championship, however May won the 18-hole contest by 2 and 1 . . . ''the spectators were treated to a fine display of golf''.[24]

MAY HEZLET
First Irish winner of Ladies British
Amateur Championship 1899.

An entry in *Nisbets Year Book* 1908 records that May Hezlet was born in Gibraltar in 1882. Her 1908 handicap was given as plus 6 and her record in the British Ladies was: Champion in 1899, 1902 and 1907, runner-up in 1904. May was also Irish Lady Champion in 1899, 1904, 1905, 1906 and 1908, runner-up in 1898. She became an accomplished golf writer contributing articles to *Golf Illustrated* and *The Irish Golfer*. In 1904 she published a book — *Ladies Golf.*

Rhona Adair: Ireland's second winner of the Ladies British Amateur Championship was a member of the famous Killymoon golfing family. Rhona Adair's father, Hugh, had laid out the first links at Killymoon in 1889. Her mother is listed amongst the attendance of the first annual general meeting of the I.L.G.U. and a Miss Adair is also listed, which may have been herself. *The Irish Golfer* 27th September 1899 reported that she had first come to notice in 1895, at the age of thirteen when she competed in the Ladies British Open Amateur Championship when it was held at Portrush. (Her father was Captain of Portrush in that year). Rhona gained the first of her two victories in this championship in 1900 when she defeated Miss E. C. Neville by 6 and 5, at Westward Ho! She was runner-up in 1901 and had her final success in 1903 at Portrush.

Rhona had an impressive succession of victories in the Irish Women's Championship, winning four successive finals from 1900 to 1903. She was runner-up in 1899 when her great rival May Hezlet was victorious. Rhona achieved fame

RHONA ADAIR

at the time for the prodigious distance she could hit the golf ball, *The Irish Golfer* regularly carried details of her prowess, the editorial of 11th April 1900 reported a win in a driving competition when she hit a "fine rasper" of 173 yards, 20 yards ahead of the others. With the primitive clubs and balls then available this drive would compare highly with any modern equivalent.

In 1907 Rhona married Captain A. H. Cuthell of the West Yorkshire Regiment and this would appear to have ended her active golfing career. Her later life was saddened by the death in action of her husband. *The Irish Field* 4th September 1915 reported he had been killed in the Dardanelles campaign. She was widowed with two children.

IRISH LADIES TEAM – FIRST INTERNATIONAL WIN 1907

In 1895 an unofficial international match was held at Portrush following the Ladies British Open Amateur Championship. The six-a-side match was won 34 holes to nil by England. A similar contest took place at Newcastle in 1899 with the English ladies again victorious by 37 holes to 18.[25] *The Belfast Newsletter* 6th May 1907 carried a proud headline when announcing "Irish Ladies Secure Triple Crown At Newcastle". This was an Irish amateur team's first ever win (men or women) in an international contest; in this case the Millar International Shield was at stake. The names of the Irish ladies were F. Walker Leigh (Foxrock), May Hezlet (Portrush), J. Magill (Co. Down), M. E. Stuart (Portrush), Florence Hezlet (Portrush), Mrs. Durlacher (Romford) and Violet Hezlet (Portrush).

THE MALIGNED LADY GOLFER

An editorial in *The Irish Golfer* 18th October 1899 under the above title reported: "Golf undoubtedly owes much of its popularity to the enthusiasm with which it has been taken up by what men are pleased to term the weaker sex. Many conscientious fathers of families can now take their families to the seaside and enjoy their rounds of golf, because their womenfolk also pursue the game, instead of boring themselves to death in seaside lodgings talking scandal or reading trashy novels. Women can now also take an intelligent part in golf

LADIES GOLF DRESS C. 1905
(Courtesy of the National Library of Ireland)

conversation and their knowledge of the game and its terms has rendered golf a topic of conversation between the sexes, which until lately it has not been. In view of these facts I wish to protest on behalf of lady golfers at the treatment they too often receive at the hands of *gentlemen* both on the green and off it . . ."

The editor, J. W. Percy, was obviously a very liberal-minded man and his periodical regularly carried material on ladies golf of the period. The edition of 24th January 1900 carried an intriguing entry regarding ladies rights at Dollymount: "The committee of the Royal Dublin Golf Club have formulated the following rules on certain vexed points:

1. That ladies be allowed to play on Dollymount on Mondays and Thursday for the whole day.
2. That ladies singles, ladies foursomes and mixed singles must allow gentlemen singles or foursomes to pass . . ."

On the same theme a very "modern" poem in *The Belfast Newsletter* 26th August 1905 expressed a wife's sentiments which surely echo in the 1980s:

THE REVENGE

I am a widow, though a wife,
  My husband's lost to me;
I seldom see his face at all,
  He's joined the B.G.C.

His talk is all of drives and putts,
  Of holing out in four,
Of bunkers, hazards, mashie shots,
  And what he calls his score.

His purse grows leaner every day,
  His golf bag fuller grows;
How many balls he's bought
  He never will disclose.

I'll join the club myself; and play
  When he is out to work;
Dusting and darning, cookery
  And washing day I'll shirk.

I'll be home at dinner time
  And in my usual seat,
And feed my truant husband well
  On excellent tinned meat.

POSTSCRIPT

Irish ladies golf continues to hold a prominent place in the sporting life of the nation. At present there are over 20,000 lady golfers under the umbrella of the Irish Ladies Golf Union which is an all-Ireland body. Great prestige has been brought to this country over the years since May Hezlet first won the Ladies British Open Amateur Championship in 1899. A total of six Irish ladies have won this prestigious event on nine occasions.[26] Eight Irish ladies have been chosen for the British and Irish Curtis Cup teams since the first event in 1932, on a total of seventeen occasions. There was an Irish representative on three of the winning teams of a total of five British and Irish victories in the event.

When the history of the Irish Ladies Golf Union comes to be written the name of a Highland officer's wife will figure prominently. The present generation of Irish lady golfers owe a debt of gratitude to Mrs. Wright who inspired the ladies of Belfast to form a golf club one hundred years ago. Countless hours of pleasure and relaxation have been enjoyed by thousands of Irish lady golfers ever since.

COMPETITORS AND OFFICIALS AT THE FIRST IRISH LADIES
CHAMPIONSHIP. CARNALEA, 1894.

FOOTNOTES

1. *Guinness Book of Golf Facts and Feats*, page 20.
2. *Royal Musselburgh Golf Club*, private history by R. Ironside, 1974, page 5.
3. *Royal Belfast Golf Club Centenary Brochure*, page 75.
4. *The Golfing Annual* 1909/10 lists the separate ladies courses, there is no mention in subsequent publications.
5. The author is indebted to Mr. G. S. Glover for research done on this newspaper.
6. *The Derry Journal* 3rd July 1891.
7. *The Irish Golfer* 21st March 1900. The first ladies committee is named in this article which reported that the ladies separate club was founded in September 1892, the men had managed the club set up the previous year.
8. *The Golfing Annual* 1894/95, the subscription was 5 shillings.
9. *Ibid.*
10. *Ibid.*
11. *The Golfing Annual* 1895/96 reported 20 lady members at Nenagh.
12. *The Belfast Newsletter* 24th December 1895 gave the result of a Malahide ladies competition, ladies may have been members of the club before 1895.
13. *The Irish Field* 1st May 1909.
14. *The Irish Times* 26th October 1894.
15. Minute book, Athlone Garrison G.C., 26th February 1898.
16. There is no mention of ladies at Dungannon in the editions of *The Golfing Annual* until 1898, when the I.L.G.U. entry lists Dungannon as affiliated.
17. *The Irish Times* 7th August 1896. Her husband, J. H. Barrington, won the competition with a nett 86 off 27 handicap.

18. *The Irish Times* 22nd April 1897.
19. *The Golfing Annual* 1893/94. Mr. W. Laidlaw Purves, Mr. Talbot Fair and Mr. H. S. C. Everard were elected Vice Presidents and representatives of South of England, North of England and Scotland respectively.
20. Minutes of I.L.G.U., by kind permission.
21. Minutes of Delegate Meeting I.L.G.U. 23rd February 1894.
22. The Minutes refer to "an animated discussion".
23. 1899 May Hezlet won, Miss Magill (R.B.G.C.) r/up; 1900 Rhona Adair won; 1901 Rhona Adair r/up; 1902 May Hezlet won; 1903 Florence W-Leigh (Foxrock) r-up; 1904 May Hezlet r/up; 1907 May Hezlet won, Florence Hezlet r/up; 1909 Florence Hezlet r/up; 1909 Florence Hezlet r/up; 1911 Violet Hezlet r/up. Source: *Guinness Book of Golf Facts and Feats.*
24. *The Irish Golfer* 20th September 1899.
25. *The Irish Times* 15th May 1899.
26. In addition to May Hezlet's and Rhona Adair's wins, documented in footnote 23 above, Mrs. P. G. McCann (Tullamore) 1951, Miss Philomena Garvey (Co. Louth) 1957 and Miss Lillian Behan (Curragh) 1985 were the other Irish winners.

Early Irish Golf

IRELAND'S EARLY CLUBS

NOTES TO APPENDIX 1

1. PURPOSE OF APPENDIX
   The purpose of this Appendix is, as far as possible, to document the founding details
   of all Irish clubs and courses instituted prior to 1923.

2. EXTINCT CLUBS AND COURSES
   Clubs founded before 1923, which are currently in existence, are shown with their
   date of affiliation to the Golfing Union of Ireland at the beginning of the listing.
   Extinct clubs and course are shown without such detail.

3. THE SPORTSMAN HOLIDAY GUIDE 1897
   This publication's full title is *The Golfers and Sportsmans Holiday Guide to Ireland
   1897.*

4. THE IRISH GOLF GUIDES
   The Irish Golfers Guide 1910 was issued by *The Irish Field*. Subsequent editions in
   1911, 1912, 1913 and 1914 were entitled *The Irish Golfing Guide*. In 1916 *The Irish
   Golfing Guide* was issued by *Irish Life*. For brevity, at times, all the above are
   referred to as *The Irish Golf Guides* in the Appendix.

ABBEYLEIX, Co. Laois.
Instituted 1895. Affiliated 1905.
   The first entry relating to Abbeyleix Golf Club is recorded in *The Golfing Annual*
   1905/06. A foundation date of 1894 is given, the Captain was R. Hampton and the
   Hon. Secretary was Rev. A. E. Bor, The Vicarage, Abbeyleix: ". . . The course
   of nine holes, circuit 2,154 yards, is at Ballymullen, one mile from Abbeyleix
   Station . . .". Later, *The Irish Golf Guides* record the foundation date as 1895.
   The Irish Field 12th March 1927 reported a recent meeting of the club at which
   it was decided to lay out a new course on Mr. Weld's land at Rathmoyle House.
   Following this, it would appear that the club went into decline for a period, probably
   during the war years. The records of the Golfing Union of Ireland reveal an
   application for reaffiliation in July 1949 from Rev. Edward O'Byrne C.C., the club
   Captain, following reconstitution.

ADARE, Co. Limerick.
Instituted 1900.   Affiliated 1932.

The Irish Golfer 5th December 1900 mentions Adare ". . . where Ben Sayers recently laid out a private course for this enthusiastic gentleman [Lord Dunraven]" Later, an article in Golf Illustrated 21st November 1902 gives a full account of the clubs origins: "The club was instituted in September 1900, but the course had been open two years previously (i.e. 1898) as a private one. The membership is now close on 60 and the management vested in a committee appointed by Lord Dunraven." The article also describes the nine holes of the course.

AGHADE, TULLOW, Co. Carlow.

The Irish Golfers Guide 1910 lists this club as founded in 1906 and states ". . . situated within three miles of Tullow Station". Lord Rathdonnel is given as Captain in the 1911 Irish Golfing Guide which also states: "This is a club organised principally for local residents but if it was nearer a town the course is one that would be very popular as it is a true natural course, offering many sporting shots."

Unfortunately, this club did not survive for too long as The Irish Golfing Guide 1916 records: ". . . owing to the war this small club had to be wound up". Later, the records of the Golfing Union of Ireland reveal that a newly-formed club at Tullow was affiliated in 1926. The Irish Tourist Directory 1937 records the continuing existence of this revived club and Thoms Directory 1940 listed M. J. McFeeley, Bridge Hotel, Tullow, as Hon Secretary of the nine-hole course. Finally Thoms Directory 1947 recorded ". . . temporarily closed".

ARDARA, Co. Donegal.

This club is first listed in The Golfing Annual 1898/99 (Vol. XII) which gives a foundation date of April 1899. However, following editions give an intriguing series of institution dates: Vol. XV lists April 1898; Vol. XVI lists January 1897; Vol. XVII lists January 1891. To add further to confusion The Irish Golfers Guide 1910 gives 1903 as the foundation date!

It would appear that this was a club associated with an hotel in Ardara, probably the "Green House" which is the listed address for the Hon. Secretary Mr. Michael McNelis from the earliest listing. The Irish Golfing Guide 1912 gives a membership of 20. No entry appears in The Irish Golf Guides 1914 and 1916, nor in The Golfers Handbook 1923.

Thoms Directory 1927 lists the club and the 1930 edition documented the Hon. Secretary's address as McNelis & Co., Green House, Ardara. A similar entry occurs in the 1932 edition; there is no further mention of the club subsequently.

ARDCARNE, Co. Leitrim.

A club of this name is listed in The Golfing Union of Ireland Yearbook 1947 with affiliation dates of 1910 and 1946. The club is not mentioned in the yearbooks 1927 to 1945 and it would seem that this was a revival of Carrick-on-Shannon Golf Club.
    *See Carrick-on-Shannon.

ARDEE, Co. Louth.
Instituted 1911.   Affiliated 1911.

This club is first listed in *The Irish Golfers Guide* 1910 as the South Louth Golf Club with a foundation date of 1911 and lists the first Captain as Captain G. Taafe, with Sir Henry Bellingham as President. The course of nine holes was adjacent to the town.

Later in *The Irish Field* 8th February 1913 Lionel Hewson wrote: "I was this week assistting the Committee of the Ardee club to lay out a new course in the Ruxton Demesne beautifully situated a few minutes walk from the centre of the town. For some three years past, the club has had a small course at the opposite end of town."

ARDFERT, Co. Kerry.

This course is first listed in *The Golfing Annual* 1896/97 which states: "There is an eighteen hole course at Ardfert Abbey. Visitors are permitted to play in the most liberal fashion". Later, *The Golfing Annual* 1902/03 lists the course as a twelve-hole one. There is no record of golf at Ardfert after 1910, when it was again listed in the *The Golfing Annual* 1909/10. *Irish Life* 12th December 1913 documents the death of the owner, Mr. Lindsey Talbot Crosbie.

GOLF AT ARDGLASS C. 1905

(Courtesy of the National Library of Ireland)

ARDGLASS, Co. Down.
Instituted 1896.   Affiliated 1897.

The Belfast Newsletter 30th April 1896 records the inaugural meeting of this club which was held in the local courthouse on the evening of 28th April, Rev. Thomas Macafee presided. A committee, headed by Dr. McComiskey, was appointed to draw up rules and make necessary arrangements. A further meeting is recorded in *The Belfast Newsletter* 6th June 1896 at which B. N. Johnson was elected President and W. P. Martin was elected first Captain.

The Golfers and Sportsman Holiday Guide 1897 records: ". . . a sporting little course of seven holes, distance about three quarters of a mile . . . a new clubhouse is in course of erection". Ladies were involved in the club from the earliest days as *The Belfast Newsletter* 16th June 1896 lists the various subscriptions among which were "Ladies 10/6d".

ATHGARVAN, Co. Kildare.

This club is first listed in *The Irish Golfers Guide* 1910 which records: ". . . another nine hole course has been opened on the Curragh near Mallicks Hotel". Later editions of the *Guide* do not list the club but Golfing Union of Ireland records reveal an affiliation date of January 1912.

It would appear that the club died circa 1922 when the British Army evacuated the nearby Curragh Camp. Local tradition records that the club was run by local business people who could not get access to the Royal Curragh Golf Club.

ATHENRY, Co. Galway.
Instituted 1902.   Affiliated 1929.

An entry for this club is first given in *The Golfing Annual* 1907/08 which lists November 1904 as the foundation date. Hon. Secretary was W. S. B. Leathan, R.I.C., and ". . . The course of nine holes varying from 111 to 480 yards (par 36) is half a mile from Athenry station". Subsequent *Golfing Annuals* until 1910 give the same date.

The club is listed in *The Irish Golfers Guide* 1910 as Athenry (Co. Galway Golf Club), which gives 1902 as the year of institution. The 1911 *Guide* records that ". . . the club is deeply indebted to Mr. J. B. Concanon, Major Hall, Mr. H. J. Concanon, Mr. J. M. Meldon and Dr. P. J. Quinlan". The length of the course is given as 2,353 yards, nine holes, which were "within half a mile of Athenry station".

The present course of this club, at Palmerston, is the fourth location since foundation, which would have been a typical chronology for many rural Irish clubs. World War One had a drastic effect, as *The Irish Golfers Guide* 1916 records: ". . . owing to depletion of members, on account of the war, and falling off of subscriptions, this club has been closed for the present".

ATHLONE, Co. Roscommon.
Instituted 1892.   Affiliated 1897.

This golf club is first listed in *The Golfing Annual* 1896/97, under the name Athlone Garrison Golf Club, an institution date of 1892 is given. The *Annual* records that the number of members was 70 and that ". . . the course, of nine holes, is about half a mile from the railway station. It is a difficult course, being round an old fortification. The hazards are walls, moats, ditches, roads, the railway, etc." The club, like the Curragh, was a military club at inception and the golf guide books of the late 1890s record predominantly military committees. Unfortunately, the earliest minute books, up to 1898, are unavailable so that the founding "officers" cannot be named. The original course was laid out amid the ruins of an old fort and its moat at the "Batteries" near the railway station. This layout may have been familiar to officers of the garrison who had served at Malta, for the original course had been laid out in 1888 by Sir Henry D'O. Torrens among the moat and ditches of an old fort.

One of the earliest mentions of the club in *The Irish Times* is 12th December 1896 when an interclub match was played against a Curragh team. Lt. Pusey of the Curragh Club (which won the match 18 holes to 12 holes) set a new course record of 41 for the nine holes. In 1904 the club changed its name to Athlone Golf Club and it was in that year that the club figured in, possibly, the earliest recorded Irish legal action for damages caused by a golfer. *The Irish Golfer* of 20th January 1904 records that, at the Quarter sessions in Athlone, Mrs. Margaret Farrell sued J. S. Vaughan, LL.D., Clerk of the Union, for £10 damages, on account of injuries sustained at the local golf "links". The accident occurred following a "slice" and a decree of £5 was given.

In 1913 the club moved to a new location two miles outside the town and Mr. W. C. Pickeman of Portmarnock assisted in the laying out (*The Irish Field* 1st November 1913). In 1938 the club finally moved to the present location at Hodson Bay.

ATHY, Co. Kildare.
Instituted 1906.   Affiliated 1906.

The Irish Times of 31st January 1906 documents the initial meeting of this club, presided over by Mr. John A. Duncan J.P. Prior to 1906 the Athy golfers had played together with the men of Carlow at Gotham which was midway between the two towns (founded in 1899). *The Golfing Annual* 1906/07 records the first amateur course record by Mr. H. F. Lesmond in October 1906 (the Captain of 1906/07). An article on the club appeared in *The Irish Field* 2nd October 1910 which gave the details of institution.

*See Carlow G.C.

ATLANTIC, Kilbrittain, Bandon, Co. Cork.

This was a proprietorial course laid out by Mr. Alcock Stanell, of Riversdale, close to the Atlantics Golf Links Hotel which was built on the "Norwegian Principle".

The Earl of Bandon was the first President of the club.

The course was listed as Kilbrittain G.C. in *The Golfing Annual* 1902/03. It is not known when the club ceased to exist after it was last recorded in *The Irish Golfing Guide* 1916.

ATLANTIC FLEET, Bere Island, Co. Cork.

The Irish Golfers Guide 1910 lists this as a nine-hole course on Bere Island ". . . most inaccessible except for residents on the island and members of the fleet". This was a Royal Navy club formerly known as the Channel Fleet G.C., which became Atlantic Fleet G.C. when the Navy was reorganised. The same publication stated: ". . . the fleet now have a course on the mainland at Castletown".

The Irish Golfing Guide 1916 listed a Royal Naval Club at Berehaven.

*See Berehaven, Channel Fleet G.C. and Royal Naval G.C.

AUGHER, Co. Tyrone.

A club with this name is listed in *The Golfing Annual* 1898/99 for the first time, no details other than the name are given. A similar entry appears in the 1900/01 edition. There is no further record of the club.

AUGHNACLOY, Co. Tyrone.

This Club is first documented in *The Golfing Annual* 1888/89 where an institution date of 23rd December 1888 is given. There were 30 members, the Captain was W. H. Mann and the President was Mr. James Pringle J.P. "The links are about two miles in extent and are on the property of the President. There are numerous hazards in the form of watercourses, rushes, hedges and trees . . . the course consists of nine holes but the number will shortly be increased . . ." In the same publication an article on golf in Ireland reported that the club had been "formed in the Autumn of 1888 by Mr. W. H. Mann, one of the County (Portrush) club's most enthusiastic members . . . and [he] had found a kindred spirit in Mr. James Pringle of Anna House, in whose demesne the course is laid out . . ."

It is of interest to note that in later editions of *The Golfing Annual* the club claimed to have first eighteen-hole course in Ireland. This claim is not borne out by the *Annuals* themselves. The Curragh Golf Club had eighteen holes in 1888, prior to the formation of Aughnacloy, and it would appear that the original course of the Royal Dublin Club in the Phoenix Park was eighteen holes from 1887 at the latest. One major claim claim to fame the club had was the fact that it was one of the nine founder clubs of the Golfing Union of Ireland in November 1891.

The Irish Golfing Guide 1910 reported that the club had been in abeyance for a few years and had been reopened in 1906 as a nine-hole course. This is not evident from the *Golfing Annuals* which continually list the club from 1889 to 1910. An entry for the club appears in each of the *The Irish Golf Guides* until 1916, which reported that the famous Aughnacloy putter was played for each May. This highly decorated putter is now in the possession of Dungannon Golf Club and was won for the first time on 11th May 1889 by Mr. H. Shaw of the Royal Belfast G.C. *The Field* 18th May 1889 recorded that there had been over 40 competitors, from the home club, Royal Belfast and the County Club (Portrush). Over 100 spectators had turned out to witness the occasion. An article in *County Life Magazine* 30th January 1964 claimed it as the oldest golf trophy in Ireland, which claim is not accurate. It certainly was not the first such trophy for open competition. The Henderson Cup was offered by the Royal Belfast Golf Club for open competition in May 1888, six months before the foundation of Aughnacloy.

Irish Life 27th January 1922 reported that the course was unique as visitors could play free of charge and the putter was still being competed for. Intriguingly, *The Irish Field* 1st November 1924 documented the fact that the "forty"-year-old course was reopened the week before with Mr. R. Montgomery, the President, driving off the first ball. The later history and fate of the club is not known.

BAGENALSTOWN, Co. Carlow.

The Irish Field of 5th February 1910 recorded the founding of a club at Bagenalstown and stated: "The links are situated between the line of the Great Southern & Western Railway and the Chairman's residence (Mr. C. R. Norton) on the Carlow Bagenalstown road." *The Golfing Annual* 1909/10 lists it as nine holes and gives A. D. La Touche as Captain. *The Irish Golfing Guide* 1916 states that the course was laid out by Mr. W. C. Pickeman of Portmarnock and that the club was affiliated to the G.U.I.

The club is listed in *Thoms Directory* 1940, a nine-hole course, with P. J. Fitzpatrick as Hon. Secretary. Its subsequent history is unknown.

BALLA, Co. Mayo.

The G.U.I. Handbook 1928 gives the institution date of this club as 1922. *The Irish Field* 20th October 1923 reported: ". . . at Balla, Co. Mayo, is the most sporting golfing community in the world. The Balla club has fifteen members and has just won the Co. Mayo Challenge Cup, a team affair. The club is affiliated too!"

Later *The Irish Field* 28th March 1925 reported: "The Balla club has lost its course. It is holding an open meeting at Mallaranny at Easter where a big dance will also take place on Easter Monday in aid of club funds." The later history of the club is unknown.

BALLINA, Co. Mayo.
Instituted 1910.   Affiliated 1924.

This club is listed in *The Irish Golfers Guide* 1911 for the first time, which gives 1910 as the year of foundation: ". . . a nine-hole course , situated within ten minutes walk of Ballina Station . . ." The President was John Garvey, Downhill, Ballina; the Honorary Secretary was John Flanagan and the Captain was H. Scroope. *The Irish Field* 19th April 1924 reported: "The Ballina new course is shaping well. Mr. John Hosford is Captain of the club. Plenty of members are joining". This was a revival of the club, *The Irish Golfers Blue Book* 1938 reported:

". . . owing to the Great War the club had to close in 1914". *The Irish Golfers Guide* also states: "Chas. H. Wilkinson (Malahide) marked out the course in September 1910 and thinks highly of it. Length of course is 2,185 yards."

BALLINASLOE, Co. Galway.
Instituted 1905.   Affiliated 1911.

Although the present club dates itself from 1905, there was an earlier club in Ballinasloe. *The Irish Golfer* of 11th October 1899 states that ". . . a club was formed in 1894 and links were procured near the town, in some pasture fields long lain fallow . . ." An entry for the club is given in *The Golfing Annual* 1909/10 for the first time. No foundation date is recorded, the Hon. Secretary was P. S. Goodwin and ". . . the course of nine holes is half a mile from the station".

The Irish Golfing Guide 1916 lists the present club's foundation date as 1905; the location is given as Garbally Demesne, given free by the Earl of Cloncarty. Writing in *Irish Golf* September 1943, Lionel Hewson states: "Quite a lot of years ago I went to Ballinasloe to lay out a course there and was looked after by Father Cogavin of the College there".

In 1937 the club moved to its present location at Rosgloss.

BALLINROBE, Co. Mayo.
Instituted 1895.   Affiliated 1902.

This is one of the oldest courses in Connaught, listed for the first time in *The Golfing Annual* 1895/96 as instituted on 3rd October 1895. The 1895 course was ". . . a private one, consisting at present of only six holes, but it is hoped the other three will be added shortly. Ballinrobe station is within two minutes walk." The first President was Col. C. H. Knox, Captain was T. Forde and Hon. Secretary was R. C. Hearne, Killoshine Cottage, Ballinrobe. There were seventy members and it is clear that there were ladies amongst them with a subscription of five shillings for the fairer sex. An extension to nine holes is recorded in *The Golfing Annual* 1896/97, with a total length of 1,900 yards.

The Irish Golfers Guide 1910 states: "The club was founded in 1895 mainly through exertions of Mr. Thos. Forde, Inland Revenue Officer, now living at Youghal, Co. Cork." *The Irish Field* 9th April 1910 documents the first competition of the club since "the opening of the new links". The *Irish Life* 23rd July 1915 states that the club ". . . is to be congratulated on the success which attended the bogey competition in aid of the Cigarette Fund for the Connaught Rangers and Mayo Prisoners in Germany . . . the club has only 40 members but raised £7.10s."

BALLYBUNION, Co. Kerry.
Instituted 1896.   Affiliated 1909.

The first entry in the *Golfing Annuals* relating to this club appears in the 1895/96 edition which gives an institution date of 1895 and no particulars forthcoming. The 1896/97 edition gives the same date and states: ". . . the course of nine holes, is over a rabbit warren, but is not particularly well cared for. It might be made an excellent course''. The writer of these few words certainly had a keen eye for golfing terrain but it was a difficult struggle for the early pioneers of this modern day mecca for Irish and foreign golfers. Subsequent *Golfing Annuals* record the institution date as 2nd April 1896.

In his history of the club, Mr. William J. McCarthy (Hon. Secretary 1928-52) states that the first committee meeting of the (old) club was held on 4th March 1896. Mr. George Hewson of Ennismore, Listowel, was the first President and Mr. McCarthy states that his father, Patrick, took over as Hon. Secretary from Mr. C. Mark Montserrat on 20th January 1897. Mr. McCarthy elder was Manager of the Listowel & Ballybunion Railway Co. (which had been built in 1888 by Charles Lartigue, a Frenchman). *The Irish Field* 26th December 1908 records that ''. . . the links were laid out about 12 years ago by P. McKenna, then professional at Portmarnock, afterwards at Lahinch, the expenses being defrayed by the Lartigue Railway Co.''

The course is listed in *The Golfing Annual* 1898/99 as one of eighteen holes ''. . . in circuit about three and a half miles''. It would appear that the club went into decline at that time, for the last minutes of the old club are dated 13th August 1898, although the *Golfing Annuals* continue to document the club/course up to 1904. Herbert Warren Wind in his *The Lure Of Golf* states that "when the club was reformed in 1906 after financial woes had brought down the original organisation, Captain Lionel Hewson, for many years Editor of the *Irish Golf* magazine, built the nine holes that became the basis of the present layout." This was one of Hewson's proudest achievements and he recalled afterwards that a large bottle of champagne was opened that day.

The "revivers" of Ballybunion in 1906 were Col. Bartholomew, an ex-Indian officer, Mr. B. J. Johnstone of the Bank of Ireland, Listowel, Mr. Patrick McCarthy, Hon. Secretary of the original club, and Mr. John Macaulay of Listowel. By 1926 the committee found that nine holes were insufficient for the needs of the club and extended the course to eighteen holes. They entrusted the work to Carter & Sons of Raynes Park, London, who were widely known specialists in laying out sports grounds. The new links was ready in 1927.

In 1936, when the G.U.I. selected Ballybunion as the venue for the Irish Close Championship of 1937, the club called in the renowned course architect Mr. Tom Simpson. After inspecting the course he had only three recommendations to make − the relocating of the second, fourth and eighth greens and some changes in bunkering. The 1937 Close Championship was won by Jimmy Bruen; however, the G.U.I. were not the first to recognise the qualities of the course. This honour goes to the I.L.G.U. who held the Irish Ladies Championship there in 1932, won by Miss Betty Latchford, a member of the host club.

BALLYCASTLE, Co. Antrim
Instituted 1891. Affiliated 1891.

Ballycastle Golf Club was instituted on the 8th May 1891 and an article in the magazine *Golf* dated 8th January 1897 carries the following account: ''. . . the making of this pretty little nine-hole course was mainly due to the energy of Comdr. Causton R.N., late in charge of the Coastguard in the district, and Lt. Cutfield, the present Coastguard officer; and about fours years ago a club was formed with Captain Causton as Secretary, which post he still retains."

A more complete account of the club's institution is recorded in *The Irish Golfer* 26th September 1900 on the occasion of a presentation to the club's founder: "Eleven years ago . . . Commander Causton R.N., the then Divisional Officer of Coastguards at Ballycastle, having been initiated into the Royal and Ancient game at Portrush, saw that the 'Warren' at Ballycastle, a stretch of sandy turf abounding in rabbit holes and bracken, could in time be coverted into excellent links for those in the locality who might be induced to take up the game. Having received from Miss Boyd permission to use this ground, he laid off the greens and with three or four other residents in the neighbourhood, established the now well known Ballycastle Golf Club. He was elected its first Honorary Secretary, and each year since its formation the members of the club have unanimously elected him the same office."

A description of the course was given in *The Golfing Annual* 1893/94: "The links are small and situated on a warren, bordering a bay, half a mile from Ballycastle Railway Station". It would appear that the ancient inhabitants of the links had been causing trouble for the golfers, however, *The Sportsmans Holiday Guide* 1897 recorded ". . . the course was formerly a rabbit warren but the troublesome bunny has been sufficiently dealt with". One year later *The Golfing Annual* 1898/99 documented the institution of the Ballycastle Ladies G.C. in 1897 . . . "The Causton medal is played for monthly".

Despite its modest beginnings, the club has an honoured position in the history of Irish golf. In November 1891, together with delegates from eight other clubs, Ballycastle was one of the founders of the Golfing Union of Ireland.

BALLYMENA, Co. Antrim.
Instituted 1904.   Affiliated 1908.
The Golfing Annual 1904/05 carries the following details: "Instituted 1904. The course of nine holes is laid out on the old race course. Gorse is the chief hazard." *The Irish Field* 10th September 1904 states: "The old racecourse at Baughshane has been secured for the Rt. Hon. Lord O'Neill of Shanes Castle and last week the links were opened by the Rt. Hon. R. T. O'Neill, the local M.P. The Captain of the club is Mr. John K. Currie.

Later, *The Irish Golfers Guide* 1910 and *The Irish Golfing Guide* 1916 give the institution date of 1902, which is at variance with the earlier references.

BALLYNAHINCH, Co. Down.
*See Spa.

BALLYSHANNON, Co. Donegal.
This club is listed in the *The Golfing Annual* 1908/09 which gives an institution date of February 1908. There were 50 members, the Captain was F. G. Townsend and

his wife was Hon. Secretary . . . "The course of nine holes, longest 440 yards, is a mile from the station". A correction for the date of institution is recorded in *The Golfing Annual* 1909/10 which lists January 1907.

The club is documented in *The Irish Golfing Guides* from 1910 to 1916; the latter stated: "The club is now closed".

BALMORAL, Co. Antrim
Instituted 1914. Affiliated 1915.

In common with many other Irish golf clubs, Balmoral does not possess its earliest minute books and details of its foundation are sparse. The club was formed in 1914 and the records of the Golfing Union of Ireland list an affiliation date of 17th November 1915.

Originally the course was leased at a rental of £297.16.0, however a special annual general meeting was held on 9th September 1918 at which it was decided to purchase the course for £8,000. The decision to form a limited company was also taken at this meeting, the minutes of which are the earliest extant records of the club. Mr. A. C. Young was Captain at this time.

BANAGHER, Co. Offaly.

The first notice of this club is recorded in the *The Golfing Annual* 1895/96 but no date of institution is given. The 1898/99 edition of the *Annual* gives the institution date as 1894 and the following information: ". . . Annual subscription 10 shillings. Hon. Secretary Very Rev. J. J. Sherrard, The Rectory, Banagher, Kings Co. The season extends from October to May." Subsequent editions of the *Annual* up to 1909/10 give the same details re the Hon. Secretary, who would appear to have been the main promoter of golf in that district. *The Irish Golfing Guide* 1910 states: "Believed to be extinct".

BANBRIDGE, Co. Down.
Instituted 1913. Affiliated 1914.

Unfortunately, the earliest minute books of this club, prior to 1922, are unavailable which makes the documentation of its foundation a difficult task. *The Irish Golfers Guide* 1914 gives an institution date of 1913, the Captain's name as D. W. Smyth and the Hon. Secretary's name as W. Haughton Smyth. It further states: "The Banbridge course is a nine hole inland one about a mile from Banbridge Station. Length of course 2,760 yards. Bogey − 37."

At present the club has twelve holes.

BANDON, Co. Cork.
Instituted 1893. Affiliated 1910.

Bandon first appears in *The Golfing Annual* of 1894/95 but the club institution date is not given: ". . . the course is situated in the Castle Bernard Demesne Co. Cork".

The Golfing Annual 1896/97 gives September 1893 as the foundation date without any other new detail. *The Sportsmans Holiday Guide* 1897 states: ". . . course within the demesne of Castle Bernard, Lord Bandon's beautiful place in Co. Cork. The green which is a 9 hole one is about 1½ miles round . . . the course where it is, is more or less a private one and supported locally. Secretary L. Hewitt Esq. J.P., Clancole, Bandon."

Until the 1908/09 edition *The Golfing Annual* continued to list the club's date and location as above. However, *The Golfing Annual* 1909/10 gives a new foundation date of 1st January 1910, the new Captain was J. J. Calnan: "The course of nine holes is in Killountain demesne, a mile from the station". (*The Irish Golfers Guide* 1910 confirms this was the Earl of Bandon estate).

This would appear to have been a reconstitution of the older club which, without doubt, is one of the oldest clubs in Munster.

BANGOR, Co. Down.
Instituted 1903.   Affiliated 1903.

The Irish Golfer 25th May 1904 recorded that Mr. F. C. Doran was the inceptor and one of the founders of the club: ". . . after a talk with a few friends, he took the responsibility of issuing the circular calling the preliminary meeting, at which he was elected first Hon. Secretary, and during his term of office as secretary the amount of work he got through was astonishing."

The club's first Captain was Mr. T. C. Connel and *The Belfast Newsletter* 15th June 1903 carries an account of the opening ceremonies of the club's first course. A membership of over 300 was recorded, an auspicious start for the new club. A ladies' club was founded in the first year, Miss H. E. McGuire was the inaugural Lady Captain. In 1904 a new clubhouse was opened under the captaincy of the founder, Mr. Doran.

Initially a nine-hole course was laid out but in 1905 a further nine were added. The present course was laid out by James Braid in 1932 following the sale of 22 acres (and the original clubhouse) and purchase of a further 66 acres of adjoining land.

BANTRY, Co. Cork.

Although the present club in Bantry was founded in 1975, golf had existed there in the 1890s. *The Sportsmans Holiday Guide* 1897 states: "There is a small club here with a course on Chapel Island, 10 minutes row from the pier. The club is chiefly supported by the officers of the Guard Ship HMS Dreadnought." An entry for the club appears in *The Golfing Annual* 1905/06 which gives January 1901 as the institution date. There were 50 members and the Hon. Secretary was J. E. Keene, Harbour View House: ". . . the course of nine holes, which is not playable in Summer, is at Gurteenroe".

The Irish Golfing Guide 1916 lists the club, without foundation date: ". . . nine holes close to Bantry Station — membership about 25". Later, the club is listed in *The Golfers Handbook* 1923, however the *Irish Tourist Authority Directory* 1937 does not mention the club.

BAR GOLFING SOCIETY OF IRELAND.

The story of the Irish Bar's contribution to golf in Ireland is told in Chapter 7; from 1891 members of the profession found that golf and the practice of law went hand in hand. The Royal Dublin Golf Club had an exceptionally large number of members belonging to the Bar (*The Irish Golfer* 18th April 1900 could state that there were 70 barristers in the club). In the 1890s the Bar had a team of its own and *The Irish Times* of 8th May 1891 records a match played at Dollymount between the Curragh Brigade Golf Club and a Bar team, which the latter won by 9 holes.

It was not until 1906 that the Irish Bar Golfing Society was instituted and *Golf Illustrated* 12th July 1907 records the name of the first President, Mr. J. H. Campbell, K.C., M.P., and the Captain was Mr. James Chambery, K.C. *The Irish Golfing Guide* 1916 states that ". . . owing to the war all competitions have been suspended and consequently no Captain has been elected for the current season. Membership 120 . . . The Bar Golfing Society of Ireland is a more or less private body, membership being confined to Barristers who are members of the Law Library and to Judges".

BELFAST UNIVERSITY, Co. Down.

*See Queens University Golf Club.

BELLINTER PARK, Co. Meath.
Instituted 1922. Affiliated 1923.

This club was a continuation of the old Navan Golf Club which had been dispossessed circa 1922. It was founded shortly afterwards by, among others, J. J. Lyons, P. J. McQuillan, Dr. F. J. Moore, T. Noonan and A. Steen. Fifty-four acres were rented from Cecil H. Briscoe at Bellinter and a nine-hole course laid out.

In the early 1960s the Land Commission acquired the entire Briscoe estate and leased sufficient extra land to allow conversion from nine to eighteen holes in 1966. At this time the name was changed to Royal Tara Golf Club.

*See Navan G.C. and Royal Tara G.C.

BELMONT, Co. Down.

This club is first listed in *The Golfing Annual* 1894/95 which gives an institution date of 1892. However, from the 1897 edition onwards, the institution date is given as 1891. *The Sportsmans Holiday Guide* 1897 states: ". . . this club have their course at Tillysburn, a station on the Belfast and Bangor branch of the Belfast & Co. Down Railway . . . The course is one of 9 holes and is rather more than a mile around." In some early newspaper accounts the club's location is given as Garnerville and in *The Belfast Newsletter* 5th December 1894 a report of the club's annual general meeting mentioned that "after negotiations with Mr. Garner the lease was extended to 31st December 1898".

The club is listed in *The Golfing Annual* 1907/1908 for the last time, the Hon. Secretary was D. B. Walkington, 61 Royal Avenue, Belfast: ". . . the course of nine holes is five minutes walk from Tillysburn station . . . in a pretty park known as Garnerville''. Belmont Ladies G.C. was listed in *The Golfing Annual* 1898/99 for the first time, with an institution date of 1894. The subsequent histories of both these clubs is unknown.

BEREHAVEN, Co. Cork.
Golfing Union of Ireland records reveal that Berehaven Golf Club was affiliated in 1939. The club would appear to have functioned until the 1970s. The Royal Naval Garrison there had a club from 1906, known originally as Channel Fleet Golf Club.
   *See Atlantic Fleet G.C., Channel Fleet G.C., Royal Naval G.C.

BESSBROOK, Co. Armagh.
Golfing Union of Ireland records list the affiliation of Bessbrook Golf Club on 17th November 1915. An entry for the club appears in the Union's *Yearbook* for 1927: A. Downey, Woodville, Bessbrook, was Hon. Secretary. There is nothing recorded in later yearbooks relating to this club.

BETTYSTOWN, Co. Meath.
   *See Laytown & Bettystown.

BIRR, Co. Offaly.
Instituted 1893.   Affiliated 1912.
The former Kings County & Ormond Golf Club changed its name to Birr Golf Club sometime between 1910 and 1914. *The Irish Golfers Guide* 1910 lists the club under the old name, *The Irish Golfing Guide* 1914 lists Birr Golf Club. Unfortunately, the club does not possess any of the older records.
   *See Kings County & Ormond G.C.

BLACKROCK, Rochestown, Co. Cork.
Blackrock Golf Club first appears in *The Golfing Annual* 1895/96 where it is listed under the Dublin clubs with the following information: "Instituted 1895. The course is situated at Mounthovel, Rochestown." All the committee are named in the entry, the Hon. Secretary was Miss. L. C. Parke, Ballinlough, and H. Humphreys, Ballintemple, was Hon. Treasurer. No Captain or President were named.

   Any native of the Douglas area near Cork city will recognise the addresses above. Both Ballinlough and Ballintemple are close to Blackrock and there is little doubt that this was a Cork city club. The *Golfing Annuals* continue to list this club under the Dublin district until 1908/09. There is no mention of the club in *The Irish Golfers Guide* 1910 or any later publication.

BORRIS, Co. Carlow.
Instituted 1907.   Affiliated 1908.

Like so many other Irish clubs the earliest Borris records are missing. However, *The Irish Field* 10th August 1907 recorded the opening of the course of the new Borris Golf Club. Later *The Irish Field* 4th December 1909 carried an acount by Lionel Hewson on a recent visit to the club. The President was Mr. W. MacMorrogh Kavanagh M.P, the Captain was Mr. S. P. Cox and the Hon Secretary was Charles Butler of Mount Leinster . . . "Mr. Kavanagh originally started golf in his park chiefly for the benefit of his sons; but, when the idea of a club was mooted he promptly offered the course and clubhouse rent free to the Borris Club . . . Mr. Charlie Butler of Mount Leinster undertook the secretarial duties which he has carried out most successfully. The club only started in 1907, but already has a membership of 100."

Although the club is listed in *The Golfers Handbook* 1923 it would appear that it had fallen on lean times as *The Irish Field* 14th February 1925 records a revival of the club under the Presidency of Major Arthur Kavanagh. A description of the course was given in the *The Irish Golfing Guide* 1916: ". . . this sporting and well kept course embraces the old military fortifications, redoubts, etc. . . . within one mile of Borris station . . ." In 1979 the nine-hole course was extended to ten holes.

BOYLE, Co. Roscommon.
Instituted 1911.   Affiliated 1924.

Boyle Golf Club is not listed in the *The Irish Golfers Guide* 1910 but is well documented in the *The Irish Golfing Guide* 1914 where the institution date is given as 1911: "A nine holes course within one mile of Boyle station . . . Open from 1st November to 1st May . . . a pavilion was erected in December 1912. The course was laid out by Messrs Vernon and Ormsby of Rosses Point."

BRAY, Co. Wicklow.
Instituted 1897.   Affiliated 1898.

The existence of an eighteenth century golf club in the town of Bray has been outlined in Chapter 2. It was not until 1897 that golf is heard of once more in this famous seaside resort.

The Irish Times 18th July 1897 carried a report on a preliminary meeting held in the Grand International Hotel "for the purpose of establishing a golf club for the district . . . Sir R. Fanning proposed and Rev. Mr. Glenn seconded 'That this meeting approves the formation of a golf club in Bray' . . ." Later on *The Irish Golfer* 13th December 1900 told the story of the club's origins: "Bray G.C. owes its existence mainly to the enterprise of Mr. J. S. Robson and Mr. D. J. Stewart who having induced the Rt. Hon. Lord Plunkett to act as President, spared no pains in arousing the inhabitants of Bray and surrounding district. The club has just completed its second year and can boast of a membership roll of 325 . . . having procured the grounds lying around Ravenswell . . ."

If the reader turns now to the map of Bray on page 10 he will immediately see that the new club had secured the land at Ravenswell which was occupied by a Mr. De Butts up to Napoleonic times at least. The 1762 course at Bray was in the area of the present Promenade but the first known member of that early club had been Elias De Butts and his residence would appear to have been Ravenswell.

*See Chapter 2 and Chapter 5 (General Torrens).

BUNCLODY, Co. Wexford.

Golfing Union of Ireland *Yearbook* 1932 gives an affiliation date of 1920 for this club. The *Yearbook* for 1927 does not list the club and there is no entry in the 1937 edition.

*See Newtownbarry G.C.

BUNCRANA, Co. Donegal.

Although the present club at Buncrana was founded in 1951, golf had an early start at this location. *The Derry Journal* 3rd July 1891 recording the institution of the Northwest Golf Club states: ''. . . the ladies have not been forgotten in the arrangements . . . as immediately adjacent to the Railway Station at Buncrana an exceedingly good nine-hole course has been laid out . . .'' Some confusion regarding the Northwest Club's location is evident when *The Irish Times* 11th July 1893 advertised a forthcoming joint open tournament at Rosapenna, Portsalon and ''Buncrana''. *The Sportsmans Holiday Guide* 1897 reported on ''Northwest Ladies Golf Club'' . . . ''The links of this club are at Buncrana. The course is a nine-hole one and the distance around is about a mile and is of a very sporting nature. It is a natural one and the turf somewhat similar to the Lisfannon Green . . .'' The subsequent history of this separate ladies course is not clear.

*See Northwest G.C. and Chapter 9.

BUNDORAN, Co. Donegal.
Instituted 1894.   Affiliated 1906.

The Belfast Newsletter 21st May 1894 recorded that ''County Donegal is rapidly becoming famous for its golf links'' . . . within the next ten days a fourth will be ready for play and visitors to Bundoran will be able to enjoy a game . . . The ground on which the course has been laid out covers close upon 100 acres and is the private property of the Irish Highlands Hotel Co. Ltd. At present only nine holes have been laid out. . . . The starting point is within 5 minutes walk of the railway station and the first hole might be termed the 'crater' from its resemblance to the well known hazard at Portrush . . . A strong club is likely to be got up in the district and the Railway Company are granting players the usual facilities.'' The club is first mentioned in *The Golfing Annual* 1894/95 which gives the institution date as August 1894; it is also recorded that the course ''was laid out under the careful supervision of Mr. G. L. Baillie''. (Baillie had been the prime mover in establishment of golf at Belfast thirteen years earlier). The Duke of Abercorn is listed first President, the Captain was J. Johnston and there was a total of 94 members.

By 1896 the Great Northern Railway Co. had taken shares in two of the Irish Highland Hotel Company's hotels at Warrenpoint and Bundoran. In 1896 the GNR presented a cup for open competition and soon the company was looking for business as far afield as London. In the *Sportsmans Holiday Guide* 1897 it is advertised that the course is "19 hours from London via Kingstown". It was 1903 before a full eighteen holes was laid out by C. S. Butchart (a Scotsman), the then professional at Newcastle.

In 1927 the club arranged for a visit by Harry Vardon, *The Irish Field* 26th March reporting that the famous man had been secured for a friendly match at Easter. Nine months later the same paper recorded, on 17th December: "As a result of Vardon's skill a fine course will in future be available for visitors".

(Courtesy of the National Library of Ireland)

BUSHFOOT, Bushmills, Co. Antrim.
Instituted 1893. Affiliated 1906.

This club is first listed in *The Golfing Annual* 1894/95 without date of foundation. The Hon. Secretary was A. H. Steen, Bushmills. Later, the minutes of the Golfing Union of Ireland 26th July 1895 list the club for the first time. A foundation date of 1893 is given in *The Golfing Annual* 1898/99 which stated: "The course of nine holes is about a mile from the Giants Causeway".

A conflict of dates of foundation is evident in *The Irish Golfing Guide* 1910 which listed 1890 as Bushmills year of institution. The entry also stated: "In summer the electric tram stops and lifts passengers every hour at the clubhouse".

CAHIR, Co. Tipperary.

The Irish Golfers Guide 1911 lists this club with an institution date of 1902 and states the course ". . . 9 holes . . . within one and a half miles of Cahir Station . . . the course is on a gravel hill, commanding fine view". Sunday play was not allowed and the club was not affiliated to the Golfing Union of Ireland. Later, *The Irish Golfing Guide* 1916 documents the club, whose Hon. Secretary's name is given as R. W. Smith Jun., Bengarragh, Cahir. *Thoms Directory* 1927 lists the club, it is not mentioned in the 1930 edition.

CARAGH LAKE, Co. Kerry.

The Irish Times 19th December 1895 reports "a new course has just been laid out by Anthony Brown of Dollymount for the Great Southern and Western Railway for the use of visitors to their Caragh Lake Hotel. The links are about ¾ mile from the hotel . . . an 18-hole course has been laid out but for the present only 9 holes of this will be used". This course is listed in *The Golfing Annual* 1895/96 and it is also listed as a course (without club mention) in the 1898/99 edition.

It is very difficult to untangle the early history of golf in this locality, the local golfers would appear to have used this private hotel course and also another course at nearby Dooks. *The Golfers Guide* 1897 lists the Caragh Lake course and also lists a course at Dooks. To add further confusion *The Sportsmans Holiday Guide* lists a course in conjunction with the Glenbeigh Hotel.

Golfing Union of Ireland records reveal that on 26th May 1903 the two separate clubs of Caragh Lake and Glenbeigh and Dooks were affiliated.

*See Caragh and Dooks, Dooks, Glenbeigh.

CARAGH AND DOOKS, Co. Kerry.

The Golfing Annuals between 1902 and 1910 list this club and give a foundation date of 1895. *The Irish Golf Guides* from 1910 to 1912 give the same information. It would appear that the Caragh Lakes and Dooks players had a loose alliance together.

*See Caragh Lake, Dooks G.C., Glenbeigh Caragh and Dooks.

CARLOW, Co. Carlow.
Instituted 1899.   Affiliated 1901.

The Irish Times Saturday 20th May 1899 gives the following account of the club's foundation: "On last (Thursday) evening a meeting was held in the Country Clubhouse for the purpose of establishing a golf club for Carlow and Athy. Dr. Brannan, Kilkea Lodge, Castledermot, and Mr. P. Lynch, Athy, were the promoters of the meeting and these two gentlemen have been most active in their efforts to introduce and render the game popular in South Kildare. Captain Stewart Duckett occupied the chair . . . It was resolved to establish a club to be styled the Royal Leinster Golf Club, with ground at Gotham midway between Carlow and Athy . . . It was further resolved to ask Lady Walter Fitzgerald (Kilkea Castle) to accept the Presidency of the Club . . . Dr. Brannan was elected Hon. Secretary . . ." An article on the club in *The Irish Golfer* 8th August 1900 related that the two prime movers, who had instituted the club, were very experienced golfers. Mr. Lynch had previously been Honorary Secretary of Bundoran G.C. whilst Dr. Brannan was a former Honorary Secretary of Greystones G.C.

It is of interest from the foregoing to see that the present Carlow Golf Club was founded by two residents of Co. Kildare and the *The Golfing Annual* of 1902/03 lists the club as a Co. Kildare club! The Royal title does not appear again in any references to the club and may have been adopted in a flurry of anti-Home Rule enthusiasm by the meeting. By 25th July 1899 *The Irish Times* was able to report the official opening of the "links" at Gotham (three miles from Carlow and seven from Athy). It was a nine-hole course ". . . it must be said for Larkin, the Bray professional who had the laying out of the Gotham links, that he made the most of the land at his disposal . . . Brown a young professional of promise has been engaged as greenkeeper and coach . . ."

The club's name was changed from Leinster G.C. to Carlow G.C. some time between 1900 and 1903, the latter title first appears in *The Golfing Annual* 1902/03. A feature article in *The Irish Field* 13th August 1910 stated that "the Athy residents supported the club till they found they required a course of their own". The new club at Athy was instituted in 1906 and this break-up had a serious effect on the older club with membership dropping to ten or twelve members. These few persevered and as Bernard O'Neill recalled in *Carlovian* in 1952: ". . . in 1921 or thereabouts, a member of vision and enterprise, the late Very Rev. M. H. Bolger P.P., decided that Carlow golfers deserved more ambitious terrain. His keen golfing eye saw first the possibilities of the Deerpark . . . its owner, the late Mr. Henry Bruen of Oak Park . . . welcomed the proposal and in 1922 the Club became tenants of the Deerpark on very generous terms". *Irish Life* 21st April 1922 reported: "Carlow are to be congratulated on its fine new 18 hole course. Mr. Barcroft was the golf architect and succeeded in laying out a remarkably good course at very low cost".

The Irish Golfers Blue Book 1939 recorded that in 1937 the club requested Mr. Tom Simpson (an internationally-famous golf architect) to suggest improvements to the course. Simpson redesigned ten greens and his plan is the basis of the present course layout.

CARNALEA, Co. Down.

This location was the home of the Royal Belfast Club from 1891 to 1926, prior to their move to Craigavad. *The Irish Field* 9th April 1927 noted the opening of Ireland's first municipal golf course at Carnalea, the Prime Minister of Northern Ireland drove the first ball. On 27th may 1927 the present Carnalea Golf Club was formed and on 1st April 1964 the club took over management of the course.

CARRICK, Co. Donegal.

The Sportsmans Holiday Guide 1897 lists this as a nine-hole course to "be open for the holiday season of 1897. The course, which is close to the Glencolumbkille Hotel, should prove an additional attraction". There is no further record of this course.

CARRICKFERGUS, Co. Antrim.

The present club at Carrickfergus was founded in 1926 but an entry in *The Belfast Newsletter* of 5th January 1892 would indicate that there had been earlier golf at this location. Referring to train fares for golfers the writer states: ". . . now that links have been opened at Carrickfergus . . ." There is no other available record on golf at Carrickfergus in the 1890s.

CARRICKMACROSS, Co. Monaghan.

This club was affiliated to the Golfing Union of Ireland at their meeting of 13th May 1912. Later, *The Irish Field* 10th April 1915 documented a match at Carrickmacross versus a Castleblaney team. The club is listed in *The Golfing Union of Ireland Yearbook* 1927. Its subsequent history is unknown.

CARRICKMINES, Co. Dublin.
Instituted 1900. Affiliated 1901.

Notification of the institution of a new Dublin club was given in *The Irish Golfer* 1st August 1900: "A new club has been formed at Carrickmines. The links are situated within seven minutes walk of Carrickmines Station on the Dublin, Wicklow and Wexford Railway. A nine hole course is now ready for play, and another nine holes will be made during the winter months. The ground, we are informed, is most suitable for play. A limited number of ladies will be admitted as associates. Mr. N. M. Hone, of Killiney, has been appointed secretary, and amongst the members of committee we see the following well known names: Messrs. H. J. Daly, Hon. Sec. Golfing Union; E. J. Figgis, R. J. Meredith, R. C. Orpen and C. Townsend, gentlemen well qualified by past experience to float a new concern. We wish the 'infant' every success."

The Irish Golfer 6th April 1904 documented the origins of the club: "It was founded about four years ago, and only those who had previously seen the ground can fully appreciate the pluck of those two sportsmen, W. H. Wilson and Andrew Armstrong, in purchasing the tenants interest in that wilderness which has been transformed . . . The ground was practically covered with bracken and a good portion of it with granite boulders, black and whitethorn and brambles . . . However almost immediately, early in 1900, a number of foundation members combined together who were not afraid to go ahead. They formed a committee and appointed one of themselves, N. H. Hone, Secretary, and to his indefatigible energy and knowledge of what work should be done and how to set about it is due the lion's share in the success of the undertaking . . ."

It was reported in *The Irish Field* of 17th January 1914 that a second nine holes were under construction at Carrickmines, however the outbreak of World War One probably terminated this expansion. *The Irish Golfing Guide* 1916 recorded a nine-hole course, which is the present day number.

CARRICK-ON-SHANNON, Co. Leitrim.
Instituted 1910. Affiliated 1910.

The Irish Golfing Guide 1911 lists this course, which was affiliated to the GUI in 1910. A short course, open only during the winter months, the Captain was D. A. Steadman D.I., R.I.C., and there were over 40 members. *The Irish Golfing Guide* 1916 gives no date for the club and states it ''. . . is situated close to the Shannon, there are a considerable number of natural hazards in the way of ditches, hedges and streams . . .'' The course had nine holes.

   *See Ardcarne.

CARRIGART, Co. Donegal.

   *See Rosapenna.

CASHEL, Co. Tipperary.

Irish Life 1st November 1912 carries the following entry: ''The residents of Cashel District held a meeting last Saturday to decide on the advisability of forming a Golf Club and we are glad to hear the decision was in the affirmative''. In the same publication on 17th October 1913 the club is recorded as hosting a visiting team from the Tipperary Club whom they defeated ''handsomely''. The club is not listed in the *The Irish Golf Guides* and there is no further record of its subsequent history.

CASTLE, Rathfarnham, Co. Dublin.
Instituted 1913. Affiliated 1913.

The official history of this club records that when Messrs. Bailey and Gibson purchased the property of Rathfarnham Castle in 1912 they intended building a garden city with a golf club at the centre of it. The initial meeting at which the club was instituted was held in the Ivanhoe Hotel, Harcourt Street. The committee was composed of five elected members and five nominated by the proprietors. At a meeting on 21st February 1913 Mr. J. McMurray was appointed the first Hon. Secretary. Some illustrious names were associated with laying out the original eighteen-hole course: Cecil Barcroft of Royal Dublin, W. C. Pickeman of Portmarnock and Tom Hood, the professional at Royal Dublin.

   The proprietor, Mr. Bailey, sold the grounds to the members in December 1917 and on 1st January 1918 the Castle Golf Club Limited came into existence.

CASTLEBAR, Co. Mayo.
Instituted 1910. Affiliated 1912.

The Irish Golfing Guide 1912 lists the club as founded in 1910: ''. . . a nine hole course within 1¼ miles of Castlebar Railway Station''. Details of the club's origins are given in the 75th anniversary brochure produced by Mr. John Egan, a member of the club for over 55 years.

   The initial meeting to form the club was held in November 1910 in the Imperial

Hotel, Castlebar. Chairman of the inaugural meeting was Rev. A. Lendrum and 32 other local gentlemen. The following were elected as the first committee: Rev. J. A. Lendrum, Dr. F. C. Ellison, H. R. Sheridan, T. G. Gahan, A. C. Vernon, J. C. Robertson, Rev. O'Brien, Dr. M. Knott and Thos. Teehan. Later, Lord Bingham was elected first President. The initial course was at Flannelly's of Moreen until the move to the present course at Rocklands, shortly afterwards. Credit is given to members of the Connaught Rangers, who were stationed in the town at the time, for helping to start the club. There was a rifle range on the course at the time which was used by the local military personnel.

In 1958 extra land was purchased, known as Rockland House, and in 1982 further land was acquired which allowed for an 18-hole course to be opened in 1984. It is clear that there was early interest in golf at Castlebar, *The Irish Times* 6th March 1898 reported that a number of golfers from the town had competed in a recent competition at Ballinrobe.

CASTLEBLAYNEY, Co. Monaghan.
Instituted 1982. Affiliated 1984.

The present Castleblayney Golf Club was founded in 1982, however *The Irish Field* 10 April 1915 recorded a golf match at Carrickmacross versus a Castleblayney team. Later, *The Golfers Handbook* 1923 documented a club there with a membership of 60, the Hon. Secretary was Frank A. Orr, Fern Villa, Castleblayney. There was a nine-hole course and Sunday play was allowed.

The Golfing Union of Ireland Yearbook 1927 lists the club and there are continuous entries until the 1950s. It would appear that the club became disaffiliated and, possibly, defunct between 1950 and 1956.

CASTLECOMER, Co. Kilkenny.

There is an intriguing entry in the *The Golfing Annual* of 1906/07: "Castlecomer Golf Club. Hon. Secretary − T. Ferguson, Castlecomer, Co. Wexford". In the index of this edition the club is also listed under Co. Wexford. Listing clubs in wrong counties is not unusual in the *Golfing Annuals*, for Banagher was listed under Co. Londonderry in several editions. However there is a doubt as to the location of this club. The club is listed in the *Golfing Annuals* until 1909/10, with the same details. There is no mention in the *Irish Golf Guides* 1910 to 1916.

GUI records show an affiliation date of 4th September 1906 but no more is heard of a Castlecomer Golf Club until the present one was founded in 1933.

CASTLEGREGORY, Co. Kerry.

The Sportsmans Holiday Guide 1897 lists a course at this location and states ". . . a very fine 18 hole course extending to about 3½ miles in circuit. It lies along the coast and is quite the first course in the Kingdom of Kerry . . . information will be supplied by S. A. Waters Esq, County Inspector, Tralee". This course was the second "links" of the Tralee Golf Club which had been founded in 1896 and the

Golfing Annuals continue to list Castlegregory until 1905. In 1907 when the Tralee Club was reconstituted it would appear that the course fell into disuse.

*See Tralee G.C.

CASTLEKNOCK, Co. Dublin.

The Irish Golfers Guide 1910 lists this club and states: "Believed to be extinct".

CASTLEREA, Co. Roscommon.
Instituted 1905.   Affiliated 1908.

This club is first mentioned in *The Golfing Annual* 1906/07 without any detail other than the Captain's name, Mr. G. W. F. Kelly. An institution date of September 1905 is listed in *The Golfing Annual* 1907/08. There were 60 members at that time, including ladies and ". . . the new course of nine holes, varying from 80 to 420 yards, is a mile from Castlerea Station". In *The Irish Field* 21st December 1907 the following is recorded: "The golfers of Roscommon have been in the wilderness for some time. Mr. T. C. Wills-Stanford has however come to the rescue in a most public spirited and sporting manner and a nine-hole course has been laid out in his demesne".

Like many other early Irish golf clubs, Castlerea appears to have had problems in establishing firm roots and *The Irish Field* account of 1907 most probably records a move from the location occupied in 1905. *The Irish Golfing Guide* 1916 stated: ". . . this course (9 holes) is laid out in the O'Conor Don's demesne". It is of interest to note that the *Golfing Annuals* from 1907, and the *Irish Golf Guides* from 1910 to 1916, record F. G. O'Donoghue as Honorary Secretary.

CASTLEROCK, Co. Derry.
Instituted 1900.   Affiliated 1902.

Although Castlerock records 1901 as the year of institution, the first public meeting held to consider the founding of a club was documented in *The Belfast Newsletter* 7th May 1900: ". . . held in the Pavilion Castlerock on the 4th inst. for the purpose of considering the advisability of laying down golf links at that seaside resort and of making the preliminary arrangements . . . after further discussion, it was agreed to ask the Belfast and Northern Counties Railway Co. if they would send Mr. Baillie, a golfing expert, to survey the ground and report as to the probable expenditure required to lay out the golf course. The following preliminary committee was appointed: Mrs. Fletcher, Mrs. Warke, Rev. J. Armstrong and Mrs. S. Ross with Mrs. Warke and Rev. Mr. Beckett as Secretaries and Rev. Mr. Beckett as Treasurer."

It is of interest to note that the founding committee was composed of two ministers, a gentleman and two ladies. *The Irish Golfer* 11th July 1900, in a column of Ladies Notes, reported: ". . . a new golf course has been laid out at Castlerock, Co. Derry, which ought to prove another great attraction to that popular seaside resort. An expert from St. Andrews went over the proposed ground, and has laid out what he describes as one of the most complete nine-hole courses in the country. A committee has been formed, and they hope to be able shortly to have everything ready for players."

*The Belfast Newsletter*17th January 1901 recorded a professional match over the new links which was being laid out by J. Coburn of Portrush. George Coburn, the professional at Portmarnock, was one of the contestants and he spoke highly of both the links and scenery. The same newspaper account reported that the official opening of the links would take place at Easter. *The Irish Field* 10th October 1908 recorded the extension of the course to 18 holes following a favourable settlement with the landlord, the same article recorded that the thanks of the members were due to the energetic Hon. Secretary, Mr. J. G. McVicker.

Catastrophe struck the club in the summer of 1913 when their clubhouse was burned down. A number of Irish clubs have suffered this calamity over the years but Castlerock quickly responded and *Irish Life* 3rd July 1914 carried a photograph of their new clubhouse.

CHANNEL FLEET, Berehaven, Co. Cork.

The Golfing Annual 1906/07 gives November 1906 as this club's institution date, the number of members was "about 150" and the club Captain's name is listed as Captain J. de M. Hutchison C.M.G. . . . The club, which is for naval officers only, has two nine-hole courses, the one at Castletown, Berehaven, Bantry Bay and the other on Bere Island."

Subsequently this club is recorded in *The Irish Golfing Guide* 1916 as Royal Naval Golf Club, Berehaven.

*See Royal Naval Golf Club.

CHARLEVILLE, Co. Cork.

The present Charleville Club was founded in 1941, but *The Irish Golfers Guide* 1910 lists a club there of nine holes, founded in 1909. The earlier club would not appear to have survived for long as it is not listed in subsequent *Irish Golf Guides* between 1911 and 1916.

CILL DARA, Co. Kildare.
Instituted 1920.   Affiliated 1922.

The magazine *Irish Life* 21st November 1913 carries an intriguing entry: "Kildare is to have a golf club. We hope in order to avoid confusion something will be done to obviate having two Kildare Clubs viz. the County and the Town". This reference was to the fact that Naas at that time was known as Co. Kildare Golf Club.

The official history of the latter club states: "The year 1913 is also memorable for the inauguration of a golf club near the town of Kildare, the present Cill Dara links. The late Dr. Coady, County Kildare Club Captain, was invited to take the helm there also." Research by the present club has revealed that an application had been made to the War Department authorities for permission to use the Little

Curragh for golf in 1914, but, they said that the application would have await "the Cessation of the Hostilities".

Unfortunately, Cill Dara Golf Club does not have any of its early records following their foundation, a rule book of the club in the Golfing Union of Ireland archives is dated 1920. The first Captain in 1920 was Mr. A. Anthony and credit is given Dr. E. Coady, J. C. Bergin, J. Doyle, F. J. and C. Burke, in addition to the founding Captain, for the institution of the club. It would appear that the 1913 attempt was frustrated by the outbreak of World War One, any golf at that time being of an "unlicensed" nature.

CITY OF DERRY, Co. Derry.
Instituted 1912. Affiliated 1912.

The Irish Golfing Guide 1912 listed this as the City of Londonderry Golf Club and stated: "This new club has lately been formed and the course was laid out by W. Park". The 1914 *Guide* recorded the following information under City of Derry Golf Club: "A nine-hole course, situated at Prehan, two miles from Londonderry . . . Hon. Secretary, A. Price, Shipquay Place, Londonderry."

The Irish Golfers Blue Book 1939 recorded: "In November 1911 a meeting was held in Londonderry when the formation of the club was decided on. Ground was taken on lease at Prehan and nine holes were laid out by the celebrated Willie Park. Later extra land was purchased and in 1930 the course was extended to 18 holes. Sand bunkers were then constructed to the plan of Mr. Harry Colt after the latter inspected the links. A new clubhouse was erected in 1922 at a cost of £2,500."

This club suffered the loss of their clubhouse in an explosion and fire in 1982, when all their club records were lost. A further nine holes were added in 1984.

CLAREMONT, Howth, Co. Dublin.

The earliest course opened by a hotel in the Dublin area is documented in *The Irish Times* of 13th August 1895: "A new nine-hole course was laid out on Friday last in the Deerpark adjoining the Claremont Hotel, Howth, by Anthony Brown, the professional at Dollymount. Mr. Holder will maintain it for the benefit of visitors to the Claremont." (The owner, Mr. Walter Holder, was the managing director of the Gresham Hotel at that time). *The Irish Times* 2nd April 1896 advertised a match between the "Claremont Golf Club and Sutton Yacht & Boat Club"; this would indicate that a club then existed in the hotel.

It was in the months of April and May 1896 that the Sutton Yacht & Boat Club first took an active interest in golf. Nothing more is heard of the Claremont golfers and it is probable that they all joined the new Sutton Golf Club when it was formed that Summer.

*See Sutton G.C.

CLAREMORRIS, Co. Mayo.
Instituted 1927. Affiliated 1927.

The club lists its foundation date as 1927, however an old entry in the files of the

Golfing Union of Ireland gives an institution date of 1918. The *GUI Yearbook* of 1925 lists the affiliation date as 1920. At some earlier date the club records a previous name of "Castlemacgarret Golf Club".

CLIFTONVILLE, Belfast, Co. Antrim.
Instituted 1911.   Affiliated 1911.

This club was founded on a site at "Deerpark" in 1911, on an 18-hole course. Unfortunately, the club's early records have been mislaid but the files of the Golfing Union of Ireland reveal that the club was affiliated on 14th June 1911. In 1924 the club moved to its present site and became a limited company. This new course was eighteen holes but ground was sold in the 1930s and nine holes were disposed of.

CLOGHER, Co. Tyrnone.

The Golfing Annual 1898/99 lists a club at this spot but gives no institution date. *The Irish Times* 10th May 1897 gives the result of a match played between Aughnacloy and Clogher, which indicates an existence previous to that date. There is no mention of this club after the 1899 listing, however in 1905 the Corick Golf Club was formed and some of the names listed in the Clogher team are again to be found in references to the latter club.

*See Corick G.C.

CLONAKILTY, Co. Cork.

The Golfing Annual 1895/96 give the institution date of this club as 1895 and states: "The course, of nine holes, is close to the town". J. McNamara was recorded as Hon. Secretary of the club. *The Sportsmans Holiday Guide* 1897 gives a lengthy account and states: ". . . the links of the Clonakilty Golf Club are within half a mile of the Imperial Hotel . . . The course all grass which is rather long for summer play but first rate from October to the middle of April . . . There are over 40 resident members. The Secretary is J. McNamara Esq. of the Imperial Hotel." The latter name would indicate that the management of the local hotel had an interest in the club.

The *Golfing Annuals* continue to list the club, with an 1895 date until the edition of 1908/09. In the following edition the club is again listed but an institution date of March 1909 is given. This would appear to have been a revival of the older club, the new Secretary was S. H. Lewis and ". . . the course of nine holes is a mile and a half from the station". *The Irish Golfers Guide* 1910 recorded that the club was extinct.

There is evidence for a pre-1895 interest in golf at this location as the visitors book at the Royal Belfast Golf Club was signed by C. Smythe, Clonakilty, Co. Cork, on 2nd December 1893.

*See Inchydoney.

CLONES, Co. Monaghan.
Instituted 1913. Affiliated 1915.

This club was instituted in 1913 with Mr. Michael E. Knight as first Captain presiding at the inaugural meeting. Nine holes were laid out at Lisnaroe, near Clones, and this remained the home of the club until the move to Hilton Park in 1929. The club was affiliated to the Golfing Union of Ireland on 17th November 1915.

CLONMEL, Co. Tipperary.
Instituted 1911. Affiliated 1912.

The Irish Golfers Guide 1911 recorded: "There is no course at present at Clonmel, but there is a decided feeling in favour of one among the residents and the only difficulty is securing the necessary ground, owing to the high value of land about the town . . . it is more than likely a club will be formed in Clonmel this year." *Irish Life* 19th July 1912 carried an article on Clonmel Golf Club and gave credit ot the County Surveyor, Mr. Hackett, for being the "instigator". There were 200 members in the club, which was very creditable for the club's first year of existence.

The Irish Golfers Guide 1914 listed the Earl of Donoughmore as President of the Club (see Knocklofty) and stated: "The scenery is very fine, the course, situated on high mountain land excellent and the air most exhilarating". Eight years later *The irish Field* 7th January 1922 recorded a traumatic period for the club: ". . . for the 3rd time in twelve months some person or persons has cut up the greens . . ." Soon afterwards *The Irish Field* 4th March 1922 documented the effect of the recently-signed treaty: "The departure of British troops brings in its trail hardship to many. Murray, the Clonmel professional, will be out of a job soon as the club cannot afford to keep a professional owing to loss of military members. Murray used to be at Stillorgan park and it is hoped some club may be able to give him employment."

The course was extended to eighteen holes in 1973.

CLONTARF, Co. Dublin.
Instituted 1912. Affiliated 1912.

The first meeting to form this club was held in the Clontarf Town Hall in January 1912. Rev. J. L. Morrow was the driving force behind the movement to form a club and he was ably assisted by an ecumenical gathering of Rev. J. Hickey P.P., Rev. P. J. Ryan C.C. and Rev. J. O'Connell together with eleven other locals. Morrow was already prominent in golf circles having been Hon. Secretary of the Golfing Union of Ireland since 1901. He was elected first President of the club, Mr. J. McNie was first Captain, with Mr. J. J. Moore, Hon. Secretary.

Mr. Picton Bradshaw leased his ground in February, at Mount Temple, for the first course of nine holes, and the public opening of the course on 25th May 1912 was performed by the Lord Lieutenant Lord Aberdeen. In 1914 when the Royal Dublin Golf Club were dispossessed by the British Army, Clontarf made the exiles honorary members and employed Tom Hood as professional (he only stayed a short while). Early in 1918 the course was under threat when *Irish Life* of 5th April 1918 stated that "would-be plotholders" wanted to secure some of the Dublin courses for cultivation and "The first of these courses for which application was made was Clontarf, which occupies 45 acres of ground". The same account tells of Rev. Morrow's spirited defence on behalf of the club, which was obviously successful.

In 1922 the club secured "Porters Field" together with the house which had been occupied by the late Master of the Rolls, Sir Andrew Porter, and were enabled to lay out a twelve-hole course. *The Irish Field* 4th February 1922 reported: "In view of this another 50 members are being admitted to the club. Mr. Colt the famous expert is to come over and assist the committee with the new course." Later, *The Irish Field* 5th February 1927 recorded the success of the club in acquiring enough land to lay out a further six holes, the basis of the present 18-hole course.

COLERAINE, Co. Derry.

This club is first mentioned in *The Golfing Annual* 1896/97 which gave no details other than the name of the club. Subsequently, similar entries appeared annually in this publication until 1901, after which nothing else is documented. This club may have been set up to use the course which had been laid out in 1896 at Magilligan. Mr. G. S. Glover, golf historian of Londonderry, reports that clubs had been set up in Limavady and Coleraine for this purpose.

*See Magilligan.

COOKSTOWN, Co. Tyrone.

The Golfing Annual 188/89 states: "Another prominent member of the County Club (Portrush), Mr. H. Adair, of Cookstown has laid out a nine-hole course near that town". *The Belfast Newsletter* 28th February 1889 mentions "golfers at Cookstown". According to *The Golfing Annual* 1893/94 the Killymoon golf Club was founded on 1st March 1890.

From the above it can be seen that golf had been played at Cookstown for some time before the foundation of the club.

*See Killymoon G.C.

COOLATTIN, Co. Wicklow.
Instituted 1949. Affiliated 1950.

At present this club's foundation date is recorded as 1949, however *The Irish Times* 5th August 1922 reported the formation of a new club at this scenic Wicklow location: "A new golf club with a representative committee from Shillelagh and Tinahely districts, with Rev. M. Fitzsimons and Mr. McKenna as Secretaries has recently been organised and has acquired beautiful grounds at Coolattin Park."

An entry for Coalatten G.C. [sic] is listed in *The Golfers Handbook* 1923 without without other detail. The club is not listed in subsequent publications until 1949.

CORICK, Clogher, Co. Tyrone.

It can be seen from an earlier entry that a golf club had existed at Clogher in 1898. *The Golfing Annual* 1906/07 lists the club for the first time, giving an institution date of August 1905. The Hon. Secretary was Rev. W. H. Bailey and there were 40 members at that time.

Later, *The Irish Golfing Guide* 1916 stated the 9-hole course was ". . . beautifully situated in Corick Demesne, convenient to Clogher station. The Hon. Secretary of the 1916 club was C. F. Moutray whose name is listed by *The Irish Times* 20th April 1899 as a member of the Clogher team, beaten by Aughnacloy in a home match. An entry in *The Irish Field* 21st October 1922 reported the club was changing its course from Clogher Park to new grounds at Corick. *The Golfers Handbook* 1923 lists the club, its later history is unknown.

*See Clogher.

CORK G.C., Co. Cork.
Instituted 1894.   Affiliated 1900.

The records of this club were lost in a fire in 1945, and ever since there has been difficulty in ascertaining the origins of Cork Golf Club. *The Golfing Annual* of 1895/96 gives the institution date as 1st November 1894 and states the nine-hole course was situated at Killahora, five minutes walk from Queenstown Junction Station. The following officers of the club are named in this publication, there is no doubt that they would have been among the key founders of the club: President, H. R. O'Kearney; Captain, G. Galwey; Hon. Secretary, G. T. Harley, 41 South Mall, Cork.

The 1894 institution date is confirmed in *The Golfers Guide* 1897, which stated that the course was at Killahora. At present the club claims a foundation date of 1888 but there is no clear evidence to support this. There is a suggestion that the club originated from a club at St. Anne's Hill but *The Golfing Annual* 1902/03 gives November 1901 as the institution date of that club, which does not appear in any earlier publication.

The club possessed a Rathconey Cup prior to the fire of 1945, which was its oldest trophy. There is an entry for a Rathconey Golf Club in *The Golfing Annual* 1894/95, no date of institution is given. This same publication carried no entry for Cork Golf Club. It is possible that the Rathconey golfers handed over the trophy on the demise of their club, however the *Golfing Annuals* continue to list this latter club until 1905.

There were a number of other pre-1895 clubs in Cork including Blackrock G.C. at Rochestown and Queenstown G.C. at Rushbrook. The latter club still existed in 1909 as *The Irish Field* of 30th October 1909 records a meeting at Fota Island, home of Lord Barrymore, for "a handsome silver cup for competition among members of these two clubs" (i.e. Cork and Rushbrook). To add further confusion, *Golf Illustrated* of 22nd February 1907 states: ". . . a club is being established at St. Anne's Hill. The prime movers in the matter are the members of the clubs at Little Island and Rushbrook".

In October 1898 the Cork golf club took possession of the present course which was one mile nearer the city than the Killahora course. A disadvantage of the older course was that it was only open for play during the winter months (*Sportsmans Holiday Guide* 1897). Mr. A. F. Sharman-Crawford J.P. (President of the club from 1898 to 1916) and Mr. H. H. Maudsley (Captain 1899) are credited with discovering the course during a trip upriver from Passage West. Tom Dunn of Bournemouth laid out the original course of nine holes, which was extended to eighteen holes at some time between 1910 and 1916. Dunn was a member of the famous Musselburgh Dunn family. He had married Isabella Gourlay, the daughter of John Gourlay (see Chapter 3).

It is unfortunate that Cork Golf Club lost its archives in 1945 as the history of golf in Cork is not well documented and there will always be dissension, with claims and counter claims of antiquity in the Southern capital.

*See Blackrock G.C., Rathconey G.C., St. Anne's Hill G.C., Chapters 5 and 6.

COUNTY ARMAGH.
Instituted 1893.   Affiliated 1893.

The Irish Field 22nd May 1909 records that Mr. Charles Burke of Ballinahor House, an enthusiastic golfer, was the first gentleman to introduce golf at Armagh. He had private links in his own grounds where he often invited his friends to play. Subsequently they decided to form a club and requested Mr. George De La Poer Beresford for use of his land which encompassed the Primate's Palace. The club was formed on 15th September 1893.

The above institution date is confirmed in *The Golfing Annual* 1894/95, however all subsequent editions carry the date as October 1894! There is no doubt about the year of institution for *The Belfast Newsletter* of 18th November 1893 has an account of the opening ceremonies of the recently formed club which were performed by the High Sheriff of the County Mr. Maynard Sinton. *The Sportsmans Holiday Guide* 1897 reports: ". . . a nine-hole course and from its situation is unplayable in the summer months owing to the length of the grass . . . the season commences on 12th November and ends on 12th May".

COUNTY CAVAN.
Instituted 1894.   Affiliated 1899.

Writing in his monthly magazine *Irish Golf* of January 1930, Lionel Hewson told the story of the early days of golf at Cavan: "It was in the middle eighties of the last century that Mr. Thomas Lough, afterwards M.P. for West Islington and Under Secretary for Education in the Campbell Bannerman ministry, laid out a nine-hole course at his Cavan residence Killynebbar, ten minutes walk from the town. At first it was used only by the Lough family and their political visitors from across Channel, as not for a year or two could any of the local residents be induced to interest themselves in the game. Eventually however a sufficient number, probably not more than twenty, came together and formed the nucleus of a modest club."

An entry for "Cavan Golf Club" appears in *The Golfing Annual* 1895/96 which stated: ". . . no particulars forthcoming". The 1896/97 edition also listed the Cavan club, giving an institution date of October 1894. A. S. Lough was the President in

1896 and there were 28 members. ". . . The course of nine holes, varying in length from 122 to 226 yards, is situated at Killynebbar, about a mile and half from Cavan Station". Later *The Sportsmans Holiday Guide*1897 recorded: "The green is only a winter one and is situated on a grass farm and in Summer time the grass is too long for play, consequently the Cavan golfing season is somewhat curtailed, play being possible only between the months of October and April . . . There is no clubhouse but the Royal Hotel supplies all necessary requirements".

At a later date the club moved to its present location at Drumelis, where an 18-hole course was opened in 1973.

It is of interest to note that the visitors book at the Royal Belfast Golf Club was signed by W. F. Johnson, Bawnboy, Co. Cavan, on 26th April 1892.

COUNTY CLUB.
*See Royal Portrush G.C.

COUNTY DUBLIN.
*See Hermitage G.C.

COUNTY GALWAY.
The Golfing Annual 1905/06 first lists this club and gives an institution date of 1884. There were 30 members and the Captain was S. Nolan, ". . . the course at Gentian Hill is the property of the Captain . . .". This was the original Galway Golf Club's course which had been "evacuated" by the majority of the members (as can be seen in that club's entry, later). Similar detail is recorded in the *The Golfing Annual* 1906/07, however no further entries occur in subsequent editions. Sebastian Nolan died in April 1907 and his attempt to keep the Gentian Hill course going obviously died with him. His claim of an 1884 institution date is without foundation and may have been an attempt to emphasise seniority over the new Galway club.

It is of interest to note that the *Golfing Annuals* from 1906 to 1908 list Athenry, Co. Galway Club and similar detail is given in the *The Irish Golf Guides* from 1910 to 1916.

*See Athenry G.C. and Galway G.C.

COUNTY KILDARE.
*See Naas G.C.

COUNTY LONGFORD.
Instituted 1900. Affiliated 1910.
In common with many other Irish golf clubs, earliest records of County Longford are missing; earliest available are for 1913. A foundation date of 1896 is claimed but this is not borne out by the contemporary golf guide books.

A listing for the club is first given in *The Golfing Annual* 1909/10, which records 1900 as the year of institution. At that time there were 20 members, the Captain was J. Boyers and the Hon. Secretary was S. Boyd, Ulster Bank, Longford; ". . . the course of nine holes varying from 95 to 414 yards is a mile from the station . . ."

Later, *The Irish Golfing Guide* 1916 reported: "The course is pleasantly situated and is given at a nominal rent by the Earl of Longford, who also generously provided a small clubhouse . . . Play begins in October and ends on May 1st".

Golfing Union of Ireland records reveal an affiliation date of 24th February 1910.

COUNTY LOUTH, Baltray, Co. Louth.
Instituted 1892.   Affiliated 1995.

An entry in *The Irish Times* 8th August 1892 announced the institution of this club: ". . . a new club has just been started under the title of Co. Louth Golf Club. The links are on the seashore at Baltray, three miles from Drogheda, where a nine-hole course has been laid out and can be seen on application to the greenkeeper J. Smith, Baltray. Gentlemen who wish can communicate with the acting Secretary G. H. Pentland, Black Hall, Drogheda." This notice in *The Irish Times* was the first move in the formation of this club; it will be noted that Mr. Pentland was acting Secretary. An article in *The Irish Golfer* 21st February 1900 recorded: "In the Spring of 1892 G. H. Pentland discovered the present links and invoked the aid of Tom Gilroy (see Mornington), who at once realised their capabilities . . . a meeting was called in Drogheda on 11th October 1892 and Co. Louth Golf Club was established. Mr. T. Gilroy was elected Captain and G. H. Pentland, Hon. Secretary and Treasurer."

The Golfing Annual 1894/95 records the course as an 18-hole one for the first time: "It is an excellent course, the soil being sandy and the turf short. The circuit is about three miles and the hazards are sandhills, bents and bunkers". Tom Gilroy is credited in this *Guide* with the first record for the new course − a 79 in May 1894.

The founder of the club, G. H. Pentland, was a prominent local landowner who had qualified for the Bar at Dublin University, but did not practise. Another of the founder members, Mr. H. J. Daly, Captain of the club in 1895, achieved high office in the administration of Irish golf. In 1899 he succeeded George Combe, the founder secretary of the Golfing Union of Ireland, a post he held for three years.

In 1914 Cecil Barcroft, the Secretary of the Royal Dublin Golf Club was called in to redesign the course and this layout remained for twenty-four years. In 1938 the famous golf architects Tom Simpson and Molly Gourley redesigned the course again, which was formally opened on 24th July that year, by the late Jimmy Bruen, one of Ireland's most illustrious golfers. Three years later the club initiated the prestigious East of Ireland Championship, which was won on the inaugural occasion by another illustrious Irish golfer, Mr. J. B. Carr.

*See Mornington.

COUNTY MEATH, Trim, Co. Meath.

This club is first listed in *The Golfing Annual* 1903/04, in the 1904/05 edition a foundation date of September 1900 is given. Entries for the club are listed in all subsequent *Golfing Annuals* until 1910. A foundation date of 1898 is given for the club in *The Irish Golf Guides* from 1910 to 1916. In the 1916 edition the name of the club is recorded as Trim Golf Club.

*See Trim G.C.

COUNTY SLIGO, Rosses Point, Sligo.
Instituted 1894.   Affiliated 1902!

The Co. Sligo Golf Club is first recorded in *The Golfing Annual* 1894/95 which gives an institution date of 1894. President of the club was Col. Cooper and Vice-President was Sir H. W. Gore Booth, Bart. ". . . The course of nine holes is situated at Rosses Point, about five miles from Sligo but as there is plenty of ground available it will before long be extended to 18 holes. The turf is of first rate quality and the hazards are bunkers, sandpits, bents, a quarry, a wall, a road and broken ground. There is no crossing. The par of the round is 38 . . ." The club is listed as affiliated to the GUI in this guide book.

An article in *The Irish Field* 19th June 1909 would indicate that golf had been played at Rosses Point earlier than 1894: "The officers of the Duke of Connaught's Sligo Own Artillery were the first to play golf on the present course, their camp having been annually pitched close to Rosses Point. It may be said that golf began there in 1890 though it was not until 1894 that Mr. George Combe proposed the formation of a club. Colonel Campbell, the club President, then set to work to negotiate a lease which was obtained." It is of interest to note that Mr. George Combe, founding Secretary of the Golfing Union of Ireland, was a key figure in setting up the club. He maintained a close interest in the club and presented the Combe Cup for competition. *The Irish Times* 24th June 1898 recorded the third half yearly competition for the cup, which had been won on the previous two occasions by Mr. J. Brabazon.

Over the winter of 1906/07 the course was extended to eighteen holes and *Golf Illustrated* 19th April 1907 carried an account of the opening: "The original course has for long been admitted to be one of the very best nine-hole courses in Ireland. The new holes have been laid out by Mr. W. Campbell, a scratch player and a member of the Oxford and Cambridge Golfing Society, and when played on for a time promise to be quite up to the standard of the old. The extended course was opened last week."

In 1926 the club decided to alter the course to keep pace with the improvements in golf equipment over the previous twenty years. H. S. Colt, the famous golf architect, was engaged and over the following two years work was carried out, which resulted in the present championship course.

The West of Ireland Amateur Open Championship was instituted by the club in 1927. This commences the golfing year for the Irish Championship circuit and is most popular among the top players in the country.

COUNTY WESTMEATH.

*See Mullingar G.C.

COURTMACSHERRY, Co. Cork.

The Golfers Guide 1897 lists a club and course at this location. There is no further record of either.

CRAIGS PARK, Co. Antrim.

The Golfing Union of Ireland Yearbook for 1931 lists this club and gives an affiliation date of 1916. The 1937 edition also reported a reaffiliation date of 1924, entries for the club cease in the 1945 edition of the *Yearbook*.

CUAN, Strangford, Co. Down.

This club is listed in *The Golfing Union of Ireland Yearbook* 1927. J. W. MacMurray was Hon. Secretary and there were nine holes. The 1928 edition recorded 1922 as the date of affiliation. An entry for the club in *The Irish Golfers Blue Book* 1939 names it as Guan G.C. which is an obvious error (although the entry is in the ''G'' alphabetical sequence). An institution date of 1922 is recorded in the latter publication. Entries for Cuan appear annually in the *GUI Yearbook* until 1947, it would seem that the club ceased to function at that time.

CULLYBRACKEY, Co. Antrim.

The records of the Golfing Union of Ireland reveal an affiliation date of 17th November 1915 for this club. There is no mention of it in *The Irish Golfing Guide* 1916. *The Golfers Handbook* 1923 lists the club giving the game F. J. Frazer as Honorary Secretary. It reported that the course of nine holes was 1¾ miles from Cullybrackey Station. A second affiliation to the Golfing Union of Ireland is documented in *The Irish Field* 2nd February 1924 and an entry in the Union's *Yearbook* 1927 listed W. J. Kernohan, Springhill, as Hon. Secretary. The club's subsequent history is unknown.

CURRAGH, Co. Kildare.
Instituted 1883. Affiliated 1898.

The story of early golf on the Curragh is told in Chapters 3, 4 and 5. Although golf was first played there in 1852 there is no evidence, at present, of a club being founded until 1883. The course itself is the oldest in Ireland and the club is second in seniority only to Royal Belfast.

An account of the club's institution is given in *The Irish Times* 12th March 1883 in a column of military news: "Maj. Gen. Fraser, V.C., C.B., Commanding Curragh Brigade has sanctioned the formation of a garrison golf club in connection with the Officers Recreation Club. Lieutenant A. G. Balfour of the 1st Battalion Highland Light Infantry, stationed in the Camp, has been appointed Secretary. The Rules of the Club will be the same as those of the Royal and Ancient Golf Club of St. Andrews.'' More detail is given in Chapter 5 of the close connections between the Royal and Ancient and Curragh clubs. It will be noted that the original rules of the Curragh were those of St. Andrews and the club is fortunate that an original bound copy of these rules has survived; the only documentation extant from its institution.

Lt. Balfour's name appears again in *The Golfing Annual* 1887/88 where he is recorded as Captain of the club; the earliest known Captain. The 1887 course was described as ''. . . eleven holes and about 2½ miles around . . . all on good turf, has a variety of hazards − gorse bushes, gravel quarry, two open ditches . . .''

The Golfing Annual 1888/89 list A. G. Balfour as Honorary Secretary once more and for the first time the course was of eighteen holes.

Ladies are first recorded as playing at the Curragh in *The Irish Times* 5th July 1890, a ladies handicap which was won by Mrs. Norman Lee (wife of the Camp Chaplain). The compeition was held on a special ladies' course of nine holes, the first such course in Ireland. From 1897 the *Golfing Annuals* list a separate ladies' course, until 1907.

The club did not open its membership to local civilians until late in the 1890s and this was restricted to the local gentry. One or two exceptions were made, one was in the case of Captain Henry Greer who had retired from the Highland Light Infantry in 1889 to commence an illustrious career in the local horse-breeding industry. He had been a fellow officer of Lt. A. G. Balfour and his wife was one of the 1890 lady golfers. During the Boer War 1899/1902, and First World War 1914/1918, Greer paid the greenkeeper out of his own pocket.

The club entered a golden period when the new King, George V, granted the Royal title to the club, on 24th September 1910. It is poignant to note that David Ritchie, the founder of the 1852 course, had died only two weeks before − forgotten except for an obituary in *The Kildare Observer* 17th September 1910. The obituary recorded: ''He claimed, and we believe rightly so, to be the oldest golfer in Ireland, as he had ample proof of playing with the late Mr. Alexander Love on links he organised at Donnelly's Hollow, Curragh, in the early fifties of the last century.''

Within four years the First World War denuded the golf club of its members and when the Armistice was signed in November 1918 the military members found themselves at war in Ireland. The last British contingent left the Curragh on 16th May 1922 and took with them any surviving records, including the Royal Charter. However, there was one item they could not take with them and that, of course, was the ''links near Donnelly's Hollow'' which had been laid out by David Ritchie in 1852 − the oldest course in Ireland. The first Captain of the club after the handover was Mr. P. O'Shaughnessy, manager of the Hibernian Bank, Newbridge.

*See Royal Curragh G.C. and Chapters 3, 4, 5, 6, 7, 9.

CUSHENDALL, Co. Antrim.

*See Glenariff.

DARTREY, Co. Monaghan.

A club of this name is listed in *The Golfers Handbook* 1923. There was a membership of 50 and the Honorary Secretary was Chas E. Murphy, Ivydene,

Cootehill, Co. Cavan. The course was nine holes and no institution date was given. An entry for the club appears in *The Golfing Union of Ireland Yearbook* 1927, which is evidence of affiliation, the Hon. Secretary was unchanged. The club is not mentioned in the 1937 *Yearbook*, although it is listed in *The Irish Tourist Directory* in that year. The subsequent history of this club is unknown.

DELGANY, Co. Wicklow.
Instituted 1908.   Affiliated 1908.

A lengthy article in *The Irish Field* 13th March 1926 documented the origins of Delgany Golf Club: "It is said that its foundation was due to the reluctance of the council of the Greystones Golf Club to allow Sunday golf . . . anyhow the first meeting was held in the Grand Hotel Greystones on 22nd February 1908 with Dr. A. M. Archer in the chair . . . The godfather of the new club was Mr. A. L. Figgiss who proposed that 'it was desirable to form a golf club to be called the Delgany Golf Club, with a course in Bellevue Demesne' . . . on 22nd July it was decided that the course should be opened for play the following Saturday . . . The first President was Dr. Archer and for the first Captain the choice of the members fell on Mr. F. W. Robertson."

This same article recorded that a committee meeting on 26th August 1909 decided to invite the famous Harry Vardon over to inspect the course. *The Irish Field* 25th September 1909 reported the famous man's arrival to make improvements on the course, originally designed by Tom Hood (professional to Royal Dublin G.C.). Club records reveal that the famous Michael "Dyke" Moran played a 36-hole challenge match against Vardon during his visit. In front of a large crowd the former British Open champion was victorious by 3 and 2.

DERRYNANE, Co. Kerry.

A course at this Kerry beauty spot is listed *The Golfing Annual* 1895/96 for the first time: "The course is a private one, laid out on the property of Mr. D. Connell, but visitors staying at the Derrynane Hotel, or bringing letters of introduction are allowed to play." *The Golfers Guide* 1897 states: ". . . a small links exists in South Kerry in one of the loveliest spots in the Kingdom — Derrynane, the home of the O'Connells. The present representative and descendant of the Great Liberator is most good natured in permitting visitors to play."

The Derrynane Golf Club was founded on 9th June 1897 and the founding committee is listed in *Golf* 2nd July 1897 — Mr. D. O'Connell, President and Captain; Miss P. O'Connell, Treasurer and Secretary; committee, Mrs. O'Connell and five other local gentlemen. Later on *The Golfing Annual* 1902/03 reported that the course was of nine holes varying from 120 to 400 yards, laid out on the property of Mr. D. O'Connell, close to the Darrynane Hotel [sic].

The Irish Golfing Guide 1916 lists the club but Mr. O'Connell died in August 1919 and the club does not seem to have survived for long afterwards.

DERRYVALE, Co. Tipperary.

The Irish Golfers Guide 1910 lists this as a private course owned by Mr. Sydney Smith, it further states: ". . . seven holes but two greens played twice, admission by invitation, members of recognised clubs always welcome". There is no mention of the course *The Irish Golfing Guide* 1916.

DONAGHADEE, Co. Down.
Instituted 1899. Affiliated 1900.

The Irish Golfer 10th January 1900 documents the beginnings of this club and states that it all ". . . is largely due to the undoubted perseverance of Mr. Adam Duffin, who overcoming obstacle after obstacle saw his efforts crowned with success when on 28th July last Lord Londonderry opened the Donaghadee links . . . Mr. Duffin being ably supported in his endeavours by Daniel Delacherois D.L., the Lord of the Manor, and Col. Delacherois J.P. The latter accepted the post of Captain."

Initially the course consisted of nine holes, on land given by Mr. W. Gabbey (at the first annual general meeting he was thanked for placing the warren at the club's disposal). *Nisbet's Yearbook* 1908 records that the club now had eighteen holes and 350 members and a new clubhouse was built "last year".

DOOKS, Co. Kerry.
Instituted 1895. Affiliated 1910.

There is a tradition in this club of the local national school children attending a game of golf at the site of the present course in 1889. It is also believed that military personnel were involved in the institution of the game there as far back as 1886. *Irish Golf* November 1936 carries an article by Lionel Hewson wherein Mrs. Hickson, the Hon. Secretary, stated: ". . . officially founded in 1895 . . . it has really been in existence for close on fifty years". Mrs. Hickson went on to state that she had played there, with the late Lord Kitchener and Messrs David Roche and C. Downing.

The Golfing Annual 1898/99 lists Dooks Golf Club as a seaside eighteen-hole course, giving F. R. Bateman as Hon. Secretary. Later on, *The Irish Golfer* 20th September 1899 carries an article on the Caragh and Dooks Golf Club: "The club was formed in 1896 under the auspices of the Director of the Great Southern Hotel at Caragh and a few of the residents in the neighbourhood and has continued to flourish since. There are at present fifty members . . . The club have a small pavilion of their own but on competition days they have the use of a 'lodge' . . . Hon. Secretary, F. R. Bateman, Glenbeigh."

The Golfing Annual 1903/04 gives 1895 as the institution date of the Caragh and Dooks Golf Club. F. R. Bateman is listed as Captain and the continuous presence of this man's name would indicate that there was only one club involved. The club accepts that Caragh Lake, Caragh and Dooks and Glenbeigh, Caragh and Dooks were all names used in the past, depending on who was running the club at the time. Unfortunately the club minute books prior to 1910 are missing, which prevents a full account of the early years being written. All documentary evidence indicates 1895 as the date of institution.

*See Caragh Lake; Caragh and Dooks; Glenbeigh, Caragh and Dooks.

DOUGLAS, Co. Cork.
Instituted 1909.   Affiliated 1911.

The Irish Field 25th September 1909 reported that very satisfactory progress was being made with the new links and clubhouse at Douglas, nine holes would be ready by Christmas and a further nine by Spring. It was also reported that Harry Vardon had laid out the course in July. *The Golfing Annual* 1909/10 lists the club with a foundation date of July 1909, there were 261 members. An entrance fee of 4 guineas was payable and the annual subscription was £4, ladies £2.

A full account of the origins of the club was given in *The Irish Field* 1st May 1926, which recorded that Douglas Golf Club was started as a limited liability company by Mr. Arthur W. Winter, Mr. J. J. Brown, Mr. P. Morrogh, Mr. W. Morrogh and Mr. Guest Lane. The first Secretary was Mr. M. W. Litton . . . credit was given to Mr. M. English for being the guiding spirit of the club for many years. The article continued . . . "When the club was formed there was land for only nine holes, which were laid out by Harry Vardon, and as well as can be remembered the nine holes were played until May 1911 when the 18 were constructed. The history of the club is somewhat obscure for in the unfortunate burning all the records perished . . . It is now known that the burning of the clubhouse was the result of a blunder in interpreting an "order" but the damage was done and seemed irreparable." This entry referred to the burning of the clubhouse during the recent Civil War.

The same article recorded that the members stepped into the breach and contributed £735 for the rebuilding of the clubhouse, which was reopened in May 1923.

DROMANA, Rush, Co. Dublin.

The Irish Times 30th October 1895 carries a charming account of this club: "On the sea beach hugged by the Dromana heights on one side and the Rush cliffs on the other and commanding a lovely view of Dublin Bay there is a very pretty golf links. Sir Roger Palmer is the President of the club and yesterday he entertained the members and presented a prize after which there was a very keen competition. After the first eighteen holes were played Mrs. Margetts, Rev. N. Brunskill, Dr. Fahie and Mr. Bradshaw were declared the best players and the cup is to be played for by these members on the next club day." The account goes on to give the names of the players amongst whom were three military gentlemen – General Stewart, Captain Thunder and Captain Fenwick.

There is no further evidence of this club's existence or demise; it may have been a private course.

DROMORE, Co. Down.

The Irish Times 10th January 1896 records the institution of this club: "A new Irish club has been formed at Dromore, Co. Down, to be called the Dromore Club. At a recent meeting of those interested in its formation the following appoints were made: President, Lord Arthur; Vice Presidents, Rt. Rev. Monsignor McCartan, Rev. Eamon Hayes and John R. Miniss; Captain, William Preston . . ." *The Golfing Annual* 1895/96 states: "Instituted 28th November 1895, the course, of nine holes, is situated on the old Loyola grounds . . . Dromore being a cathedral city and the burial place of the celebrated Bishop Jeremy Taylor".

The club is listed for the last time in *The Golfing Annual* 1907/08 and *The Irish Golfers Guide* 1910 recorded the club as "believed to be extinct".

DUBLIN G.C., The Phoenix Park, Co. Dublin.

At its foundation in May 1885, the Royal Dublin G.C. was originally named the Dublin Golf Club. In May 1891 the club was authorised to use the prefix Royal.

DUBLIN SCOTTISH, Co. Dublin.

If the club had survived it would have been the second oldest in Dublin and one of the earliest in Ireland. *The Irish Times* 6th October 1890 records: "The members of the above club played their first annual handicap medal on Saturday at Baldoyle, the winner being Mr. John M. Fisher". Seven months later *The Irish Times* 20th April 1891 stated: "The Captain's medal (D. MacRae) was competed for at Sutton on Saturday 16th and was won by Mr. John Jameson".

At present Sutton Golf Club possess a copy of a lease dated 23rd May 1890 between Lord Howth and Mr. J. McAdams of the Dublin Scottish Golf Club for use of "Cosh" (Cush Point) from 1st June 1890. The rent was one shilling per month. After its 1891 mention of this club *The Irish Times* does not record any mention of golf at Sutton until 1896 when the present Sutton Golf Club was founded as an offshoot of the Sutton Boat & Yacht Club.

Mr. John Jameson, who is mentioned above, was most probably the owner of the area of Portmarnock which would later become the home of that famous club.

*See Portmarnock G.C. and Sutton G.C.

DUBLIN UNIVERSITY G.C., Co. Dublin.
Instituted 1894. Affiliated 1896.

The Golfing Annual 1894/95 lists the founding committee of this club, the President was Dr. A. Traill and the Captain was Mr. B. O'Brien. There were thirty members. In effect this was a club within a club as they had no home of their own and were given the privilege of playing over the Royal Dublin course at Dollymount.

From the beginning this club had a major part to play in the early development of golf in Ireland. *The Irish Golfer* 1st November 1899 carries an article by Cecil Barcroft (a former Captain of this club and one of the early pioneers of Irish golf) which states: ". . . great impetus was given to the game by the foundation of the

Dublin University Golf Club . . . the club has furthered interclub matches with all its power". This is borne out in the columns of the *The Irish Times* from 1895 onwards, when many interclub matches, featuring Dublin University, are recorded.

The Belfast Newsletter 16th November 1895 recorded that ". . . for its membership, this new club, started a year ago, has probably the largest amount of golfing talent in the country". This was certainly confirmed when Mr. James Stewart Moore, a member, won the Irish Close Championship of 1896. Later on *The Irish Golfers Guide* 1910 records that the club was "open to all of the University up to M.A." The Captain of that year was Lionel Munn, one of the major figures in Irish golf of the early 1900s.

Soon afterwards, the First World War was to have a dramatic effect on the club, with the *The Irish Golfing Guide* 1916 reporting: "This club has ceased to exist for the time being, practically all its members being in His Majesty's forces". The periodical *Irish Life* 5th November 1915 states: "Lt. Gerald Johnston (who enlisted after the war began) is the first Irish golfer to receive a distinction for bravery, the M.C. . . . played on Dublin University team v. Carlow in the Barton Cup last year".

The club was resuscitated after the war and continues to play a major role in Irish golf.

DUBLIN UNIVERSITY GOLF SOCIETY, Dublin.

The Irish Field 26th June 1909 records the institution of this society whose object was "to unite all past and present Trinity players and to promote interclub matches". Mr. D. M. Wilson K.C. was the first Captain and the Hon. Secretary was Cecil Barcroft. An exact foundation date of 5th February 1909 is given in *The Golfing Annual* 1908/09.

After the initial enthusiasm, the society had lost ground by 1912 when *The Irish Times* of 16th November asked: "What has become of the Dublin University Golf Society formed some three or four years ago. It was to have played a series of matches but it seems to have died soon after its birth". The society is recorded in the *Irish Golf Guides* 1910 to 1916, however, in *Irish Golf* April 1930 Lionel Hewson reported that the society had continued until the war and that it was revived at a meeting in Trinity College on Monday 26th December 1926. Judge Denis Pringle played a prominent part in this revival.

*See Dublin University G.C.

DUFFERIN, Killyleagh, Co. Down.

The Golfing Guide 1897 states: ". . . a new course has been opened at this place in Co. Down. The President is the Marquis of Dufferin and Ava, who has given the ground". Later on, *The Golfing Annual* 1898/99 gave the institution date of 1st November 1896 . . . "The course of nine holes, varying in length from 150 to 300 yards". Similar entries occur in subsequent *Golfing Annuals* until 1910. There is no listing for the club in the *Irish Golf Guides* 1910 to 1916.

DUNDALK, Co. Louth.
Instituted 1904. Affiliated 1905.

Golfers at Dundalk are probably unaware that golf was first played there in 1895 or 1896. An article in *The Irish Field* 31st July 1909 tells the story: "Golf was first played at Dundalk when the 13th Hussars were stationed there and the prime movers were Capt. MacLaren (of polo fame), Mr. P. L. MacArdle, J. St. P. MacArdle and that well known Co. Down sportsman Col. Wallace. This semiclub died a natural death from want of support".

The Army Lists of that period show that in 1894 the 13th Hussars had been on the Curragh and in 1895 they were transferred to Dundalk where they stayed until early in 1897 when they moved to Dublin. It was obviously during 1895 or 1896 that the golfers of this Regiment were active in Dundalk.

The game was not revived until late in 1904 and *The Golfing Annual* 1904/05 records 7th December 1904 as the institution date. Mr. V. S. Carroll is listed as Captain with Mr. P. L. MacArdle as Honorary Secretary (a link with the earlier golfers). The *Annual* states: "The course, of nine holes, is in the Deer Park, within five minutes of the station. It was laid out by G. Coburn (professional at Portmarnock)."

Golf Illustrated 21st June 1907, in an article about Michael Moran becoming assistant to Tom Hood at Royal Dublin, recorded: "Moran was engaged by the Dundalk club during the past Winter, but during the Summer play is abandoned owing to the grass". *The Irish Field* 31st July 1909 reported on an improved situation: ". . . hitherto it has not been opened for Summer play but this year the club have bought a large mower and the course is in capital order for play all year round".

The Irish Field 21st October 1922 reported that Tom Shannon and James Martin had laid out a fine course for the new Dundalk Golf Club (recently formed as a limited company): "It is very pleasantly situated and commands grand views of Dundalk Bay and the Mourne Mountains. The course is just 6000 yards long and is laid out in two loops".

*See Chapter 6.

DUNFANAGHY, Co. Donegal.
Instituted 1906. Affiliated 1920.

There is tenuous evidence that a club existed here in 1897 as *The Sportsmans Holiday Guide* records: "There is a sporting nine-hole course here extending to about a mile and three-quarters in length. The local club is naturally a small one, Dunfanaghy being only a small village on the shores of an inlet of Sheephaven . . . but owing to there being a first rate hotel in the village the list of members is greatly increased during the Summer and Autumn months". *The Golfers Guide* 1897 states: "The links are in connection with Starrett's Hotel" and does not mention a club.

Later, *The Golfing Annual* 1906/07 records the institution date as 1906 and gives the Captain's name as Major Edgeworth-Johnstone; the Honorary Secretary is listed as Mr. J. A. Sterritt (a connection with Starretts Hotel, above?). The following acount is given: "The course of eighteen holes, is bordered by the Atlantic on the one side and by Derryveagh Mountains on the other, and has splendid natural bunkers and hazards.

DUNGANNON, Co. Tyrone.
Instituted 1890.   Affiliated 1891.

This club has the distinction of being one of the founders of the Golfing Union of Ireland in November 1891. It was exactly twelve months earlier that the club was founded on the 22nd November 1890 on the ground given by the Earl of Ranfurly. This man brought further honour to the club by being chosen as the first President of the Union. He was also listed as first President of the club in *The Golfing Annual* 1890/91, the first Captain was John R. McDonald J.P. The Hon. Secretary was Rev. Edward F. Campbell and there were nine holes.

The Golfing Annual 1893/94 describes a twelve-hole course . . . "but by taking in six of the holes, in a second round, the orthodox eighteen are secured . . . a very commodious clubhouse was opened recently . . . at the sole cost of the President, the Earl of Ranfurly". By 1896 the course had reverted to nine holes and there was no change until the club created eighteen at their present location, Mullaghmore, in 1963. (The club was located at Drumcoo from 1918 until 1953).

One of the early pioneers of Irish golf, Cecil Barcroft was a member from 1892 and Captain in 1897 (see Dublin University and Royal Dublin).

A ladies' branch is first listed in the *The Golfing Annual* 1903/04, however Dungannon ladies' club is listed as affiliated to the ILGU in 1896.

DUNGARVAN, Co. Waterford.

The present club at Dungarvan claims a foundation date of 1924, however *The Golfers Handbook* 1923 lists a Dungarvon G.C. (Co. Waterford).

DUN LAOGHAIRE
Instituted 1909.   Affiliated 1910.

The Irish Field 11th December 1909 announced under the caption "Kingstown have a club" that a proposal to form a club had been taken at a recent meeting there. The inaugural meeting had taken place two days earlier when fifty-one residents of the district attended at the Royal Marine Hotel. Major Bryan Cooper M.P. chaired the meeting at which the Earl of Longford K.P. was elected first President of the club. A famous name in Irish golf journalism became the first Captain of the club, Captain Lionel Hewson, M.V.O. This man had written for *The Irish Times, The Irish Field* and later edited *Irish Life* which also had a fine golf column. He founded *Irish Golf* in 1928.

Initially nine holes were laid out on the ground leased at Eglinton Park and Highthorn. However *The Irish Field* 26th November 1910 reports on an extraordinary annual general meeting to be held on the following Monday to consider extending to eighteen holes. The members agreed to the proposal, and a further forty acres were leased on the other side of the Glenageary Road. After

World War One, Harry Colt, the famous British architect who in 1922 designed the new course at Sunningdale, was commissioned to redesign the Kingstown course which remains largely unchanged to this present day. (Colt's masterpiece was his work on the Pine Valley course in New Jersey which had taken seven years to build when opened in 1919).

The club changed its name from Kingstown to Dun Laoghaire Golf Club in 1951.

DUNMANWAY, Co. Cork.

The Golfers Handbook 1923 lists this club, without giving a date of institution: "Private club, membership 20, Hon. Sec. H. C. O'Callaghan, 9 holes".

The latter history of this private club is unknown.

DUNMORE, Co. Galway.

The Irish Golfing Guide 1914 lists the Dunmore Club and gives the following information: "A nine-hole private course situated at Quarter, about a quarter a mile from Dunmore. It is perfectly natural and rather difficult course, is well drained and possesses fine natural bunkers. It is ten miles from Tuam. Mr. T. I. Norman acts as Hon. Secretary."

The further history of this club is unknown.

DUNMURRY, Belfast, Co. Antrim.
Instituted 1905. Affiliated 1905.

The Golfing Annual 1904/05 gives the institution date of this club as 6th February 1905, the first Captain's name is recorded as Mr. J. Williams and ". . . a course is being laid out, and is expected to be ready for play by 15th May". Somehow the institution date was incorrectly given in *The Golfing Annual* 1906/07 as 20th May 1905 (probably the course opening day). Dunmurry's first course of nine holes had a length of 2,650 yards.

Like so many other Belfast golf clubs the men who guided the formation of this club were some of the leading industrialists of the city, amongst whom were J. Milne Barbour (first President), J. Williams (first Captain), T. R. Bristow, F. W. Ewart, E. J. Travers, J. Stoupe, F. McCance and Malcolm Gordon.

The original course had been leased from Sir Robert Anderson but after two years part of it had to handed back for building purposes. Over the years, since then, additional land was purchased until the present eighteen-hole course was opened in 1977. (Harry Colt, the famous British golf architect was engaged to redesign the course in the late 1920s when additional land had been purchased). One of the club's most talented players was Max McCready who won the 1949 British Amateur Championship at Portmarnock.

DURROW, Co. Laois.

The Irish Golfers Guide 1911 lists this club and gives an institution date of 1906. it had nine holes beside Attanagh Station on the G.S.W. Railway. The Hon. Secretary was Dr. D. J. O'Brien, The Square, Durrow; the Captain was A. F. Smyth. Men's fees were 10 shillings and ladies' 5 shillings. Sunday play was allowed and the club was not affiliated.

An entry for the club appears in *The Irish Golfers Guide* 1912, however there is no further mention any later publications.

EDENDERRY, Co. Offaly.
Instituted 1910.   Affiliated 1928.

The Irish Field 22nd October 1910 reports: "The Honorary Secretary for the new golf club at Edenderry in Kings County is a Mr. A. J. Roche and he informs us that the course will be open for play on 1st Novmember. The course is over 2,400 yards in length. Among the officials are Mr. T. O. K. White, Captain; Mr. R. G. Brown, Treasurer. The fees are low and the club should have good support in the district."

Later, *The Irish Golfing Guide* 1916 lists the club as "Edenderry and District Golf Club" and Mr. White is listed as that year's Captain also. A bogey of 41 is given for the course which was 1½ miles for Edenderry Station. The present club records earlier locations as Carrick and before that The Derries. It is of interest to note that between 1932 and 1946 *Thoms Directory* lists Francis Mulvin of Clonmore as Captain of the club.

ENNIS, Co. Clare.
Instituted 1897.   Affiliated 1910.

The Sportsmans Holiday Guide 1897 states: "There is a nine-hole course here to which visitors are made welcome". Later, *The Golfing Annual* 1898/99 gives an institution date of 1897 for Ennis Golf Club but carries no other details. Subsequent *Golfing Annuals* do no list the club.

Ennis Golf Club is listed in *The Irish Golfers Guide* 1914 for the first time, which gives an institution date of 1907 (obviously a revival date). There was a membership of ninety and the nine-hole course measured 2,500 yards. Men's and ladies' subscriptions were the same at ten shillings and there were three ladies on the committee.

ENNISCORTHY, Co. Wexford.
Instituted 1906?   Affiliated 1925.

A golf club at Enniscorthy is first listed in *The Golfing Annual* 1906/07 which gave no institution date. *The Golfing Annual* 1908/09 listed 1906 as the date of institution, the Hon. Secretary was F. P. Roche, The Castle, Enniscorthy, and there were 50 members . . . "the course of nine holes is three quarters of a mile from the station". The same details are recorded in subsequent *Annuals* until 1909/10. Some years later *The Irish Field* 22nd February 1913 stated: "Golf has languished for some time past at Enniscorthy owing to the course being most unsuitable and play only allowed from December to April. Ground for a new course has been secured near the town . . . Mr. W. C. Pickeman of Portmarnock has been asked to lay out the course and promises to do so.

The Irish Golfing Guide 1916 stated that the club was two miles from Enniscorthy station with a bogey of 36. Later, *The Golfers Handbook* 1923 lists the club with 9 holes and 1¼ miles from the station. However, this course and club must have fallen on hard times as the present club have no knowledge of an existence previous to 1925. The Golfing Union of Ireland records give an affiliation date of 1908 for the older club.

It is of interest to note that the visitors book of the Royal Belfast Golf Club was signed by a Mr. C. A. Symes of Enniscorthy on 24th April 1890.

ENNISCRONE, Co. Sligo.
Instituted 1922.   Affiliated 1931.

It is not known who instituted golf at Enniscrone, but local tradition records 1918 as the year in which the game was first played there. *The Western People* of 19th August 1922 reports as follows: "Enniscrone Golf Club – Medal competitions . . . competitions will be held over the above links on Thursday 24th August and Sunday 27th inst. All wishing to compete will please notify the Secretary and send club handicaps before 20th. Further particulars on application to the Secretary".

Apart from this account there are no details available on the founders of golf at Enniscrone and it was not until 1930 that a permanent home was secured at Bartra. The club was affiliated to the GUI in 1931.

ENNISKILLEN, Co. Fermanagh.
Instituted 1896.   Affiliated 1911.

An article in Enniskillen's local newspaper, *The Impartial Reporter* 19th March 1896 recorded the inception of the town's golf club: "On Monday afternoon a number of gentlemen met in the Townhall Enniskillen, for the purpose of taking steps if possible to establish a golf club in the town. Mr. William Teele J.P. in the chair . . . Mr. Andrew Stuart, Manager of the Ulster Bank, explained exactly the purpose in view and mentioned that negotiations had already been commenced with Mrs. Hurst, Killyhevlin, for a portion of her large field, bordering on the Dublin Road opposite Lord Belmore's Demesne. . . . Mr. McCoy kindly consented to act as Hon. Sec. in this matter. One or two suggestions were made regarding other sites not suitable for the club and ultimately a committee was formed to take the matter into consideration."

Unfortunately the early minutes of the club have disappeared and it would appear that there may have been a temporary gap in continuity. *The Irish Golfing Guide* 1911 recorded: "Founded 1911. A nine holes inland course has been laid out by the club, which has only just been formed. The Hon. Secretary is Mr. O. A. Pringle, Willoughby House, Enniskillen, *The Irish Golfing Guide* 1916 recorded that the club's course was at Killyhevlin, which was the original 1896 course location.

In 1944 the club moved to it present location at Castlecoole where a nine-hole course was laid out. Work is progressing on laying out a further nine holes which should be open in 1988.

FERBANE & MOYSTOWN, Co. Offaly.

This club is first mentioned in *The Irish Golfers Guide* 1910 which gives the name as Moystown G.C., instituted 1907. There were nine holes, within two miles of Beltown station and the Captain is listed as E. W. Perry. It would appear that this was a private course as it is listed as not affiliated and had a membership of 30. Six years later *The Irish Golfing Guide* 1916 gives the name as Ferbane & Moystown G.C. with Mr. Perry still Captain of the club. There were still thirty members but the war had caused inflation of the subscription from 10 shillings to 25 shillings for men and the ladies paid 10 shillings, up from 5 shillings. The course bogey was 38 and the club had not affiliated.

The Irish Tourist Authority Directory 1937 lists the club with nine holes, its later history is unknown.

FERMOY, Co. Cork.
Instituted 1893.   Affiliated 1905.

The formative years of golf at Fermoy are closely linked with the presence of British Regiments stationed there. Unfortunately, the records of the present club do not extend beyond 1905 and there is therefore no evidence to support the local legend that the first club was formed in 1887. The earliest reference to a club is to be found in *The Sportsmans Holiday Guide* 1897, which does not give a foundation date and states: "The Fermoy golf course is situated at the race course about a quarter of a mile from the (railway) station. The course is all grass and is situated on the highest ground about Fermoy . . . there are nine holes". No Captain's name is given and the Honorary Secretary's name is given as W. Sherrand. The club is listed in the *Golfing Annuals* from 1898 onwards, without a foundation date. A foundation date of 1903 is first given in *The Golfing Annual* 1905/06, however this was clearly a revival date. (The club may have succumbed during the South African War, 1899/1902, when the garrison would have been depleted). *Nisbets Golf Yearbook* 1908 lists 1893 as the institution date and this is also recorded in *The Irish Golfers Guide* 1910 and *The Irish Golfing Guide* 1916. Until 1934 the club played over nine holes at the Sandpit on the Duntaheen Road. An entry in *The Irish Golfers Blue Book* 1939 recorded: ". . . the present course was constructed in 1934, situated at the highest point on the Northern side of the town . . . the Fermoy Aerodrome adjoins the course". In 1970 the club moved once more to its present location at Corrin, where an eighteen-hole course was laid out.

The Irish Golfer 25th April 1900, in an article on Col. H. D. Cutbill, Hon. Secretary of the (Royal) Co. Down G.C., stated that he had served with the 86th Regiment (Royal Irish Rifles) and had begun to play golf in 1892, at Fermoy. It was in 1892 that the first record of golf at Fermoy is documented in *The Irish Times* of 11th May, which carries details of a match between "Officers 1st Seaforths v.

Lismore Golf Club, played at Fermoy yesterday''. The article goes on to record a handsome victory for the officers by 65 strokes, a repeat of a previous match at Lismore which they had won by 65 strokes.

See Chapter 6 for further information on military golf at Fermoy.

FETHARD, Co. Tipperary.

Irish Life 6th February 1914 reports: ''An influential meeting was held in Fethard at the end of January . . . the meeting decided to establish a club and appointed Mr. Cyril L. Baker Hon. Sec.'' Later the *The Irish Golfing Guide* 1916 lists the club as having a nine-hole course one mile from Fethard Railway Station. In a further lengthy article *Irish Life* 7th June 1918 carries a feature on the Fethard and Tipperary Golf Club and states: ''. . . (the club) has had this year a considerable accession of new members. Thursday is the 'club day' and on that day tea is served in turn by lady members''.

There is no further record of this club.

FINGLAS, Co. Dublin.

The Irish Golfing Guide 1911 gives an institution date of 1911 for this club which was within ten minutes walk of the Glasnevin Tram. Mr. J. B. Patterson was the Hon. Secretary and the course was 2,700 yards long. Initially the course, which was proprietorial, had nine holes but *Irish Life* 28th November 1913 in a report on the club's annual general meeting states that ''the club will be playing soon on an 18-hole course''.

Unfortunately, the First World War had a drastic effect and *Irish Life* 13th October 1916 records: ''We are told this club is closing down after the end of the year owing to loss of members. This is due, some say to the high cost of living, consequent on the war . . . the course was recently extended to 18 holes . . . many members are going to join Clontarf, Hermitage and Sutton''.

This club was also known as the North Suburban Club.

FINTONA, Co. Tyrone.
Instituted 1904.   Affiliated 1926.

This club claims to have begun in 1896, however the official club history states: ''. . . little is known of the early years of its existence since the records, extant, do not regress beyond 1939 – apparently a former secretary of the club used the earlier records to fuel the burning of rubbish in his back yard''. The official history goes on to state: ''Bankers, clergy, teachers and business people constituted the bulk of the early membership; the earliest trophy (men's) extant, a challenge cup, was presented in 1913 by C. W. L. Browne Lecky''.

Irish Life 4th September 1914 carries a report on this club which clarifies some of the early history. The club was a private course owned by the above-named Mr. Browne Lecky. The course, of nine holes, was open all year round and had been laid out ten years before ''under the supervision of Mr. Taylor''. This would give an institution date of 1904 and not 1896 as believed by the club. For the first time *The Golfing Annual* 1909/10 listed Fintona Golf Club, no institution date is given. The Hon. Secretary was J. Anderson and "the course of nine holes adjoins the station". Golfing Union of Ireland records give an affiliation date of 1926 for the club.

FONTHILL, Chapelizod, Co. Dublin.

If this club had survived it would have been one of the earliest in Dublin, however there is no record of it after 1907. *The Irish Times* 31st October 1894 records a monthly handicap competition won by Mr. J. Hitchcock with a nett score of 80 off a handicap of 40 "on their links at Chapelizod". Three other names are mentioned, Mr. J. Godley, Mr. J. Harrison and Mr. D. W. Christie. The club is first listed in *The Golfing Annual* 1895/96 but no details are given. Again in *The Irish Times* 27th November 1894 a monthly handicap result is given and the same four names, only, are listed. Mr. Godley won the second event with 73 nett off 45. One could speculate that this was a private golf club, with only four members. The last mention of the club is in *The Golfing Annual* 1906/07 which states: "No details".

FORTWILLIAM, Co. Antrim.
Instituted 1891.   Affiliated 1895.

This golf club was "first" founded on 16th October 1891 according to the records of the club, although the *The Golfing Annual* 1894/95 gives the date as 14th November 1891. Eleven gentlemen of the Antrim road area met in No. 1 Custom House Square on the inaugural date and the chair was occupied by Mr. J. T. Reade.

Initially nine holes were laid out on land between Fortwilliam Park and Parkmount but the course was only open for the Winter months, November to March − the landowner requiring the land for "grazing and/or hay" during the Spring and Summer. An article in *The Northern Whig* November 1891 carries a description of the course, which was laid out on the lands of Mr. John McFerran at Barnageeha.

The golf club continued until 1897, in which year the ground was taken over as building land in the outward expansion of Belfast and it was not until January 1903 that moves were made to revive the club. The first general meeting of the revived club took place on 10th January 1903 and in February 1903 C. S. Butchart, professional to the (Royal) Co. Down Golf Club "attended for one day and constructed the course"! Fortwilliam's new course consisted of nine holes and *The Irish Field* 28th June 1924 documented the opening of the new clubhouse and extension of the course to eighteen holes.

It is of interest to note that during the period after the demise of the original club, some of the members continued to play and keep the old memories alive. *The Irish Golfer* 19th February 1902 carried a letter from J. S. Reade to the Golfing Union of Ireland: ". . . since then members have been forced to play over the links of Royal Portrush and County Down. Would it not be reasonable to again take 'Fortwilliam' under its protection on the renewal of the annual subscription. Thus this historic club would be placed in the same position as 'Trinity' . . . P.S. The club will be open for matches during Easter".

Lady members were admitted to the club from the earliest days, *The Golfing Annual* 1894/95 recorded their subscription as five shillings per annum, which was half the men's.

FOTA ISLAND, Co. Cork.

The Belfast Newsletter 1st November 1886 reported: ". . . since November 1881 when the Belfast club was instituted . . . no less than three additional courses have been laid down in different parts of the country. The second was at Fota Island . . . one of our London contemporaries noticing an opening game there in 1883". This would appear to be the earliest reference to golf in the Cork area and was possibly related to the activities of General Sir Henry D'O Torrens (see Chapter 5). It was not until June 1883 that golf was documented at Kinsale (see Kinsale).

Later, *The Irish Times* 6th January 1906, under the heading "New Links At Fota", records: "In the demesne at Fota, Lady Barrymore has laid out a golf course of nine holes which compares favourably with any inland links . . . upon them will be played next month a stroke competition under handicap for a valuable silver cup kindly presented by Lady Barrymore. The entries will be open to members of Cork and Rushbrook golf clubs only".

It is obvious that the earlier Fota course had not survived and that fleeting mention in the *The Belfast Newsletter* remains an enigma for Cork historians to explore.

*See Chapter 5.

FOXROCK, Co. Dublin.
Instituted 1893.   Affiliated 1894.

The Irish Times 9th February 1893 under the heading "A New Club For Foxrock" announced: "A golf club has been started at the Foxrock estate belonging to the Royal Exchange Assurance Company, College Green. The links are situate opposite the race course at Leopardstown . . . they have been laid out by Mr. Brown, the well known professional golf player and they have been pronounced by him to be all that could be desired. The club, we are informed, will be a proprietary one." By 15th March *The Irish Times* reported that the course was open for play and that "there are separate links for use of young players".

One year later the club employed Curley as professional from Dollymount, however he did not have a lengthy tenure as *The Irish Times* 28th August 1894 reports that ". . . Mungo Park the newly appointed 'pro' has the green in good order and as a coach is most successful, his North Berwick training making him an excellent exponent of iron play". Mungo of course was the famous Musselburgh professional who had won the British Open in 1874, however he too did not stay long as *The Irish Times* 13th August 1895 reports that Mungo was now at Portmarnock.

The club's first president was Sir. C. Barrington, with Maj. H. Domville as his Vice-President, the first Captain was C. J. Wallis and ladies were admitted from the very beginning.

The Golfing Annual 1894/95 reported ". . . there is a clubhouse and ladies pavilion". *The Sportsmans Holiday Guide* 1897 reported ". . . the course which consists of nine holes . . . the distance round is about 1½ miles . . . The hazards consist of ditches and stone walls".

Later, *The Irish Field* 9th May 1908, in feature on the club, records: "The Royal Exchange Insurance company Ltd. at one time owned most of the land about Foxrock and its board displayed remarkable business acumen when it decided to start a golf club in order to attract building on their land. The club was thus a proprietary one in the first instance . . . the proprietary club came to an end in 1905 and became the present institution.

GALWAY, Co. Galway.
Instituted 1895.   Affiliated 1899.

The history of golf in Galway is not easy to document and the earliest record of the game in the city is related in the memoirs of Lt. Col. H. F. N. Jourdain, last commanding officer of the Connaught Rangers whose headquarters were in Renmore Barracks: "Golf was at this time just beginning to get a foothold in the West of Ireland and I made a nine-hole course with a famous young golfer of the 15th Regiment . . .". This would probably have been in 1894, as the 15th (East Yorks) did not arrive to Ireland until after September 1894 (Army Lists). Jourdain himself had been commissioned into the Connaught Rangers in February 1893.

A club at Galway is first mentioned in *The Sportsmans Holiday Guide* 1897 which states: "The Galway Golf Club, which has only been quite recently formed, has its course, which is a nine-hole one, on Glentain [sic] Hill . . . the distance round is about one mile and hazards consist of boulders and bushes . . . Secretary George Good, Bank of Ireland, Galway". Later, an article in *The Irish Golfer* 22nd January 1902 on Mr. J. M. Meldon records: "He was one of the founders of Galway Golf Club. The idea originated with Captain Henley a gentleman who, we may say, has done much for golf in the West of Ireland. He called together a few likely young sportsmen, supplied them with a club and ball apiece and told them to 'blaze away' on the ground which now forms Galway links."

Captain Henley was obviously a key figure in the origins of Galway golf and on his death *The Irish Golfer* 9th December 1903 relates: "Captain Henley gave up his military career some time before he came to Galway. Originally he joined the 82nd Regiment . . . he was afterwards transferred to one of the West Indian Regiments . . . Captain Henley was a well known personality in Galway, everybody liked 'Joe' . . . a practically perpetual Captain of Galway Golf Club he was mainly, indeed almost entirely, responsible for the success of that institution."

A foundation date of 1895 is first recorded in *The Golfing Annual* 1898/99 which gives the Captain's name as S. M. Nolan. This would have been Sebastian Nolan who was proprietor of the course, subsequently his name appears in various *Golfing Annuals* as President of the club. Mr. Nolan was a very tempestuous character and Lionel Hewson tells a story in *The Irish Field* 17th July 1909: "Many amusing stories are told of the old club landlord. One is about a duel that nearly took place between him and a gallant Colonel, which fortunately did not come off, though one gentleman recommended a dozen golf balls each and a driver at ten yards distance as a good method of settling any knotty point.''

Captain Henley's death in late 1903 would appear to have been crucial in the chronology of Galway golf, as his beneficial influence was missed. *The Irish Field* 5th March 1904 records: ''. . . owing to being turned off the links, the Galway club − till they acquire a new course − are like Mahomet's coffin. The club sustained a great loss in the death of their esteemed Captain a few months ago, although a worthy successor has been found in Commander Dundas R.N. He is without a 'command' till such time as the new links are discovered.'' Mr. Nolan's course continued to exist and various competition results were published in *The Irish Field* until his death in April 1907 after which the ''old'' course ceased to exist.

The ''new'' club's birth is documented in *The Irish Field* 13th May 1905 when a new committee under the Presidency of The Hon. Robert Dillon was elected at a meeting held in the Royal Hotel on 9th May. It is also related: ''. . . a committee which had accompanied Larkin, the Bray professional, that day over a promising new course on Mr. M. Lynch's property at Barna reported on the suitability of the ground.''

The Irish Field 19th April 1924 reported on the proposed purchase of Col. O'Hara's property at Salthill. Just one year later *The Irish Field* 9th May 1925 recorded: ''. . . the old course at Barna has been abandoned, nine new holes opened, of eighteen . . .''. In 1926 the course was extended to eighteen.

*See Co. Galway G.C.

GARRON TOWER, Co. Antrim.

The Irish Golfer 30th August 1899 announced the formal opening of this links by Col. McCalmont M.P. It had been the former residence of the Marchioness of Londonderry but had been recently converted into a golfers hotel. This links was listed, as Garron Point, in the *Golfing Annuals* from 1902 until 1910 but there is no mention in *The Irish Golfers Guide* 1910 or later Irish *Guide* books. The course was of nine holes varying in length from 85 yards to 440 yards.

GLENARIFF, Cushendal, Co. Antrim.

The Irish Field 10th December 1910 documents a meeting held in Cushendall for a proposed new golf course at Glengariff, no further detail is given. Later *Irish Guide* books do not list the club, however the records of the Golfing Union of Ireland reveal that the Glenariff Golf Club was affiliated on 9th September 1912.

GLENBEIGH, Co. Kerry.

There is difficulty in distinguishing the various place names associated with golf in the Glenbeigh and Dooks area. *The Sportsmans Holiday Guide* 1897 reports: ''There is a first rate course of nine holes here in connection with the Glenbeigh Hotel . . . the course is about one and a half miles around and commands beautiful views of mountain, sea and wood . . . Full particulars can be obtained from the manager of the hotel''.

It will be noted that the Caragh Lake course opened by the Great Southern and Western Railway in 1895 is listed, separately, in *The Sportsmans Holiday Guide* 1897 and that this would indicate the existence of two separate courses in the locality. There is no reference to Glenbeigh course in any *Golfing Annual* edition. Later, the name is listed in the *The Irish Golfing Guide* 1916 under Glenbeigh, Caragh and Dooks (1895) but this would appear to relate to the club previously listed as Caragh and Dooks.

*See Caragh Lakes and Dooks.

GOREY, Co. Wexford.

The Golfing Annual 1906/07 lists this club as instituted in October 1906 and gives the name of the first Captain as Maj. A. W. Richards; it further states: "The course of nine holes is on Creagh Hill and commands views of the Irish Sea." *The Irish Golfers Guide* 1910 records: ". . . a course that exists for local residents". A greater claim to fame is recorded in *The Irish Field* 7th February 1914 when Mrs. E. A. L. Turner was appointed Captain of the club (this must be one of the first such appointments in Irish golf).

The club is listed in *The Irish Golfing Guide* 1916 under the Captaincy of Dr. James Dwyer. However, the Tillage Legislation of 1918 must have had a drastic effect on the club as *The Irish Field* 23rd February 1924 records: "Gorey, I hear, is again forming a club. The last one died owing to the land being taken for agriculture".

The Irish Field 11th April 1927 recorded a visit by Lionel Hewson to the revived club "that was formerly existing in the town and is only in existence about two years . . . Mr. W. T. Williamson is Honorary Secretary, there is a two room clubhouse . . . the course is laid out in large fields adjoining the picturesque residence of Mrs. Lea Wilson". This revived club was listed in the *Irish Tourist Directory* 1937, its later history is unknown.

The earlier Newborough Golf Club, near Gorey, may have had a pre-1907 connection with this club.

*See Newborough.

GRANGE, Co. Dublin.
Instituted 1910.   Affiliated 1911.

An article in *The Irish Field* 25th November 1911 extols the wonders done in a year on "this pleasant course" and further states "the club is a direct result of the rather ill starred Kilmashogue Club". The Kilmashogue Club has been founded in 1908 as a proprietary club and had attracted, initially, quite a few members, however by November 1909 the club was in difficulty and some of the members began to look further afield.

In April 1910 a meeting was held at the home of Rev. Henry Cave and a decision was taken to form a new club. Mr. Douglas Rowley, the then owner of Marley Grange, agreed to lease ground for 21 years from July 1910 and so the club was born. The first President was Major Guinness (who is documented in *The Irish Field*

13th November 1909 as President of the aforementioned Kilmashogue Club). Tom Hood, the professional of the Royal Dublin G.C. laid out the course of nine holes which were ready for play in March 1911.

Following the purchase of Marley Grange in 1925 by R. K. Love the club were enabled to prepare a second nine holes which were opened later that year. In 1927 James Braid remodelled the eighteen holes for a fee of 35 guineas and the present-day course is basically his design.

GREENCASTLE, Co. Donegal.
Instituted 1892.   Affiliated 1896.

A lengthy article in *The Belfast Newsletter* 30th April 1895 extolled the pleasures of playing golf at this Donegal links: "The Belfast player wishing to pay Greencastle a visit should proceed to Bellarena, a station on the Belfast and Northern Counties line, a few miles beyond Coleraine and drive to Magilligan Point five miles distant where he can be ferried across in a few minutes to the first teeing ground. The course is on the property of Rev. T. McLelland who generously gives to the local club not only the use of the links but also that of a small clubhouse entirely rent free. At present the course covers about 60 acres but it is intended shortly to take in an additional twenty acres, so as to lengthen a few of the holes . . . players during a few days sport on a green that they will have almost to themselves could not be do better than to visit Greencastle where they will receive a hearty welcome from Captain Crosbie J.P. and other members of the club".

This club is first mentioned in *The Golfing Annual* 1896/97 which gives an institution date of 1893. There were 42 members at the time and the Captain was P. Crosbie, more than likely the Captain Crosbie mentioned above. The course was a nine-hole one. A set of accounts presented in 1893 for expenditure in 1892 is in the club's possession. This is evidence of a pre-1893 foundation date.

The Sportsmans Holiday Guide 1897 records that the average length of the holes was 350 yards and "there is a small but very comfortable clubhouse to which visitors are admitted". Later, *The Irish Golfing Guide* 1910 gives an institution date of 1892 and fours years later the *The Irish Golfing Guide* 1914 records that the course had now been extended to eighteen holes.

1892 is also given in *The Irish Golfing Guide* 1916 as the club's institution date and the course was still an eighteen-hole one at that time. However, *The Golfers Handbook* 1923 records the return to a nine-hole course, which was the result of compulsory tillage during the First World War.

GREENISLAND, Co. Antrim.
Instituted 1894.   Affiliated 1896.

The Belfast Newsletter 11th June 1894 reports as follows: "On Saturday last a number of local gentlemen met at the 'Knockagh' in connection with the formation of this new club and inspected the proposed links . . . it was resolved, at a meeting held subsequently — Mr. Berkeley D. Wise C.E. in the chair — to form the above club provided satisfactory arrangements can be made with the holders of the land".

Later, *The Sportsmans Holiday Guide* 1897 records: "The Greenisland club has its links close to Greenisland station . . . The putting greens mostly articifical, have been laid with seaside turf. There is an excellent clubhouse. The course, which consists of nine holes, commands fine views."

Modern-day environmentalists would be intrigued to know more concerning the seaside turf mentioned above. The "secret" is revealed in an article in *Irish Golf* April 1928 when "Pedes" reports: ". . . during 1894 Mr. Day's (Alex G. Day, professional at Royal Belfast) services were called upon to lay off the nine-hole course at Greenisland, through the instrumentality of Mr. B. D. Wise, Chief Engineer of the Northern Counties Railway, and Mr. Stuart Kelly . . . Mr. Wise provided all the material, labour and donkeys to haul the material from the station to the links. He also brought the turf for the construction of the greens all the way from Magilligan Strand, by rail free of cost to the club".

The club is first listed in *The Golfing Annual* 1895/96 where the President is named as Colonel McCalmont C.B. A total membership of 168 is recorded. A total of 120 lady members is given in the 1896/97 edition of this publication, for the first time.

*See Magilligan Links.

(Courtesy of the National Library of Ireland)

GREENORE, Co. Louth.
Instituted 1896. Affiliated 1896.

The Irish Times 23rd October 1896 records: "The London and North Western Railway have been for some time at work laying out a twelve-hole golf course and erecting a clubhouse at Greenore. On Saturday a meeting of the local residents of Dundalk, Newry and district was held in the Greenore Hotel for the purpose of forming a golf club to be called Greenore Golf Club . . . Lord Rathmore was elected President and Lords Kilmorey, Russell of Killowen with James Gray esq. were appointed Vice Presidents.

Later, *The Irish Field* 14th May 1910 tells us: "The mere building of the railway was not sufficient to bring golf, and it was not till Mr. G. L. Baillie, whose name is well known in golf club promotions, travelled on the line that the possibility of golf was noticed. Having seen the possibilities Mr. Baillie acted. The first circular convening a meeting to consider golf was signed by him and dated September 1896 . . . It was Mr. Baillie, as far as I (Lionel Hewson) can gather, who succeeded in increasing the course to 18 holes in 1897."

This club was owned and maintained by the London and North Western Railway Co. and throughout the golf publications of the 1890s and 1900s the railway hotel and golf course were widely advertised. Between July 1900 and October 1907 four lengthy articles on Greenore golfing holidays appeared in *Golf Illustrated*.

Ladies were admitted to the club from the beginning and *The Irish Times* 9th November 1898 reports the opening of a new ladies' clubhouse. The first Captain was Mr. R. Dempster of Newry.

GREYSTONES, Co. Wicklow.
Instituted 1895. Affiliated 1897.

The Irish Times 26th January 1895 reported: "A number of gentlemen interested in the now fashionable pastime of golfing have secured a fine piece of ground suitable for links on the Burnaby estate and they propose to form a club and with that object a meeting will be held at 7 o'clock this evening in the Grand Hotel, Greystones. Amongst those who are taking an active part in connection with the formation of the club are Dr. Norman Thompson, Delgany and Messrs. David J. Stewart, Bray; Robert Gore, Bray; Arthur Hughes, Greystones".

The ground for the club had been secured by the Grand Hotel (now La Touche) in a lease dated 5th June 1894. A further report in *The Irish Times* 13th March 1895 states: "This club has been formed under the most favourable auspices. There are about 100 original members. The links are very convenient to the station on the Burnaby estate, being a nine-hole course". Rt. Hon. Viscount Powerscourt was the first President of the club, the first Captain was Mr. D. J. Stewart and the official opening of the course took place on 8th June 1895. A report of the event was carried in *The Irish Times* five days later: ". . . as a result of the splendid weather which prevailed, larger numbers of ladies and gentlemen enjoyed themselves in witnessing the play . . . we observed that the Royal Dublin, Portrusk, Portmarnock, Foxrock and Aughnacloy golf clubs were represented in the open competition".

The club is regularly mentioned in the *The Irish Times* after this with open

competitions being held for prizes presented by the Dublin, Wicklow and Wexford Railway Co. In the age of steam, the railway company were conscious of increasing the traffic on their trains. In 1914 the course was extended to eighteen holes and despite the effect of World War One, which seriously affected the intake of green fees, the club survived very well. (*The Irish Golfing Guide* 1916 records a membership of 178 men and 176 ladies).

GROVE, THE, Belfast.

The Golfing Annual 1891/92 records the existence of this early private course: ". . . of the Private courses in Ireland The Grove, Belfast, the charming residence of W. B. Ritchie is *facile princeps*, the Saturday At Homes, with golf as the *Pieces de Resistance*, forming one of the social features of the Northern capital."

HEADFORT, Co. Meath.

Although the present golf club at Headfort was not founded until 1928, *The Irish Field* 19th August 1905 reported: "The Marquis of Headfort who has been greatly fascinated by the Royal and Ancient game . . . has a private links laid out at his Irish seat in Co. Meath". Later, in 1907 the Marquis is recorded as opening the new

Navan course for which he presented the Headfort Cup. In 1922 the Marquis became first President of the Killua Castle Club, he had been Captain of Co. Louth G.C. in 1908.

*See Killua Castle G.C. and Navan G.C.

HEATH, Co. Laois.
Instituted 1930. Affiliated 1931.

Current golfers at The Heath would be surprised to know that the seventh oldest golf club in Ireland was the Queen's County Heath G.C., founded in November 1889! The present club records its institution date as 1930, however this was a "revival" date, the second in its history. (Further detail on the institution of the original club is given in Chapter 5). *The Field* 29th August 1891 gives an account of a recent competition for the Emo Challenge Cup, presented by Viscountess Carlow and to be played for annually until won three times by the same person. This competition was open to lady and gentlemen members and was won for the first time by Captain Millington of the 4th Leinster Regiment (a Militia Battalion).

An entry for the club in *The Golfing Annual* 1892/93 names the President as the Earl of Portarlington, the Captain was Colonel Cosby, the Hon. Secretary was Captain H. Armstrong, Rathleash House, Portarlington. There 73 members and there were three ladies on the committee, including Lady Goring . . . "The course consists of nine holes situated on the Great Heath of Maryborough . . . luncheon may be procured at the green . . ." *The Golfing Annual* 1894/95 reported: ". . . there is an excellent clubhouse, originally the Grand Stand, when races were held on the Heath. The club day is Tuesday".

Later editions of *The Golfing Annual* continue to record the existence of the club up to 1910, Rev. J. J. Kearney was listed as Hon. Secretary in that year. *The Irish Golfing Guide* 1910 lists Maryboro Golf Club (the pre-Treaty name for Portlaoise) and gives an institution date of 1903. Captain for 1910 was Rev. J. J. Kearney C.C. and the Hon. Secretary was Richard Bull of Rockview. This reverend gentleman proves the continuous link with the old Queens Co. Heath club. Maryboro G.C. is documented in *The Irish Golf Guides* 1911 to 1916 with the same officers and committee. Its subsequent demise is unrecorded.

The present club was formed in 1930 and the location of its clubhouse is in exactly the same position as the old Grand Stand of 1889!

HELEN'S BAY, Co. Down.
Instituted 1896. Affiliated 1897.

This club is first listed in *The Golfing Annual* 1896/97 which gives an institution date of 1st April 1896 and states: "The course extends over some 60 acres of park land rented from the Marquis of Dufferin and is bounded on the north by the sea. The clubhouse is close to the Helen's Bay Station".

The earliest minute books of the club only exist from January 1906, which makes life difficult for the historian. Luckily *The Irish Field* 12th June 1909 carried an article on the origins of the club: "The club was formed in 1895 [sic] and was originally intended as an attraction and recreation for the local residents in what was formerly known as 'Clandeboy' and it was never expected to have more than 30 or 40 members at the most. However the idea was enthusiastically supported by all and sundry, to the surprise of the promoters the list went on increasing until over 150 were on the roll. The late Marquis of Dufferin and Ava was a most generous supporter of the club from its inception and it was largely through his kindness in granting use of land etc. that the promoters were enabled to carry out their scheme . . . Col. Sharman Crawford whose beautiful estate immediately adjoins the links also gives his warm support and the late Mr. G. Herbert Brown became first Captain''.

An article in *The Irish Golfer* 14th March 1900 recorded that G. Herbert Brown was Captain for the first three years of the club's existence, from 1896. He was a key figure in the birth of the club, which has remained unchanged as a nine-hole course at the same location near Bangor.

HERMITAGE, Co. Dublin.
Instituted 1905.   Affiliated 1906.

When this club was first mentioned in *The Irish Times* 5th December 1905 it was named as County Dublin Golf Club, however after objections from the Royal Dublin Golf Club the name was changed to Hermitage in 1906. The original title "might have caused confusion". One other unfortunate memory of its first year of existence was the untimely death of the founding Captain, Mr. James Walsh, which is documented in *The Irish Field* 20th October 1906.

The origins of the club can be dated to 1904 when a group of Lucan Golf Club members decided to form a club of their own and took some land at Ballydowd, close to the present course. Nine holes were laid out but in 1905 when the club wanted to acquire more land they were unable to come to an agreement with the landlord. One of the Ballydowd members was Mr. James Crozier and, when approached, he agreed to let his land, in addition to allowing use of a clubhouse.

Nine holes were laid out initially by James McKenna, the professional at Carrick-mines, and in 1907 the course was extended to eighteen. By 1914 the course had matured to such a degree that the Golfing Union of Ireland selected Hermitage as venue for the Irish Native Amateur (Close) Championship. Lionel Munn had the impressive margin of 10 and 8 in the 36-hole final against the Earl of Annesley. (The unfortunate Earl, from the Co. Down family, was killed in action three months later).

During the First World War the old mansion was given over by Mr. Crozier for use as a convalescent home by disabled soldiers. Play continued on the course with some difficulties, at times, caused by the erratic behaviour of some of the "visitors". There was pressure for a period to hand over some of the course for tillage under the emergency legislation of the period. Luckily the club survived unscathed.

HOLYWOOD, Co. Down.
Instituted 1904.   Affiliated 1904.

When the Royal Belfast Golf Club was founded in 1881 the site of its first course was Kinnegar, Holywood. By 1892 the club were forced to move on account of the course being used for its primary purpose as a military rifle range. It was to be another twelve years before golf was again played in the Holywood area.

The Irish Field 6th January 1912 records that the club was founded in 1904 by Mr. J. K. Stephen (Captain 1912) with other local gentlemen who made arrangements with Mr. Henry Harrison the ground landlord. Mr. Harold Reade (the Irish Close Champion 1897, 1899 and 1903) and C. S. Butchart (professional at Royal Co. Down) laid out the original course. The first Captain was Mr. H. L. Garrett who was one of the prime movers in the founding of the club. A lengthy account of the club's first annual general meeting was carried by *The Belfast Newsletter* 1st August 1905 which recorded a total of 212 members and an income surplus of £12.15 shillings. A very successful first year.

In March 1923 the club was formed into a limited company and bought some extra ground for £6,000, a further nine holes were laid out making an eighteen-hole course for the first time. In addition a new clubhouse was built, which was burned down in October 1945. Unfortunately, as a result of this fire many of the club's early records were destroyed.

HOLYWOOD LADIES G.C., Co. Down.

In the Autumn of 1887 Miss C. E. McGee visited the Kinnegar, Holywood, which was home to the Royal Belfast Golf Club. She had been invited by Dr. William F. Collier, one of the founder members and was amazed to see the sight of a lady playing golf. The lady in question was Mrs. Wright, wife of a Captain in the Gordon Highlanders, then stationed in Belfast.

Miss McGee later recorded: "We were introduced and she inspired me with a wish to play the game". (See Chapter 9 re first lady golfer in Ireland). This pioneering Ulster lady, who was to become the first Honorary Secretary of the Holywood Ladies Golf club, the first such club in Ireland, recorded her memories in a letter to Miss Leah Garratt on the occasion of the Royal Belfast Ladies Golf Club's 25th anniversary in 1913. As a result of Miss McGee's enthusiasm a meeting was held in the Autumn of 1888 in the home of Mrs. R. Young, Hillbrook, Holywood and a committee was formed. The *Royal Belfast G.C. Centenary Book* tells the story: "With Mrs. Young as Hon. Treasurer and myself as Hon. Secretary the first meeting of Holywood Ladies Golf Club was held. We received much kindness and encouragement from some members of Royal Belfast Golf Club, especially from Mr. Henry Gregg and Mr. Henry Herdman, the Hon. Secretary, who gave us valuable help and information. Needless to say it was uphill work as there were many prejudices in those days regarding 'petticoats on the links' as we were dubbed by some opposing members. Club rules, of which we were ignorant, had to be studied and I always think it was the strict observance of those rules which contributed to the success of our undertaking and to the winning over of those who thought a ladies' club impossible . . ."

At that time the ladies of the Holywood Ladies Club had use of the Kinnegar course on certain days. When the Royal Belfast Golf Club moved to its next home at Carnalea in 1892, the ladies' club followed and thereafter was known as the Royal Belfast Ladies Golf Club.

HOWTH, Co. Dublin.
Instituted 1911.   Affiliated 1919.

The Irish Field 12th March 1910, under the heading "Golf On The Hill Of Howth", documented a proposal for a new course and Lionel Hewson reported that he had a map in front of him, by Johnnie McKenna. Hewson was critical of the intended name of Kilrock G.C. Later, *The Irish Field* 19th November 1910 reported that the project had languished during the Summer but a new course was to be laid out and the names of a provisional committee headed by Mr. Gaisford St. Laurence and Rt. Hon. Justice Boyd are given. Finally, *The Irish Golfing Guide* 1911 states: "A course has been chosen on the Hill of Howth and Mr. Barcroft (Secretary of Royal Dublin G.C.) has laid out nine sporting holes".

This first course was laid out as a proprietorial venture by Mr. Butson, a former employee of the Jameson family and a keen golfer. Members were invited to join at an annual fee of 2 guineas. Unfortunately, *The Irish Golfing Guides* 1912, 1914 and 1916 do not contain any entries relating to the club, whose first Captain, Mr. Eddie Stuart was elected in 1916. However, *The Irish Field* 24th April 1915 recorded that the affiliation of Howth G.C. to the G.U.I. was on the agenda for a meeting of the Leinster Branch.

Howth Golf Club bought out Mr. Butson's interest in 1918 and in 1926 the club employed James Braid (winner of the British Open on five occasions) to plan an extra nine holes. His fee was 28 guineas! Mr. William T. Cosgrave, the then president of the executive council, opened the additional nine holes in June 1929.

INCHYDONEY, Clonakilty, Co. Cork.

A club with the same name is listed in *The Irish Golfers Blue Book* 1939, with an institution date of 1932. The course of nine holes "was laid out by Tom Travers of Dun Laoghaire. The clubhouse is situated 300 yards from Inchydoney Hotel". The latter date mentioned was probably a revival date and most probably the course was connected to the hotel.

The club is listed in the *Golfing Union of Ireland Yearbook* until 1946, its subsequent history is unknown.

*See Clonakilty.

ISLAND, Malahide, Co. Dublin.
Instituted 1891.   Affiliated 1901.

Mystery surrounds the origins of golf on the Island, Malahide and various theories have been advanced regarding the common factor which led a number of gentlemen to develop a course at this location. The earliest mention of the Island in the golfing journals of the day was carried in *The Sportsmans Holiday Guide* 1897: "The links which are reached by a ferry boat are considered to be the best natural links in the Province of Leinster. The turf is excellent and affords great scope for brassey play. The greens are without exception large and natural. This is an eighteen-hole course and the distance round is about three miles."

A visit by the famous golfer Harold Hilton (winner of the British Open, as an amateur, in 1897) is documented in *The Irish Times* 14th May 1902. He is quoted as saying ". . . truly interesting golf . . . with money spent on the green there is the making of one of the finest links in the Kingdom . . . The present course, sporting and interesting though it be is but the crudest attempt at a golf course when compared with the ideal course which a Tom Morris or Willie Park would see in and lay out upon the 'Island' . . ."

Part of the reason for the poor state of the course in 1902 was the way in which the club was run by the original founders. A detailed article in *Irish Life* 8th September 1916 reported: ". . . not only is the course unique but the constitution of the club is also unique. The actual members are a few gentlemen who act as a sort of permanent committee . . . these gentlemen founded the club in 1891 and all the others who play regularly on the Island are associates. The number of associates are 150 gentlemen and an equal number of ladies . . . associates are proposed and seconded in the usual way and elected once a year. But the committee exercise the right of asking any associate not to renew his subscription. Thus we find an absence of the grumbling and protesting which we so often find in many golf clubs."

The Golfing Annual 1900/01 lists the club for the first time and gives an institution date of 1892, however, the later *Irish Golf Guides* of 1910 to 1916 give 1891. This date is also given in a comprehensive article on the club in *The Irish Field* 8th May 1926 which finally reveals the common bond which had led to the founding of the club: "The Island is one of the oldest golf clubs in Ireland, having been formed in 1891. At the time there was no such thing at Dollymount as Sunday golf although many of the the members of Royal Dublin were not adverse to playing the game on the Sabbath; and thus it was decided by some of the latter that the best way to solve the difficulty would be to form a golf club where the game would be permitted on Sunday.

To the enterprise of ten men we owe the inception of 'The Island' club — Messrs. James. R. Bristowe, J. R. Law, J. R. Blood, J. H. Barrington, Thos. Stewart, H. J. Daly, Daniel Martin Wilson, W. S. Hayes, Godfrey Fergusson and David T. Moore . . .".

An entry in *Irish Golf* March 1952 noted the handing over of the affairs of the club to the members: "The Island Golf Club Malahide syndicated for the last fifty years, will soon pass into the hands of a council elected by the associate members, who will become full members . . . This was decided at a meeting in Dublin recently . . . The President will be Lord Talbot De Malahide; Captain, Norman Chance; Hon. Sec., George Watson . . ." Since that date the course has been transformed into one of the finest links in the country.

KENMARE, Co. Kerry.
Instituted 1903.   Affiliated 1922.

Writing in *Irish Golf* February 1947, Lionel Hewson stated: "Once upon a time somewhere down the beginning of this troubled century, a party of enthusiasts started the Kenmare club. They were Rupert, Colomb, Henry Perceval Maxwell, Stephen O'Brien Corkery, J. Minhear, Tom Taylor, 'Michael D' and a few more including the late Percy Joy. We got the necessary ground for some absurdly cheap rent from the Lansdowne estate and went ahead."

The *Irish Golfer* 9th November 1904 records that the club came into existence on 10th October 1903 and *The Golfing Annual* 1903/04 gives the Hon. Secretary's name as P. Joy . . . "the course of nine holes is close to the Southern Hotel". Mr. Joy was obviously a central figure as *The Irish Times* 16th November 1905 reports: ". . . owing to his transfer elsewhere, Mr. Joy D.I., R.I.C., has just relinquished the Hon. Secretaryship and at a meeting of the club a vote of thanks was passed emphasising the gratitude Kenmare owes to him for having instituted the club".

KILBRITTAIN, Bandon, Co. Cork.
*See Atlantic G.C.

KILKEE, Co. Clare.
Instituted 1896.   Affiliated 1910.

The origins of golf at Kilkee are vague and the present club claims an institution date of 1889. Most of the club's earlier records have not survived and there is no direct documentary evidence for this date apart from a reference in *The Irish Golfer* 18th October 1899. In the article, which gives biographical material on Mr. Alexander Shaw (founder of Limerick and Lahinch), it is stated: ". . . some ten years ago Mr. Shaw might have been seen learning the alphabet of golf on the breezy down of Kilkee, under the tuition of Mr. Douglas Driver of Dallar . . ."

The next reference to golf at Kilkee is in an article in *The Limerick Chronicle* 17th September 1892 entitled "Golf At Kilkee" which states: "The first golf tournament on these links took place on 12th and 13th inst:

First Day	A. McLeod	Nenagh	104-4-100
	Dr. Watson	Kilkee	10-Scr-104
Second Day	Mr. Cyril Andrews		120-25-95
	Mr. Francis	(Visitor)	106-3-103

(a list of other competitors follows) . . . Mr. A. W. Shaw was umpire and Wm. Fitzgerald was Treasurer and Secretary and the course was 16 holes". (The above was kindly supplied by Mr. Tom Lillis, Hon. Secretary, Kilkee G.C.).

It can be seen that Alexander Shaw was active in this golf competition at Kilkee; in *The Irish Golfer* article quoted above it is also stated: "The Limerick Golf Club, which played in the Winter over the racecourse and in the Summer over the downs of Kilkee, was founded in 1891 . . . it was soon found difficult during the Summer months, when the racecourse was heavy with grass, to keep up the play of the club at the distance of Kilkee and it was decided to find some seaside course nearer

Limerick.'' Kilkee, then, was the earliest Summer abode of the Limerick golfers (before they found Lahinch), and *The Limerick Chronicle* article above would appear to document one of their competition days there. There is no doubt that Kilkee golfers will dispute those findings and adhere to their claim of a local origin for the game.

For the first time, *The Golfing Annual* 1895/96 (published April 1896) recorded: ''. . . a nine-hole course, with good bunkers and hazards, has been laid out along the cliffs across the Bay from Kilkee . . .'' No other detail is given and there is no mention of a club. *The Irish Times* 28th August 1895 carries the result of a golf competition at Kilkee (without mention of a club) ''held during the course of the week in the West End links which have undergone large and extensive improvement''. These entries would indicate that golf had continued at Kilkee after the departure of the Limerick golfers and the following year the first club was formed, *The Sportsmans Holiday Guide* 1897 recorded: ''The club has only recently been formed (May 1896) and the course was laid out last June . . . a nine-hole one and is situated along the cliffs''.

This club would appear to have succumbed after a few years as *The Irish Times* 15th May 1903 reported: ''. . . a new club has been formed, of which Rev. R. S. S. Ross Lewin is Hon. Secretary and a new course has been laid out, conserving the best features of the old''. For thirty-four years the club remained at this site until the present course at East End was chosen.

*See Lahinch G.C. and Nenagh G.C.

KILKENNY, Co. Kilkenny.
Instituted 1896.   Affiliated 1910.

Most Kilkenny golfers would be unaware that the club was first formed in 1896, all recent documentation on the club's age has indicated 1901 as the institution date. However *The Irish Times* 6th April 1896 carries a full account of the foundation: ''This newly formed club was opened on Thursday last (2nd April) by E. Smithwick esq. J.P. in the presence of a large number of members and friends. The links is a nine-hole one and difficulties are varied. The limit of membership has already been reached and candidates are now waiting for vacancies. Much of the success of the club is due to Mr. Smithwick (whose name is a household word) who gave the ground free for the promotion of a links. Mr. C. J. Power on behalf of the members of the club heartily thanked Mr. Smithwick for his kindness and Mr. Smithwick, having replied, hit off the first ball and declared the links open.''

The location of the course is given in *The Golfers Guide* 1897 as ''Kelcrune'' . . . ''There is no clubhouse and headquarters is in town at the Victoria Hotel''. *The Golfing Annual* 1896/87 stated: ''The course of nine holes, varying in length from 120 to 350 yards, is about a mile and a half from Kilkenny Station''. The course was on the land of Mr. E. Smithwick who is listed as Vice President, the President being the Marquis of Ormonde and the Captain was J. J. Smithwick. Without doubt there was a strong local brewery interest in the club.

Subsequent *Golfing Annuals* continue to list the club up to 1907, however *The Irish Field* 21st August 1909 carries a full article on the club and, giving 1901 as the club institution date, stated: "Golf in Kilkenny owes much to the exertions of Mr. J. J. O'Connell who learned the game on the capital course at Dooks . . . the first course was opened in 1901 at Richview, but the great difficulty was the rich grassy nature of the ground. This course was given up in 1902 and ground at Garrinagreene was chosen for a new one. Unfortunately, this was available only in Winter months . . . in the Spring of 1908 a general feeling prevailed that a permanent all the year round course should be found. A keen Kilkenny golfer, Mr. James Smithwick came forward and offered the present excellent course on very liberal terms. the course is at Kilcrene Lodge about one mile from the station . . .''.

The Irish Field 1st November 1924 recorded the next move: "Up till this year Kilkenny only had a course available in the Winter months. The club now has a nine-hole course available all the year round. . . . The course is only (of) nine holes, laid out by Mr. Barcroft, and was opened last Spring. This was the present course at Newtown, which was extended to eighteen holes in 1938.

Why *The Irish Field* of 1909 failed to uncover the 1896 origins of the club must remain a mystery, the Smithwick connection had remained from the earliest years. This would be an example of the pitfalls which await researchers into early golf club history.

KILLAHORA, Co. Cork.

The Irish Golfers Guide 1910 lists this club as "extinct", however there would not appear to have been a Killahora club as such. In *The Sportsmans Holiday Guide* 1897 the location for the Cork Golf Club is given as Killahora ". . . within 10 minutes walk of Queenstown Junction Station . . . the green is only open for play during Winter months, the grass being too long in the Summer". In 1898 Cork Golf Club moved to its present location at Little Island, and, it would appear that golf became extinct at Killahora after that.

KILLALOE, Co. Clare.

The first mention of golf at this location is given in *The Irish Golfer* 2nd May 1900: "In addition to the attraction of fishing, The Shannon Lake Steamers Co. have laid out golf links on the shores of Lough Derg on which the visitors to this company's new Lakeside Hotel are entitled to play free". A club is listed in *The Golfing Annual* 1902/03, without giving a foundation date, the Hon. Secretary's name is listed as R. Newman, Provincial Bank, Killaloe. Further, the same *Annual* lists the club as affiliated to the Golfing Union of Ireland.

The Golfing Annual 1905/06 gives an institution date of 1901. Later, *The Irish Golfing Guide* 1916 lists the club and, giving 1900 as the institution date, states "no entrance fee during continuance of war". What happened to this club afterwards is not known.

KILLARNEY, Co. Kerry.
Instituted 1893.   Affiliated 1909.

Nature's bounty has always been acknowledged when the name of Killarney is mentioned and this is specially true when knowledgeable golfers visit the area. In *The Irish Times* 27th May 1894 a letter written by Walter Butler, Captain of the club, is reproduced. The letter had recently appeared in the magazine *Golf*: "Sir, It may be of interest to some of your readers to know that in addition to the enchanting scenery of Killarney the visitor who has the good fortune to be a golfer can now have all the delights of 'Ye Royal and Ancient Game' on capital links — The Earl of Kenmare has given the use of his Deer Park and has become President of the local club, which is established. There is ample space in this beautiful park for a course of eighteen holes but the committee are working prudently and are endeavouring to make the teeing grounds and putting greens for nine holes as perfect as possible . . . the view from the putting green on Turret Hill is of the most superb imaginable. No matter how exciting the match there are few who do not pause to glance around at the glorious prospect — the distant mountains encircling the glittering lakes — and to inhale the fresh breeze straight up from the sea."

The club is first mentioned in *The Golfing Annual* 1893/94 which gives an institution date of December 1893. Forty members had joined the club in its first year at an annual subscription of ten shillings. Three years later *The Irish Times* 13th January 1896 reports: "Lord Kenmare gave permission to have the grass cut right throughout the links and not only that but lent a large pair horsemower for the purpose . . . the grass is now quite close except for the first 120 yards from each tee".

An article by Lionel Hewson in *The Irish Field* 10th October 1908 gives an insight into the foundation of the club; however, for the first time an institution date of 1891 is given which is at variance with entries in all previous golf guidebooks. The article stated: "Though the present club was formed in 1891 there had for a long time been a good deal of promiscuous golf played about Killarney. Mr. W. Butler of the Munster and Leinster Bank used to be a prime mover in the old days. Others who were connected with the early days of Killarney golf were Miss O'Connell (now Lady Tucker), D. M. Moriarty, the brothers Downing, Major Hewson and residents who, alas, have left the Killarney District."

In the following year *The Irish Field* 2nd October 1909 carries the news that Killarney was to be extended to eighteen holes thanks, once again, to the generosity of the Earl of Kenmare: ". . . his son Lord Castlerosse is already a young player of much promise". Work on the enlarged course was completed in September 1910 and in November, that year, Willie Park visited to give advice on bunkering and other matters. In the *The Irish Golfing Guide* 1916, the club Hon. Secretary reports that "Park was astonished at the sandy nature of the soil, quite expecting to find a clay or mud course so far inland. The trueness of the greens, with their sea links grass especially took his fancy. He predicts a great future for the Killarney links."

1936 was an historic year in the development of the club when, due to a number of circumstances, the committee found themselves looking for a new location for their course. Lord Castlerosse, mentioned above, was a keen golfer. A rotund boisterous character, he had been writing a widely read gossip column in one of the major London newspapers. He readily agreed that the Western Demesne could be used for the new golf course and took an active interest in the club. Under his direction the Killarney Golf Club Ltd. was formed, Sir Guy Campbell and Henry Longhurst advised and the new course was officially opened on 3rd October 1939, one of the gems of international golf. In 1971 an additional eighteen holes was opened which combined elements of the old course.

KILLINEY, Co. Dublin.
Instituted 1902.   Affiliated 1904.

An article in *The Irish Golfer* 4th May 1904 documented the origins of this club: "In the summer of 1902 Capt. E. P. Stewart, Mr. George Cashin and Mr. George F. Stewart took up the idea of forming a golf club at Killiney and having inspected a tract of land, had it inspected by James McKenna of Carrickmines Golf Club, who pronounced it well suited for the purpose. These gentlemen, who are the trustees of the club, then secured a lease of the ground, and convened a meeting of the residents to start the project: this was done by 49 gentlemen forming a guarantee fund for three years, they becoming the original members of the club. The next step was the laying out of the course by J. McKenna . . . as possession could not be obtained till the Winter, the course was not ready to be opened till Easter Monday of 1903, but on that day a fairly playable course was started with . . .".

The same article recorded a 1904 membership of 188 members and 169 lady associates, besides juvenile and temporary members. Later, World War One had a dramatic effect on the club and *Irish Life* 11th May 1917 reported: "This club, being composed largely of military and professional men was very seriously affected by the War. It cetainly showed distinct evidence of neglect when I was there last Summer . . . Recently a circular was sent to members which suggested that the only course open to members was to close down or allow the club to continue as a proprietorial concern or increase the subscription to four guineas for ten years . . . about fifty members responded to this appeal."

The Irish Field 5th April 1924 recorded the final important development: "The club has bought its course and can be congratulated on its wisdom. This proceeding of course did away with the banning of Sunday golf". The first Secretary of the club was Mr. S. Martin Ashlin who built himself a house beside the course, to give full attention to the business of the club.

KILLORGLIN, Co. Kerry.

A golf course existed at this town in the mid 1890s; it is documented in *The Sportsmans Holiday Guide* 1897 which states: "There is a nine-hole course here which is open to visitors at any of the hotels. The course is considered to be a very sporting one".

It would seem that this course was a commercial enterprise which does not appear to have survived for long. There is no mention of the course in any of the guide books.

KILLUA CASTLE, Co. Meath.

The Irish Times 3rd June 1922 carries a report on the institution of this club which was "seven miles from Kells and three from Athboy . . . the membership roll is close to two hundred members. The President of the club is the Marquis of Headfort . . . He drove the first ball on Wednesday. Mr. S. B. Murray is Captain and Mr. C. Y. Spratt is Hon. Secretary . . . Mr. Hackett is the owner of the land . . .''.

Affiliation to the Golfing Union of Ireland took place in 1923. A listing for the club appears in Golfing Union of Ireland yearbooks until 1940 but there is no entry for the club from 1942 onwards. It would appear that the club succumbed during the war years.

KILLYLEAGH, Co. Down.

*See Dufferin Golf Club.

KILLYMOON, Cookstown, Co. Tyrone.
Instituted 1890. Affiliated 1891.

Some detail on the earliest mention of golf in the Cookstown area is given in Chapter 5. It can be seen that Mr. H. Adair was a prime figure at that time. For the first time a "Killymoon" Ladies Golf Club is listed in *The Golfing Annual* 1890/91: "no particulars forthcoming". The club's entry in *The Golfing Annual* 1892/93 gives 1st April 1890 as the date of institution, the President was Mervyn S. T. Moutray, the Captain was J. B. Gunning Moire and H. Adair is listed as a committee member: "There are two courses, each of nine holes for ladies and gentlemen, situated in the park of Killymoon Castle, one mile from Cookstown". *The Belfast Newsletter* 26th February 1891 recorded a club competition which "took place in the beautiful demesne of Killymoon, which is placed at the disposal of this flourishing young club by its owner Mr. Moutray".

Just nine months later Hugh Adair and A. W. Gaussen represented the club at the founding meeting of the Golfing Union of Ireland. In this regard the club holds an honoured place in Irish golf history. It is also of historical significance that Hugh Adair, the club's founder, instituted a ladies' open scratch medal competition just a year after the foundation of the club. *The Belfast Newsletter* 14th May 1891 recorded the first competition, open to "All Ireland". There were 14 entries from Dungannon, Hollywood, Aughnacloy and Killymoon and the winner was Miss Garratt from Hollywood (Royal Belfast). This was the first such open ladies' competition in Irish golf history. Later, Rhona Adair, a daughter of the founder, became the second Irish winner of the Ladies British Amateur Championship, in 1900. May Hezlet and Rhona were to dominate ladies' international golf for over ten years before World War One.

The club has never changed location from its institution, however an article in *The Belfast Newsletter* 27th June 1894 reported: "The Cookstown Golf Club, which was established this season, has removed to new links, the old ground being found unsuitable. An extensive grazing farm of 150 acres close to the town has been secured and the links will soon be opened by the Captain, Mr. Hugh Adair J.P."

This intriguing entry adds mystery to the chronology of Killymoon golf. Was there a move to a new location for a period? Was a second club founded in 1894?

In 1920/21, the "old nine" of the course was laid out by John Adair, a grandson of the founder, thus the Adair connection with the club continues to the present day.

KILMASHOGUE, Rathfarnham, Co. Dublin.

The Irish Field 26th June 1908 reported: "It is only the other day so to speak that Kilmashogue club came into being and it owes its origins to the fact that Mr. O'Brien Butler, the well known Irish composer, finding he had a portion of his estate ideally situated for an inland golf course . . . set about at once to have the land transformed into one. He sought the willing advice of Mr. Pickeman of Portmarnock". The club was affiliated to the Golfing Union of Ireland in September 1909, however, the club was in difficulty at this time. An article in *The Irish Field* 13th November 1909 commented on proprietary clubs not being successful, lacking the esprit de corps of private clubs. In addition the club was relatively inaccessible, *The Irish Golfers Guide* 1910 stated the course "is situated about three miles from Rathfarnham". A year later *The Irish Golfers Guide* 1911 reported that there were 80 men and 35 lady members: "It started as a proprietary club but is now in the hands of an elected committee".

There is no further mention of the club in later guide books and an article in *The Irish Field* 25th November 1911 reported that the new Grange Golf Club had been founded "as a direct result of the rather ill starred Kilmashogue club".

*See Grange Golf Club.

KILREA, Co. Derry.
Instituted 1920.   Affiliated 1920.

Golfing Union of Ireland records reveal an affiliation date of 1920 for this club, which would also appear to have been its year of institution. *The Golfers Handbook* 1923 listed nine holes for the club, ¼ mile from Kilrea station. The Joint Hon. Secretaries were W. H. Gracey and T. C. McKeag.

It would appear that the club may have ceased to function for a period after this. Golfing Union of Ireland records list an application for the club for reaffiliation on 28th February 1953.

KILWAUGHTER CASTLE PARK, Larne, Co. Antrim.

The Irish Golfer 4th April 1900 carries an article on Larne Golf Club in which it is stated: "Prior to this date (1894) a few ardent sporting spirits enjoyed the privilege of playing over the private links at Kilwaughter Castle Park, by consent of the late Mr. T. J. Galt Smith".

KINGS COUNTY AND ORMONDE, Birr, Co. Offaly.
Instituted 1893.   Affiliated 1912.

This club is first listed in *The Golfing Annual* 1895/96 which gives an institution date of 1894. The President of the club was the Earl of Rosse, Mr. J. E. Dykes was Captain and there were 90 members; Mrs. W. K. Marshall was the Honorary Secretary. Further details were: "The course of nine holes, varying in length from 170 yards to 520 yards, is laid out at Baronne Court, about two and a half miles from Parsonstown (sic). The hazards consist of walls, hedges, streams and rocks. The grass is short both in Summer and Winter, and the turf is good throughout . . . a new clubhouse is in process of construction . . ."

An article in *The Irish Times* 26th October 1894 gave details of the first annual general meeting of the club: "The Earl of Rosse K.P., H.M.C. as President of this flourishing club, presided at its first annual meeting in Dooleys Hotel, Birr on Thursday. There was a large attendance of members. Mrs. N. K. Marshall of Baronne Court submitted the report for the past year . . . the last named lady, on whose grounds the links are situated was reelected Hon. Secretary and accorded a voted of thanks for the active interest she has taken in promoting the club's interest. A vote of thanks to Lord Rosse for presiding terminated the proceedings".

It is obvious from the above article that the club had been in existence since 1893, unfortunately the early records of this club (now known as Birr Golf Club) and its title deeds have been lost. Later *Golfing Annuals* give a foundation date of September 1893. *The Irish Golfing Guide* 1911 records a nine-hole course "within two miles of Birr Station". *The Irish Golfing Guide* 1914 records an eighteen-hole course "situated at the Glenns, Birr". From this evidence it would appear that the club moved to its present location between 1911 and 1914, at which time it also changed its name to Birr Golf Club.

*See Birr G.C.

KINGSTOWN, Co. Dublin.

*See Dun Laoghaire.

KINSALE, Co. Cork.
Instituted 1897.   Affiliated 1912.

Golf was first played at Kinsale by the 2nd Battalion Kings Own Borderers early in 1883 (see Chapter 5). This was a military club, which had no geographical roots other than the current location of that Regiment. Documentation of this Regiment's golfing exploits is carried in *The Field* 16th June 1883 which records that their links was located at the "Musketry Camp" about four miles from Kinsale, where an eight-hole course was laid out. The Regiment was stationed at Kinsale from April 1883 to Autumn 1884, when it transferred to Dublin.

There is no further record of golf at Kinsale until an entry in *The Sportsmans Holiday Guide* 1897 recorded: "The Kinsale Golf Club links are situated on the glacis at Charles Fort and command extensive views of the Atlantic, Kinsale Harbour and town, the Royal Naval Reserve Battery etc. The course is one of nine holes and is about one mile in circuit. There is no club house but visitors will be able to supply all requirements at the sign of the Kinsale Arms Hotel. Visitors wishing to avail themselves of the course must be introduced by a member of the club. Secretary Captain Shattock R.A., Charles Fort, Kinsale.''

This entry is most interesting from a number of points. The Secretary was a Captain of the Royal Artillery (R.A.) who would have been a member of the garrison. The description of the course would categorise it with similar arrangements in the fortifications at Malta and Athlone (see Athlone). An institution date for the club is not given in the above entry, which therefore must remain a tantalising mystery until further evidence is uncovered.

There is no mention of this early Kinsale club in any of the *Golfing Annuals* and *The Irish Golf Guides* 1910 to 1916 do not list any details of a golf club there. Unfortunately, the minute books of the present club only extend to 1932, which leaves the origins of the club obscure. The present club claims an institution date of 1912 for their nine holes at Ringenane, however there is little doubt that this club's origins certainly go back to 1897.

*See Chapter 5.

KIRKISTOWN CASTLE, Co. Down.
Instituted 1902.   Affiliated 1903.

Unfortunately, this club does not possess its early records, a situation common to many other Irish golf clubs. The club tradition credits the foundation of the club to seven gentlemen from Portaferry.

The first entry relating to Kirkistown Castle Golf Club appears in *The Golfing Annual* 1903/04 which gives an institution date of 3rd September 1902. J. Greer is listed as the Captain and the Hon. Secretary was F. M. Allen of Nunsquarter, Kirkcubbin, Co. Down. There were 56 members who paid an entrance fee of £1.1 shilling and a similar sum as annual subscription. The *Guide* also states: "The course of nine holes, at Kirkistown is about four miles from Portaferry, where there is a hotel. The course commands lovely views of the Isle of Man, Mull of Galloway etc. and is an excellent seaside green.''

The course was extended to eighteen holes in 1929.

KNOCK, Belfast, Co. Down.
Instituted 1895.   Affiliated 1896.

The Belfast Newsletter 31st December 1894 reported: "On Saturday last a meeting of gentlemen interested in the formation of a golf club at the Knock was held in the lecture hall adjoining Dundelea Presbyterian Church . . . on the motion of Mr. Peddie seconded by Mr. Todd, Mr. Hanna was called to the chair and he explained they were met for the purpose of seeing if a golf club could be formed at the Knock . . . Dr. King Kerr said the grounds could be had for £77 per annum. Mr. Bailey said the grounds could be made ready for playing for about £26. On the motion of Mr. Peddie, seconded by Mr. Buchanan, it was unanimously agreed to form a club . . . Dr. King Kerr, Messrs. Todd, Peddie, Malcolm and Buchanan were appointed as committee to negotiate for the renting of the ground and drafting of rules. Dr. King Kerr was appointed Secretary and Mr. Hanna Treasurer. It is expected that the links will be in order for playing from about the end of January . . .''

There is no doubt, from the above account, that the institution date of this club was December 1894; however *The Golfing Annual* 1895/96 and all subsequent editions list May 1895. *The Sportsmans Holiday Guide* 1897 states: "The Knock Golf Club have their links on the shores of Belfast Lough, three miles (10 minutes by train) from Belfast. The course of nine holes is about a mile and half around, the lengths of the holes varying from 100 to 350 yards . . . there is a nice pavilion . . .''

Knock's first course was located at Cherryvalley beside Knock Railway Station. An article in *The Irish Golfer* 14th February 1900 documented an early move for the club: "The club was formed in 1895 when the golf fever in Ulster was at its height and its formation was chiefly due to the popular Honorary Secretary Dr. King Kerr along with the assistance of Mr. R. Webb (uncle to the famous golfing family), Mr. Peddie, Mr. Todd, Mr. Buchanan and Mr. Calder, who along with the advice of Mr. Baillie . . . laid off the old course . . . The opening ceremony of the club under Mr. Webb's Captaincy, was a memorable one as it was the largest gathering of golfers ever held at a junction of its kind in Ireland. . . . The club's enjoyment of this pretty course was not of long duration, for in less than three years the committee were compelled to prospect for pastures new, owing to the ground being taken for building purposes; However . . . the new links is situated only ten minutes walk from Knock Station . . . and is situated in a delightul spot.''

Again, 1895 is given in the above account and it would appear that the committee decided to document the club's foundation for the inauguration date of the original course. This new course was located in the Shandon Park estate and it is interesting to note that G. L. Baillie, a founder of the Royal Belfast Golf Club and a key pioneer in the spread of early Irish golf, was involved in the preparation of the original 1895 course.

In 1920 the club moved to its present location at Summerfield.

KNOCKLOFTY, Clonmel, Co. Tipperary.
The Irish Golfing Guide 1911, referring to Clonmel, recorded: "Lord Donoughmore has a Private course in his demesne at Knocklofty, which is four miles from Clonmel. One may play there on invitation.''

LAHINCH, Co. Clare.
Instituted 1892.   Affiliated 1895.
From its earliest days, Lahinch captured the imagination for the golfing public in Ireland. This was due to a number of factors not least of which was the imagination and initiative displayed by the "founding fathers", who had the foresight to call in the most famous professional of the era to pronounce blessings on the course. The Limerick Club, of which Sir Alexander Shaw was founder Captain, had played on Kilkee during the Summer of 1892 (see Kilkee). An article in *The Irish Golfer* 18th

October 1899 documents the origins of Lahinch: "It was soon found difficult during the Summer months, when the racecourse (at Limerick) was heavy with grass, to keep up the play of the club at the distance of Kilkee and it was decided to find some seaside course nearer Limerick. Some traveller to the Cliffs of Moher possessed of a golfer's eye, had seen on the coast, somewhere between Ennistymon and the Cliffs what presented all the natural features of a golf course. A search party consisting of Messrs. Shaw and Plummer was dispatched and on the north side of Lahinch village they made the grand golfing discovery of the century."

The story is taken further in *The Irish Field* 29th May 1909: ". . . on 26th March 1892 Sir Alexander Shaw went out with the late Mr. Plummer the Hon. Secretary of the Limerick Golf Club . . . whilst driving from Ennistymon they passed what was then a dreary desolate piece of land, a mass of sandhills. Struck with the possibility, they stopped and made inquiries and the result was a second visit on the 9th April when an eighteen-hole course was marked out. Mr. MacFarlane of the Blackwatch played the opening match with Mr. W. F. McDonnell on Good Friday of that year. These players liked the course even as it was. The Blackwatch (Regiment) were then at Limerick and gave every assistance to the members of the Limerick club who, for the first year, managed the Lahinch Club as part of their own club."

In all of the foregoing, there is one major point of chronological detail which might be questioned. The Limerick Golf Club was instituted in December 1891 and

GOLFING LAHINCH. Co CLARE. 4151 W.L.

(Courtesy of the National Library of Ireland)

the earliest article above refers to that club's golfers playing at Kilkee in the Summer. This could only have been in the Summer of 1892 as their club had not been in existence the previous summer. There is no doubt that as late as September 1892 some of the Limerick golfers, including Sir Alexander Shaw, were playing at Kilkee (see Kilkee, entry in *Limerick Chronicle* 17th September 1892). It must therefore be presumed that the Limerick golfers were playing at both Kilkee and Lahinch during the Summer of 1892. The Blackwatch Regiment departed Limerick for Mary Hill Barracks Glasgow in January 1893, therefore they would not have been involved in an 1893 discovery of Lahinch.

In his book *The Life Of Tom Morris*, Rev. W. Tulloch records (page 262): "In June (1894) he was in Ireland. The members of the Royal Dublin Golf Club gave him a warm welcome as he came to Dollymount, brisk and hale, from Lahinch, in the county of Clare (where he had just laid out a capital links of 18 holes) . . .". One month later *The Irish Times* 23rd July 1894 reported: ". . . and it is proposed to hold a meeting in September for the Championship of the South of Ireland open to all amateurs. It is hoped that most of the clubs of Ireland will be represented as the splendid links are most suitable for a championship meeting, being pronounced by Tom Morris to be one of the finest clubs in the United Kingdom."

For some unknown reason the first South of Ireland Championship did not take place until September 1895, one year later, being won on the inaugural occasion by Dr. G. S. Browning who beat a fellow Lahinch member W. F. McDonnell by 2 and 1. A major boost was given to the club later that year, as recorded in *The Belfast Newsletter* 12th November 1895: "The Great Southern and Western Railway . . . have agreed to give to golfers Friday to Tuesday tickets from Kingsbridge to Lahinch Co. Clare, a distance of 175 miles for one guinea first return. As Lahinch links are one of the best courses in the country . . . this concession will be a decided advantage to the golfing public." A further major boost is recorded in the magazine *Golf* 10th July 1896 (which had wide circulation in the United Kingdom) . . . "Mr. Gerald Balfour Chief Secretary for Ireland, who, like his brother, is a good golfer, has taken rooms at the Royal Golf Hotel, Lahinch . . .".

The Royal Golf Hotel had been built by a syndicate headed by Sir Alexander Shaw, in which he seems to have been a major shareholder. He was Captain of the club from 1893 to 1901 and President from 1893 to 1923, certainly one of the key figures in early Irish golf.

In late Autumn 1906, Charles Gibson of Westward Ho was called in to review the layout of the course and he supervised the re-orientation of the links to incorporate more of the famous sandhills. Gibson's revision remained in play until 1927 when Dr. Alister Mackenzie was invited to advise on improvements. At a cost of £2000, a major transformation was performed by this master golf architect (who had been resposible for laying out the Augusta National and Cypress Point courses in the U.S.A.). The present "old" Lahinch links is basically Mackenzies work and all that remains of Old Tom Morris's work is the 6th "Dell" Hole.

Right up to the present day the South of Ireland Championship remains one of the most popular events on the Irish golfing calendar. The success of this club and the championship it hosts every year is a credit to that hardy band of Limerick golfers who, tired of long grass in the Summer of 1892, sought and found the answer on Dan Slattery's ground at Lahinch.

*See Kilkee G.C., Limerick G.C., Chapter 6.

LARNE, Co. Antrim.
Instituted 1894.   Affiliated 1895.

This club's foundation is recorded in *The Belfast Newsletter* 10th November 1894: "During the past few weeks a number of gentlemen have been actively engaged in the promotion of a golf club in Larne. A committee was formed and a guarantee list opened and now everything promises fair and it is expected that the club will be in working order before next Summer. The following are the office bearers: Captain, Mr. William Rankin; Vice Captain Mr. Alfred Fisher; Sec. Mr. John F. Cousins; Treasurer Mr. W. N. Brown . . . ground has been secured on the farm of Mr. N. Holmes, Islandmagee . . . a deputation consisting of Messrs. W. Rankin, W. N. Brown and J. W. McNinch recently waited on the Directors of the Belfast & Northern Railway and . . . applied for a grant in aid . . . The Directors after carefully considering the matter directed that they would be pleased to contribute £20 a year for 5 years."

The Irish Golfer 4th April 1900 carries a lengthy article on the origins of the club: "Prior to this date (1894) a few ardent sporting spirits enjoyed the privilege of playing over the private links at Kilwaughter Castle Park by consent of the late Mr. J. Galt-Smith. When however it was known that suitable ground for a links had been discovered nearer home all golfers and would be golfers readily joined the newly formed club . . . with the assistance of Mr. G. L. Baillie a very sporting nine-hole course was soon in playing order and a neat commodious clubhouse erected from a plan gratuitously designed by Mr. J. F. Peddie . . . Col. James McCalmont M.P. drove off the first hole on 1st June 1895 . . . The site occupies the most northern portion of Island Magee and is reached by ferry from Larne harbour for the moderate sum of one penny."

A short description of the early course is given in *The Golfing Annual* 1895/96 : "The course of nine holes, is situated on Island Magee, to the North of Larne Lough and commands views of the Antrim coast, Mull of Kintyre, Ailsa Craig, and the Scotch coast. The hazards are bushes, an old road, a hill and a chasm. The par of the round is 32 . . ." There were 200 members paying a subscription of one guinea.

An institution date of 1929 is given in *The Irish Golfers Blue Book* 1939, which would indicate a revival at that time.

LAYTOWN & BETTYSTOWN.
Instituted 1909.   Affiliated 1909.

Golf had first been played in the Laytown and Bettystown area by Tom Gilroy and his family in the 1880s (see Mornington). The game had continued to be played by the Gilroys until late in 1895 when the family emigrated to England. An entry for Bettystown G.C. first appears on *The Golfing Annual* 1908/09 which gives an institution date of 1908. No names are given for Captain or Hon. Secretary.

The Irish Field 25th September 1909 carries an article on the founding of the present club: ". . . a chance remark of Captain Lowry, a merchant service skipper, to his friend Captain Lyons when walking together over the present course led to the latter starting the present course of nine holes . . ." The founding officers of

GOLF AT LAYTOWN C.1912

(Courtesy of the National Library of Ireland)

the club are given in the same article as: Captain, Patrick J. Tallan; Hon. Treasurer, J. Lyons; Hon. Secretary, J. F. Smyth. Later, *The Irish Field* 13th September 1913 carries an interesting feature on the club: "The golf course at Bettystown is to be extended to eighteen holes. When this is accomplished it will undoubtedly be one of the best seaside courses in the country. The additional ground lies on the South side of the Boyne exactly opposite the Baltray course. . . . Over twenty years ago there was a golf course of nine holes over the ground now to be taken in, having been made and kept up by Mr. Tom Gilroy who was one of the founders of the Royal Dublin course . . . as Mr. Gilroy had some trouble with local people, who did not approve of golf, he after a year or so gave up the course on that side of the Boyne and had one laid on the other side which is now the course of the Co. Louth Club (see Co. Louth) . . . Some of the greens are still to be seen but it would be very difficult if not impossible to trace out the exact course."

The club is listed in *The Golfing Annual* 1909/10 which gives an institution date of April 1909. A membership of 200 is recorded and . . . "The course of nine holes, varying from 110 to 450 yards . . . is still rather rough. The hazards are bunkers and sandhills". *The Irish Golfing Guide* 1914 reported: "The great possibilities of the place strike one at once, as there is ample room for an eighteen-hole course. The neat little clubhouse is close to the last green and first tee . . ."

The Irish Field 14th April 1923 reported: ". . . a club pavilion, where refreshments may be had, is being erected''. One year later the same paper reported on 19th July 1924 that an additional nine holes had been opened. Finally, *The Irish Field* 17th January 1925 recorded: "It is a satisfactory to hear that the club has succeeded in buying land on which the 18 holes are situated".

*See Mornington, Chapters 5 and 6.

LEINSTER G.C., Co. Carlow.

This club, which had been founded in 1899, changed its name to Carlow G.C. circa 1902. *The Golfing Annual* 1902/03 records it as "Carlow (late Leinster) G.C."

*See Carlow G.C.

LEOPARDSTOWN, Co. Dublin.

Modern day racegoers to Leopardstown are familiar with the sight of golf greens and bunkers within the area of the racecourse. However many would not be aware that the first determined effort to plant golf there had taken place almost one hundred years ago.

The Irish Times 16th July 1891 reports: "The racecourse at Foxrock will afford in a very short time a new attraction to the numerous members of the Leopardstown Club and their lady friends. Part of the course has been laid out as a golf links and although the turf is not the short crispy turf of a seaside green, the fine air of a district midway between mountain and sea and the superior clubroom accommodation fully compensate for its lack of sand and bunker. Nine holes have been put down and the aggregate length of the round will be over a mile and a half . . . The opening meeting has been fixed for Saturday 25th inst. when a number of valuable prizes open to members of all recognised golf clubs will be competed for. The Dublin, Wicklow & Wexford Railway Company . . . has kindly consented to issue tickets to Foxrock at special fare to members of the club who become golf subscribers.''

A lengthy article in *The Irish Times* 27th July 1891 describes the opening of the links, Mr. Tom Gilroy won the competition with a nett 100 off plus 2. There were twenty competitors. It is of great interest to note that a Mr. Baillie is named as "golf superintendent'' at Leopardstown in this article. This surely must have been G. L. Baillie who had devoted himself to the spread of golf courses in Ireland from his earliest days at Royal Belfast Golf Club.

There is no further account of golf at Leopardstown in contemporary newspapers, possibly the elite of South Dublin were not yet ready for golf. Foxrock Golf Club was founded two years later.

LETTERKENNY, Co. Donegal.
Instituted 1913. Affiliated 1913.

There is no record of this club in the early *Irish Golf Guide Books*, nor is it listed in any of the *Golfing Annuals* prior to 1912. However, without question, golf was being played in Letterkenny in 1894. Writing to Maj. Gen. A. C. H. Stewart, landlord of the Rockhill House estate, the land steward Mr. Robert R. Robinson stated in a letter dated 9th April 1894: "I write and beg to say Mr. Chambers Manager of the Ulster Bank, Dr. Carre and a few others have been playing golf in the Lawn, starting at McDaid's old Lodge and going across into the Fort Field. . . . They say it is splendid golfing ground and are envious to get what they call six pots made in it. This I refused letting them do until I hear from you . . .''. The mention of "pots" in the letter is intriguing, quite possibly the golfers were using buried jampots as holes.

The present club has no record of its foundation and its earliest minute books date from 1929. A local legend exists of an original course of three holes at Windyhall and an even earlier course at Ballyraine. A foundation date of 1913 is listed by the club and this is supported by an entry in *The Irish Field* 14th November 1913 which reported a match played at the club between Cromwell of Royal Co. Down and ''the Stabane professional Martin''. However *The Irish Golfers Blue Book* 1939 gives an institution date of 1902.

In 1967 the club moved from its nine-hole course at Crievesmith to its present eighteen-hole course at Barnhill.

LIMERICK, Co. Limerick.
Instituted 1891.   Affiliated 1909.

As with so many other Irish clubs, Limerick have no earlier records than 1901. This loss is most regrettable from a national point of view as the early golfers at Limerick played a major role in the development of golf at Lahinch. The Blackwatch Regiment's part in this club's institution was another link in the military involvement in spreading the game throughout the country.

In May 1891 the Blackwatch Regiment moved to Limerick from Belfast and amongst their ranks were many keen golfers. When the Regiment was stationed in Dublin, in 1887, they had presented a medal for competition by members of the Dublin Golf Club. *The Irish Golfer* 18th October 1899 recorded: "The Limerick Golf Club which played in the Winter over the racecourse and in the Summer over the downs of Kilkee, was founded in 1891 by Messrs. A. W. Shaw, M. Gavin, Capt. Willington and Richard Plummer. The time was favourable for such a movement, for the Blackwatch had just been quartered in Limerick and it numbered several enthusiastic and expert golfers. Munster golfers gratefully remember the names of MacFarlane and Wylie.''

An account of the origins of golf at Limerick is given in *The Golfing Union of Ireland Yearbook* 1967 where credit is given to the Murray family for introducing the game to the city. The Murrays had moved from Scotland to Castleconnell in 1888 and the eldest three sons were children of Mrs. Murray's previous marriage to a Mr. Driver. It is of interest to note that *The Irish Golfer* 18th October 1899 recorded that ''. . . some ten years ago Mr. Shaw might have been seen learning the alphabet of golf on the breezy downs of Kilkee under the tuition of Mr. Douglas Driver of Dallar . . .'' This would confirm the Driver connection with early golf in the Limerick area.

The Driver brothers were very friendly with the Phelps family of Limerick who were members of the Limerick County Club. Following contact between the members of this club and the Blackwatch officers who had arrived several months earlier to Limerick, a public meeting was called for the Library of the Old Athenaeum on 12th December 1891. Alexander Shaw presided over the meeting and was elected Captain together with a committee of seven which included a Blackwatch officer (probably Lieutenant MacFarlane). There is no doubt that Alexander Shaw (later knighted and a Vice President of the Golfing Union of Ireland) was the guiding spirit behind the move to create a golf club in Limerick. *The Golfing Annual* 1892/93 records him as both Captain and President of the club, a foundation date of 11th December 1891 is also given. Later, *The Golfing Guide* 1897 listed him, still in office as President.

The initial location of the club at the racecourse near Ballinacurra House, off the Patrickswell road, was not very hospitable. *The Irish Golfer* October 18th 1899 reported: "It was soon found difficult during the Summer months when the Racecourse was heavy with grass to keep up the play of the club at the distance of Kilkee and it was decided to find some seaside course nearer Limerick". From this account it can be seen that the Limerick golfers were adventurous spirits who travelled as far as Kilkee to keep up the game. *The Limerick Chronicle* 17th September 1892 records a competition at Kilkee and among the names are several of the Limerick golfers, with other visitors from Nenagh and Kilkee itself.

The entry for the club in *The Golfing Annual* 1892/93 recorded a membership of 140, which was very creditable. This edition was published in April 1893 and the following information would have referred to the experiences of the previous year: "The course at Ballinacurra is one of nine holes, the hazards being hedges and walls. It is, however, only playable in Winter and Spring. The Summer links of the club are at Lahinch, Co. Clare, thirty-six miles from Limerick, and consisting eighteen holes, over a natural golfing country . . ." Alexander Shaw is credited with the discovery of the Lahinch links in *The Irish Field* 29th May 1909, together with Richard Plummer, in March 1892. From *The Irish Golfer* and *The Irish Field* accounts it would appear that both Kilkee and Lahinch were being visited in the Summer of 1892 as an alternative to the Limerick course. *The Golfing Annual* 1893/94 records the same committee for both Limerick and Lahinch golf clubs giving a foundation date of March 1892 for the latter. Present-day Lahinch golfers owe a debt of gratitude to the zeal of Alexander Shaw and his friends from Limerick.

Limerick Golf Club's present location at Ballyclough is the eighth since 1891. An article in *Irish Golf* March 1944 recorded: "The first course was in the racecourse grounds. Then it went to a site near the tennis club which complained about its courts being hacked to bits. Then began many wanderings which ended at Ballyclough, the present course . . ." *The Golfing Annual* 1902/03 recorded the club's location as "Newcastle about 2½ miles from Limerick Station".

Ballyclough became the club's home in 1908 and in March 1919, the farm on which the present course is located was purchased from a Mrs. Crawford. A nine-hole course was opened in March 1920. Lionel Hewson recorded the work of extending the course to eighteen in *The Irish Field* 30th August 1924. Mr. Fred Ballingal, Lord Dunraven's agent at Adare, had laid out the new course, which was officially opened on 11th June 1925.

*See Kilkee, Lahinch, Chapter 6.

LISBURN, Co. Antrim.
Instituted 1891. Affiliated 1905.

Although the present Lisburn Golf Club records its foundation date as 1905, golf had been played there at least fourteen years before. Lionel Hewson wrote in *Irish Golf* September 1934: "On a portion of ground used by the club today, formerly part of the Manor House Park, a small band of enthusiasts started to play golf in 1890. The game was then unknown locally; but the prime mover was a Scotsman Mr. Hugh Shaw, who had won his way to almost first rank before he moved to Lisburn. As late as 1910, after his return Scotland, he won the open News Of The World Cup against a representative field and for some years held the record for Ralston . . . In those days the ground was not available in Mid Summer but as the soil is sandy and the subsoil sand, it is really at its best at other times. . . . The early club collapsed in 1896 and it was not till 1905 that the present one arrived . . . the course was first laid out by Mr. J. L. Baillie (sic) . . ."

Hewson's account of the earlier golf club in Lisburn is confirmed in *The Golfing Annual* 1892/93 which has an entry for Manor House Golf Club, instituted 1891 . . . "No particulars forthcoming". *The Field* 30th April 1892 carries a result from this club in which it stated: ". . . the winter season of the club is drawing to a close". Later *The Golfers Guide* 1897 recorded a foundation date of 18th March 1891 for Lisburn G.C. An entry for the Lisburn Club in *The Golfing Annual* 1893/94 gives a foundation date of 1st January 1893, the Captain was R. H. Bland, Hon. Secretary was J. M. Barbour and H. Shaw was listed on the committee . . . "Location for the course − Manor House demesne . . . There is a clubhouse on the green, which is only open for play from Nov. 1 to May 1 . . ."

These entries confirm the continuity of golf in Lisburn from 1891 and it will be noted that the 1894 location was still the "Manor House" which was the title of the original club. There is no listing for Lisburn in the *Golfing Annuals* after 1896 until the revival of 1905. The present club was revived at a meeting held in the Lisburn Courthouse on 3rd April 1905 when a decision was made to form a club and lease 40 acres at the "Manor Lands" for 20 years. This was the same land which had been used as a course fourteen years before. President of the new club was Mr. Harold A. M. Barbour M.A. and the Captain was Mr. George H. Clarke.

In 1971 the club sold its original course and purchased the present land at Magherageery. Fred Hawtree designed the eighteen-hole layout which was officially opened for play on 6th June 1973.

LISDOONVARNA, Co. Clare.

There was an attempt to emulate Lahinch's success in 1906 when a local Lisdoonvarna hotel proprietress called in Harry Vardon to lay out a course there. *The Irish Field* 17th March 1906 carries the following: "The new links laid out by Harry Vardon at Thomond House (the up to date sanatorium which Mrs. Bulger intends opening this season at Lisdoonvarna, Co. Clare) are most promising . . . Vardon visited last October . . ."

Mrs. Bulger was a lady with "connections" and these are recorded in *The Irish Field* 14th July 1906 when an account is given of a visit by the Lord Lieutenant of

Ireland and his wife (Lord and Lady Aberdeen) . . . "under the conduct and tutelage of Mr. A. W. Shaw, who has done splendid pioneer work for Munster they visited far famed Lahinch on Tuesday and on the following day bestowed the royal blessing on the youngest of Irish courses at sweet sounding, health giving Lisdoonvarna . . . Vardon is staying at Thomond House . . .''. *The Golfing Annual* 1907/08 lists a club at the resort, the annual subscription was one guinea, the course was nine holes and the Hon. Secretary was Dr. O'Sullivan. An institution date of 1906 is given.

Despite the prestigious opening ceremony the exercise of golf must have proved too onerous for the Edwardian clientele visiting the famous "waters" of Lisdoonvarna. *The Irish Golfers Guide* 1910 stated ". . . believed to be extinct". This was not the end of golf at the resort as *The Irish Field* 26th May 1923 reported on a successful dance held to aid the golf club fund: "Those interested in the club are Messrs. O'Loughlin, Maguire, Lynch and Sheedy. The last named the Honorary Secretary". Later the same paper reported on 18th August 1923: "Lisdoonvarna boasts a nine-hole golf course now. It was laid out by Willie McNamara of Lahinch. Sulphur water and dancing seem to be the chief things in Lisdoonvarna, but golf is coming along steadily . . ."

The club is mentioned again in *Thoms Directory* 1940, with nine holes and J. Sheedy as Hon. Secretary. Similar information is given in the 1946 edition. Lisdoonvarna's subsequent history is unknown.

LISMORE, Co. Waterford.
Instituted 1965. Affiliated 1967.

A golf club existed in Lismore long before the present club was established in 1965. *The Sportsmans Holiday Guide* 1897 records: "The Lismore golf club have their course about half a mile out of town on very high ground, overlooking the valley of the Blackwater and commanding fine views of the surrounding country. The number of holes is 8, the distance around is about one mile and the holes average a little over 200 yards in length."

No foundation date is given in the above account and the first entry in *The Golfing Annual* 1898/99 only states: "The course is a small one, of nine holes". Despite the paucity of information in these early guide books there is substantial evidence to prove that a club existed here in the very early years of the 1890s. *The Irish Times* 11th May 1892 has an intriguing entry which documents a golf match between the Officers 1st Battalion Seaforth Highlanders versus Lismore Golf Club: "The above, which was a return match, was played at Fermoy yesterday under the most auspicious circumstances. At the match played at Lismore the Seaforths won by 43 strokes . . ."

It is clear that a club was active in Lismore from early 1892, at least, and one of the players recorded as playing in the Fermoy match was Sir Richard Musgrave. *Nisbets Golf Yearbook* 1908 records the Honorary Secretary of the club as Sir R. Musgrave and also states: "At present this club is in abeyance but it is hoped to reopen this year". A foundation date of 1898 is also given in this guide book, which is clearly incorrect, and is further proof of the dangers of relying on one particular source for information. *The Irish Golfers Guide* 1910 reported that the club was "believed to be extinct".

The Irish Field 19th March 1921 reported: "It is good to hear that the Lismore club has again reopened after closing for five years". Later, *The Golfers Handbook* 1923 records the club, with a membership of 50 and the Hon. Secretary was F. C. Guest. *The Irish Tourist Authority Directory* 1937 listed the club with nine holes. An entry for Lismore G.C. is given in *Golfing Union of Ireland Yearbooks* 1945 and 1946   after which the club would appear to have succumbed until its present revival.

*See Fermoy and Chapter 6.

LIVERY HILL, Stranocum, Co. Antrim.

This club is first listed in *The Golfing Annual* 1907/08 which gives an institution date of 1907. There were 40 members, the Captain was Rev. J. S. Pyper and Hon. Secretary Dr. R. C. Millar . . . "The course of nine holes is situated under the shadow of Knocklayde, half a mile from Stranocum Station".

Subsequent editions of *The Golfing Annual* list the club until 1910. *The Irish Golfers Guide* 1910 listed the club as Livery Hill, Dervock . . . "believed to be extinct".

LUCAN, Co. Dublin.
Instituted 1897.   Affiliated 1905.

The foundation of the first club at Lucan is recorded in *The Irish Times* 29th September 1897: "New Links At Lucan — A new and excellent golf course has recently been laid out at the Moor of Meath Lucan and on Saturday the opening ceremony was performed by Captain Colthurst-Vesey . . . a few of the holes will undoubtedly bear improvement, but they will not be wanting, and in time the links should make a pretty inland course . . . altogether great credit is due to the Honorary Secretary Mr. Gray, for his indefatigible exertions in the promotion of the links . . . The visitors were entertained to tea in the clubhouse, by the members and Miss Smith of the Spa Hotel also looked after their wants." *The Golfing Annual* 1898/99 lists this club as "Moor of Meath Club" but does not give the names of any club officers.

Later, *The Irish Golfer* 13th June 1900 records the move of the club to its present location: "The new links of the Lucan Golf Club were formally opened on Whit Monday . . . the links are prettily situated on the slopes opposite the Lucan Spa hotel . . . The course is a nine-hole one . . . considering the very short time that has elapsed since work on the course was begun, the condition of the greens and course generally is very good . . . This is to be attributed to the energy of the Honorary Secretary Mr. A. Grey D.I. of Lucan. The directors of the hotel have given the members every material assistance in their endeavours to make the club a success."

An article in *The Irish Golfer* 28th July 1900 clarifies what happened to the old course when it reported: "This is the second golf links formed in the Lucan district, as some three years ago a course was formed on the Moor of Meath, about three miles from Lucan. The turf there was suitable for both Summer and Winter play, but, owing to the inaccessibility of the place, one by one of the members dropped off until the club was well nigh extinct. Some six months ago the present ground was rented, the first tee being a cleek shot from the Spa Hotel . . . The club is not yet strong enough to take over the ground entirely, but no doubt the Hotel Company will ultimately do so, and when this is done we can safely predict for the Lucan golfers, golf of the very best.''

From the foregoing, it can be seen that Mr. Gray had been a key figure in the early life of this club. However, the turn of the century move did not solve Lucan's problems and it would appear that the club died for a short period. *The Irish Times* 10th January 1902, under the heading ''Lucan Redivivus'', reported: ''We are pleased to hear that the Lucan club has been reorganised . . . the Committee have acquired the lands immediately adjoining the well known Spa hotel and have laid out an excellent nine-hole course . . . The Hon. Secretary is Mr. F. M. Mooney, Leixlip Castle.''

There is an article on the club in *Golf Illustrated* 1st February 1907 which adds mystery of Lucan's ongoing: ''Five years ago a nine-hole course was laid out adjoining the Spa hotel and a club was formed''. This information would not appear to be correct and one wonders was there a deliberate attempt to erase all memory of the club's previous existence. The same article states: ''Recently, the course has been reconstructed under the direction of James McKenna, the professional of the Carrickmines club and on Saturday last an opening competition was held . . .''.

LURGAN, Co. Armagh.
Instituted 1893.   Affiliated 1894.

An entry in *The Belfast Newsletter* 16th November 1893 records the institution of Lurgan Golf Club: ''. . . a club has just been formed in Lurgan for the practice of the Royal and Ancient game, under exceedingly favourable circumstances. The number of players almost reads one hundred, and sixty acres of excellent ground with numerous hazards has been secured in the demesne for links. The ground has been laid out under the personal supervision of the Captain, Mr. H. J. McGleagh who has taken much interest in the foundation of the club . . . the links were formally opened on Saturday last by Mr. James Malcolm D.L. President of the club.'' *The Belfast Newsletter* 12th November 1894 records: ''. . . the gentlemen who inaugurated the club were fortunate to secure over 66 acres in the beautiful demesne formerly owned by Lord Lurgan but now held by three gentlemen of the town, Messrs. McCaughey J.P., Malcolmson and Clarke . . .''.

Irish Golf September 1934 in an article on the club states: ''. . . on 8th September 1893 nine gentlemen met in Mr. N. G. Leepers rooms and decided to form a golf club in Lurgan . . . the first competition for which there were 30 entries was played in the following November. The standard of play was not very high but Mr. Thomas Dickson, the Irish native champion won with a score of 92.''

The annual general meeting of the club is reported in *The Irish Golfer* 6th December 1899 and the loss of the old course is documented: ''The club had been obliged to give up their links in Lurgan Demesne where a capital nine-hole course had been laid out by Captain Greer and Mr. H. G. MacGeagh . . . a great deal of anxiety had been manifested by members when they were informed that the club would have to give up its links in the Lurgan Demesne but happily . . . they had been able to obtain ground at Grace Hall, the owner of which gave members every facility for enjoyment of the game.'' *The Irish Golfer* 27th June 1900 reported that this was . . . ''an excellent green consisting of 9 holes and being 2,500 yards in length . . .'' The same magazine stated that the club professional was W. D. Daly of Musselburgh (father of Alec and Christopher, professionals at Royal Belfast and Malone respectively).

In 1923/24 the club moved once again and this time they returned to their alma mater in the Demesne where a nine-hole course was laid out. *The Irish Field* 9th May 1925 reported the opening of the new links and clubhouse. The course was extended to 18 holes in 1971/72.

For a period there were two golf clubs in the Lurgan area, the other club being the Woodville G.C.

*See Woodville G.C.

MAGILLIGAN, Co. Derry.

The opening of this links is recorded in the *Coleraine Constitution* 15th August 1896: ''On Saturday last between thirty and forty players mustered to compete in the inaugural match on these links. Shortly after twelve o'clock the first ball was driven off by Captain Crosbie J.P., the Castle, Greencastle. Work had only been commenced on the ground on the 1st July and general admiration of the state of the course, especially of the putting greens, was expressed by all the players. Mr. W. H. Webb, Randelstown, last year's champion, carried off the scratch prize with a score of 82. . . . The golf course is to be run as an open links, for which day and weekly tickets will be issued . . .'' It can be clearly seen that this was to be a public course open to all who were prepared to pay. In this regard it would appear that Magilligan was the first venture into the field of municipal golf.

The prime mover in the creation of this course was none other than G. L. Baillie of Royal Belfast fame. His interest in this project was revealed in a *Belfast Newsletter* article dated 18th May 1896 when he advertised a trip to the proposed new links and also to Greencastle. In another account of the opening of the course *The Belfast Newsletter* 10th August 1896 records: ''The course is a full one of eighteen holes . . . 200 acres of magnificent golfing ground close to Magilligan Point have been secured on lease for a period of 21 years principally from Mr. George Leek of Bellarena. The course has been laid out by the golfing expert Mr. G. L. Baillie who is also acting secretary of the new link . . .''

There is no further mention of this course after an entry in *The Golfing Guide* 1897, which gives no details. Mr. G. S. Glover of Derry states: ''. . . during the next three years the ground staff fought a losing battle against the rabbits in their very natural habitat. The rabbits won, not even the extensive trapping, which was a local feature, could hold them at bay''. Rabbits had been a feature at Magilligan long before as is clearly to be seen in Arthur Young's *A Tour In Ireland* (1776) where he tells us: ''. . . at Magilligan is a rabbit warren which yields on average 3,000 dozen per annum . . . the warren is a sandy tract on the shore and belongs to the bishop . . .''

*See Coleraine and Greenisland.

MALAHIDE, Co. Dublin.
Instituted 1892. Affiliated 1896.

Malahide was one of the earliest locations in Ireland at which golf was played. An article in the paper *Sport* 18th July 1885 on the institution of the Dublin Golf Club records: "Last year (i.e. 1884) not a few visitors to and inhabitants of Malahide were startled by the apparition of a well known Dublin citizen playing a game which was aptly described as 'a cross between hurley and hole and taw' over the sandbanks along that almost unrivalled strand . . ."

Unfortunately the name of this early pioneer is not recorded in the newspaper account, more than likely he was one of the band of expatriate Scotsmen who would become prominent in the early Dublin clubs. It was to take another seven years before a serious attempt was made to start the game again at Malahide and the story is told in *The Irish Golfer* 24th January 1900: "The club owes its origins to the Reverend William Reid (now a valuable member of the Committee), who when on a visit to his brother-in-law Mr. Nathaniel Hone, now of St. Doloughs Park, but then residing at Malahide saw, with a Scotsman's eyes, the capabilities of the stretch of sand dunes lying to the east of the town, for the Royal and Ancient game. Mr. Hone took up the project and enrolled a small band of embyro golfers, which has now grown into one of the largest and most influential of the clubs, with a nine-hole

OLD COURSE AT MALAHIDE PRIOR TO DAMAGE BY STORM C. 1906
(Courtesy of the National Library of Ireland)

course, in Ireland. . . . The Malahide club instituted in 1892, is almost unique in one respect, that its lady members pay the same entrance fee £2 and annual fee £1 as the gentlemen but they also have similar rights and privileges in every way except that they cannot serve as officers of the club . . .''

The Irish Times 12th January 1906 recorded an important step for Malahide: ''. . . the club have acquired 16 acres of additional land on the South West side of the clubhouse, which is admirably suited for golf . . . Three new holes will be laid out on this ground and six on the ground heretofore played over.'' This move may have been precipitated by the inroads of the sea on the old course. Eventually by 1927 the club was forced to abandon the sea holes completely.

In common with many other Irish clubs, Malahide does not possess its early records, however *The Irish Times* from 1894 onwards contains regular reports of golf activities there. From an early date ladies' competition results appeared and this club together with Foxrock had a key part to play in the early development of ladies' golf in the Dublin area.

The club's founder, Nathaniel Hone, was one of Ireland's most famous artists. He married Magdalen Jameson in 1872, a daughter of the famous whiskey distiller and owner of the nearby Portmarnock links where golf had been played in 1858.

*See Portmarnock.

MALLOW, Co. Cork.
Instituted 1892. Affiliated 1898.

The present club at Mallow dates itself from 1947, however golf had been played there over fifty years before. An entry in *The Golfing Annual* 1895/96 is the earliest mention of the former club and gives an institution date of October 1892: ''The course, of eighteen holes, is about half a mile from the town, and the hazards are quarries, brooks, the Fermoy Railway etc. Play takes place all the year round''. President of the club at that time (May 1896) was R. E. Longfield; Captain, F. J. F. Smith and Hon. Secretary was R. H. Spratt, Bank of Ireland.

Further detail is given in *The Golfers Guide* 1897 wherein the Honorary Secretary's name is again recorded as R. Spratt, Bank of Ireland, Mallow; the President was R. E. Longfield D.L. and the Captain was F. J. F. Smith. This entry also gives a membership of 70, men's subscriptions being £1 and 12/6 for ladies. The course was only nine holes and closed from May to September. For some reason the club had been reduced to nine holes and excluded from the course for the Summer; more than likely the landlord had reviewed the terms of his lease.

The club is continuously mentioned in *The Golfing Annuals* up to 1907 and in *The Irish Golf Guides* from 1910 to 1916. *Irish Life* 5th November 1920 recorded the election of Mr. K. B. Williams J.P. as Captain. Later, *The Golfers Handbook* 1923 listed the club with nine holes a quarter of a mile from the railway station.

The Irish Field 29th March 1924 reported: ''. . . a new course is to be laid out at Mallow . . . I believe it is to be 18 holes . . .'' It would appear that the club became defunct around this time and it was not until 1947 that the present club was revived.

MALONE, Belfast, Co. Down.
Instituted 1895.   Affiliated 1895.

One of the notable facts about the foundation of this club is that there was no course available prior to the decision to form a golf club. The institution is recorded in *The Belfast Newsletter* 29th April 1895: ". . . on Friday last the 26th inst. a meeting of the promoters was held in the National Schoolroom, Malone Road. The Rev. R. W. Seavers B.D. Rector of St. John's church occupied the chair. . . . it was unanimously resolved that such a club should be forthwith established and that its designation be 'Malone Golf Club', membership of which should be open to ladies and gentlemen . . . a committee was appointed to make all requisite inquiries as to the best and most suitable of certain sites available in the neighbourhood for the new golf links . . . Mr. Ernest Young was elected Captain, Mr. W. A. Chapman Honorary Treasurer and Mr. Joseph Pyke Honorary Secretary . . ."

The new committee selected ground at Newforge Lane and laid out nine holes. In a very short period it was discovered that the area was unsuitable and *The Belfast Newsletter* 8th January 1896 reported on a special meeting "to remove to more suitable and convenient ground at Stranmillis Road . . ." within a very short period the new course was in play, the opening day receiving due notice in *The Irish Times* 4th June 1896 . . . "the growth of this club has been so great that the short nine holes course at New Forge was found quite insufficient and the club are to be congratulated on having secured an 18 hole links of such excellent quality so near Belfast as Strandmillis (sic) . . . the greens promise to be very good and the course extends to almost 2½ miles in length. A wooden clubhouse has been erected . . . Mr. Ernest Young, Captain, drove off the first ball . . ."

It is clear that Ernest Young was the key figure in the foundation and promotion of Malone G.C. An article in *The Irish Golfer* 7th November 1900 reported that he had first begun playing on the old Kinnegar course of Royal Belfast in 1885. G. L. Baillie had been his tutor and in 1890 he had succeeded that great pioneer of Irish golf when he took over the duties of Hon. Secretary of the new Co. Down G.C. at Newcastle. Ernest Young found Newcastle and Royal Belfast clubs too distant and, for this reason, decided to form a club nearer to the city.

There is no doubt that this club had a healthy start, *The Golfing Annual* 1896/97 records a membership of 450 with an entrance fee of £2.2s and an annual subscription of £2.2s. A ladies' club is also listed in this same publication.

In 1919 the club moved once more to the Harberton Estate where an eighteen-hole course was laid out. Finally, in 1962 the club moved to its present location at Ballydrain, Upper Malone.

MARKETHILL, Co. Antrim.

Golfing Union of Ireland records reveal an affiliation by this club on 28th August 1911. There is no further information on the founding date of the club.

MASSEREENE, Co. Antrim.
Instituted 1895.   Affiliated 1896.

The Irish Times 28th August 1895 announced ". . . a new golf club to be called the Massereene Golf Club has been formed at Antrim. The course is an eighteen-hole one on the borders of Lough Neagh and ought to prove superior to most inland courses as many of the holes close to the lake resemble seaside holes. The hazards are sand bunkers and plantations. The club has been most generously treated by Lord Massereene who has given the ground forming part of his demesne for a nominal rent. The opening meeting will be held on Saturday for which the Northern Counties Railway have arranged to stop the golfers express at Antrim." An entry for the club in *The Golfing Annual* 1895/96 lists Lord Massereene as first President, H. M. D. Barton was Captain and the Hon. Secretary was L. J. Holmes. The latter had won the opening competition with a nett 76 off 22 handicap.

The Golfing Annual 1906/07 records a reduction of the course to nine holes and it was not until 1964 that an extension to eighteen holes was opened. In 1961 additional land had been purchased and F. W. Hawtree (sen.) was engaged on the planning and construction of the new layout.

GOLF LINKS, ANTRIM, 3187. W.L.

(Courtesy of the National Library of Ireland)

MIDLETON, Co. Cork.

Golf at Midleton is first documented in *The Irish Times* 28th April 1896, in connection with a "links" at Midleton College: ". . . an extended nine-hole course has recently been laid out on these links, which now undoubtly makes them the best school links in Ireland". This entry is an intriguing one as the presence of other school golf courses is not documented at that time.

Some years later, *The Irish Golfing Guide* 1910 documents the Midleton Golf Club and gives an institution date of 1909: ". . . Nine holes inland, close to the town and five minutes from Midleton railway station. Honorary Secretary, Thomas Forde; Captain, T. Forde . . . members 120 . . . a compact course, with good natural and artificial hazards". There is an entry for the club in *The Golfing Annual* 1909/10 which confirms the above detail. The annual subscription was £1.10s. for men and £1 for ladies.

The club is not listed in *The Golfing Handbook* 1923, however *The Irish Field* 5th November 1921 records the club conferring honorary life membership on Mr. W. Bren, following his recent transfer from the town. It would appear that the club succumbed shortly after Mr. Bren's departure.

MILFORD, Co. Donegal.

A Milford Golf Club is recorded in *The Irish Golfers Guide* 1910 which gives 1908 as the date of institution. The Captain's name is listed as Dr. J. Patterson and the President was the Earl of Leitrim. The club was affiliated to the Golfing Union of Ireland. Further detail is given in *The Golfing Annual* 1909/10 which gives 1908 as date of institution and recorded 60 members; the Hon. Secretary was M. A. McGreadie, The Hotel, Milford, and "the course of nine holes varying from 160 to 410 yards, adjoins the hotel". Clearly the club and course were closely associated with the hotel.

It is of interest to note that·the Earl of Leitrim was closely associated with this club as Tom Morris had been brought over to lay out a course at the nearby Mulroy House by the Earl in 1891 (see Rosapenna). Milford Golf Club is again listed in *The Irish Golfing Guide* 1916 but the later history of this club is unknown.

MILLPARK, Roscrea, Co. Tipperary.

The Irish Golfers Guide 1910 records: "This club was started again in 1904, the course having been laid out some years previously but lapsed for want of members . . . Hon. Secretary R. A. Bolton, Dungan Park . . ." Millpark G.C. is listed in *The Golfing Annual* 1909/10 with an institution date of 1904. There were 30 members and the course of nine holes was two miles from the station.

It would appear that for a number of years (circa 1900 to 1910) Roscrea had the luxury of two local golf courses. *The Irish Golfers Guide* 1911 documents an amalgamation of this club with the other local club with a course at Derryvale being chosen as the new "home".

*See Roscrea.

MILLTOWN, Co. Dublin.
Instituted 1907. Affiliated 1907.

Like a number of other Irish golf clubs Milltown lost its early records in a tragic fire in 1958. However, the golf journals of the day recorded the inauguration of this club for posterity. *The Irish Field* 5th October 1907 reported: "Twas in February that Mr. J. H. Callan and a few friends, including Mr. J. Smalley entered into an agreement to lease the lands at Milltown for a golf course and in September a course is in almost perfect condition for play and a handsome commodious clubhouse is opened at one of the pleasantest functions I have attended . . . Milltown will make itself felt in metropolitan golf. It is distinctly the most accessible green of this class within a few minutes of the train . . . The course laid out by Mr. W. C. Pickeman (of Portmarnock) has its greens well placed in the corners of the fields. The new clubhouse designed by W. O'Connor and erected with loving care by Dr. Barry, is handsome and commodious . . . at a cost of something like £2,000 . . . sufficiently large to meet the requirements of its 350 members . . . Unfortunately Mr. W. Murray J.P., the President, was called to London but Mr. F. E. Davies, the Captain, performed the ceremony as a scratch man should. The Honorary Secretary is Mr. J. H. Callan, Hon. Treasurer Mr. J. E. Walsh . . ."

An article in *Golf Illustrated* 21st June 1907 reported that "the members have been playing the course for some weeks . . . the Milltown club had the unique experience of having its membership full 'ere it was able to begin play on its course."

A full account of the origins of the club is given in *The Irish Field* 16th January 1926 which recorded: "Milltown dates from the beginning of 1907 — to be accurate from January 11 of that year, when the first meeting was held in the Leinster Club, with Mr. T. Baker, who was connected with the *Freemans Journal* in the chair . . . we find that at the first meeting at which it was decided to form the club there were present Messrs. T. Baker, Fred E. Davies, J. Callan, Wm. M. Battersby (of Messrs. Battersby & Co.), John Smalley, E. J. Walsh and Wm. J. Carberry. They formed a select but experienced band of golfers . . . when they however hit on the ground at Mount Temple there was then available for golf only sufficient land for nine holes but the preliminary meeting did not hesitate for they reasoned and wisely that in the not distant future there might be an opportunity of securing enough of the land adjoining, to extend the course to eighteen holes . . ."

Wise indeed were the founders, for *The Irish Times* 9th December 1922 reported on plans to extend the course to its present eighteen holes.

MILLTOWN MALBAY, Co. Clare
*See Spanish Point and West Clare Golf Clubs.

MITCHELSTOWN, Co. Cork.
Instituted 1910. Affiliated 1924.

In common with many other Irish golf clubs, Mitchelstown does not possess it earliest records. A foundation date of 1908 is claimed, however *The Irish Field* 22nd

October 1910 reported: "New Southern club . . . at a public meeting in the Town Hall Mitchelstown it was unanimously decided to form a club at Mitchelstown. The project starts with every sign of success. The Rev. Canon Courtenay-Moore, Brigtown, was in the chair at the meeting which brought the club into being . . . The chairman dwelt upon the advantages that would accrue to the town and district and remarked upon the success of the Mitchelstown Lawn Tennis Club. The general tone of the meeting was enthusiastic and it was pointed out that land suitable for a course could be readily obtained. It was decided that the subscription would be £1 and 10 shillings for gentlemen and ladies respectively."

The original course was in the area of Ballinwilliam, now a housing estate, up to 1917. In that year the present course was made available by Col. King Harman of Mitchelstown Castle. Club records are complete only from 1917.

MOATE, Co. Westmeath.
Instituted 1900.   Affiliated 1940.

The Irish Golfer 23rd January 1901 recorded: "During the past month the Royal and Ancient game has established a firm footing in the sporting little town of Moate, Co. Westmeath. Links have been secured along a line of gravel hills adjacent to the town and no exertion has been spared by the Hon. Secretary to make them as perfect as possible. They afford quite a diversity of hazards . . . The club is under the Presidency of C. O'Donoghue esq. Ballinahown Court and the Captin H. A. S. Upton esq. Coolatore is backed up by a strong committee. Already the club numbers over fifty members."

Entries from the club are continuously recorded in the *Golfing Annuals* from 1901 to 1910. Men's subscription in 1901 was £1 and ladies 10/- . . . "the course of nine holes is about half a mile from the railway station".

The club is listed in *The Irish Golf Guides* 1910 to 1916 and in *The Golfers Handbook* 1923. A listing appears in the *G.U.I. Yearbook* 1927 and the nine-hole course is included in *The Irish Tourist Directory* 1937. At present the club's foundation date is given as 1940 which would indicate a break in continuity shortly before that date.

MOHILL, Co. Leitrim.

The Irish Field 24th April 1915 records a match between teams from Carrick-on-Shannon and Mohill. The former club had been founded in 1910, there is no further record of a club at Mohill.

MONAGHAN, Co. Monaghan.

The history of early golf at Monaghan will probably never be fully ascertained. It is in *The Golfers Annual* 1892/93 that a golf club is first noted there, with the intriguing entry . . . "no particulars forthcoming". A similar entry is to be found in the 1894/95 edition of the *Annual*.

Further mystery is added in an article in *The Belfast Newsletter* 11th November

1895: "The grounds of the County Monaghan club were formally opened with a competition by stroke under handicap. Unfortunately the day was wet and stormy which accounts for the high scores of some of the members". The following members are mentioned: W. Kerr, Dr. Henry, W. A. Parke, Mr. McWilliam, P. Rafferty and J. Behan. The mystery is compounded in *The Golfing Annual* 1895/96 which gives an institution date of 1895 and lists the Honorary Secretary's name as W. Kerr.

It is clear that a club existed at Monaghan prior to 1895 as evidenced in the earlier *Golfing Annuals* but no other record of the earlier club is documented. The 1895/96 *Annual* states: "The course is laid out on ground given by the use of Dr. Hall". There is a listing of the club in subsequent *Golfing Annuals* up to 1910 and *Golf Illustrated* 10th May 1907 reported that Monaghan club would be seeking affiliation at a forthcoming meeting of the Golfing Union of Ireland. The *Golfing Annuals* from 1908 to 1910 show the club affiliated.

The Irish Golfers Guide 1910 lists Monaghan Golf Club as extinct and it was not until 1916 that another club at Monaghan was instituted.

*See Rossmore G.C.

MONKSTOWN, Co. Cork.
Instituted 1908. Affiliated 1908.

The Cork Constitution 7th April 1908 carries a lengthy account of the first general meeting of this club. The chairman was Mr. A. H. Exham who had been a member of a sub-committee of the Monkstown Improvement and Amusements Committee tasked with investigating the setting up of a golf club. Other members of the sub-committee were A. G. Boumphrey, J. S. Cummins, G. A. Goulde, J. H. Hogan and J. F. Maguire.

The club is first documented in *The Golfing Annual* 1907/08 which, intriguingly, gave an institution date of 1907 and named the Hon. Secretaries as J. S. Cummins and A. G. Boumphrey. One year later *The Golfing Annual* gave a foundation date of April 1908, there were 350 members including ladies and ". . . the course of nine holes is in Lord De Vesci's demesne, with the old castle, built in 1643 as the clubhouse".

The 5th Viscount De Vesci had agreed to lease Monkstown Castle and grounds as a pavilion and course and after the election of the Viscount as first President and Mr. J. F. Maguire as first Captain . . . "The members present then inspected the castle expressing much approval of the main hall in which the meeting was held, also dressing rooms, kitchen etc. while other wandered over the links now almost complete for the opening ceremony on Saturday next the 11th inst."

Initially a nine-hole course of 2,500 yards was laid out by the club professional Peter O'Hare, who had come from Greenore and J. Brown the professional at Little Island. On 14th April 1908 the course was opened by the Vice President Mr. Exham who had been a key figure in the foundation of the club.

In April 1959 the club purchased the castle and the land for £4,000 from the De Vesci estate. Later in 1966 a 62-acre farm at Parkgarriff was purchased for £12,500 and the following year Monkstown Castle and 32 acres were sold for £22,000. An eighteen-hole course was laid out on the newly-acquired land, combining elements of the old course which remained in the club's ownership.

MOOR OF MEATH, Lucan, Co. Dublin.

A club of this name is first listed in *The Golfing Annual* 1898/99, with an institution date of 1897: "The course is laid out on the Moor of Meath, and will in time make a good inland green". Similar detail is given in the 1900/01 edition. *The Irish Times* 29th September 1897 records the foundation of the club at this location. In 1900 the club moved to the area of the Spa Hotel in Lucan, where it remains to the present day, under the name it assumed at that time.

*See Lucan.

MORNINGTON, Co. Meath.

One of the key figures in the spread of early golf in Ireland was Mr. Tom Gilroy, who in 1885 had settled at Mornington, four miles from Drogheda. In November 1886 a return match was played on a links here between the Royal Belfast Golf Club and the Dublin (later Royal) Golf Club (see Chapter 5). A newspaper account dated 30th October 1886 in the Royal Perth's Golf Society's scrapbook stated: "This links is without doubt the nearest approach to that of St. Andrews, the premier of Scottish greens . . . it abounds in legitimate hazards, the bunker, the rabbit scrape, the water, the furze. Here is not only opportunity for the long driver and stealthy putter but as too many of the Belfast team found, for the successful player of the sand iron and niblick. The Belfast team left on Saturday morning at seven o'clock and met the Dublin men at Drogheda about ten. Both teams then drove along the Boyne to Mornington House, the residence of Mr. Thomas Gilroy (late of Dundee), whose guests they were for the day. The match ended in favour of Dublin by 11 holes . . . after the match the teams returned to Mornington House, where they were most hospitably entertained."

In an article on Tom Gilroy in the magazine *Golf* 17th February 1893, the writer stated: "There may be seen (at Mornington) fluttering in the breeze . . . the flags of an excellent fourteen-hole course which Mr. Gilroy has laid out upon his property; the tee for the first hole being about two hundred yards distant from the entrance gates of Mornington House, sometimes Coney Holl, where Mr. Gilroy now resides".

An article on the Laytown and Bettystown Golf Club in *The Irish Field* 13th September 1913 reported: ". . . over twenty years ago there was a golf course of nine holes over the ground now to be taken in, having been made and kept up by Mr. Tom Gilroy who was one of the founders of the Royal Dublin course . . . as Mr. Gilroy had some trouble with some local people, who did not approve of golf, he, after a year or so gave up the course on that side of the Boyne and had one laid out on the other side which is now the course of the Co. Louth club . . . some of the greens are still to be seen but it would be very difficult, if not impossible, to trace out the exact course."

For whatever reason,Tom Gilroy decided to depart the area permanently and *The Irish Times* 19th December 1895 regretfully recorded the departure of the Gilroy family to England. The Mornington course which had started off with such promise did not see golf again until the present Laytown and Bettystown course was laid out in 1909.

*See Laytown and Bettystown; also Chapter 5.

MOUNTBELLEW, Co. Galway.
Instituted 1906. Affiliated 1930.

The Irish Field 10th November 1906 reports: ". . . a meeting of the above club was held in Mannions Hotel during the week. President Sir Henry Grattan Bellew; Vice President Lord De Rythyn; Captain Mr. Nernon. A vote of thanks was passed to Sir Henry Grattan Bellew for giving use of the Deer Park grounds for the golf course". This is the first record of a club at Mountbellew and for the first time *The Golfing Annual* 1906/07 lists the club, without giving an institution date. Similar entries occur in the *Golfing Annuals* up to 1910. There is no mention of the club in any of the *Irish Golfers Guides* 1910 to 1916 and it would appear that the early club was short-lived.

The present Mountbellew Golf Club was founded in 1929 and the course was laid out on land rented from Col. Bellew at £18 per annum. The pioneers were Ned Donoghue, Dr. Matt Crowe, James Haverty, Micky Gilmore, Maurice Hegarty, Father Matt Loftus, the Naughton family, Nellie Mannion and the staff of the Bank of Ireland.

MOYSTOWN, Co. Offaly.

*See Ferbane and Moystown G.C.

MULLINGAR, Co. Westmeath.
Instituted 1894. Affiliated 1895.

The Irish Times 5th April 1895 reported: "Yesterday a large number of the County aristocracy assembled at Newbrook racecourse for the purpose of inaugurating the Westmeath Golf Club. The following were amongst those present: Rt. Hon. Lord Greville, Hon. Miss Veronique Greville, Mrs. Swift (Lynn Lodge), Mr. and Mrs. A. E. Triscott . . . Tea having been partaken in the Grand Stand, an adjournment was made to the course and the President (Lord Greville) having opened the links, delivered a brief address on the enjoyment of golfing and wished the club every success. Play was then indulged in for some hours. The Hon. Secretary, Mr. A. R. Triscott, is sparing no effort to secure the success of the club and is ably seconded by several ladies and gentlemen who hope in the near future to be in a position to take part in some of the metropolitan matches."

An entry for the "Westmeath Club" in the *The Golfing Annual* 1895/96 gives 1894 as the institution date and states: "The course has recently been improved and the greens protected against cattle". *The Sportsmans Holiday Guide* 1897 gives the club's name as the Mullingar Golf Club and records: ". . . a nice nine-hole course on the Gaybrook (sic) Racecourse about a mile out of town. The course commands fine views of lakes Owel and Ennal . . . the distance round is about 1½ miles''.

The Irish Times 30th April 1900 reported a match on the club's new course at Mount Prospect, the property of Mr. Killian. This site was the club's home until 1909 when a new course was laid out on the lands of Mr. J. T. Roche at Lynn, one mile outside the town. *The Irish Golfers Guide* 1910 reported there were sixty men and twenty lady members and there was ". . . no record as the old course has been abandoned. A new nine holes course was laid out by Mr. W. C. Pickeman in September last and should soon be ready for play.''

There a further move by the club in 1919 when a nine-hole course was laid out on the lands of Mr. Peter Gaynor, beside Lough Owel. This was a most picturesque setting but the presence of the Midland & Great Western Railway through the centre of the course prevented further development. Increasing interest in the game led to the Captain of 1935, Mr. J. R. Downes, and a hard-working sub-committee seeking a suitable location for an eighteen-hole course. As a result they were successful in obtaining the property of Col. Howard Bury at Belvedere. James Braid, five times winner of the British Open Championship, was invited to design the new course. The new course was opened in 1937 and has since then become one of the finest inland courses in the country.

There is some confusion over the institution date of the club, which is not surprising due to so many temporary abodes being occupied. *The Irish Golfing Guide* 1910 recorded a date of 1887 which is in conflict with the earlier published date of 1894 in the *Golfing Annuals*. However, *The Irish Times* account of 1895 is a clear evidence of the opening of the course of a recently established club at Mullingar. *The Golfing Annual* 1905/06 gives an exact foundation date of 18th October 1894.

MULRANY, Co. Mayo.

The present club at Mulrany was founded in 1968, however golf had been played there over sixty years before that date. Details of the earlier course are first recorded in *The Irish Field* 7th August 1909: ". . . quite a good nine-hole course existed up till 1907 at Mallaranny (sic) in conjuction with the Midland Great Western Railway but owing to some difficulties, now happily overcome, the course was given up for two years. This year the Railway company have arranged with various tenants who own the necessary strip of seaside land''.

The Irish Golfers Guide 1910 states that the railway company had "a nine-hole course in conjunction with their fine hotel at Malaranny. Owing to scarcity of residents in the neighbourhood the course is chiefly used by visitors''.

From the above it can be seen that this was a proprietorial course, organised by the Midland Great Western Railway Co. mainly for the visitors to their hotel. No foundation date is given and there is no mention of a club's existence in the entries of the early Irish *Golf Guides*. The course is listed in *The Irish Golfing Guide* 1916 but there is no record of the later history of the course.

MUSKERRY, Co. Cork.
Instituted 1897.   Affiliated 1910.

The Irish Times 18th September 1897 recorded: "The newly established Muskerry Golf and Lawn Tennis Club have now decided on taking over the golf links at Leemount, near Coachford, Co. Cork, for the use of the members . . . formed quite recently now numbers 72 members under the Presidency of Sir Augustus Warren with Mr. H. W. Gillman as Honorary Secretary and the club supplied a longfelt want amongst the resident gentry throughout Muskerry". The club is listed in *The Golfing Annual* 1898/99 which lists Mr. Gillman as Honorary Secretary but little other detail. Following this there is a gap until *The Golfing Annual* 1906/07 when the club's institution date is given as 1907 and the Honorary Secretary is given as Dr. A. Hudson, St. Ann's Hydro, Blarney. An exact foundation date of April 1907 is given in *The Golfing Annual* 1907/08.

It would appear that the earlier club had ceased to function in the early 1900s and a revival is confirmed in *Golf Illustrated* 26th April 1907: ". . . a new golf course has been laid out at Coachford Junction station, six miles from Cork on the Muskerry Light Railway. It will be opened next month as the headquarters of the Muskerry Golf Club, of which Sir George Colthurst is President and Dr. Ainslee Hudson of St. Ann's Hill the Hon. Secretary. John McNamara, a brother of Willie McNamara of Lahinch is professional to the club. The course of eighteen holes is 5,200 yards in length . . . a commodious clubhouse is projected and owing to its great accessibility, the new club promises to be a real acquistion to golfers in County Cork".

In the interim years after the demise of the earlier club, another club was founded at nearby St. Ann's Hill with that name.

*See St. Ann's Hill.

NAAS, Co. Kildare.
Instituted 1896.   Affiliated 1907.

A comparison of the early *Golf Guides* reveals a conflict of dates for the institution of this club which was known as Co. Kildare Golf Club until 1966. *The Golfing Annual* 1898/99 gives 1897, the 1902/03 edition has two listings for the club giving 1897 and 1895. Later *The Irish Golfers Guide* 1910 gives 1894.

In a letter to the editor of *The Irish Field,* published in in the edition of 3rd October 1908, Mr. E. I. Gray corrected an earlier account of the foundation of the club: "Your correspondent states that Messrs. Gray and McCann were chiefly responsible for the forming of the club in 1896. Neither McCann, or myself, had anything to do with it. It was first put on foot by a great enthusiast Mr. Mansfield D.L., our President, who was ably assisted by Mr. J. S. Shannon now manager of the Hibernian Bank at Loughrea. They got together a very small club at Halverstown, that existed only on sufferance and despite the fact that the rent was only something like £6 a year, it was with great difficulty raised . . ."

It can be seen that 1896 is the acknowledged institution date given in this early account, the first course was laid out in that year at Halverstown. In 1903 George

Coburn, the professional at Portmarnock, laid out a new nine-hole course for the club at the Decoy (*The Irish Field* 12th March 1904).

Like so many other Irish clubs, difficulties with leases and restrictions in use of the land created major problems for this club. *The Irish Field* 27th July 1912 records the next move of the club to the Knocks, this was a nine-hole course laid out by W. C. Pickeman of Portmarnock. In 1922 there was a further move to Monread where Cecil Barcroft had laid out a nine-hole course. Finally in 1940 the present course at Kerdiffstown was acquired and on 8th June 1941 it was officially opened.

NAVAN, Co. Meath.

The Golfing Annual 1906/07 lists this club with an institution date of January 1907. In the following edition an amended foundation date of December 1906 is recorded. The first Captain is given as Capt. J. R. Roberts and a membership of 25 . . . "The course of nine holes varying from 200 to 400 yards is about a mile from the Great Northern and Midland Great Western Stations . . . the course is only open from November 1st to first week in April".

An account of the opening of the club's new course is given in *The Irish Field* 23rd November 1907: "The links situated close to Navan were opened on Friday by the Marquis of Headfort in the presence of a representative company. The greens were well disposed, the lengths varying from 150 to 400 yards. Lord Headfort in his opening address congratulated the members on the excellence of the links and paid compliments to Major Roberts and to the Secretary Mr. Lord. . . . His Lordship drove the first ball in the competition for the Headfort cup, presented by himself to be won twice in succession or four times altogether in one year . . . Mr. J. C. Hanbury, Co. Meath Club was first winner".

The Irish Golf Guides from 1910 to 1916 continually list Captain Roberts as the club Captain and in the latter year a membership of 60 men and 16 ladies was recorded. Following the First World War, land and cattle values increased and the landowner, Mrs. Swan, finally ejected the club circa 1922.

Following this break-up of the club the members moved to Bellinter and reformed themselves as Bellinter Golf Club.

*See Headfort G.C., Killua Castle G.C., Bellinter G.C.

NENAGH, Co. Tipperary.
Instituted 1892. Affiliated 1929.

The present Nenagh Golf Club dates its foundation from 1929 and the club's history brochure states ". . . our club was fortunate to take over an established nine-hole course of some merit, from the old club which existed prior to 1929 . . . the first AGM was held on 23rd February 1929 . . . the officials appointed were, President Lord Dunally . . ."

The Golfing Annual 1895/96 documents the earlier Nenagh Golf Club for the first time and an institution date for 13th October 1892 is given. The President is listed as Lord Dunally and here can be seen the link with the later club. A membership of 49 is given, which included 20 ladies, and ". . . the course, of nine holes, adjoining the town. It is a rather difficult round, the hazards being walls, hedges and drains. . ." In addition, the Captain is named as H. Waring and the Hon. Secretary was J. W. C. Barry, Provincial Bank of Ireland, Nenagh.

In *The Limerick Chronicle* 17th September 1892 the names of A. McLeod, Nenagh, and Capt. Waring R.N., Nenagh, are given as contestants in a golf competition at Kilkee, these same gentlemen are named as committee members in *The Golfing Annual* 1896/97. *The Irish Times* 12th April 1895 for the first time records an interclub match at Nenagh when the home club were successful against a Roscrea team. Two years later *The Sportsmans Holiday Guide* 1897 stated: "The Nenagh Golf Club have a sporting nine-hole course close to the town . . . the amateur record of the green is 45 which gives a pretty fair idea of the difficulties that the golfer has to contend against here. The course is only in its infancy as yet, having been formed as recently as 1892".

Later editions of *The Golfing Annual* continue to give 13th October 1892 as the institution date and the 1898/99 edition lists the club as affiliated to the Golfing Union of Ireland for the first time. However, later editions of the *Annual* and of the *Irish Golf Guides* from 1910 to 1916 do not record affiliation. *The Golfing Annual* 1907/08 reported that the club had occupied a new course 1½ miles from the railway station. *Irish Life* 20th February 1920 carries a brief article which reveals the plight of the club at that time: ". . . a letter from the Nenagh club (to the Golfing Union of Ireland) stated how they had been obliged to give their course for cultivation during the war but were now able to resume, having secured suitable ground. It was unanimously decided that Nenagh be reinstated as an affiliated club".

NEWBOROUGH, Gorey, Co. Wexford.

The Irish Times 15th January 1898 has an entry relating to this club: "On Thursday last (gentlemen's competition day) a very exciting match took place on the above links. The light was fading as the last green was reached and Mr. Tuke was declared the winner. The tired competitors were then entertained to a most enjoyable tea given by Mrs. Turner of Clonattin."

The Golfing Annual 1898/99 gives an institution date of November 1894 which would make this club one of the earliest Leinster clubs. Miss M. E. Guise, Gorey, is listed as the Honorary Secretary and . . . "The course consists of nine holes". Succeeding *Golfing Annuals* until 1905/06 continue to list the club, without giving any additional information.

There is no listing of this club in the *Irish Golf Guides* from 1910 to 1916.
*See Gorey Golf Club.

NEWMARKET, Co. Cork.

A club of this name is listed in the index to *The Sportsmans Holiday Guide* 1897. No other detail is given.

NEWPORT, Co. Tipperary.

An entry in *The Irish Times* 31st March 1899 is the first record of the existence of this club. The article related the result of a match versus the Nenagh Golf Club which was won by the latter by 19 holes . . . "The links are charmingly situated on the Clamaltha river, within a mile of Newport . . . Considering these links were only opened last October, the greens and everything connected with the course reflects the greatest credit on the energetic Honorary Secretary, Mr. P. A. Blaischeck, Newport".

An entry for the club is first given in *The Golfing Annual* 1908/09 which gives the Hon. Secretary's name as C. J. Dwyer, Churchfield House, Newport. . . . "The course is a Winter one of nine holes". *The Irish Golfing Guide* 1916 records: "This club has ceased to exist for the present". It can be seen from *The Irish Times* account that the course was first instituted in October 1898, which was probably the year of the foundation of the club.

NEW ROSS, Co. Wexford.
Instituted 1905.   Affiliated 1912.

New Ross Golf Club is first listed in *The Golfing Annual* 1908/09, no institution date is given. J. M. Roche was the Hon. Secretary and "the course of nine holes is a mile and a half from New Ross Station". *The Irish Golfers Guide* 1910 gives an institution date of 1905 and recorded that the nine-hole course was three-quarters of a mile from the railway station. The 1911 *Guide* lists the Captain as P. J. Roche and he is also listed as Captain in the 1912 edition. *The Irish Field* 22 September 1917 reported a revival of the club with Dr. O'Regan as President and Mr. W. H. Howard as Hon. Secretary. This revived club would appear to have fallen on hard times. *Irish Golf* 1929 recorded: "New Ross has had disappointments in recent years in the way of golf but the inhabitants have not sat down under them. It is excellent news that a new club has been formed with a strong committee. A new site for a course has been chosen . . . Mr. R. H. Corbett is Honorary Secretary and Mr. P. J. Roche is Captain."

It can be seen that Mr. P. J. Roche was the link with the previous club.

NEWRY, Co. Armagh.

The Belfast Newsletter 3rd October 1892 carries the following: "A largely attended meeting was held last Monday in the Town Commissioners rooms for the purpose of starting a golf club in Newry. Mr. Dempster was voted in the chair. The following appointments were made: Committee Messrs. Hunter, Moore, Dempster, K. Moore, Burrows, Erskine, Carvill, Mainwaring and W. S. Walker Hon. Secretary and Treasurer. A course of nine holes has been laid out on the drill fields, the use of which has been kindly given by Mr. R. Dempster."

A further entry in the same paper's edition of 22nd October 1892, in regard to an open competition, reports: ". . . the links situate in the Military field off the Camlough road . . ." An entry in *The Irish Times* 28th October 1892 records that a competitor from Newry had entered an open competition of the Royal Dublin Golf Club.

The club is not listed in any of the *Golfing Annuals* from 1893 to 1910 and the *Irish Golf Guides* from 1910 to 1916 do not mention it. An entry for a Newry Golf Club appears in *The Golfers Handbook* 1923, which may have been a revival, but the subsequent history of this later club is unknown.

NEWTOWNBARRY (Bunclody), Co. Wexford.

One of the earliest records of this club's existence is a competition result in *The Irish Times* 19th February 1906 which was won by Capt. C. V. Cameron with 73. *The Irish Golfers Guide* 1910 gives an institution date of 1904 for the club . . . "a nine holes inland course situated at Newtownbarry House demesne, about seven miles from Ferns Station". The Honorary Secretary's name is listed as Rev. R. Talbot and the President was R. Hall-Dare D.L. Sunday play was allowed without caddies and ". . . chief fixtures are during the Spring and Winter. The course is prettily situated on the banks of the Slaney and is well kept. A variety of hazards render the course thoroughly sporting. There is much local interest in the game".

The course is listed in *The Irish Golfing Guide* 1916 with R. M. Hall-Dare still in office. Later, *The Golfers Handbook* 1923 lists the club with a membership of 84. It is continually documented in *Thoms Directories* until 1946. *The Irish Golfers Bluebook* 1939 described it as a "most picturesque course on the banks of the Slaney". (This would indicate that there had been no move since 1910).

The Golfers Handbook 1963 has an entry for the club, there were 50 members and the Joint Secretaries were Rev. James Quigley and E. A. Owens. Subsequent history of this club is unknown.

NEWTOWNSTEWART, Co. Tyrone.
Instituted 1914. Affiliated 1918.

The magazine *Irish Life* 16th October 1914 documented the foundation of this club and the generosity of the Duke of Abercorn was acknowledged. The inaugural meeting was held in the Abercorn Hotel on the 9th October and the Duke was elected first President of the club. Two men are credited with the foundation of the club in addition to the Duke, Mr. H. Kiernan of the Northern Bank and Mr. W. Ross Henderson (Captain in 1922).

Initially a nine-hole course was laid out . . . "ten minutes cycling distance from the town". In 1970 the course was extended to eighteen holes.

NORTH SUBURBAN, Co. Dublin.
*See Finglas G.C.

NORTH-WEST, Lisfannon, Co. Donegal.
Instituted 1891.   Affiliated 1891.

This club belongs to that select group of nine clubs which founded the Golfing Union of Ireland in November 1891. At that time the North-West Club was less than nine months old itself. *The Derry Journal* 25th February 1891 documents the preliminary meeting, held in the Guildhall, Derry: ''. . . for the purpose of starting a golf club in the neighbourhood of Derry. The following were present: Mr. Thomas Hayes J.P. (in the chair), Colonel Perry, Professor McMaster, Dr. Reid, Dr. McCullagh and Messrs. R. S. Smythe, Andrew Johnston, James Stewart, Harold Chambers, F. Dawson, A. Hogg, G. D. Coates, R. L. Hogg, Charles R. Tillie, John Patton and Gilbert V. Craig.'' The meeting was informed of inquiries made by the Lough Swilly Hotel Company about use of land but the tenants had refused to sign agreements and ''asked for an increase in rent''. The meeting was adjourned for a fortnight.

When *The Derry Journal* next reported on the venture it was in its 3rd July edition: ''The course at Buncrana having been carefully surveyed and laid out by Thompson, the professional at the County Club, Portrush, is now open for play . . . The total length of the nine-hole course is 2,622 yards, absolutely without a cross and can boast of two holes, 515 and 412 yards in length respectively . . . The ladies have not been forgotten in the arrangements in connection with the club as immediately adjacent to the railway station at Buncrana an exceeding good nine-hole course has been laid out and is rapidly being got into order. As an indication of the advance of golf in the North, we may mention that the new club has already enrolled upwards of seventy members. Owing to the magnificent and natural character of the links, as well as the surrounding beautiful scenery, it certainly may look forward to a brilliant future.''

The official opening of the Lisfannon course was documented in *The Derry Journal* Wednesday 5th August 1891: ''. . . formally opened on Monday . . . besides the members and their friends, there were golfers present from Portrush, Belfast, Aughnacloy and Randalstown . . . the roll of membership is very near a hundred, including the fifteen lady members of the club. Two portions of ground are available for golfing, the gentlemen's links at Lisfannon and the ladies' links at Buncrana. The latter portion of ground, which has been kindly placed at the disposal of the club by Mr. George H. Mitchell J.P. has not yet been laid out, but the former, the use of which has been granted by Captain Norman, has been carefully arranged . . .''

The inaugural competition was won by J. Black with 88 nett off a 30 handicap. Later that evening the inaugural dinner was held in the Lough Swilly Hotel, presided over by G. H. Mitchell J.P., one of the Vice Presidents. The first Captain, Mr. Thomas Hayes, Chief Inspector R.I.C., acted as ''croupier''. R. L. Hogg and in particular G. V. Craig, the Joint Honorary Secretaries, were greatly praised.

Apart from being a founder club of the Golfing Union of Ireland, North-West has the distinction of having one of the earliest separate nine-hole courses for its lady members (see Royal Portrush, Killymoon and Thomastown). Within a very short period the fame of the course was advertised abroad and the magazine *Golf* 13th November 1891 carried a lengthy account of golf there. In each successive *Golfing Annual* until 1910, the ladies' nine-hole course is documented. However, the *Irish Golf Guides* 1910 to 1916 do not mention it and in 1938 the present course was extended to eighteen holes.

*See Buncrana.

OMAGH, Co. Tyrone.
Instituted 1910.   Affiliated 1911.

The present Omagh Golf Club dates itself from 24th February 1910 when a general meeting was held in the Courthouse, Omagh, however *The Irish Field* 2nd October 1909 reported the foundation of Tyrone Golf Club on 24th September 1909 at which meeting Capt. Auchinleck had been elected President and Mr. F. Shields was elected Captain. Capt. Auchinleck had agreed to give suitable land for a course. G. L. Baillie, the founder of golf at Belfast was employed to lay out the golf course.

It is of interest to note that two golf clubs at Omagh were listed in *The Irish Golfers Guide* 1910, the newly-founded Tyrone G.C. (renamed Omagh G.C. at the general meeting in February 1910) and a club captained by Dr. H. B. Fleming. The foundation date of the latter club was given as 1892, the Honorary Secretary was Miss Fleming, Palisade House, Omagh. There were 20 lady members and 25 men and . . . ''The club exists for the benefit of members and friends and is run on modest lines''.

An entry in *The Golfing Annual* 1891/92 confirms the earlier existence of golf here: "Omagh is the proud possessor of two nine-hole golf courses, one of which is of a semi private nature. The holes are judiciously placed on both courses". *The Belfast Newsletter* 1st May 1891 lists an Omagh Golf Club with a membership of 20 and names the Honorary Secretary as Capt. H. H. Stewart. The earlier Omagh Golf Club is recorded as an affilated club in *The Golfing Annual* 1896/97 and is continuously listed until the 1909/10 *Annual*, which gives an institution date of 1892. *Nisbets Golf Year Book* 1909 also confirms this institution date. However it would appear that by 1909 the older club had become a private family-run concern, which did not cater for the needs of the locality. Sadly, *Irish Life* 5th February 1915 recorded the death in action of the present club's founder President, Capt. Auchinleck.

In May 1983 the course was extended to eighteen holes.

ORMEAU, Belfast, Co. Down.
Instituted 1893.   Affiliated 1894.

The Belfast Newsletter 24th September 1892 reported that a deputation had gone to the Parks Committee of Belfast City Council re the proposed golf links at Ormeau Park and that they were hopeful of the outcome. Later, *The Irish Golfer* 14th October 1899 stated: "Ormeau possess one supreme advantage over most of the important courses in the North of Ireland. It lies inside the municipal boundary of no mean city . . . being one 20 minutes walk from the Belfast exchange . . . The club was founded in 1893 under the Captaincy of Mr. James Woodside . . . the outlook from the clubhouse is a very charming view of wonderful scenery, contributed to by the tall ancestral trees of the old Donegall estate, now the Ormeau Park."

The club's entry in *The Golfing Annual* 1893/94 lists December 1892 as the date of institution and records a membership of 160. . . . "The course is a nine-hole one of about one mile and a quarter in length. The hazards are whins, streams, trees and hedges . . . There is a clubhouse on the ground".

A ladies' club is documented in *The Golfing Annual* 1895/96: "There is separate accommodation for the ladies in the clubhouse".

OTWAY, Co. Donegal.
Instituted 1893.   Affiliated 1893.

Otway Golf Club have a legend that golf was first played in the area in the 1850s when British officers of the local Martello Tower (built c. 1805) played golf in the area. There is an amazing entry in *The Irish Golfers Blue Book* 1939 which gives an institution date of 1873. It was also claimed that the club had minutes going back to 1884. There is no tangible evidence of this early golf and the first documented club was founded in 1893, according to the present club's records.

The Golfing Annual 1893/94 gives an institution date of December 1892, the President was Mr. W. E. George and the Captain was Major Batt. The club had 15 members and . . . "The green record is 34 by Dr. J. Patterson on August 13 1893

. . . The course of nine holes is situated on the shore of Lough Swilly and hazards are numerous. Rathmullen is twelve miles from Londonderry where train may be taken to Fahan and from there by steamer to Rathmullen. The links are two miles from Rathmullen.''

It is obvious that this club, with only fifteen members, situated in an area difficult of access, is a fine example of the tenacity of early golfers. The Major Butt mentioned above was most probably one of the Batt family, inadvertently mispelled. This family have had a long established connection with the area, *Griffiths Valuation* 1858 records Thomas Batt as a substantial landholder. *The Golfing Annual* 1898/99 lists Lt. Col. T. E. Batt as Honorary Secretary and *The Irish Golfing Guide* 1916 has C. L. Batt as a committee member. All of the *Golfing Annuals* from 1894 to 1910 record December 1892 as the date of institution. The *Irish Golf Guides* 1910 to 1916 give 1893.

OUGHTERARD, Co. Galway.

The present club at Oughterard dates from 1973, however *The Irish Field* 23rd June 1906 states: "Golf continues to hum in Galway and at Oughterard a golf course is shortly to be laid out near this picturesque little village of that name, some 17 miles from Galway". *The Golfing Annual* 1906/07 records the club for the first time and gives an institution date of 1907, no other detail is given. There is no entry for the club in the *Golfing Annuals* after 1909. Subsequent history of the earlier club is unknown.

PHOENIX PARK, Dublin.

Some recent golf publications have claimed that Scottish regiments played golf in the Phoenix Park in the 1850s. No evidence has been quoted for such claims, although it is quite probable that the game was played there at that time. Evidence of the establishment of a military golf club there in 1884 is outlined in Chapter 5 and it is clear that this was pointed out by one of the speakers at the founding meeting of the Dublin Golf Club on 15th May 1885 (see Royal Dublin). That the two clubs merged in 1885 is clear and the later institution date became accepted.

The Dublin Golf Club departed the Phoenix Park, finally, in early 1889 when the new links at Dollymount had been acquired. Lord Cadogan, who was Lord Lieutenant from 1895 to 1902, reintroduced the game during his term of office. George Sayers of North Berwick had been coming over annually to give lessons to his family prior to 1900, as can be seen in Chapter 7. *The Irish Golfer* 5th February 1902 reported: "The Duke and Duchess of Connaught (brother of King Edward VII) and Lady Cadogan are amongst the regular attenders at the golf links in the Vice Regal Lodge, Phoenix Park". It is most likely that Sayers laid out this course.

The golfing interests of the following two Viceroys are outlined in Chapter 7 also. Lord Dudley (1902-1905) was a golf fanatic and Lord Aberdeen also was a keen golfer. Ireland's first President, Dr. Douglas Hyde, also had an interest in golf and he organised a course at the ex Vice Regal Lodge after taking office. In the National Library of Ireland, ms. 14900, Mr. A. J. Nowlan recorded: ''. . . on the appointment of Dr. Douglas Hyde **as first** President of Ireland, his secretary Mr. McDunphy applied to the Board of Works to have a small golf course provided in the Presidential grounds. The President, a lover of the open air life, used to play a good deal of golf at his home in Roscommon . . . the site agreed on began at the rear of the residence, meandered near the pleasant wooded grounds and ended near the entrance to the house. Fifteen bunkers were raised with the aid of soil brought from the wilderness and the turf rolled back from the surface . . . the course was in use in May 1939 . . ."

*See Royal Dublin G.C.; also Chapters 5 and 7.

PORTADOWN, Co. Armagh.
Instituted 1894.   Affiliated 1902.

There are many difficulties in recording the history of golf at Portadown, there is conflicting documentary evidence regarding the chronology of golf in the locality. The official club brochure records: ". . . as far back as 1900, golf came to Portadown when a number of gentlemen established a course at Lisniskey. It became an organized club in 1905 and affiliated to the Golfing Union of Ireland". However, *The Golfing Annual* 1902/03 records a golf club at Portadown, the Honorary Secretary was J. McMechan, Belfast Bank, Portadown.

There is little doubt that a golf club existed in the town at a much earlier date. *The Belfast Newsletter* 2nd March 1895 reported: "The members of this club (Portadown) held their annual meeting in the Young Men's Institution. There was a large attendance, thus testifying to the healthy interest which is taken in the club by the young men of the town. The chair was occupied by Mr. John Lutton (Captain) who from the formation of the club some fifteen years ago has always evinced a desire to promote the welfare of the organisation. The Secretary's report was read by Mr. Waugh. The statement of accounts was presented by Mr. T. Alexander and showed the club to be in a prosperous condition. The following office bearers were elected for the ensuing year: President, Charles Johnston J.P. . . . Captain, John Lutton . . ."

The above report was inaccurate in one respect, referring to the formation of the club "fifteen years ago". This would have dated its foundation to 1880, older than Royal Belfast. It is probable that there was a transcription error, and "fifteen years" could have been "fifteen months", or, "five years". This early club is not documented in any of the *Golfing Annuals* and is not recorded again in *The Belfast Newsletter*.

Entries for the Portadown Club are given in successive *Golfing Annuals* from 1907 to 1909, in which year there were joint Secretaries, Mr. V. Wilson and Mr. R. Richardson. The course location was given as Drumcree. An article in *The Irish Field* 23rd November 1907 under the heading "New Club at Portadown": ". . . a meeting having been held in the Town Hall on the 18th inst. to further the purpose. The Chairman of the Town Council, Mr. H. Richardson was in the chair and said the movement had been on foot for some time and he thought the matter would be taken up heartily provided that suitable grounds could be got . . . Mr. Valentine Wilson was appointed secretary to the meeting . . ." *The Golfing Annual* 1909/10 lists the "new" club and gives an institution date of 1908.

Golfing Union of Ireland records reveal an affiliation date of 20th May 1902, *The Irish Field* 18th March 1916 also documents a further affiliation. The present club records a move to Mahon in 1919 and finally to its present location at Carrickblacker in 1934. An eighteen-hole course was laid out, using the old greens from Mahon, and officially opened in 1936.

During the Second World War nine of the holes were closed, flax and potatoes were grown on the disused area of the course. In 1974 the course was once again extended to eighteen holes.

PORTARLINGTON, Co. Laois.
Instituted 1908. Affiliated 1911.

The Irish Field 9th July 1910 carried an article on this recently founded club, giving an institution date of 1909: "For some time previous to 1909 there was a strong desire for a golf club prevalent among the residents of the Portarlington district, but it was not until last year that Cannon Cole, Mr. Cobbe, Mr. O'Donnel and Rev. H. Beauchamp took the matter seriously in hand and started the club. A meeting was called in Portarlington and a committee was formed. The Rev. J. L. Morrow (Hon. Secretary G.U.I.) then laid out a course in the Garryhinch Demesne, which is about two and a half miles from the town and station . . ."

It is of interest to note that the Irish Golf Guides from 1910 to 1916 record 1909 as the club institution date as it would appear that *The Irish Field* article, quoted above, was inaccurate. In the 5th December 1908 edition of this same sporting paper the following article is carried: "Portarlington although a favourite residential town for leisured or retired families, has been long in taking its place in the ranks of provincial town possessing golf courses . . . a demesne of liberal extent has been rented within an easy cycle run, or even walk, of the town. Lord Portarlington, the Rev. Father Beauchamp Hon. Secretary of the club with a number of others, have heartily taken up the promotion of Portarlington Golf Club and now everything gives promise of success. The ground which consists of old pasture, provides a mossy turf, which grows grass slowly even in Summer . . . There is a handsome lodge at the gate which will serve for a time as a clubhouse. The Hon. Secretary of the G.U.I. last week laid out the course . . ."

For the first time the club was documented in *The Golfing Annual* 1908/09 which gave 1908 as the year of institution. Rev. H. Beauchamp was Hon. Secretary. The "handsome" gate lodge, mentioned earlier, is the nucleus of the present fine clubhouse and the club continues to enjoy the same original course.

PORTMARNOCK, Co. Dublin.
Instituted 1894. Affiliated 1895.

The Portmarnock golf club which is widely acclaimed as having one of the premier golf courses in the world might never have come into being if the British War Department had had its way! *The Irish Times* 22nd December 1891 records the opening of an inquiry at the police barracks Baldoyle "to receive objections against

PORTMARNOCK G.C. OPENING DAY, SEPTEMBER 1894.
Captain's match at 5th. George Ross, first Captain, on extreme left. John Petrie playing.
(Presented by Gordon Ross, 1944).

the Secretary of War Department purchasing under the compulsory powers
conferred on him by the Barracks Act 1890, near Portmarnock the property of John
Jameson esquire''. The inquiry continued to take evidence in June 1892 with Mr.
John Jameson giving evidence that his father had acquired the lands, comprising 580
acres in all, in the year 1847 and built a substantial dwelling house there. Many local
fishermen also gave evidence and pointed out the dangers of placing a rifle range
in the area with so many boats fishing the traditional grounds. The objections were
successful and the future of Portmarnock as a golf links was thus secured.

Unfortunately for the historian, the minute books of the early years of this club
are missing, a common fact for many other Irish clubs. Fortunately *Golf Illustrated*
30th November 1906 carries a full account of the formation of the club: ''. . . as
the train on the main line from Belfast to Dublin draws near the junction station of
the Howth branch, the traveller today gets a brief glimpse of the Portmarnock links
and clubhouse. Such an accidental glimpse given, over twelve years ago, to the eyes
of Mr. W. C. Pickeman led to the discovery of the Portmarnock course and the
formation of the golf club. Mr. Pickeman who has since its formation been the
Honorary Secretary of the club, and is at present its Captain, first visited the ground
on September 10th 1894 and at once called a meeting of his Scottish and Irish

friends. Twenty two responded, sixteen being Scotch three Irish and two English. all agreed to cooperate in establishing a club and appointed a deputation to wait on Mr. John Jameson D.L. of whose demesne St. Marnocks, the Portmarnock links forms a peninsula jutting out towards the sea. Mr. Jameson who remembers golf being played on these sand dunes by his father and his guests while he was yet a boy, so facilitated matters that agreements between the club and Mr. Jameson and his tenants were drawn up and signed on October 1st 1894 and before the close of the year a meeting of the young club was held and the following officers were appointed: President Mr. John Jameson D.L.; Captain Mr. George Ross; Trustees Walter Hume and J. C. Anderson; Hon. Treasurer Mr. A. Walker, Hon. Secretary Mr. W. C. Pickeman. . . . although the society was mainly composed of Scots, an Irishman Mr. George Ross was elected Captain and for three years held the office. Mr. Pickeman laid out the original course of nine holes which won the approval of Mungo Park (the Open Champion of 1874) who was called in as consultant green architect. At Easter of 1896 the full course of 18 holes and the clubhouse were opened . . . a young fellow named Brady from Dollymount was the first professional.''

The Irish Times 28th December 1894 records the formal opening of the new links and the same paper's edition of 13th August 1895 reported: ''The course is being quickly brought into excellent condition by Mungo Park and promises yet to take a good position among the Irish links''. Park at this time would appear to have been ''poached'' from the Foxrock Club where he had been employed since August 1894 (see Foxrock). The first annual general meeting of the club is reported in *The Irish Times* 24th January 1896, when the Hon. Secretary reported a membership of 150. He also reported on the considerable difficulty experienced by members as to the ferrying from Sutton Station (see Sutton) and arranging satisfactory terms with the tenants. He also reported that the new clubhouse would cost £500 and that ground for the new nine holes had been presented by Mr. Jameson for a nominal £10, the only stipulation being that there would be no Sunday play!

The course is described in *The Golfing Annual* 1896/97: ''. . . eighteen holes, varying in length from 150 to 520 yards, extending to three and a quarter miles, and is bounded on three sides by the sea. The course is not unlike Troon and the greens are excellent''. Some of the difficulties with the early course and the journey to the links were documented in a reflective article in *The Irish Times* 30th January 1903: '' 'Twas no easy matter to induce men to take a sea voyage to the peninsula in the early days when the club was originated. When they were there it was hard to convince them that the moss which lay as soft as rich eiderdown over the whole links would ever be transformed into the true golfing turf. 'Twas pioneer work. What made the success of Portmarnock was the men who in the little 'Shanty' in which Mungo Park and his wife were the presiding geniuses . . .''

In 1898 Portmarnock's new links was recognised by the Golfing Union of Ireland when it was added to the rota of Irish championship courses, the others being Portrush and Newcastle in the North and Dollymount in the South. The 1899 Irish Amateur Open Championship was held there when John Ball Jun. beat F. W. Williamson 12 and 11 in the final. In 1949 the British Amateur Championship was won at Portmarnock by Max McCready, this was the first occasion on which this prestigious tournament was played in Ireland (later played at Portrush in 1960 when

Joe Carr won). Further prestige was added when the Dunlop Masters was held there in 1959, Christy O'Connor winning with a final round of 66 from Joe Carr.

Golf had first been played by the Jamesons at Portmarnock in 1858 (see Chapter 4) and the family, of whiskey fame, were generous benefactors to the club from its inception in 1894. It was John Jameson's spirited defence in June 1892 which preserved this world famous stretch of golfing terrain. Unfortunately, the present Jameson family have no recollection of the earlier golfing days on this links.

*See Dublin Scottish G.C., Sutton G.C. and Chapter 6.

PORTSALON, Co. Donegal.
Instituted 1891.   Affiliated 1891.

This club has the distinction of being a founder member of the Golfing Union of Ireland, in November 1891. At that time the club itself was only a few months old and its foundation is documented in *The Belfast Newsletter* 26th August 1891: "The latest but by no means least addition to the golf courses of Ireland is to be found at Portsalon on the Northwest shore of Lough Swilly . . . It has become widely known within the past two or three years principally owing to the erection of an excellent hotel. . . . We understand the golfing fraternity are indebted to Captain Kenneth McLaren for the discovery of this new ground. . . . The holes are eighteen in number, with a circuit of over three miles beginning and ending at the clubhouse, which is one minute's walk from the hotel . . . a club is being organized with Col. J. D. Barton of Greenport, on whose property the links are situated, as Captain and Mr. Henry Chichester Hart J.P. of Carrablagh, Portsalon as Hon. Secretary . . ." An entry for the club in *The Golfing Annual* 1892/93 listed 25 members paying one guinea per year. The Captain was Col. Barton and the Hon. Secretary was unchanged.

An article in *The Field* 30th April 1892 extolled the virtues of this new golf course and on many occasions the course featured in the pages of the magazines *Golf* and *Golf Illustrated* between 1897 and 1904. *The Irish Golfer* 1899 carries an article on golf at Portsalon: "There is first class accommodation for over 40 guests in the roomy shooting lodge which Col. Barton, the owner of most of the land hereabouts, turned into an hotel . . . it stands high above the harbour and commands a beautiful view of the Lough and of the links. The links are free to all guests staying at the hotel, for a nominal six pence a day. Seven golfing days in the week may be had here . . . while the Queen's writ runs in Donegal, the Anathema Maranatha of the General Assembly does not and erring Scotchmen, having escaped its jurisdiction have more than once engaged on a Sunday, with a profane motive, in a good tussle over 18 holes . . ."

It is of interest to see that Sunday golf was being advertised as a means of attracting visitors. In addition, Portsalon, North-West and Rosapenna golf clubs engaged in a joint open competition which was widely reported from 1893 onwards. The Barton family connection continued for many years, *The Irish Golfing Guide* 1916 records the Captain and Honorary Secretary as Major B. J. Barton D.S.O. and also . . . "The course was chosen in 1905 and 1912 for the Irish Ladies Championship".

PORTSTEWART, Co. Derry.
Instituted 1894. Affiliated 1895.

The Coleraine Chronicle 26th August 1894 reported: "Portstewart is at length bestirring itself. It, too, is to have a golf links. A printed circular is about to be issued suggesting the formation of a club and golfers and others will be invited to join, the proposed subscription being 10/6 annually" With the famous Portrush course in full swing not far from this holiday resort, the residents had, belatedly, decided that golf as an amenity would be good for the town as the article makes clear . . . "In Scotland, almost every seaside town of any pretension has its golf course and there is no reason why Portstewart should not also provide an attraction of this kind".

This same newspaper in its edition of 4th May 1895 records a general meeting of the club, which makes it clear that the foundation date of the club was September 1894: ". . . on the motion of Mr. Lyle, seconded by Mr. O'Neill, the chair was taken by Mr. Montagu, J.P. who briefly explained the steps which had been taken for the organisation of the club since its origination in September last and the terms upon which the ground for the links had been leased. The club had, he said, been formed principally for the benefit of Portstewart and the success which had already been attained was most gratifying, the membership now being about 130. The business of that meeting was the election of officers and the adoption of rules and bye-laws. The annual general meeting would be held each September."

At this meeting Mr. R. A. C. Montagu was elected first Captain, Mr. Marcus Gage J.P. Hon. Secretary and Mr. George Wilson Hon. Treasurer. Later, *The Golfing Annual* 1895/96 giving an institution date of 1895 reported: "The course consists of nine holes, but it will shortly be extended to eighteen holes". This course extension did not take place until 1907 when a separate eighteen-hole course was laid out near the town. The club now has two full eighteen-hole courses.

PORTUMNA, Co. Galway.
Instituted 1907. Affiliated 1926.

Portumna Golf Club claims an institution date of 1907, unfortunately the club is not documented in any *Golfing Annual* between 1907 and 1910. The *Irish Golf Guides* 1910 to 1916 do not list the club. An entry for the club in *The Irish Golfers Blue Book* 1939 gives an institution date of 1912 and reported: "The old course was abandoned in 1934 and the Earl of Harewood then let a portion of his demesne for the new course which opened in 1935".

Writing in his magazine *Irish Golf* in February 1948, Lionel Hewson wrote: "Portumna has always interested me, if only that my efforts may have improved the course". Hewson also related that the course had escaped being tilled during the recent World War following his intercession with Lord Harewood. Golfing Union of Ireland records reveal an affiliation date of 1926.

QUEENS COUNTY (HEATH), Co. Laois.
*See Heath G.C.

QUEENS COLLEGE, Belfast.
Instituted 1907.   Affiliated 1907.
This club claims an institution date of 1907, Golfing Union of Ireland records reveal that the club was affiliated on 17th January 1907. *The Golfing Annual* 1906/07 lists the club and names J. L. Jackson as Honorary Secretary. Later, *The Irish Golfers Guide* 1910 reported that the members played on the Malone course.

QUEENSTOWN, Co. Cork.
*See Rushbrooke G.C.

RANDALSTOWN, Co. Antrim.
*See Shanes Park G.C.

RATHCONEY, Co. Cork.
Details about this early Cork club are only to be found in the early *Golfing Annuals* and *Golfers Guides*, there is no mention of the club in any Irish publication. Rathconey Golf Club is first listed in *The Golfing Annual* 1894/95 with the intriguing entry "no particulars forthcoming". The *Golfing Annuals* continue to list the name of the club until 1906 but give no other detail. *The Golfers Guide* 1897 lists the club also but no detail is recorded.

RATHFARNHAM, Co. Dublin.
Instituted 1899.   Affiliated 1908.
For some years past this club's foundation date has been recorded as 1896, however *The Irish Times* 5th April 1899 documented the details of its institution: "It has been decided to establish a golf links at Butterfield, Rathfarnham the land of which containing about 50 acres were duly surveyed by T. Hood professional of Royal Dublin Golf Club, who indicated the best positions for the greens and tees and reported that a very pretty and sporting course with 9 holes, to start with, could be had. Mr. John Lumsden and other competent authorities also kindly inspected the grounds . . . the greens and tees have been made and the course is now ready for play. . . . The club being a proprietary one, the liability of the members will be limited to their subscriptions, the present proprietor Mr. P. V. Bogue undertaking to keep the links in perfect order for a term of years. The following gentlemen have consented to act as a committee for 1899: Sr. F. Shaw Bart; Messrs. F. Franklin; F. P. Dickson, W. D. Murphy; Dr. Albert Croly; Dr. Robert Browne and Mr. P. V. Bogue Proprietor and Secretary."

The Irish Golfer 6th September 1899 reported that Mr. Bogue promised to keep the links in good order until 1st November 1902. Later, *The Irish Golfer* 31st January 1900 credits Mr. John Lumsden, the founder of the Royal Dublin Club, with the discovery of the course "just one year ago". The same article records: ". . . although it is not more than 10 months in existence it already numbers 120 members including several ladies". *The Irish Golfer* 11th April 1900 carries an account of the clubs first annual general meeting, which was chaired by Dr. Browne and the new Captain Mr. H. Bishop was nominated by the outgoing Captain (the first) Mr. W. D. Murphy.

As with many other proprietorial courses, the initial Rathfarnham Golf Club was not a success. *The Golfing Annual* 1904/05 gives an institution date of 1st May 1903 for the club and an article in *The Irish Field* 26th September 1908 reported: "The present club has only been in existence since 1903 but previously to that a Mr. Bogue ran a proprietary club which fell through for a variety of reasons . . . The four gentlemen who signed the present lease are Dr. Robert Brown, Dr. L. G. Gunn and Messrs. G. N. McMurdo and F. P. Dixon. The membership amounts to 210 of which some 90 are ladies."

The revived club continued to play over the old course, beside the River Dodder until 1965/66 when road widening caused a move to their present location at Newtown.

RENVYLE, Co. Galway.

Writing in *Irish Golf* December 1943, Lionel Hewson stated: "There was no golf at this wild weird spot near Clifden. About 1908 the owner of the Renvyle, Miss Blake, sent an SOS to me to come and layout a course for her. It was a long journey ending at night amidst the noise of exhuberant waves. The old house and its lady impressed me but I slept well and was up betimes to cast an eye about for possible golfing holes . . . I must draw a veil over it all. The poor old lady was terribly upset but golf courses don't grow on a two acre field. A £100,000 might have built a course for her but lack of money made her try running a hotel. Life is full of disappointments."

Hewson was slighly unfair to Mrs. Blake, who was obviously a persistent lady. *The Sportsmans Holiday Guide* 1897 reported the existence of a golf course at Renvyle: ". . . at present it consists of 11 holes but alterations and extensions are talked of . . . the course extends along the seashore and is a little over a mile in circuit . . . Further particulars from Mrs. Blake, Renvyle House Hotel, Letterfrack . . . There is at present no subscription . . ."

Later *The Irish Golfers Guide* 1910 lists Renvyle Golf Course and gives an institution date of 1909 . . . "a 9 hole mixed sea and inland course . . . Hon. Secretary Mrs. Blake, Renvyle House Hotel, Letterfrack . . . a pleasant little course, commanding superb views of sea and mountain". The course is listed in *The Irish Golfing Guide* 1916 but the later history is not known.

RIVERSIDE, Portmarnock, Co. Dublin.

This club was one of the several proprietary golf clubs founded before the First World War. An article in *The Irish Field* 18th September 1909, giving an institution date of 1908 for the club, stated: "Last year some friends of Mr. W. L. O'Neill remarked he should utilise his land at Riverside as a golf course. Messr. John Fairclough and F. Walker were the first gentlemen who saw the possibilities of a pleasant little course at Riverside, situated 12 minutes from Portmarnock''. The Captain named in the article was John Fairclough, one of the proposers of the club. *The Irish Golfing Guide* 1916 recorded that the course was ''a nine hole sea course . . . within 7 minutes walk of Portmarnock Station and the course is quite close to that of the Portmarnock Club. The surroundings are quite pleasant and a neat little clubhouse meets the wants of the members in a temperate way. The club is run on simple lines, being more an opportunity of friendly gatherings than a means of serious golf; but though the course is short it bristles with bunkers and therefore is quite a good test of an accurate short game''. The Honorary Secretary's name is listed as W. L. O'Neill, who was the proprietor of the links.

Irish Life 10th January 1919 recorded: '' . . . since the war began several Dublin clubs have closed down including Riverside''. The club appears to have been revived after the war as there is an entry for Riverside in *The Golfing Handbook* 1923 which lists W. L. O'Neill as the Hon. Secretary. There were 150 members at this time. The later history of this club is unknown.

ROBIN HOOD, Inchicore, Co. Dublin.

The Irish Golfers Guide 1911 gives an institution date of 1910 for this club: ''. . . a nine hole inland course situated at the village of Fox And Geese about 1½ miles from the Inchicore Tram. Hon. Secretary G. D. Williams . . . Captain J. L. J. Jones''. The club is listed in the index of the 1914 *Guide* but there is no entry in *The Irish Golfing Guide* 1916.

Writing in *The Irish Field* 27th March 1926 re the formation of Newlands Golf Club, J. P. Rooney stated: ''It is really in its sixteenth year for it was in 1910 that the Robin Hood Club, of which it is a foundation, was started. Situated a mile or so from the Inchicore tram terminus, is a piece of ground forming a triangle, which was originally a quarry . . . this was the site selected for the original Robin Hood Golf Club, but sixteen years ago there were not the same facilities for getting to remote localities which there are now and after remaining at the quarry for a few years the committee had to abandon the project and the club came to an untimely end. William Butler, the doyen of Irish professional golfers, who began his career as a caddie at Hoylake, was attached to the club, and when it closed its doors he migrated to Finglas . . . But it was not until 1920 that another attempt was made to get it on its feet. Among those who took an active part in reconstituting the club were Mr. Fleming and Mr. P. C. Roberts and so successful were the promoters that the club flourished for close on five years. The Committee were, however, ambitious and with an increasing membership role it became evident that additional land would have to be obtained and the course extended, if the competition were to be relieved. But they were doomed to disappoinment in that direction and were obliged to look further afield. Ultimately they found themselves as tenants of Newlands . . . the turf of the old course is that of close dwarf growth which is more like turf found on the seaside . . . in November 1920 the course was laid out by Ben Sayers and in the January following was ready for play for there was little difficulty in making good greens on such turf and as for bunkering, it needed none. The disused sandpits formed, in themselves, trouble galore . . .''

ROSAPENNA, Co. Donegal.
Instituted 1895. Affiliated 1898.

The intriguing story concerning the discovery of this links is documented in *The Sportsmans Holiday Guide* 1897: "The Rosapenna golf links were discovered quite by chance by Tom Morris of St. Andrews. A few years ago, this veteran golfer being employed by the late Lord Leitrim to lay out a nine hole course in the neighbourhood of the Manor House, after completing his task was taken to Rosapenna to see the beautiful scenery to be found there. His practiced eye was at once struck by the adaptability of the ground to the requirements of the game, and with his prophetic instinct he predicted before long the redcoats would be seen driving the gutta over its fine slopes . . . there are 18 holes and the circuit is about 3½ miles. It has been found necessary to lay only 3 greens, the other 15 being natural and remarkable for their size and quality. The turf is excellent and of a true golfing nature. There is no clubhouse the first tee and home green being the hotel door."

In the *Golfing Annuals* between 1893 and 1896 the course is listed under Carrigart, without reference to a club. *The Golfing Annual* 1898/99 gives an institution date for the club of 1895 and records the Honorary Secretary's name as Rev. M. Vance. *The Irish Golfers Guide* gives no date of institution but lists that year's Captain as A. Manning, the President was C. J. Stewart and the patrons were the Earl of Leitrim and the Earl of Dartmouth.

The exact date of Tom Morris' discovery is not clear but the Earl of Leitrim wrote to Lionel Hewson, as reported in *Irish Golf* June 1939, that the course had been started in 1891 by his father, with the help of Tom Morris. From an early date the course was popular with golfers and *The Irish Times* 11th July 1893 reported a joint open competition over the Rosapenna, Portsalon and Buncrana links.

ROSCOMMON, Co. Roscommon.
Instituted 1904. Affiliated 1915.

Irish Golf February 1937 recorded: "The Roscommon club was started in 1904 with a six hole course at Ballingard. Eventually it moved to its present site at Moate Park, Lord Crofton's home". Lord Crofton was club President from 1904 to 1912 and the earliest recorded Captain was John Hughes, District Inspector R.I.C., in 1910. Credit for the foundation of the club is given to a group of private citizens, whose names are unrecorded. The club is first listed in *The Golfing Annual* 1908/09 which stated: ". . . the course of nine holes adjoins the station". In the following year's *Annual* the Hon. Secretary is given as W. C. Smith and Sunday play was allowed.

In 1948 the club purchased its course at Moate Park.

ROSCREA, Co. Tipperary.
Instituted 1892. Affiliated 1911.

Like so many other older Irish clubs, Roscrea has no documentation on the early years of their golf club. *The Golfing Annual* 1895/96 records the existence of Roscrea Golf Club for the first time and gives an institution date of 1892. There were

53 members, President was W. P. H. Lloyd Vaughan, Hon. Secretary was T. R. Ely, Ballaghmore Castle. No Captain was named. A short description is given: ". . . nine holes, is undulating, with short grass. The hazards consist of banks, trees and rabbit warrens. Roscrea station is one and half miles distant". The club is listed as affiliated to the Golfing Union of Ireland in this *Annual*.

Earlier, *The Nenagh Guardian* 17th November 1894 documents an interclub match versus Nenagh Golf Club and gives the names of the Roscrea team as Powell, Smith, Bridge, Ely, Eaton and Perry. The Nenagh team won by 16 holes to 11. Later, *The Irish Golfers Guide* 1897 records: "Instituted 1893 − The links is at Golden Grove, one and half miles from Roscrea, and there are nine holes, the longest 420 yards and shortest 90 yards . . . the greenkeeper has a comfortable cottage, where there is a room for members, and tea is provided. . . . President W. P. H. Lloyd Vaughan D.L.; Hon. Sec. J. Robt Ely J.P. Ballaghmore Castle, Roscrea; Hon. Treas S. E. Smith . . . Greenkeeper Jones Thompson. Membership about 50 . . ."

It would appear that this early club had difficulties around the turn of the century, *The Irish Golfers Guide* 1910 lists the club as Mill Park Golf Club and states: "This club was started again in 1904, the course having been laid out some years previously, but lapsed for want of members. One and a half miles from Roscrea . . . Hon. Secretary Captain R. A. Bolton, Dungar Park, Roscrea". The following year, *The Irish Field* 5th August 1911 reported: "The Roscrea district is very wisely amalgamating the two existing private clubs and establishing a public club. The representative meeting called to discuss the matter decided on taking Derryvale as the site for the new course."

*See Millpark.

ROSSES POINT, Co. Sligo.
*See Co. Sligo Golf Club.

ROSSLARE, Co. Wexford.
Instituted 1905.   Affiliated 1908.
Writing in *The Irish Field* 3rd April 1926 J. P. Rooney stated: "It was in 1905 that the game was introduced and to private enterprise its present popularity is due. Mr. (James) Farrell in conjunction with that well known sportsman Mr. M. J. O'Connor, conceived the idea of forming a proprietary club of which Mr. Charles M. Barry was the Hon. Secretary, but owing to financial troubles the life of the club was a short one, and the end came at the close of 1906."

The Golfing Annual 1905/06 has the following entry re this first Rosslare club: "Instituted 1905. The course of 18 holes stretches along the burrow, and is bounded on the east by sand dunes and on the west by wooded country. The clubhouse is only half a mile from the station."

J. P. Rooney's article continues: "Fortunately for the future of the game at Rosslare, when the proprietary club came to an end, Mr. Barry continued to look after the upkeep of the course and kept it open until 1908, when the present club

ROSSLARE GOLF CLUBHOUSE C. 1910

(Courtesy of the National Library of Ireland)

was formed. The founder of the club practically was Sir William Paul who was President up to his death in 1912 and he had the very active cooperation of a very able lieutenant in Mr. J. B. Pettigrew, who held the position of Hon. Secretary to 1922. Following the preliminary meeting which was held in Wexford and of which there is unfortunately no record available, the first general meeting took place in Whites Hotel Wexford . . . the following were elected President, Sir William Paul; Captain, R. W. Elgee Jun; Hon. Secretary, J. B. Pettigrew . . . The work of planning the links and laying it out was entrusted to Mr. Pettigrew, who showed a thorough knowledge of the game and of golf architecture . . . another who rendered the club splendid service in attending the links was J. J. Ennis the groundsman . . . at the start the membership consisted of 60 men and the same number of ladies . . . Course extension to 18 holes was originally proposed in 1913 but the war and other difficulties such as tenants grazing rights held the project up and in overcoming the latter difficulty, Mr. John English rendered the club great assistance . . .''.

ROSSMORE, Monaghan, Co. Monaghan.
Instituted 1916.   Affiliated 1920.

The periodical *Irish Life* 25th August 1916 recorded the foundation of this club "at a largely attended meeting held in the Westenra Arms Hotel, Monaghan, over which Lord Rossmore presided, it was unanimously decided to form a golf club in the town

. . . Lord Rossmore had presented a course in Rossmore Park free of rent and also a pavilion and a subscription of £10 towards the initial expenses of the club''. The same account recorded that Lord Rossmore was elected first President of the club. *Irish Life* 8th September 1916 reported that the new course was being laid out by J. L. Morrow, Hon. Secretary of the Golfing Union of Ireland and that he hoped to have the assistance of Barret of Carrickmines.

There was an earlier club at Monaghan, listed in *The Golfing Annual* 1895/95, however *The Irish Golfers Guide* 1910 reported: "believed to be extinct".

*See Monaghan G.C.

ROSSNOWALAGH, Co. Donegal.

The Golfers Handbook 1923 lists this club with Miss S. Jennings, Warren Lodge, Rossnowalagh, as Hon. Secretary. There were nine holes and the course was ¾ mile from the local station. *The Irish Tourist Authority Directory* 1937 lists the club, its subsequent history is unknown.

ROSTREVOR, Co. Down.

The Belfast Newsletter 23rd May 1892 reported on the proposal to form a golf club at Rostrevor: ". . . our own Lord Mayor has generously granted the free use of the grounds at Ballydesmond his lately acquired estate, about two miles beyond Rostrevor for the purpose, and the opening meeting and competition are announced to take place on Saturday week 4th June . . . nine holes have been laid down, but there is ample space for a full course of eighteen holes''.

Two weeks later *The Belfast Newsletter* 6th June 1892 reported on the opening of the club: "Mr. W. J. Hall D.L. Narrow Water, was called to preside, the land had kindly been placed at the disposal of the club by the Lord Mayor of Belfast Mr. Daniel Dixon J.P. . . . Mr. Thomas J. Dixon proposed that a golf club be formed to be called the Rostrevor Golf Club . . . E. Greer J.P. proposed that Rt. Hon. Daniel Dixon, Lord Mayor of Belfast, be President of the club, proposed by Dr. Vesey that Maj. John Ross of Blandensburg be Vice President of the club . . . Mr. W. J. Watson J.P. M.R.I.A. proposed that Maj. Hall D.L. Narrow Water be the Captain of the club''. One week later *The Belfast Newsletter* 14th June 1892 reported: "Though only a week old this club has already over 80 members . . . several of the local ladies taking part''.

This club certainly had a prestigious beginning, *The Golfing Annual* 1894/95 gives Maj. Hall again as Captain for that year (1895) and states: "The course which formerly consisted of 12 holes has been altered to 9 . . . the round is a sporting one and is over 1½ miles in length''. All was not well with the club, however, and *The Golfers Guide* 1897 stated: "The Rostrevor Golf Club has been dissolved in consequence of a change in the ownership of the links''. It is of interest to note that G. L. Baillie was involved in the beginning of the club, *The Golfing Annual* 1892/93 reported that the course record (12 holes) had been set by him in August 1892 . . . "the former secretary''.

*See Royal Belfast G.C.

ROYAL BELFAST, Belfast, Co. Down.
Instituted 1881. Affiliated 1891.

With the foundation of Belfast Golf Club in November 1881 the modern era of Irish golf began. As outlined in Chapter 2, the first recorded golf club in Ireland was the Bray club of 1762. Despite all of the documented golf on the Curragh from 1852 to 1875 there is no evidence that a club was founded there until 1883. Therefore the honour of being the oldest existing club in Ireland rests with the present Royal Belfast Club.

The Field 19th November 1881 records the foundation of the club as follows: "Belfast Golf Club. To the already numerous and fast increasing list of golfing societies throughout the United Kingdom has now to be added the one bearing this title. At a meeting held in the Chamber of Commerce on Wednesday last under the Presidency of the Mayor (Mr. Edward Porter Cowan) the club was formally constituted and if local influence, unanimity and enthusiasm avail anything Belfast Golf Club ought to have a successful career. The Kinnegar at Hollywood, permission having been kindly granted by Captain Harrison J.P. will be headquarters and from personal knowledge of the spot we can vouch for its capability of being easily converted into a first-class golfing arena."

The newly selected course was laid out by G. L. Baillie and Walter D. Day, a famous old Musselburgh professional and clubmaker, who had been invited over by the former. This work was carried out early in 1882. The Kinnegar which had been chosen as the site was also in use as a military training area and rifle range. This would lead to problems for the club later on.

In 1885 the club received permission to use the prefix Royal, the first Irish club to have this honour. The President of the club, Captain Harrison took the opportunity of a visit to Belfast docks by the Prince of Wales to request him to become patron of the club. *The Saturday Review* 26th July 1890 described the course: "The golfer has not yet not yet displaced the Royal Armagh Militia, whose tents are 'teed up' all over the Kinnegar during a month or so in Summer. But this matters little, because the Kinnegar is only a Winter course. The grass grows long in Summer which is as much to say that the soil is clay, not the royal sandy links of Newcastle or Portrush. Still there is broken ground and whin which form good hazards and in Winter months the Kinnegar is no bad test of golfing qualities. There is a most comfortable little clubhouse."

The next step in the life of the club is documented in *The Field* 29th October 1892, which carried a report on the Autumn meeting: "The move from the Kinnegar at Holywood (where golf was first regularly played in Ireland by the Belfast club and which had to be given up recently owing to its acquisition by the military as a rifle range etc.) is likely to be advantageous to the club. The new course is beautifully situated close to the sea at Carnalea, about twelve miles from Belfast . . . and although the club have only had possession of it for three or four months a great amount of work has been done on the putting greens etc. in the time. On account of the limited extent of ground available and only allowing for nine good holes, it has been decided to limit the membership to 200 resident and 100 non resident."

The members enjoyed their golf at Carnalea for 33 years, however by 1925 encroachment by the public on holidays and weekends had caused major nuisance for the club. In that year it was decided to purchase the 140 acre estate and house at Craigavad which had been owned by the Rt. Hon. J. C. White, a former Lord Mayor of Belfast. The members subscribed £11,500 by debentures, for the purchase and for the construction of the course. H. S. Colt, the internationally famous golf architect, carried out the design of the course which was opened for play in May 1927.

A further distinction for the club occurred on 13th November 1891 when, with eight other Ulster clubs, it co-founded the Golfing Union of Ireland. Mr. Henry Herdman, Captain in 1893 and 1894, represented the club at the historic inaugural meeting. The Royal Belfast Ladies Golf Club, previously named Holywood Ladies Golf Club, were a major force in the foundation of the Irish Ladies Golf Union in 1894. The club provided the first officers of the Union and the first Irish Ladies Championship was played at Carnalea in 1894. Miss Clara Mulligan of the home club was the first winner, she was also first secretary of the Irish Ladies Golf Union.

The part played by Mr. G. L. Baillie in the spread of early Irish golf is dealt with in Chapter 6; without question this Musselburgh man had a major role in the development of the game. Sir James Henderson D.L., proprietor of *The Belfast Newsletter* and Captain of the club in 1887 was another towering figure, who for many years was an advocate for the game in the sports columns of his paper.

*See Carnalea, Royal Co. Down, Royal Portrush; also Chapters 5, 6 and 9.

ROYAL BELFAST LADIES, Belfast, Co. Down.

The story of the development of ladies golf at Belfast is documented in the Holywood Ladies G.C. entry. In 1892, when the Royal Belfast G.C. was forced to move to its new course at Carnalea, the ladies followed and they renamed themselves the Royal Belfast Ladies G.C. The original Holywood Ladies G.C. was the first ladies club in Ireland.

*See Holywood Ladies G.C. and Chapter 9.

ROYAL COUNTY DOWN.
Instituted 1889.   Affiliated 1891.

Background information on the setting up of the original golf course at Newcastle is given in Chapter 5. There were very close ties with the Royal Belfast Club and G. L. Baillie, one of Irish golf's outstanding pioneers. The institution of County Down Golf Club was noted in the golfing columns of *The Field* 23rd March 1889: "Ulster can now boast of four golf clubs — the Royal Belfast, the County at Portrush, Aughnacloy and the County Down. The last named, though only opened on Saturday last, promises to be the most successful of the lot. At the initiatory meeting presided over by Lord Annesley, it was announced that over fifty members had been enrolled, many of them leading gentlemen."

Shortly afterwards the "grand old man" of golf, Tom Morris, was called in to look over the new course and his visit, too, is documented in *The Field* 20th July 1889: "Tom spent Tuesday and Wednesday at Newcastle and was immensely pleased, not only with the capabilities of the ground, but with the magnificence of the surrounding scenery. The course at Newcastle is at present a nine-hole one, but,

GOLF LINKS. NEWCASTLE Co. DOWN. 6253 W.L.

(Courtesy of the National Library of Ireland)

on Morris's suggestion an additional three holes will at once be added. He also mapped out six other holes and these will be brought in during the Autumn and Spring, so that by next Summer a full round of eighteen holes will be in use.'' It is of interest to note that the provisional committee had employed Morris at "an expense not to exceed £4''.

The first Captain of the club was Mr. Armar Lowry-Corry who took office in March 1890. On the following 26th July the full eighteen-hole course designed by Tom Morris was officially opened. G. L. Baillie was a joint Secretary of the club until October 1890, he had been a key figure in organising the club and, having achieved his objective, had other golf business to attend to. In November 1891 the club sent George Combe and Dr. Magill to attend the inaugural meeting of the Golfing Union of Ireland. Combe was elected first Honorary Secretary of the new organisation and was to become a major influence in Irish golf affairs during his seven years in office. (He was captain of the club in 1895/96 and 1904).

In April 1894 the ladies club was formed and in the Autumn of 1897 the present clubhouse was opened. Prior to this the Co. Down Railway had provided facilities at the nearby station. A second eighteen-hole course was laid out in 1900. In May 1907 Ben Sayers visited the links, from Scotland, and as a result some alterations were made to the course. April 1908 was an historic month for the club, when King Edward VII conferred the title "Royal". At this time there were only three other Irish Royal clubs, the Curragh became the fifth in 1910. In 1926 a further remodelling of several of the championship course holes was carried out by H. S. Colt.

International recognition of the championship status of the course was first granted by the Ladies Golf Union (L.G.U.) in 1899 when the Ladies British Amateur Open Championship was held at Newcastle. On that occasion a young Irish girl became the youngest ever winner, May Hezlet from Royal Portrush. The L.G.U. were so enamoured with the course that the event was staged at Newcastle on six further occasions up to 1963. In the Curtis Cup contest of 1968 the United States triumphed by 10½ to 7½ against the United Kingdom and Ireland at this renowned course. Finally, in 1970, the men recognised the status of Royal County Down when Michael Bonallack won the British Amateur title there. On any world ranking of prominent golf courses Royal County Down consistently rates a position in the top echelon.

*See Curragh and Royal Belfast; also Chapters 3, 4, 5 and 6.

ROYAL CURRAGH, Co. Kildare.

On 24th September 1910 the title Royal was conferred on the Curragh Golf Club. The various *Irish Golf Guides* from 1910 to 1916 record this as the name of the club. It is poignant to note that David Ritchie, who had laid out the first course on the Curragh in 1852, died only two weeks before the granting of the title.

When the British Army evacuated the Curragh on 16th May 1922 the Royal Charter would appear to have become a "spoil of war". When the new committee took office at the end of that year, the name of the club had reverted to the former − Curragh Golf Club.

ROYAL DUBLIN, Co. Dublin.
Instituted 1885.   Affiliated 1892.

In the material recorded on golf in the Phoenix Park (see Phoenix Park) it can be seen that a military golf club had existed there from some time in 1884. Unfortunately, for the historian, the original records of the Royal Dublin Golf Club were lost in a clubhouse fire on 2nd August 1943. However, the beginnings of the club were noticed in several papers of the day and later in *The Irish Field* of 2nd January 1926 a fine article by J. P. Rooney documented the beginning of the club quoting generously from the minute books which were then available.

The Irish Times of 18th July 1885 reported: "Although not quite foreign to the metropolitan district, golf is a game which has yet to gain a habitation and a name in the vicinity of Dublin and judging by the well directed efforts which of late have been made to promote it here, it will ere long take its place amongst our popular sports. Mr. Lumsden, the manager of the Provincial Bank, College Street, has been exerting himself to this end, and we are glad to say that there appears every prospect of his well timed and energetic action being crowned with success. The work of organisation has resulted in the formation of a golf club, of which is Excellency, the Lord Lieutenant is Patron, Col. Stevenson, President, and Mr. John Lumsden, Captain. The committee consists of Mr. David T. Arnott, Mr. John D. Carnegie,

Mr. George M. Ross, Mr. William Megaw, Mr. Fred Cochrane, Mr. J. Malcolm Gillies, Mr. George McKenzie, Mr. Robert Law, Dr. Arthur Benson, Mr. James Stewart and Mr. Vernon Kyrke. The Hon. Secretary is Mr. Robert H. Charles of 2 Lower Baggot Street and the Hon. Treasurer is Mr. B. H. Hall 48 Dame Street . . . The course on which play will take place is situate on a very suitable piece of ground in the Phoenix Park, where a handsome pavilion is now approaching completion.''

The Irish Field 2nd January 1926, as mentioned above, carries a comprehensive account of the development of the club, the founding meeting of which took place on 15th May 1885 at No. 19 Grafton Street: ''Mr. John Lumsden was the convenor at the meeting and in his opening statement from the chair said that the object of the club would be to establish the good old Scotch game in Ireland where it had already been introduced by military and where, he was certain, from the support it already received, it would quickly become popular . . . The names of the forty one members having been handed in the meeting then separated and so was formed the Dublin Golf Club . . .

''At the AGM which was held in the clubhouse the following January Mr. Lumsden presented to the club the Lumsden medal which is still competed for at Dollymount [6 Author's note: All the club's trophies were destroyed in the 1943 fire but have since been replaced] . . . In Winter the course was reduced to twelve holes owing to difficulty of upkeep. There was always a deal of trouble with the staff and resignations were frequent. At the next AGM there was a balance against the club of 15/6 and then it was decided to reduce the number of holes to nine.

''In March (1887) the officers of the Blackwatch presented to the club a handsome gold medal which became known as the Blackwatch medal. All the time the club had difficulty in keeping the course in order owing to the grass being so heavy and in the minutes of the Committee meeting of October 1888 we find a reference to a letter from the Park Bailiff that he was sorry that the club had been inconvenienced by the unusual growth of grass for the past four months and stated that they were bringing in a large number of cattle and that things would probably improve in a short time . . . But the President made a statement to the meeting explaining his action regarding a course at Sutton on the property of Lord Howth and that permission had been received to play over the ground at a nominal rent of one shilling per month, three months rent in advance being paid by him. The meeting approved the action of the President and so it was decided to vacate to the ground at Sutton but at the same time the committee agreed to retain the Park course for a year or so to enable the members to decide what was best to be done, both courses in the meantime to be kept in play . . .''

Here we can see that in October 1888 the Dublin G.C. were on the move to Sutton where a course was laid out at Cush Point. This change obviously did not meet with the approval of the members as *The Irish Field* relates: ''. . . on 19 January 1889 a meeting of the committee was held 'for the purpose of considering the advisability of changing the course from Sutton permanently to the Bull' . . . Mr. Lumsden explained the steps he had taken to obtain permission from Colonel Vernon and the Port and Docks Board to play over the ground, and announced that for a nominal rent he had secured permission to play over as fine a golf course as was to be found anywhere . . . The Sutton course was not a success for it was out of reach of the majority of the playing members, and as permission had been obtained from Colonel Vernon and the Port and Docks Board to play at Dollymount for £1.1s. (£1 to Col. Vernon and 1 shilling to the Board) he had no hesitation in recommending the Bull to the club. Mr. Petrie suggested that the services of Tom Morris be engaged for laying out the course but further consideration of the matter was postponed owing to expense.

"Ultimately it was resolved to remove the club to the Bull and to discontinue paying rent for the Sutton course, the warmest praise being given to Mr. Lumsden 'for never ceasing to promote the welfare of the club'. The arrangement of the holes on the new course was left to the President (Mr. Lumsden) and the Captain (Mr. Gilroy) on the motion of Mr. Kyrke seconded by Mr. J. Lumsden Jun."

The Field 23rd March 1889 recorded the members' reaction to the new course: "The club opened their new course at Dollymount on Saturday last, with the usual monthly handicap and members were loud in their expressions of delight at the change from the Phoenix Park. The new course has every natural advantage and probably there are not more than three others that golfers would consider superior. The handicap produced eleven competitors, Mr. Gilroy being first, with a rather astonishing score of 79."

After this move, the club's fortunes went from strength to strength over the following twenty-five years. On 14th May 1891 the title Royal was conferred on the club in a letter signed by E. Leigh Pemberton and addressed to the club care of Mr. A. J. Balfour who was Chief Secretary to Ireland from March 1887 until October 1891 (see Chapter 7).

Balfour was a fanatical golfer and his presence in the club was a tremendous stimulant for the game in Dublin. Tom Gilroy, who laid out the first course in 1885, with John Lumsden, was Captain of the club in 1888, 1889 and 1894. He, too, was a key figure in the early years of the club, as indeed he was a towering personality in the formative years of Irish golf (see Chapters 5 and 7).

Various professional groupings within the club fostered the game among their professional companions, notably among the members of the Irish Bar. *The Irish Times* 11th May 1891 reported: "Those members of the Bar who belong to the club have presented a massive silver cup, of beautiful design, to be played for under handicap limited to 25 strokes, twice a year in May and November (see Bar Golfing Society of Ireland and Chapter 7). At all times, the military garrison in Dublin provided a very active membership, it has already been mentioned that the Military Club had amalgamated with the club in 1885. In addition to the Blackwatch medal another regiment, the 1st Battalion Coldstream Guards, presented "a very valuable silver cup", as reported in *The Irish Times* 9th May 1892 (it was won by an officer of that regiment, Hon. H. R. Hamilton Baillie, on its inaugural day in June that year).

From its earliest days, Vice Regal interest in the club had always been prominent, the first patron had been Lord Spencer, followed by Lord Carnarvon. The keenest of them all was Lord Dudley, who was Viceroy from 1902 to 1906, of whom many anecdotes are told (see Chapter 7).

John Lumsden was a leading figure in the development of golf in the metropolitan area for many years, founder Captain of the club, he became a Vice President of the Golfing Union of Ireland in 1891. It is clear that he had the full confidence of the members during the negotiations to find new locations for the club in 1888/89. He was also responsible for laying out several other courses in the Dublin area and deserves to be remembered as a leading "disciple" of early Irish golf (see Chapters 5 and 7).

Through the years the club's professionals, also, were instrumental in laying out golf courses all over the province from Anthony Brown in 1896 to George Coburn to Tom Hood. The latter was professional to the club in 1914, in which year the club underwent its greatest test. *Irish Life* 25th September 1914 reported the loss the members had suffered as a result of war breaking out: ". . . from tomorrow 26th, until further notice, Dollymount will cease to be a golf course. Huge ramparts have been erected right across the course from the Sloblands at the 14th to the Sandhills at the 5th. Behind these ramparts nimble markers will indicate to the recruits, firing from what used to be the 18th fairway, the success or otherwise of their efforts . . ." All of the other clubs in Dublin and surrounding towns rallied to the help of the Royal Dublin members, making them welcome into their clubs. However, it would not be until April 1920 that the club were able to return to their former home. *Irish Life* 7th January 1921 reported that Cecil Barcroft, the club Secretary, and Anthony Babington had called in H. S. Colt (the famous golf architect) to help in the redesign of the course.

From then on the club and course have played a significant part in the development of the game in Ireland.

*See Phoenix Park and Sutton; also Chapters 5, 6, 7 and 8.

ROYAL HOSPITAL, Kilmainham, Co. Dublin.

An attempt was made to create a golf course at the Royal Hospital, which was headquarters of the British Army in Ireland until 1922, during the period when the Duke of Connaught was Commander in Chief. The Duke, who was a brother of King Edward VII, was a keen golfer and *The Irish Golfer* 9th May 1900 reported that "during his (George Sayers) recent stay in Dublin fulfilling an engagement to give tuition in golf to the family and guests of the Lord Lieutenant of Ireland and Countess Cadogan . . . laid out a nice course for their Highness Duke and Duchess of Connaught on their private ground at Dublin".

Later, *The Irish Times* 24th January 1902 recorded the sad fate of the course: "The private course laid out for HRH The Duke of Connaught and Strathearn, Commander of the Forces, at the Royal Hospital has been a failure owing to the rankness of the grass and other difficulties and the Duke and Duchess who are both good players accordingly visit the Lodge (Vice Regal) course when they wish to enjoy a game".

ROYAL IRISH CONSTABULARY GOLF ASSOCIATION.

This police golfing association is first listed in *The Golfing Annual* 1907/08 and is mentioned in successive editions until 1909/10. No detail is given. Later *Irish Golf Guides* fail to mention the association.

ROYAL PORTRUSH, Co. Antrim.
Instituted 1888. Affiliated 1891.

The origins of golf at Portrush are credited to two local personalities, Col. J. M. McCalmont M.P. and Mr. J. S. Alexander. *The Field* 19th May 1888 noted the foundation of this now world-famous course: "A club under the name of 'The County Club' has been very successfully started in County Antrim, Ireland. A ground has been laid out close to the railway station at Portrush, well known by tourists visiting the Giants Causeway. The course is a remarkably good one of nine holes . . . on Saturday last 44 players, mostly members of the Royal Belfast Club, visited Portrush to compete for a handsome silver cup, presented by Mr. J. S. Alexander of Portglenone House, Captain of the County Club, and several handicap prizes . . ."

From this account it can be seen that Royal Belfast figured prominently in the inauguration of the new club, the minutes of the former club's meeting on 3rd May 1888 record: ". . . the Secretary announced that the Portrush links would be opened on 12th May and that the Northern Counties Railway Company had kindly offered a free pass to all members of Royal Belfast Golf Club for that day". Here, too, it can be verified that the railway companies were keenly interested in the promotion of golf in order to boost the number of passengers using their services.

Tom Gilroy was a founder member of the new club and *The Field* 16th June 1888 recorded his win in the first monthly competition of the club: ". . . several old

golfers present from a distance pronounced the course for its size, one of the finest in the three Kingdoms, having the natural bunker hazards of Prestwick and a springy turf superior even to that of St. Andrews . . . The lowest actual score of the day was made by Mr. T. Gilroy who finished the two rounds in 84. This scratch score (plus 4) was not equalled by any of the players and Mr. Gilroy therefore becomes the first winner of the Silver Cup.''

Tom Morris's visit to the club was documented in *The Field* 20th July 1889: ''Portrush had the benefit of Tom's presence on Thursday and Friday. The green there could be hardly surpassed for its size. Every hole has it accompanying hazard . . . the ground there was considered by Morris as already being well laid out, and the alterations he suggested referred principally to the changing of the teeing ground so as to elongate several of the holes.''

The course at that time was closer to the town than at present and had been extended to eighteen holes. The early success of the club was reflected in *The Field* 19th April 1890 and it is interesting to see that Portrush was being considered as the St. Andrews of Ireland at that time: ''The County (Antrim) Golf Club is in the van of the movement and with its unrivalled links at Portrush and an enterprising Council, it is not difficult to surmise where the future St. Andrews of Ireland is destined to be. The County Club is not yet quite two years old (in fact a cleek or a niblick was an unknown weapon in Portrush two years ago); its members, numbering 200 are now the happy possessors of a four mile course of eighteen holes, laid out under the supervision of the veteran Tom Morris, and a comfortable clubhouse, where the weary golfer may refresh the inner man . . .''

This same article carried an account of the competition held on the course for the Henderson Cup which had been presented by the proprietor of *The Belfast Newsletter* for open competition, played at various venues annually (see Chapter 5). The winner at Portrush was Tom Gilroy and in giving the result this same article carried an intriguing final sentence: ''The Council of the County Club are now taking the preliminary steps towards the foundation of an Amateur Championship of Ireland, open to all the world''.

The Field article quoted above is clear evidence of the ''global'' vision of the club's Council. Earlier, *The Irish Times* 17th September 1889 had reported the presentation of a ''magnificent challenge cup by Mr. J. S. Alexander D.L., ex Captain, open to all Irish Clubs''. It is therefore no surprise to note that the Chairman of the founding meeting of the Golfing Union of Ireland (reported in *Golf* 27th November 1891) held in Belfast on 13th November 1891 was W. H. Mann, the Captain of the County Club. Resolution number 15 of that meeting was ''That the Union take steps to establish an Irish Championship open to members of all recognised golf clubs, to be competed for on a links appointed by the Union''. It is now clear, also, that this club were prime movers in the foundation of the oldest Golfing Union in the world.

In September 1892 the Ladies Club of the Royal County Golf Club was founded, having been instituted in November 1891 as a branch of the men's club. The club had received the Royal title in that same year and in 1895 the club's name was changed to Royal Portrush golf Club. Two lady members of the club brought great honour to Irish golf in the years 1899 to 1907. Firstly, Miss May Hezlet won the Ladies British Open Amateur Championship in 1899, a win she repeated in 1902 and 1907. Miss Rhona Adair won the same championship in 1900 and 1903 (see Chapter 9). By 1894 the ladies at Portrush had a separate eighteen-hole course of their own in addition to a separate clubhouse. It is of interest to note that the 1895 Ladies British Championship was held at Portrush on this course, the first Irish course to host this prestigious championship.

Over the years the course were altered and moved further towards the East where there were large sandhills on higher ground. Between 1929 and 1932 H. S. Colt (the famous golf architect who also laid out the new Royal Belfast course in 1926) redesigned the Dunluce course and the status of the layout was confirmed when the British Open Championship was held at Portrush in July 1951. This was the first time that this prestigious championship was held in Ireland.

*See Chapters 5 and 6.

ROYAL NAVAL CLUB, Berehaven, Co. Cork.

This club is listed for the first time in *The Irish Golfing Guide* 1916 which states: "This club is mainly for the use of officers of H.M. Fleet. There are nine holes which have been laid out within the past few years, three miles to the east of Castletown. Formerly the club existed as the Atlantic Fleet Club, and had a nine-hole course on Bere Island. Going further back, it was known as the Channel Fleet Club but the redistribution of the fleets necessitated a change in its nomenclature. The Hon. Secretary is Lt. Cdr. C. R. S. Sharp R.N. H.M. Coastguard, Castletown-bere. The C.I.C. of the Home Fleet is the President. The Vice Admiral Commanding Queenstown and all Rear Admirals Home Fleet are Vice Presidents . . ." There is no further record of the history of this club which would, obviously, have ceased to function in 1922.

ROYAL TARA, Navan, Co. Meath.
Instituted 1922.   Affiliated 1923.

In the early 1960s the Land Commission acquired the Briscoe estate, near Bellinter, on which the local club had their nine-hole course. Sufficient extra land became available to allow expansion to eighteen holes in 1966/67 at which time the club changed its name to Royal Tara.

The original Bellinter Park Golf Club had been formed circa 1923 from among the dispossessed members of the Navan Golf Club, which had been founded in 1907. There are no "royal" connections with this club other than its proximity to the former residence of the High Kings of Ireland at Tara.

*See Bellinter Park G.C. and Navan G.C.

RUSHBROOKE, Cobh, Co. Cork.

This club is listed in *The Sportsmans Holiday Guide* 1897 as Queenstown Golf Club which states: "The course is situated on the hills overlooking the Lee, and commands fine views of Monkstown Bay, Passage, and far away views of the river as it winds up to Cork. The links are open from October to April. There are 9 holes, and the course is about 2 miles. The hazards consist of stone walls and furze bushes. There is a Clubhouse on the ground. Visitors introduced by members may play free for one week and after that period the charge is 5/- per month.''

The Golfing Annual 1905/06 lists the club for the first time and gives an institution date of 1892. At this time the club had 120 members and the Hon. Secretary was Dep.-Inspec.-Gen. E. Meade, R.N., Rushbrooke (this may have denoted Naval connections with the club, the large Naval base at Queenstown was nearby). The *Annual* also stated: ''The course of nine holes, varying from 120 to 400 yards (par 34) is 200 yards from Rushbrook Station''.

A further mention for the club is given in *The Irish Field* 30th October 1909 when Lady Barrymore, for the fourth time, offered a handsome silver cup for competition between the members of the Cork and Rushbrooke clubs to be played for at Fota (see Fota). The club is recorded in *The Irish Golfers Guide* 1910, which gives an institution date of 1891; the Captain is named as Col. G. Coates. There was a professional named H. F. Lafolly and the club was affiliated to the Golfing Union of Ireland. The various *Irish Guides* up to 1916 list the club which ''is only open for play from October to May''. However the later history of the club is unknown.

*See St. Anne's Hill G.C.

ST. ANNE'S, Bull Island, Co. Dublin.
Instituted 1921. Affiliated 1923.

St. Anne's Golf Club records 1921 as their date of institution, their first Secretary was T. Murray. One of the earliest mentions of the club is given in *The Irish Field* 27th January 1923: ''. . . at the far end of the Royal Dublin course is another course run by a few enthusiasts and I am told the golf is quite good''. At first, the St. Anne's golfers played over three holes and over the following five years this was increased to nine.

The Irish Golfers Blue Book 1939 reported: ''At the close of the Great War when the Military Authorities restored the Royal Dublin links to the club a number of young men resident in Clontarf and Dollymount were found playing already daily on the links. . . . the club could have asserted their rights but they adopted a sympathetic and sporting attitude towards the 'newcomers', offered them a lease on the ground beyond the ninth hole on very reasonable terms and assistance in laying out the course for themselves . . . no sooner was the lease granted than the members of St. Anne's set about their task . . . they 'took off their coats' at it . . . evening after evening they tramped or cycled to St. Anne's (not by any means a short walk) to perform their allotted tasks and before many months they had a lovely course (in the rough) and a comfortable if modest clubhouse.'' An institution date of 1920 is given for the club in this same publication.

ST. ANNE'S HILL, Blarney, Co. Cork.

This club is first mentioned in *The Golfing Annual* 1902/03 which gives an institution date of November 1901. The Honorary Secretary's name is given as Mrs. Pike, Kilcrenagh, Carrigrohane, Co. Cork, and ''the course of nine holes, is about a quarter of a mile from St. Anne's Hill Station, on Muskerry Light Railway. Blarney Station is distant two miles."

Similar details appear in subsequent *Golfing Annuals* until the 1909/10 edition, no mention of the club appears in subsequent *Irish Golf Guides*. However, *Golf Illustrated* 22nd February 1907 carries an entry: "A club is being established at St. Anne's Hill. The principal movers in the matter are members of the club at Little Island and Rushbrook . . ." This new club was, more than likely, the revival of the old Muskerry Club which had succumbed after being founded in 1897. *Nisbets Golf Year Book* 1908 gives the Hon. Secretary's name, of the revived Muskerry Club, as Capt. Dundas. St. Anns Hill (sic).

It is most probable that the St. Anne's Hill Golf Club merged with the new Muskerry Club circa 1910.

*See Muskerry G.C.

SAINTFIELD, Co. Down.

This club is listed in *The Golfing Annual* 1896/97 which gives an institution date of March 1896, the President was Major J. N. Blackwood-Price; Captain, J. Napier; Treasurer, R. A. Harbinson and the Hon. Secretary was C. A. Moorehead with an address at Rowallane Saintfield. The following detail is given: "This course, of nine holes, in the Rowallane Demesne, lies midway between Saintfield and Ballynahich Junction Stations, which are one mile off. Although an inland green, the turf is very good". From this entry it would appear that the club was playing over the demesne belonging to the Honorary Secretary.

The club is listed in the *The Golfing Annual* 1909/10, where the Hon. Secretary's name is given as L. Napier, Bank House, Saintfield, Co. Down. However, the club is not mentioned in any of the later *Irish Golf Guides*. The subsequent history of the club is unknown. It would not appear to have been affiliated to the Golfing Union of Ireland.

ST. JAMES GATE, Co. Dublin.

It may be of interest to note that such a club existed. *The Golfing Annual* 1906/07 gives an institution date of 1906 for the club and states "Membership confined to employees of Guinness Brewery". No names are given in this entry, however the institution of this club which was clearly organised by the workers of the Guinness Brewery as a vehicle by which they could play competitive golf.

The problems created by the foundation of this club were outlined in an article in *Golf Illustrated* 25th January 1907, which reported on a recent meeting of the Golfing Union of Ireland: "A lengthened debate took place on the proposal to affiliate the St. James Golf Club. Hitherto the only club formed for play and unpossessed of a green, which had been affiliated, was Dublin University. At last week's meeting Queens College Belfast was also affiliated. Despite these precedents, St. James Gate was refused affiliation by a majority, and a property qualification for clubs established for the first time. Notice of motion was however given to change the rules so as to admit all clubs in Ireland."

No entry relating to this club appears in the later *Irish Golf Guides*, the subsequent history of the club is unknown.

SCRABO, Newtownards, Co. Down.
Instituted 1907. Affiliated 1908.

For some reason *The Irish Golfers Guide* 1910 gives 1897 as the institution date of this club and subsequent *Irish Golf Guides*, until 1916, give the same date. The club's own records are complete and they document that the first meeting to found a local club was held in the Town Hall, Newtownards, 13th December 1907. William Sibbald Johnston J.P. chaired the first meeting at which it was agreed to form "The Scrabo Golf Club", the local Scrabo Hill was chosen as the site for the course. The first Captain was William Sibbald Johnston, Lord Londonderry K.G. was first President.

Newtownards Golf club is documented in *The Golfing Annual* 1907/08. In the following *Annual* it is listed as Scrabo Golf Club and September 1907 is given as the date of institution. G. L. Baillie, the co-founder of the Royal Belfast Club and a key figure in early Irish golf course architecture, was employed to lay out a nine-hole course on the inhospitable hill at Scrabo. The sum paid for his services was £2.2.0. By April 1908 the course had been sufficiently cleared of rocks and ferns that the members were able to play. Lady Londonderry formally opened the course on 11th June 1908 and a cup presented by the family is still played for annually. The course remained a nine-hole one until 1971 when a second nine was added.

What is of historic interest concerning golf at Scrabo is the fact that, just over three hundred years before the foundation of the club, a local school at Newtownards was gifted land by Hugh Montgomery . . . "for recreation at goff, football and archery", the first recorded mention of the game in Ireland.

*See Chapter 1.

SHANES PARK, Randalstown, Co. Antrim.

This club's entry in *The Golfing Annual* 1892/93 gives 22nd December 1891 as the institution date and ". . . no particulars forthcoming". The institution date given in the following year's edition was January 1890 and all subsequent editions list this date. In 1893 there were 61 members, the Captain was C. J. Webb and the Hon. Secretary was W. H. Webb (who would become Irish Close Champion in 1895 and 1898). The course record of 71 had been set on 5th April 1892 by the same W. H. Webb. Further detail, which did not include the number of holes, was given: "The course is situated in Shanes Castle Park, about five minutes walk from Randalstown Station, and is one of the best inland courses in Ireland, the ground being of a sandy nature, and grazed by sheep for over twenty years".

The Golfing Annual 1896/97, for the first time, lists this as an eighteen-hole course and all subsequent *Golf Guides* up to 1916 record details on the club. *The Irish Golfing Guide* 1916 recorded: "This club was founded by the Webb family. Mr. W. H. Webb was Irish Close Champion twice and his brother a runner-up one year.

The course is in the demesne of Lord O'Neill on the shores of Lough Neagh . . .
owing to the small number of members and the low fees it is left pretty much to
nature as regards upkeep. The grass is kept short by grazing and the greens are good,
if a trifle mossy . . . The Shanes Park Golf Club having been taken over by the War
Office is practically non existent at present and has been so since October 1914. The
military, with the help of the members of the old club, are making a new links in
an adjoining position of the park for the use of the convalescent soldiers of the
Scottish Command Depot stationed here, and these links will probably be taken over
by the Shanes Park Golf Club when the war is over . . .''

The club was revived after the war and *The Golfing Handbook* 1923 recorded W.
Murphy as Hon. Secretary of the revived club, there were nine holes. Subsequently
the club is documented in *Thoms Directory* until 1946 when the Hon. Secretary was
listed as Miss Rea, 8 Shanes Street, Randalstown. The course was a nine-hole one
at that time. The club was not listed as affiliated to the G.U.I. in the years after 1937.

SKERRIES, Co. Dublin.
Instituted 1905.   Affiliated 1908.

The Golfing Annual 1906/07 gives an institution date of 10th November 1905 for
Skerries Golf Club: ''. . . Par 35. The course of nine holes, varying from 133 to
400 yards, is a mile from Skerries Station . . .'' Details of the club's foundation are
given by J. P. Rooney in *The Irish Field* 10th April 1926: ''The golf club was
formed in 1905, the idea originating with Messrs. R. E. Maunsell, T. S. F.
Battersby K.C. and the late Henry Evans. . . . The lease of the ground was obtained
from Lord Holmpatrick and the course formally opened by him on April 14th of the
following year (1906). The first meeting of the promoters was held in the residence
of Mr. Battersby in Upper Mount Street on October 26th 1905, those present being
Messrs. Battersby, E. H. Bailey, Maunsell, Evans, R. A. Butler and J. A. Taylor.

In the natural order of things the choice of President fell on Lord Holmpatrick who
has held the position ever since and the first Vice President was Mr. E. H. Woods,
the Captaincy being voted to Mr. A. S. Hussey while the members of the committee
were Messrs. Battersby, Maunsell, Evans, Butler, W. Bailey, Taylor, H. Moore and
Dr. B. P. Healey. The first Honorary Secretary and Treasurer was E. H. Bailey . . .
and he still holds both positions . . .

When the course was laid out, the committee wisely availed of the services of
Mr. W. C. Pickeman who at the time was one of the recognised authorities on course
construction and later on Mr. Barcroft was consulted regarding improvements . . .
the course was further improved by the adoption of plans of Mr. Colt who went over
the ground in 1922 . . .''

In 1971 the club extended the course to eighteen holes on additional land
purchased from the Holmpatrick estate, the original nine holes had been purchased
in the 1940s. It is of interest that two of the top ''home'' golf architects, Pickeman
of Portmarnock and Barcroft of Royal Dublin (see Chapter 7), had helped lay out
the original course. H. S. Colt was the internationally famous English golf architect
whose masterpieces included the new course at Sunningdale, work on Pine Valley
and the Dunluce course at Portrush.

It is of historical interest to note that the first proposal to introduce golf to the area is recorded in *The Irish Field* 13th March 1897: "Capt. O'Dwyer of Skerries announces in the daily press the forming of Skerries amusement committee . . . a suggestion may be worthy of notice by the sporting fishing port, namely to have facilities for golf also a feature of that programme".

SKIBBEREEN & WEST CARBERY, Co. Cork.
Instituted 1905.   Affiliated 1931.

The Golfing Annual 1905/06 records the first mention of a golf club at Skibbereen and gives an institution date of 1905. The Honorary Secretary's name was Lieutenant S. T. Stephens, Skibbereen, there were 56 members and "the course consists of nine holes". No other detail was given.

Later, *The Irish Golfers Guide* 1910 lists the club as West Carbery Golf Club without giving a foundation date and ". . . a nine-hole course ¼ mile from Skibbereen Station". *The Irish Golfers Guide* 1911 lists a Captain's name for the first time, Mr. R. P. Chambers, under the West Carbery title. The following year's *Guide* gives the same Captain's name, as does the 1914 *Guide* and the 1916 *Irish Golfing Guide*.

The club moved to its present location at Licknaher in 1935, prior to that time the course was at Castlelands.

SOUTH LOUTH, Co. Louth.

*See Ardee Golf Club. *The Irish Golfers Guide* 1910 lists that club as South Louth Golf Club.

SPA, Ballynahinch, Co. Down.
Instituted 1907.   Affiliated 1907.

The Belfast Newsletter 11th May 1907 documented the opening of this club's original course: "The new course of nine holes opened at Ballynahinch should prove an important attraction. It is on the short side, the longest being only 230 yards and the bogey as low as 35, but it is a very sporting links . . . the Ulster Spa should soon find the benefit of having the all powerful attraction of golf as well as drinking water . . ."

The club acknowledges that a local hotelier — Miss Moore — was deeply involved with a local committee in the formation of the original club. For the first time *The Golfing Annual* 1908/09 recorded the name of club officials, the Captain was D. S. Ker and the Hon. Secretary was Rev. D. S. Taylor. An institution date of 1st February 1907 was listed.

The establishment of this club at the prominent Ulster Spa closely paralleled the setting up of a club at Lisdoonvarna, the famous Co. Clare health resort. (This latter club did not survive). Between 1963 and 1967 the present Spa course was constructed on a site nearer the town of Ballynahinch. This course was opened on 30th September 1967 by the Earl of Clanwilliam.

SPANISH POINT, Milltown Malbay, Co. Clare.
Instituted 1896.   Affiliated 1915.

A golf club at Milltown Malbay is listed in *The Golfers Guide* 1897 under the name West Clare Golf Club. No institution date is given, only the following detail: "This is a nine-hole course, finely situated on the shores of Malbay. Hazards are hills, sandpits and bents. It is free to visitors staying at the Atlantic Hotel". *The Sportsmans Holiday Guide* 1897 lists Milltown Malbay golf course and states: "The course, which is a nine-hole one, was laid out at considerable expense by a professional, who has varied it as much as possible . . . It is free to visitors staying at the Atlantic Hotel, which is also situated on the bay, not far from the high-water mark. The distance round is about 2000 yards, or a little over a mile . . . There is no clubhouse, the hotel acts as such . . . visitors other than those resident in the hotel must make their own terms with the manager, as there is no fixed tariff for out-siders . . ."

From the foregoing, it would appear that this early Milltown Malbay course was closely linked with the management of the local Atlantic Hotel and was probably run by the hotel. This, however, is not confirmed by *The Golfing Annual* 1898/99 which lists Spanish Point Golf Club for the first time and gives an institution date of 1896: "The course is the property of the proprietor of Miltown House, who only makes a small charge for retaining control and wishes visitors to enjoy play at little expense". An entrance fee of 2/6 with a similar annual subscription is listed. No details of committee or officers are given.

No further change in detail is recorded in *The Golfing Annuals* until the 1906/07 edition when the Honorary Secretary's name is given as Mrs. E. C. Moroney, Milltown House. Apart from this no other significant fact is given. Later, in *The Irish Golfers Guide* 1910 the club's name is given as the West Clare Golf Club with the same Honorary Secretary. For the first time a Captain is named, Mr. Ernest Ellis. This man is also recorded as Captain in *The Irish Golfing Guide* 1911.

No mention of Milltown Malbay, Spanish Point or West Clare Golf Club is given in the *Irish Golfing Guides* 1912, 1914 or 1916. Unfortunately, the present club has no early records and they credit the foundation of the club to Robert B. Barclay and Capt. Ernest Ellis, in 1912. The latter would surely have been the Captain of the West Clare Golf Club recorded in *The Irish Golfing Guide* 1911, in itself proof of a pre-1912 existence.

STEWARTSTOWN, Co. Tyrone.

This club is listed in *The Golfing Annual* 1903/04 and is listed in subsequent editions until 1909. No details are given in any edition.

STILLORGAN, Co. Dublin.

The following intriguing entry was carried in *The Irish Times* 31st January 1893: "Stillorgan Golf Club. This club at present limited to forty members has recently been formed and includes most of the distinguished old Scottish (golfers) residing in Dublin. A nine-hole course, which the committee hope to secure permanently, has with the kind permission of Mr. Darley been laid out adjacent to Stillorgan Station by the green committee, with the assistance of such veterans of the links Mr. John Lumsden, Mr. Charles and the Captain of the club Mr. Petrie. The ground is naturally adapted for golfing, almost every hole being well defended, with natural hazards of a formidable nature − disused sandpits, water ponds, whin bushes and hedges . . . these with clear bracing mountains and natural surroundings render the course a most enjoyable one. Special first class railway tickets have been granted by Mr. Payne and pending the erection of a comfortable clubhouse, a room for members has been kindly given by Mrs. Skehan in her house at the railway level crossing. The following are the officers and committee: President and Vice Presidents, Mr. John Mooney, Mr. J. Malcolm and Mr. William Perrin. Captain, Mr. J. Petrie; Hon. Secretary, Mr. J. C. Anderson; Committee, Messrs. Brown, William Comerford (Rathdrum) . . . Professor Doherty, John Lumsden . . . T. R. McCullough, P. J. Smyth, George Ross . . . The ground is now quite ready to play over though the greens are still rough. The opening meeting will shortly be announced when the Stillorgan gold medal, presented by the President, will be played for . . .''

This article is both mysterious and historic, firstly because no other documentaiton on this club is carried in any contemporary golf guide books or in later editions of *The Irish Times*. The later founded Stillorgan Park G.C. would not have been connected. Without doubt the founding committee contained some illustrious names of the golfing fraternity of the day, John Lumsden, founder of the Royal Dublin Club; John Petrie, this new club's first Captain had been Captain of Royal Dublin in 1891; George Ross was founder Captain of Portmarnock in 1894. Whatever happened to the club is a mystery, if it had survived this Stillorgan Golf Club would have been one of the oldest in Dublin.

*See Stillorgan Park Golf Club.

STILLORGAN PARK, Stillorgan, Co. Dublin.

The Irish Field 10th July 1909 carries an article on this recently founded club, for which an institution date of 1909 is given. The name of the first President was W. J. Shannon; Captain, Dr. R. C. Peacocke and the Hon. Secretary was A. B. Corr. The course lay midway between Stillorgan Railway Station and Blackrock and had been founded in April that year ''at the instigation of a few residents in the district''. The course was a nine-hole one with the very creditable membership of 220 men and 170 ladies.

Later, *The Irish Field* 10th April 1914 recorded the forthcoming opening of a full eighteen-hole course at Stillorgan Park. However, the imminent outbreak of the Great War was to have a drastic effect on this outlying club which *Irish Life* 4th January 1918 documented: ''I have to record the demise of the Stillorgan Park Golf Club . . . (it) suffered from the disadvantage of not being very accessible. It was not very enticing to walk uphill for twenty minutes in order to play golf and although outside cars were available few members care to add a permanent tax to their subs in this way. Some time ago the proprietor added a second nine in the hope that with increased membership the club would ultimately thrive. But the course never very attractive from a golf point of view, was not greatly improved by its additional length. No doubt the new stimulus given to the Castle Club by its change in management influenced the committee in its decision to close the club.'' From the above it can be seen that this was a proprietary club.

STRABANE, Co. Tyrone.
Instituted 1909.   Affiliated 1910.

Irish Life 6th December 1912 recorded the origins of Strabane Golf Club: ''This club (founded in 1909 by Mr. L. J. Passmore) originally had its course close to the town of Strabane, and was a winter course only. In November last year (i.e. 1911) it had the good fortune to secure 35 acres of very suitable land at Carricklee one mile from Strabane, the property of Mr. E. C. Herdman D.L. whose friendly interest has been in no small degree responsible for the club's present successful position. Play is now possible throughout the year . . . Mr. L. J. Passmore the founder is Honorary Secretary and well fits the position being the leading player of the club.''

The Golfing Annual 1908/09 gives an institution date of 1st February 1909 for the club, the first Captain was W. B. Smyth. There were 150 members including ladies and . . . ''the course of nine holes varying from 120 to 305 yards, lies along the banks of the Mourne, about ten minutes walk from the station''. *The Irish Golfing Guide* 1916 listed the Carricklee course as 2,400 yards long and . . . ''hillock bunkering is a feature of the course''. In 1953 the club moved to its present site at Ballycolman when a renewal of the old lease was not possible. In 1974 a full eighteen-hole course came into play and the present club is thriving and expanding.

SUTTON, Co. Dublin.
Instituted 1896.   Affiliated 1896.

Unfortunately for the modern historian, the earliest minute books of the Sutton Golf Club have been mislaid over the years. It is doubly misfortunate as Sutton is one of the oldest golfing locations in Dublin. For this reason some confusion exists regarding the present club's origins.

Golf was first played over Cush Point during the period October 1888 to March 1889 when the, then, Dublin Golf Club were in the process of terminating play over the first course in the Phoenix Park. *The Irish Times* 2nd January 1926 reported: ''The Sutton course was not a success for it was out of reach of the majority of the playing members, and as permission had been obtained from Mr. Vernon and the Port and Docks Board to play at Dollymount . . .''

The present club have discovered that Cush Point was again leased by Lord Howth for golf in 1890, to Mr. J. McAdam. This was for the Dublin Scottish Golf Club, whose Captain's medal was played for at Sutton on 16th April 1891 (see Dublin Scottish Golf Club). It was five years later that *The Irish Times* 2nd April 1896 recorded golf being played there again: ''Sutton Yacht and Boat Club . . . the committee of the above have made arrangements for a series of competitions on Good Friday, Saturday and Easter Monday over their golf links on the Burrow . . .''

The foundation of the golf club was noticed by *The Belfast Newsletter* 12th May 1896: "The newest of County Dublin clubs is the Sutton Yacht and Boat Club Golf Club. To give variety to their members the . . . club have acquired the land adjoining their comfortable clubhouse . . . and they have made a short nine-hole course . . . already the new movement has largely added to the membership of the club . . ."

Some confusion regarding the golf club's foundation date arises from its initial entries in the *Golfing Annuals*. The edition of 1896/97 gives 1895 while 1898/99 gives April 1893. The former *Annual* lists the President as Lord Howth, no Captain is mentioned and the Honorary Secretary was J. H. Fleming.

Happily all mysteries are solved in a fine piece written by J. P. Rooney in *The Irish Field* 13th February 1926 on the history of the club. It is clear that the writer had the full minute books available to him for his research . . . "The first meeting of the Sutton Club was called for the purpose of forming not a golf club but a yacht and boat club. It was held at Glenburn, Sutton on September 6th 1894, the presiding genius being Mr. J. H. Fleming. The club was inaugurated on the motion of Mr. R. P. Jacobs and it was Mr. E. S. Lauder who gave it its name . . . Mr. Lauder was appointed first Commodore."

"At the time the Portmarnock Club had been formed and figures prominently in the early minutes of the yacht club, for we read that at a meeting of the committee of the latter which was held in November 1894 a letter was read from Mr. Pickeman, Secretary to Portmarnock, inquiring upon what terms the yacht club would permit their club man to ferry members of the golf club across the channel. In reply the yacht club wrote that the committee were willing to allow use of their path, landing stage, man and boat at a charge of sixpence per head.

"In all likelihood had the Portmarnock Golf Club agreed to the terms of the yacht club there would have been no golf club started at Sutton, for the members of the yacht club would have availed themselves of the privilege of going across the channel at the reduced entrance fee, and later events would not have happened. . . . Apparently there were members in the Sutton Club who were determined to form an opposition to the Portmarnock Golf Club . . . and a resolution to the effect that on payment of a small extra subscription members of the Sutton Yacht and Boat Club could have the privilege of playing golf in the Burrow; that gentlemen desiring to make use of the links should first become members of the yacht club and pay the fees in addition to the sum fixed for golf.

"A committee of five was formed to frame the rules for the golf club and, in that way, the golfers began to oust the yachtsmen. That was on January 20th 1896. Shortly after, a committee was elected to manage the affairs of the golf club and the names of the five were . . . Rev. James Wilson, the rector of Sutton, E. Pentland, J. Holden, J. L. Jamison (sic), J. H. Fleming . . . January 2nd 1897 was a red letter day in the history of Sutton Golf Club for on that date the name of the club was changed to Sutton Boat and Golf Club on the motion of Mr. Pentland seconded by Mr. F. C. Hicks. The first Captain of the newly named club was Mr. Dilworth . . . the golf subcommittee was elected as follows, W. J. Dilworth, George Ross, J. L. Jamison and J. H. Fleming . . . The course was originally planned by Mr. Dilworth . . ."

An entry in *The Irish Golfer* 15th November 1899 relating to George Ross, mentioned above, who was first Captain of Portmarnock Golf Club from 1894 to 1896, adds a final mystery regarding the first captaincy of the Sutton Club: "Duty done after two years Mr. Ross relinquished his Captaincy much to the regret of members and anxious to further the Royal and Ancient game in every way was induced to take the helm of affairs at Sutton by becoming their first Captain and in conjunction with Mr. J. H. Fleming, he soon, with his previous experience, got things into proper order".

*See Dublin Scottish G.C., Portmarnock G.C. and Royal Dublin G.C.

SWINFORD, Co. Mayo.
Instituted 1922.   Affiliated 1922.

The origins of golf at Swinford are vague but Dr. E. Mulligan, who died in 1920 is reputed to have been a keen enthusiast when he had returned to the town some years previously. 1917 would appear to have been the first year in which golf was recorded in the locality. In April 1919 the area known as Brabazon Park was leased to the local community as a public park, by the Convent of Mercy.

As recorded in the club's 50th anniversary brochure: "The newly arrived nuns were astonished at the sight of reputable citizens 'hitting a little white ball round the park'. During the 'Troubles' the Argyle and Sutherland Highlanders who were billeted in Swinford took their time off on the golf course and the local IRA retaliated by ploughing up the greens. In 1922 Swinford G.C. was affiliated to the Golfing Union of Ireland. The earliest recorded officials were Paddy McManus, who was Secretary, and C. A. Bowles who was possibly Captain . . . construction of the (new) pavilion began, which was ready for the new season of 1930. Paddy McManus called on the services of Major Benson of Rosses Point to design a new course. The result was the present course."

TANDRAGEE, Co. Armagh.
Instituted 1920.   Affiliated 1920.

In 1911 the Duke of Manchester brought over Mr. John Stone, the professional at Sandy Lodge Golf Club, to lay out a private course on his estate at Tandragee. Green fees were allowed to play on the course, the money being collected by Mr. Stone, his wife and two daughters.

In 1920 a club was formed by the local players and affiliation to the Golfing Union of Ireland took place in 1922. For some time afterwards the Duke contributed annually to the upkeep of the course. *The Golfers Handbook* 1923 recorded a membership of 100 and the Hon. Secretary was William McMahon.

In October 1975 the club purchased the course from the representatives of the Duke of Manchester.

THOMASTOWN, Co. Kilkenny.

The existence of a golf club at Thomastown is recorded in *The Golfing Annual* 1892/93 which lists "Thomastown Ladies Golf Club . . . no particulars forthcoming''. Similar detail is given in the 1895/96 edition. For the first time the 1896/97 edition gives an institution date of 1891 for the Thomastown Golf Club. There were forty members, with a committee of twelve, of whom five were ladies. Miss G. Hunt was the Honorary Secretary and her home address was Belmore, Thomastown; this lady may have been the connection with the previously named ladies club . . . "The course, of nine holes, is one mile from Thomastown, where there is a good hotel''.

C. R. Fleming is listed as the club Captain in *The Golfing Annual* 1902/03 and later *The Irish Golfers Guide* 1910 states: "This is a sporting course commanding fine views. It lies chiefly on the side of a hill and the principal hazards are stone walls, furze and bracken. The length of the course is about 2,300 yards. The course is open only from December to May.'' An institution date of 1888 is given by this same *Guide*, which is another example of the contradictory information given possibly by an Honorary Secretary who had no recourse to original minute books.

The Irish Golfing Guide 1916 also records 1888 as the club institution date and also states: "The Thomastown golf club has been closed since the beginning of the War''. An entry in *The Golfers Handbook* 1923 proves that the club was revived, it records: "Secretary A. Brown, 9 holes. Station Thomastown (1½ miles)''. Listings for the club appear later in *Thoms Directory* 1940 and 1946 and *The Golfers Handbook* 1963. The last named Honorary Secretary in 1963 was P. Norton, Jerpoint West, Thomastown. There were nine holes and the course was half a mile from the railway station. Subsequent history of the club is unknown, if it had survived Thomastown G.C. would have been one of the oldest golf clubs in the South of Ireland.

THURLES, Co. Tipperary.
Instituted 1909. Affiliated 1909.

Unfortunately, the early minute books of this club have been mislaid, consequently the origins of the club are unclear. Luckily the first Honorary Secretary forwarded material to the editor of *The Golfing Annual* and in the 1909/10 edition the club is documented for the first time. An institution date of 1st January 1909 is listed, there were 75 members at the time (i.e. early in 1910), the Captain was R. H. Spratt and the Hon. Secretary was S. R. Thorp, Railway Cottage, Thurles . . . "the course of nine holes is a mile and a half from Thurles Station. Sunday play''. The annual subscription was one guinea for men and ten shillings and six pence for ladies. Earlier, *The Irish Field* 9th September 1909 had recorded the affiliation of the new club to the Golfing Union of Ireland.

Entries for the club appear in *The Irish Golf Guides* from 1910 to 1916 with similar detail regarding the course location. The club records the following locations for its course — 6 holes at Loughtagalla, 9 holes at Leugh, 12 holes at Dovea from 1929 to 1943, Turtulla since 1943. *Thoms Directories* give the following information re the club: 9 holes 1932, 18 holes 1935, 18 holes 1940. It is clear that the course had been nine holes until extended between 1932 and 1935.

In *Irish Golf* January 1944, Lionel Hewson wrote: "Once I laid out a nine-hole course on a pleasant site at Thurles. It was a pleasant visit and led to an excellent lunch at the College with Fr. O'Connor as host. Now it is good news to hear that the club has bought Turtulla House and lands for £6,000 . . . the old course and some of the newly acquired land will be sold''.

TIPPERARY, Co. Tipperary.
Instituted 1896.   Affiliated 1906.

Tipperary Golf Club is first listed in *The Golfing Annual* 1896/97 which gives 25th January 1896 as the date of institution. President of the club was Lt. Gen. Dunham-Massy, Captain was T. E. Willington and there were sixty members . . . ''The course, of nine holes, is very hilly, and there are plenty of natural hazards. On account of the grass, the course is more a winter than a summer green. Tipperary Station is distant half a mile.''

The Golfing Annual 1898/99 recorded, for the first time, that the cup presented by the officers of the East Yorkshire Regiment had been competed for. This regiment was stationed in the local military barracks during 1898 and 1899. The Boer War had a dramatic effect on the club, as *The Irish Golfer* 21st March 1900 recorded: ''The Tipperary club is so depleted through its members having gone to the front that there is great difficulty in keeping up even the name. The Golfing Union of Ireland has made the club an honorary member of the union so long as its members are fighting for their country.''

It would appear that at around this time the club records went astray as *Nisbets Golf Yearbook* 1908 gives an institution date of 1890 for the club. This date, also given in *The Irish Golf Guide Books* 1910 to 1916, is at variance with the consistently reported date of 1896 recorded in the *Golfing Annuals* from 1896 onwards. It is of interest to note that the Mess Records of the 1st Battalion Seaforth Highlanders do not record any golfing activities at Tipperary following their move there. The battalion, who had arrived from Fermoy in October 1893 where they had been actually playing golf, departed in January 1894.

*See Fermoy G.C.

TOOME, Co. Antrim.

The Belfast Newsletter 27th July 1896 reported: ''Toome Club. The opening meeting of this recently formed club was held on 25th inst. . . . the links are on a strip of land which was left dry when Lough Neagh was drained some years ago. Being pure sand it has grown over with short turf similar to seaside courses and in summer when other inland courses are unplayable it is at its best . . . The first ball was driven by Mr. Hugh Adair, Glenavan, Cookstown at 2 o'clock.''

The Golfing Annual 1896/97 lists the club and records 1896 as the institution date but gives no details of Captain or Committee. *The Sportsmans Holiday Guide* 1897 lists a course at Toomebridge and adds some mystery . . . ''a new course is being laid out here close to the shore of Lough Neagh and will consist of nine holes . . . It will be open for play in the Spring of 1897.''

Successive *Golfing Annuals* up to 1906/07 document the club but give no information on Captains or Committee. The club would appear to have been revived in 1909 as *The Golfing Annual* 1909/10 gives that year as an institution date. No names are listed. Finally, *The Irish Golfers Guide* 1910 states "Believed to be extinct".

TRABOLGAN, Co. Cork.

Cork was not short of entrepreneurs in the 1890s and some of them decided to invest in a golf course near Trabolgan as reported in *The Irish Times* 5th July 1896: "New Links For Cork. To meet a long felt want of a seaside course accessible to golfers in the city and County of Cork a syndicate was recently formed who have arranged with Lord Fermoy for a lease of ground for a golf links near Roches Point. The course is within the demesne of Trabolgan and will eventually be extended to 18 holes. Meantime an excellent nine-hole course has been laid out by Anthony Brown, the Royal Dublin professional and clubmaker."

The Belfast Newsletter 9th July 1896 also noted this new development and stated: "When the greens have been brought into condition the links will be excellent for testing play . . . when the membership justifies the expenditure, a suitable clubhouse with bedrooms attached will be built. Meantime a clubroom has been secured and arrangements made for board and lodging, as many as 12 or 15 golfers at a time . . . the annual subscription has been fixed at 2 guineas and a limited number will be admitted without entrance fee. The Earl of Bandon has consented to be President."

Nothing further on this venture is recorded.

TRALEE, Co. Kerry.
Instituted 1896.   Affiliated 1907.

Present golfers of this club may be unaware that the first Tralee Golf Club had two courses as early as 1897! *The Golfing Annual* 1896/97 gives 1st October 1896 as the institution date, the first President was F. C. Sandes, Hon. Secretary was S. A. W. Waters, Chute Hall, Tralee, and a Captain's name is not given. There were 120 members paying a subscription of ten shillings. Also recorded is the following detail: "The club have two courses — the one, of nine holes, close to Fenit Station, seven miles from Tralee, and the other of eighteen holes, half a mile from Castlegregory Station, sixteen miles from Tralee. The Fenit course is laid out on a peninsula in Tralee Bay, and is bounded on three sides by the Atlantic. The round extends to one and a half miles and the greens are rapidly getting into trim. The Castlegregory course lies between the seashore and one of the best trouting lakes in Kerry. The round, which extends to two and three quarter miles, bristles with hazards in the form of sandhills and bunkers . . . the only drawback is the distance from town; but no doubt a hotel will be built in time."

The Golfing Annual 1898/99 records two changes. Firstly, the club membership had fallen to 80 and the nine-hole course at Fenit was gone, instead there was now a nine-hole course in the Sportsfield, Tralee. A further change was recorded in *The Irish Times* 1st February 1898: "Mr. Waters tendered his resignation as Honorary

Secretary consequent on his change of residence to Dublin. Mr. Charles Downing was unanimously elected his successor''. It is most likely that the old club gradually faded away after Mr. Waters' departure, *Golfing Annuals* up to 1905/06 list the club but give no details regarding Captains or Committees.

Golf Illustrated 22nd February 1907 in recording the establishment of a ''new'' club at Tralee, confirms the demise of the previous club: ''During the past week we have learned of the establishment of two new clubs. Tralee in Co. Kerry is at last turning its eyes from the scenery to the golf ball. Land has been secured close to the County town; sufficient members (120) have also been enrolled to make the club financially strong. At a public meeting last week the golf club was organised.''

The Golfing Annual 1906/07 also records this as a reconstitution (1907) and the Honorary Secretaries were H. C. Hardy, Clinch Hall and C. F. Downing, Meadowlands, Tralee. This course was within a quarter of a mile of the railway station (*The Irish Golfers Guide* 1910). It is interesting to note that C. F. Downing was the previously listed Hon. Secretary of 1898.

Lionel Hewson told of the next move of the club in his magazine *Irish Golf* January 1944: ''Early visits had been paid but when I laid out the present course times were difficult in this country . . . laying out that course in Oak Park was a little upsetting as men sat around on the demesne walls watching me measuring etc. and bullets used to fly in those days on little provocation.'' Hewson was obviously referring to the ''Troubles'' period and the inferences of his remarks related to a traumatic incident which occurred on the course in 1921 (see Chapter 7). *Irish Life* March 1923 recorded this new venture: ''The Tralee club has been sportingly embarked on an 18 hole course in the pretty Oak Park Demesne . . . Mr. Dan Downing had much to do with the new departure''.

A further move for the club was recorded by Hewson in *Irish Golf* February 1948: ''Tralee Club is making a new course at Lasseugh, having given up the Oak Park one which was my effort in the troubled times. The club has bought the land.'' The club's final move was made in 1984 to its new links course at the Barrow, Ardfert. Designed by the renowned Arnold Palmer, this magnificent new course is on the opposite side of Tralee Bay where the first course was laid out in 1896.

TRAMORE, Co. Waterford.
Instituted 1894.   Affiliated 1905.

The Golfing Annual 1896/97 documents the existence of a Waterford and Tramore Golf Club for the first time in the list of clubs affiliated to the Golfing Union of Ireland. No entry is made for the club in the alphabetical club material. Eventually in *The Golfing Annual* 1902/03 an institution date of 1892 is given for this club. However, an entry in *Through The Green Isle* by Mr. J. Hurley published in 1896 refers to the ''recently established golf club'', from this a foundation date of 1894 is accepted by the club.

For the first time, an entry for the club appeared in *The Irish Times* 15th April 1896: ''This club has secured the services of David Herd of St. Andrews, not the least distinguished member of a well known golfing family . . . it is expected that Waterford golfers will improve very much in their style of play by his presence among them for the next six weeks . . .''

The Irish Times 2nd January 1897 carried a report which gave details of a recent tragedy which had befallen the club: "On St. Stephen's Day the members of this club held their first meeting since the disastrous storm of last September (1896) which ruined their clubhouse and completely covered some of the best greens with shingle. However new holes have been made and the course altered. In a short time the links will be as good as they were before the inundation." After this, it would appear that the club went into decline and was revived. *The Irish Times* 1st January 1902 reported: "The first a.g.m. of the recently revived Tramore Golf Club took place in the Grand Hotel, Tramore, on Monday . . . on the resuscitation of the old club in October 1900 the course which was laid by Herd in 1892 and which was altogether destroyed by the severe gales of 1896, was adhered to as much as the circumstances would permit . . . the course is situated on the Burrow, the golf club house, last green and first tee being only a stone's throw from the Grandstand of the well known racecourse . . . The course is on land belonging to Mr. Martin J. Murphy J.P. . . . at a rent of nothing a year." Later that year *The Irish Times* 25th October 1902 reported a move by the club: "Tom Hood of Royal Dublin has been here for the last few days laying out a new eighteen-hole course and he thinks it will be amongst the best in Ireland". According to *The Golfing Annual* 1902/03 this course was within half a mile of Tramore station.

An entry in *The Irish Field* 16th May 1908 gives the first hint of the origins of golf at Tramore: "Mr. Burke, the present General Manager of the National Bank had a great deal to do with the starting of golf at Tramore, as he and his son used to play there as far back as 1891, though no attempt at a course. Then Tom Hood of Dollymount laid out a course which was neither nine or eighteen holes, but something between. Commander Buchard R.N. next took up the running of the links and the first real match was played on 31st December 1899 . . . The club was started in all seriousness in 1904." It is clear that the writer had not been well briefed on the local club's history, as there are numerous contradictions in the report. Once again the difficulties for a historian are illustrated; however, there is one germ of truth relating to the originator of golf at Tramore. *The Golfers Guide* 1897 records Mr. William Lambert Burke, Manager, National Bank, Waterford, as Treasurer for that year. Most probably he was the "founding father" of the club mentioned in *The Irish Field* article.

The later *Irish Golf Guides* give 1904 as the club institution date, which is clearly inaccurate, even for a reconstitution date. *The Irish Golfing Guide* 1911 lists a nine-hole "sea course", and the following year *The Irish Golfing Guide* 1912 records another tragic episode in the club's history: "A new course has been laid out by Willie Park, owing to the inroads of the sea on the old course. The new course promises well and commands beautiful views of sea and land". This new links, which was close to the racecourse, remained the club's home until 1936.

The Irish Golfers Blue Book 1939 reported that it had been decided to construct a new eighteen-hole course in 1937: "The new links designed by Capt. H. L. C. Tippet, Walton Heath, has been constructed on 130 acres of natural golfing country".

TRIM, Co. Meath.
Instituted 1900.   Affiliated 1970.

An article on the County Meath Golf Club in *The Irish Golfer* 17th February 1904 recorded the beginning of golf at Trim: "The surrounding countryside, on the whole, from its rich pastoral quality is unsuitable for golf, and it was not until Mr. Devereux Emmet, an enthusiastic American golfer came to reside temporarily in the locality that the present links were discovered . . . (he) saw that within minutes walk from the town a tract of light land . . . of ample area for a nine-hole course . . . He at once laid it out, and after arranging with the tenant invited his friends to share the privilege. Soon the present club was established and it is now in a flourishing condition . . . It may be interesting to note that the links are within what was formerly the glebe lands of Laracor, Dean Swift's Parish, as are Stella's Cottage and the remains of the Dean's House."

The Golfing Annual 1903/04 lists the club for the first time under the Co. Meath title and gave an institution date of September 1900, Mr. J. C. Hanbury was Captain. A move to a new location at Oakstown is recorded in *The Golfing Annual* 1904/05. There were 61 members and Mr. Hanbury was still Captain. This gentleman is credited with being Captain of the club from its foundation until 1905. The foundation date given in the *Golfing Annuals* is contradicted by the *Irish Golf Guides* from 1910 to 1916 which give 1898. A change in name to Trim Golf Club is recorded in *The Irish Golfing Guide* 1916.

In 1925 the club ceased to function due to a general lack of interest in the sport, this was followed by a revival in 1934 when Mr. A. J. Malone was installed as Captain. The revived club played over a course at Doestown, two miles from Trim. However, difficulties beset the club sixteen years later and the club closed once again in 1950 due to lack of interest.

Finally, in 1968, Mr. Peter McConville initiated moves to revive golf at Trim and following a public meeting in September 1968 a 54-acre farm was purchased for £13,000. £6,000 of this sum had been provided by local people in the form of interest-free loans. A nine-hole course was laid out by Mick McGuirk from County Louth and the Captain, C. J. Tyrrell (who had been Captain in 1950), had the pleasure of opening the new course in July 1971.

TUAM, Co. Galway.
Instituted 1904.   Affiliated 1907.

Credit for the introduction of golf to Tuam is given to James McDonnell, a prominent local businessman, and also to Henry Concannon, a solicitor. They had become acquainted with the game while in Harrogate on holidays in 1903, brought clubs and balls back with them and commenced the game locally. This is confirmed in *The Irish Golfer* 9th November 1904 which records the founding of Tuam Golf Club: "James MacDonnell gave use of ground at Cloonasgragh Hill free". Shortly afterwards *The Irish Field* 26th November 1904 reported: "The Tuam Golf Club is now fairly launched . . . the course has been carefully laid out . . . many influential people in the neighbourhood too are interesting themselves in the welfare of the club amongst others Colonel Nolan who is a brother of Sebastian Nolan, the owner of Galway links (see Galway) and well known to the Irish Turf.''

The Golfing Annual 1906/07 lists the club for the first time and gives an institution date of October 1904. At this time there were sixty members. Later, The Irish Golfers Guide 1910 recorded that a new clubhouse was being erected, a sign of solid progress. Cloonascragh remained the club's home, as a nine-hole course, until 1937. In 1938 the club moved to Mayfield, remaining there until 1975. Barnacurragh became the present home in 1975, when a nine-hole course was laid out. This was extended to eighteen in 1978.

Present Tuam golfers will be interested to note that the visitor's book of the Royal Belfast Golf Club was signed by James McLean, Tuam, on 22nd April 1890. This would indicate very early interest in the game by a local.

TULLAMORE, Co. Offaly.
Instituted 1896. Affiliated 1899.

The official brochure of Tullamore Golf Club published in 1935 states: "Golf was introduced into Tullamore in the year 1886 by Colonel R. A. Craig, when on a visit to the Rectory. A few holes in a field on the Geashill Road represented the first links in the neighbourhood, and there Colonel Craig and a few friends drove their gutty balls with the old fashioned clubs of the period . . . After a short time they changed the scene of operations to the fields near the ruin behind the Distillery, where they were joined by a few military officers . . . The next move was to Tinnycross. A small club was formed and a regular course was made — a very rough and hilly affair, but productive of good fun for a couple of years. At the end of that time move number 3 was effected to the racecourse at Ballykilmurry, where a pleasant little nine-hole course was laid out and a small pavilion erected.''

The Irish Times 12th May 1896 reported an interclub match between the Tullamore and Banagher golf clubs: ". . . a few days ago over the links of the Tullamore club at Ballykilmurry. Though the weather was inclement, the play was watched with much interest by a number of visitors". Banagher won by 31 holes to nil. It is of interest to relate this entry with the historical account carried in the 1935 brochure. It will be noted that a club had been formed when they were at Tinnycross and this would have been some years before 1896 when The Irish Times account places the club at Ballykilmurry. There would seem little doubt that the club was formed some time before 1896.

There is no entry for the club in the Golfing Annuals until the 1900/01 edition, which does not give a date of institution but lists W. Morton, H.M. Prison, Tullamore, as the Honorary Secretary. The club appears in subsequent editions until 1906/07 when the Captain's name is listed, for the first time, as J. W. E. Dunsterville.

The present club records a revival date of 6th March 1906, due to a lapse of interest in the game for some years previous to that date. This is verified by The Golfing Annual 1907/08 which also reported the course of nine holes was three miles from the town. The 1906 course was of nine holes on land given rent free by Captain Briscoe at Screggan. This was the club's home for the next twenty years. An interesting entry in The Irish Field 20th July 1921 described the course at the time of the Anglo-Irish War: "The longest hole at Tullamore is 396 yards, the length of the nine holes being 2,509 yards. Though on the short side the course does not lack interest . . . An Honorary Officer of the club thought he would motor out the three miles to the course when the Truce was declared. Owing to trenched roads etc. the speedometer registered 23 miles by the time the course was reached". During the ensuing Civil War, the golf club was singled out for attention and *The Irish Field* 2nd September 1922 recorded the destruction of the clubhouse by arson. (This was also the fate of Douglas G.C.).

The Irish Field 29th August 1925 reported: "I hear that at Brookfield only a couple of miles from the town the club can get sufficient land at reasonable rent to lay out 18 holes". The club brochure takes up the story at this point: ". . . a site nearer Tullamore, was needed, too, and this was found in Brookfield, which largely through the efforts of Mr. Henry F. Brenan, was secured from Lady Bury . . . a new links (18 holes) was planned and constructed by Captain Hewson (*Irish Golf*) whose name is a household word in golfing circles. He was ably assisted by Mr. J. S. McCall of the club, who spared no effort."

TULLOW, Co. Carlow.
*See Aghade G.C.

TYRONE, Omagh, Co. Tyrone.
The Irish Golfers Guide 1910 records: "A new club is being formed at Omagh under the above (Tyrone) title. Mr. F. Crawford, Omagh, is Secretary. Mr. G. L. Baillie, Belfast, has laid out a course which he thinks will prove satisfactory." Previously, *The Irish Field* 2nd October 1909 reported: "A club has been formed at Omagh. Captain Auchinlech has agreed to give a suitable course . . . The club to be named Tyrone Golf Club . . . Captain Auchinlech was elected President, Mr. F. Shields Captain and Mr. F. Crawford Honorary Secretary."

It would appear that this was the inauguration of the present Omagh Golf Club; *The Irish Golfers Guide* 1910 also recorded the existence of an Omagh Golf Club, with an institution date of 1892: "The club exists for the benefit of members and friends and is run on modest lines".

*See Omagh Golf Club.

UNIVERSITY COLLEGE DUBLIN.
Instituted 1931.   Affiliated 1931.
Lionel Hewson wrote in *Irish Golf* January 1945: "UCD was possessed of a golf club before the last war. Professor J. N. Meehan and the venerable Professor W. D. O'Kelly were prime movers in starting it and I rather think that Michael Smyth now surgeoning in London, was the first Honorary Secretary. There were only a dozen or so in the Society and one of the original lot was J. B. McArevey . . . The Hermitage Golf Club very kindly fixed up the Society members at a guinea each . . .

Committee meetings were held at 86 St. Stephens Green where some strange things happened . . .''

Golfing Union of Ireland records reveal an institution date of 1931 with affiliation in the same year.

VALENTIA, Co. Kerry.

This club is first documented in *The Golfing Annual* 1906/07 which gives an institution date of November 1906. The annual subscription was ten shillings and there were 60 members . . . ''The course of nine holes, is two and a half miles by boat and car from Valentia Harbour Station . . .'' That the Honorary Secretary's name was mispelled as F. S. Rill, Reenglas, Valentia Island is clear from later *Irish Golf Guides*. Ladies are listed as members in the *Golfing Annuals* from 1907 to 1910, subscription 5/-.

The Irish Golfers Guide 1910 gives 1907 as the institution date and names the Honorary Secretary as F. Spring Rice. Further detail is also given: ''Eighteen tees have been made so as to vary the 2nd nine. Summer play has been most restricted hitherto from long grass. No sheep are on the land at present which is what is required to keep it playable throughout the year''. This *Guide* also records that the course was situated on the property of the Knight of Kerry.

Later, *The Irish Field* 5th February 1927 recorded: ''Valentia Island is one of the most ungetatable places in the South and yet the game flourishes there. Indeed, no later than last week Bernard Daly of the Tralee Club went out there on invitation to lay out a new course to take the place of the old one, which had existed for many years.''

The Irish Tourist Directory 1937 lists a nine-hole course at Valentia. *Thoms Directory* 1940 also lists the course, the 1946 edition recorded G. H. Edmond of the Cable and Wireless Station as Hon. Secretary of the nine-hole course. Its subsequent history is unknown.

WARRENPOINT, Co. Down.
Instituted 1893.   Affiliated 1894.

Warrenpoint Golf Club is listed in *The Golfing Annual* 1894/95 for the first time, the date of institution is given as 1893. There were 75 members, the President was Major Hall and the Captain was Colonel Cattell . . . ''The course of nine holes is one minutes walk from Warrenpoint Railway Station. There are plenty of hazards in the shape of roads, ditches and hedges. There is a good clubhouse.''

The club is listed in the various golfing annuals until 1897. *The Golfing Guide* 1897 gives 1892 as the institution date. Around this time it would appear that the club suffered a setback, an article in *The Irish Times* 4th November 1898 reported: ''The opening meeting of the above new club (Warrenpoint Club) was held yesterday, T. J. Marron with the useful handicap of 20 made the round of 18 holes in the nett score of 81 and was declared the winner. The Great Northern Railway Company and the Irish Highlands Hotel Co. have generously subscribed £50 each towards the formation of the club, which has added a new and principal attraction to Warrenpoint.''

The revival of the club is confirmed in *The Golfing Annual* 1898/99 which gives an institution date of June 1898. The Captain at this time was G. H. Alderdice . . . "The course of eighteen holes, is within 3 minutes walk of Warrenpoint Station and adjoins the demesne of Captain Hall".

Once more the club would appear to have encountered difficulties, as subsequent *Golfing Annuals* fail to record the club until the 1904/05 edition which gives 1905 as the date of institution and . . . "The course is being laid out on land belonging to Captain Hall D.L., J.P.". *The Irish Golfer* 15th February 1905 recorded that a meeting had been held to try and revive the game at Warrenpoint and *The Irish Times* 9th June 1905 carried an account of the opening of the lately formed club.

The Irish Golfers Guide 1910 recorded that the nine-hole course was five minutes walk from the station, which would indicate that from its inception in 1893 the course was located very close to its original site. The Hall family were, also, very closely associated with the institution and revivals of the club. In 1925 the course was extended to eighteen holes under the direction of Lionel Hewson.

WATERFORD, Co. Waterford.
Instituted 1912.   Affiliated 1912.

A perusal of the early *Irish Golf Guides* will fail to reveal any mention of Waterford Golf Club; however, the history of the club is well documented by the club in its souvenir brochure for the 25th Anniversary Waterford Crystal Scratch Tournament. When the first club was formed at Tramore in the early 1890s it was named the Waterford and Tramore Golf Club, which would indicate that there was a strong element from the County town involved in the origins of that club.

The first meeting to form a local town club at Waterford itself was held on 8th March 1912 in the Imperial Hotel. Mr. H. J. Forde is credited with the idea of starting the club and he chaired the founding meeting, at which he was able to state that suitable land was available at Mount Misery for £35 per year. As a result the Waterford Golf Club was formed. At a formal meeting on 29th March 1912 the provisional committee reported that 47 acres had been rented. An election took place to fill the positions of officers and committee and the rules of the new club were read and adopted. The first President was Mr. A. E. Graves, the Captain was H. Tooms and Honorary Secretary was A. E. Walker.

Cecil Barcroft, Secretary of Royal Dublin, was invited to lay out the new course. (Barcroft was on the Leinster team which won the first Interprovincial match versus Ulster in 1896 and was Captain of Dublin University G.C. in 1897 and also of Dungannon the same year). The plan was submitted in April 1912 and work commenced. Late in 1912 the committee decided to call in Willie Park of Musselburgh. Park had won the British Open in 1887 and 1889 (the last year in which the championship was played over the historic old Musselburgh course).

This newly-designed course was opened in July 1913, stretching over 3,000 yards. *The Irish Golfers Blue Book* 1939 recorded that in 1935 it was decided to extend to 18 holes and one of the most prominent golf architects and former golfing great, James Braid, was invited to design the additional nine holes. (Braid won the British Open five times, the last occasion being the 1910 event at St. Andrews).

WATERFORD & TRAMORE, Co. Waterford.
*See Tramore G.C.

WATERVILLE, Co. Kerry.
Instituted 1902. Affiliated 1925.

The Sportsmans Holiday Guide 1897 lists a course at this picturesque Kerry resort: "There is a private course here consisting of nine holes, pleasantly situated on Innystrand. To the north are sand dunes, and on the other sides bog or moorland. The green is considered a sporting one and the views from it are very fine while the Atlantic breezes that blow across it are invigorating and refreshing. The hazards are such as are usually to be met on seaside courses . . . Golf owes it origin in this part to the exertions of the Rev. J. G. Fahy, the Rectory, who first introduced it, and during the summer season it forms no slight addition to the native charms of Waterville . . . owing to the course being a private one, a small charge is made to visitors per round."

Later, *The Golfing Annual* 1904/05 records a golf club here, for the first time: "Waterville G.C. . . . There is a golf course here". *The Irish Golfer* 26th November 1902 recorded that "in December 1901 these links were laid out by James McKenna, professional attached to Carrickmines".

Later, *The Golfing Annual* 1906/07 records A. Holt, Waterville as Honorary Secretary of the club: ". . . the course consists of nine holes. Visitors one shilling a day". For the first time, an institution date of 1902 is given in *The Irish Golfers Guide* 1910 which also recorded that the "nine hole sea course" was one mile from the village. Mr. A. Holt continued as Honorary Secretary and the President was the Marquis of Lansdowne.

The Irish Golfing Guide 1916 names new officers for the first time, the President was D. Herbert, Waterville; Captain was William Jones and the Honorary Secretary was A. Duffield. Further detail was ". . . Fine natural links, with splendid clubhouse, situated among the sandhills on Ballinskelligs Bay . . . a considerable sum has been spent in improving these fine natural links. A spacious clubhouse has been built."

Waterville Golf Club currently gives a foundation date of 1925, however *The Golfers Handbook* 1923 lists an entry for the club, the Hon. Secretary's name was A. G. Lawrence. Sunday play was optional on the nine-hole course and the green-keeper was P. O'Reilly. The present course was laid out in the early 1970s by the eminent Irish golf architect Eddie Hackett, when a full eighteen was brought into play. Modern Waterville golfers should feel very grateful to Rev. Fahy for his keenness and foresight way back in the 1890s.

WEST CARBERY, Skibbereen, Co. Cork.
*See Skibbereen and West Carbery G.C.

WEST CLARE, Miltown Malbay, Co. Clare.
*See Spanish Point G.C.

WESTPORT, Co. Mayo.
Instituted 1908.   Affiliated 1927.

Westport Golf Club is first listed in *The Irish Golfers Guide* 1910, which gives an institution date of 1908. The course was nine holes . . . "2½ miles from Westport Station". A. G. Simpson, Bank of Ireland, Westport, was the Hon. Secretary/Treasurer and the Captain was W. H. Darley Livingstone. There were 70 members. The *Irish Golf Guides* for 1911 and 1912 record the same names as Captain and Hon. Secretary, which would indicate that they were also the inaugural officers of the club. There was no entry for Westport in the 1914 or 1916 *Guides*, it is possible the club became defunct with the outbreak of World War One.

In 1926 the club was restarted when a nine-hole course was opened at Carraholly, 3½ miles North of Westport. *The Irish Golfers Blue Book* 1939 listed eighteen holes for the club. Finally, in 1973, the club moved one mile to its present eighteen-hole championship course, now considered one of the premier courses in the country. The Irish Close Championship was held there in 1977 and 1985.

WHITEHEAD, Carrickfergus, Co. Antrim.
Instituted 1904.   Affiliated 1905.

The initial letter dated 27th July 1904 circulated to residents of Whitehead, notifying them of a meeting on 29th July, was signed by J. McLaughlin, J. Waterson, W. Martin J.P. and F. Koeller. The club is fortunate to possess its original minute books and the inaugural meeting is well documented. Among the officers elected were Col. James McCalmont M.P. as President and James Waterson as first Captain.

For some reason, the official opening of the club's first course did not take place for nearly one year and the current records of the club do not mention the exact location or number of holes laid out. However, all is revealed in *The Irish Golfer* 28th June 1905 which contains a very lengthy article on the inauguration of the new course: "The links are situated at no great distance from Blackhead, the lighthouse on the promontory standing out conspicuously. . . . considering the limited time during which Messrs. Morrow and son have been engaged in bringing the ground to order, very good progress has been made. . . . The nine-hole course is partly uphill for the first three or four holes and there are sufficient difficulties in the form of hedges and ravines. . . . Mr. R. B. Urquhart, Belfast, erected the handsome pavilion which adorns the grounds and which provides ample accommodation for both ladies and gentlemen."

A full list of the attendance is given in the account, with included details of the opening competition, won by T. McKeagu with a nett of 93. The ladies putting competition was won by Mrs. Chapman; it is clear from the article that a ladies club formed part of the original club as the lady Captain named was Mrs. Smiley of Belair and the Marchioness of Donegall was Lady President. *The Irish Golfer* article recorded the official opening as follows: "On behalf of the club Dr. Martin then presented to Col. McCalmont, a handsome silver mounted cleek, with which the gallant member drove off the first ball amid much cheering.''

The Golfing Annual 1905/06 recorded: ''The course of nine holes is a short distance from Whitehead station and commands a splendid view of the sea''. The annual subscription was one guinea for men and ten shillings and sixpence for ladies.

In 1909 the course was moved to the Marquis of Donegall estate where it remained until 1936 when the club moved once more to Bentra. This was a nine-hole course designed by James Braid. In 1973 the present course at Muldersleigh was developed and the eighteen holes were opened in 1974.

WICKLOW, Co. Wicklow.
Instituted 1904.   Affiliated 1906.

A perusal of the early *Golf Guides* will give contradictory institution dates for this club. *The Golfing Annual* 1905/06 lists the club for the first time, with an institution date of 1904 and Captain Harrington as Captain. Mr. T. A. Tombe was Hon. Secretary and the nine-hole course ''(circuit 2400 yards) is on the high lying coast towards Wicklow Head, about a mile from Wicklow Station''. Later, the *Irish Holiday Guides* from 1910 to 1916 record 1905 as the year of foundation.

An article in *The Irish Field* 30th May 1908 gives a comprehensive account of the formation of the club the previous year, which would indicate 1907 as the date of institution. Lionel Hewson wrote: ''. . . walking out on the first tee one is faced by a magnificent view, stretching right away to the Hill of Howth . . . The first thing that strikes one is the bravery of those who were responsible for making the course. The difficulties must have been well nigh inconceivable, and Mr. W. O'Shaughnessy told me this was the case, as dense furze covered the whole course. He remarked that Mr. H. Toppin, the former D.I. at Wicklow, and the present Secretary Mr. T. A. Tombe were primarily responsible for the commencement of the club, but I fancy Mr. O'Shaughnessy had a finger in the pie also. . . . Last year, 1907, a meeting was called, and subscriptions taken. Lord Fitzwilliam and two other gentlemen took debenture shares to all amount large enough to buy the land and the building which is now the clubhouse . . . as before remarked, the gorse covered ground required herculanean labour to clear it and in 1907 it was always necessary to have a forecaddie to watch the balls. The fact that I enjoyed many rounds without losing a ball testifies to the clearance that has been effected. Mr. Toppin the D.I., with an unfailing supply of matches was largely responsible for a good deal of the clearance . . . The course (of nine holes) was laid out by Tom Hood of Dublin . . . membership 120 . . . Sunday play with caddie allowed . . .'' It would appear that this *Irish Field* account referred to a move by the club in 1907, the *Golfing Annuals* from 1906 to 1910 confirm 1904 as the year of institution.

This same *Irish Field* article records the Earl of Wicklow as club President and Mr. T. A. Tombe, Rossanagh Cottage, Rathnew, as Hon. Secretary. No Captain's name is given.

From an early date the attractions of golf at Wicklow were advertised widely, *Golf Illustrated* 28th January 1910 carried an article on the course listing its merits for visiting golfers.

WOODBROOK, Co. Wicklow.
Instituted 1920.   Affiliated 1921.

Golf at Woodbrook owes its origins to Sir Stanley Cochrane, of mineral water fame. Cochrane was an enthusiastic sportsman and because of his wealth was able to develop first-class cricket facilities at his residence, near Bray. Some of the top international cricket teams played here in the years before the First World War. Sometime after 1912 a private course was laid out at Woodbrook, where Sir Stanley used to entertain his friends. The inspiration for Sir Stanley's interest in golf is credited to Brian Brooks-Alder who became his private secretary later.

The present Woodbrook Golf Club date themselves from 1921, however *Irish Life* 5th November 1920 carries an account of the club's institution: "A meeting was held at Woodbrook, Bray on Thursday at which it was decided to form the Woodbrook Golf Club. The rules submitted to the meeting were adopted and the following officers were elected. President Sir Stanley H. Cochrane Bart. D.L.; Captain Richard P. Pim; Honorary Secretary and Treasurer George Revell, 7 Galtrim Road Bray. The meeting appointed a committee and elected a number of members. The Woodbrook course is situated on most favourable ground. It commands a glorious view of the sea and mountain. It is one of the longest nine-hole courses around Dublin. . . . Woodbrook must no doubt be regarded as a proprietary course but with such an enthusiastic sportsman as President, Woodbrook Club is certain to flourish."

It is interesting to note that the offical club history compiled by Paul MacWeeney states that the club did not affiliate to the Golfing Union of Ireland until 1926, in which year the club became an "open" club. In addition he also states that the first election of officers did not take place until 1927, surely Richard Pim, the first elected Captain in 1920, would feel aggrieved! *The Golfing Union of Ireland Yearbook* 1928 gives 1921 as the club's affiliation date.

WOODENBRIDGE, Co. Wicklow.
Instituted 1897.   Affiliated 1899.

As is common with several other Irish clubs, the origins of golf at Woodenbridge are shrouded in the mists of antiquity. The club claims as its date of institution an 1884 invitation reputed to have been extended by Col. E. A. R. Bayly of Ballyarthur, Woodenbridge, to Sir Stanley Cochrane at Woodbrook House asking if Sir Stanley would field a team of gentlemen to play golf at Woodenbridge. This original letter would no longer appear to exist, however there is no evidence in contemporary or subsequent golf publications to support the claim to an 1884 club institution date.

The club's centenary brochure states: "By 1892, Colonel Bayly found the environs of Ballyarthur too restricted for his pasttime and decided to build a private course ¼ of a mile to the West at Woodenbridge". *The Sportsmans Holiday Guide* 1897 recorded: "A nine-hole course is being laid out in the Vale of Ovoca, rendered famous by Moors 'meeting of the waters'. With the additional attraction which a golf course affords, Woodenbridge should soon rise in fame as a pleasant holiday resort, especially as there is such a good hotel so handy to the station viz the Woodenbridge Hotel".

The club is first documented in the *The Golfing Annual* 1898/99 which gives an institution date of 1st July 1897. All subsequent editions of *The Golfing Annual* also give this date. Vol. XII lists the Honorary Secretary as A. Tailyour, Lamberton, Arklow and there were 50 members. C. E. Day held the "green record" with 34 for the par 33 course . . . "The course of nine holes, varying in length from 92 to 430 yards, is within 100 yards of Woodenbridge Station". The C. E. Day mentioned above was most probably Christopher Day, who had come to Ireland from Musselburgh in 1896 to act as professional at Greenisland. In 1898 he moved to Malone. An article in *The Irish Field* 25th July 1908 credits Tailyour and Day with laying out the course.

In *The Irish Golfer* 3rd October 1900 there is a fine article on the club which commences: "This club was formed about three years ago. The original members numbered only about six or seven. Owing to the kindness of Colonel E. R. Bayly, Ballyarthur, Co. Wicklow, the President of the club, who permitted grounds of his adjoining the Woodenbridge Railway Station to be turned into a golf links, the difficulties attached to the formation of the club were speedily got over. It has improved every year, so that now there are about sixty members. The links, a grassland course, are beautifully situated, bounded on one side by the woods of Ballyarthur and on the other side by the river Ovoca; the greens are carefully kept and the sod on them is considered to be second to none on any inland links in the country."

An article in *The Irish Field* 25th July 1908 confirms 1897 as the institution date: "The club was started in 1897 and owes a great deal to the late Colonel Bayly who did all in powers to further its interests, giving the land free".

WOODVILLE, Lurgan, Co. Armagh.

The Golfing Union of Ireland Yearbook 1928 lists this club, giving an affiliation date of 1918. An entry in *Irish Life* 23rd December 1921 reported that the club had received a handsome cup from its president Lord Lurgan.

It would appear that for a period the Lurgan area enjoyed the facilities of two golf clubs. *The Golfers Handbook* 1923 listed both the Lurgan and Woodville golf clubs, the latter having a membership of 200 and the Hon. Secretary was C. W. Neill. There were nine holes and the course was 5 minutes walk from the station. Entries for the Woodville Club appear in *Thoms Directory* up to 1930, after which only the Lurgan G.C. is listed. The subsequent history of this club is unknown.

*See Lurgan.

YOUGHAL, Co. Cork.
Instituted 1898.   Affiliated 1912.

The origins of golf at Youghal can be traced back before the turn of the century when the *The Sportsmans Holiday Guide* 1897 carried the following: "There is no regular club in Youghal but a course has been laid out by residents and is free to all-comers. It stretches along the sea shore on a soil eminently suitable for the game. A club is in course of formation and by the commencement of the coming season (1897) a proper provision will be made for tourist golfers. The course is about two miles only and consists of nine holes. The hazards consist of intersecting roads, ditches and patches of bushes . . ."

An article in *The Irish Times* 22nd October 1898 recorded the next phase: "A meeting was held in the Town Hall Youghal on Thursday evening for the purpose of forming a golf club, suitable links having been found close to the railway station and overlooking Youghal Bay. In the absence of the Earl of Shannon, the chair was taken by Mr. H. F. Allen J.P. and a committee was appointed to carry out the objects of the club. The Rt. Hon. Earl of Shannon was appointed President. His Excellency Sir Henry Blake Vice President; Mr. S. Sealy Allen Hon. Sec.; and Mr. A. B. Graves, Hon. Treasurer."

An entry for the club is first given in *The Golfing Annual* 1898/99 without institution date. The 1906/07 edition gives a foundation date of 1888 which is clearly an error for 1898. A match against a team from "Little Island" is documented in *The Irish Times* 21st April 1900. The Cork team had a close victory by one hole. In the years following it would appear that the club went into decline, *The Irish Golfers Guide* 1910 reported: "Youghal has, we believe, a six hole course".

Following a meeting held in the Mall House on 20th March 1911, chaired by Mr. R. Carey, Chairman of Youghal U.D.C., *The Irish Field* 2nd July 1911 reported: "Youghal now possess a nine-hole course and comfortable clubhouse". Affiliation of the club to the Golfing Union of Ireland was noted by *The Irish Field* 27th January 1912. An entry from the club appears in the 1932 edition of *Thoms Directory*, there is no listing in the *G.U.I. Yearbooks* between 1935 and 1939. The club was reaffiliated to the Union in 1940, probably after a revival.

Early Irish Golf

CHRONOLOGICAL INDEX OF CLUBS AND COURSES

NOTES TO APPENDIX 2

1. Entries in italics signify establishment of course only.

2. Entries with * signify year of affiliation to Golfing Union of Ireland, actual year of institution unknown.

3. Entries with ° signify a local legend for existence of a course.

1606:   *Newtownards.*
1762:   Bray.
1852:   *Curragh* (D. Ritchie).
1858:   *Curragh* (J. Gourlay, professional), *Portmarnock.*
1875:   *Curragh* (Revival by 91st Highlanders).
1881:   Royal Belfast.
1883:   Curragh, *Fota,*° *Kinsale.*
1884:   Phoenix Park (Military), *Woodenbridge.*°
1885:   Royal Dublin.
1886:   *Cavan,*° *Mornington, Tullamore.*°
1888:   Aughnacloy, Portrush, *Sutton.*
1889:   *Dooks,*° *Kilkee,* Queens Co. Heath, Royal Co. Down.
1890:   Dublin Scottish, Dungannon, Killymoon, Shanes Park.
1891:   Ballycastle, Belmont, Fortwilliam, *Leopardstown,* Limerick, Lisburn, North West, *Omagh,* Portsalon, The Island, Thomastown.
1892:   Athlone Garrison, *Carrickfergus,* Co. Louth, Greencastle, Lahinch, Lismore, Malahide, Mallow, Monaghan, Nenagh, Newry, Omagh, Roscrea, Rostrevor, Rushbrooke.
1893:   Bandon, Birr (Kings Co. and Ormond), Bushfoot, Co. Armagh, Fermoy, Foxrock, Killarney, Lurgan, Ormeau, Otway, Stillorgan, Warrenpoint.
1894:   *Ballinasloe,* Banagher, Bundoran, Cork, Co. Cavan, Co. Sligo, Dublin University, Greenisland, Larne, *Letterkenny,* Mullingar, Newborough, Portadown, Portmarnock, Portstewart, Rathconey, Tramore.
1895:   Abbeyleix, Ballinrobe, Blackrock (Rochestown), Caragh Lake, *Claremont Hotel,* Clonakilty, *Derrynane,* Dooks, Dromore, Galway, Greystones, Knock, Malone, Massereene, Rosapenna.

1896:   *Ardfert*, Ardglass, Ballybunion, Coleraine, Dufferin, Enniskillen, Greenore, Helens Bay, Kilkee, Kilkenny, *Magilligan, Midleton*, Naas, Saintfield, Spanish Point, Sutton, Tipperary, Toome, Trabolgan, Tralee, Tullamore.

1897:   Bray, *Carrick*, Corick, Courtmacsherry, Derrynane, *Dunfanaghy*, Ennis, Kinsale, Moor of Meath (Lucan), Muskerry, Newmarket, *Renvyle, Waterville*, Woodenbridge, *Youghal.*

1898:   Ardara, Newport, Youghal.

1899:   Carlow, Donaghdee, *Garron Tower*, Rathfarnham.

1900:   Adare, Carrickmines, Castlerock, Co. Longford, Killaloe, Moate, *Royal Hospital*, Trim.

1901:   Bantry, St. Anne's Hill.

1902:   Athenry, Atlantic, Cahir, Killiney, Kirkistown Castle, Waterville.

1903:   Bangor, Kenmare.

1904:   Ballymena, Dundalk, Fintona, Holywood, Newtownbarry, Roscommon, Tuam, Whitehead, Wicklow.

1905:   Castlerea, Ballinasloe, Dunmurry, Hermitage, New Ross, Rosslare, Skerries, Skibbereen.

1906:   Aghade, Athy, Channel Fleet, Dunfanaghy, Durrow, Enniscorthy, Gorey, Lisdoonvarna, Mount Bellew, Valentia.

1907:   Borris, Ferbane and Moystown, Livery Hill, Milltown, Navan, Portumna, Queens University Belfast, Scrabo, Spa.

1908:   Ballyshannon, Delgany, Kilmashogue, Milford, Monkstown, Portarlington, Riverside, Westport.

1909:   Charleville, Douglas, Dun Laoghaire, Laytown and Bettystown, Midleton, *Mulrany*, Stillorgan Park, Strabane, Thurles.

1910:   Athgarvan, Bagenalstown, Ballina, Carrick-on-Shannon, Castlebar, Castleknock (extinct), Derryvale (extinct), Edenderry, Grange, Mitchelstown, Omagh (see 1892), Robin Hood.

1911:   Ardee, Boyle, Cliftonville,* Clonmel, Finglas, Howth, Market Hill,* *Tandragee.*

1912:   Carrickmacross,* Cashel, City of Derry, Clontarf, Waterford.

1913:   Banbridge, Castle, Clones, Dunmore.

1914:   Balmoral, Fethard, Newtownstewart.

1915:   Bessbrook,* Cullybrackey,* Inchydoney* (see Clonakilty).

1916:   Craigs Park,* Rossmore.

1917:   Nil.

1918:   Claremorris, *Enniscrone*, Woodville.*

1919:   Nil.

1920:   Bunclody,* Cill Dara, Kilrea,* Tandragee, Woodbrook.

1921:   St. Anne's.

1922:   Balla,* Bellinter Park (Royal Tara), Coolattin, Cuan,* Enniscrone, Killua Castle, Swinford.

BIBLIOGRAPHY

BOOKS:
A Genealogical History of the Family of Montgomery. Emilia G. S. Reilly (1842).
A History of Golf, The Royal and Ancient Game. Robert Browning. Dent (1955).
Balfour. Max Egremont. Collins (1980).
Early Golf. Steven J. H. Van Hengel. Van Hengel (1982).
Edward VII, Prince and King. Giles St. Aubyn. W. M. Collins & Co. Ltd. (1979).
Fifty Years of Golf. Andra Kirkaldy. T. Fisher Unwin Ltd. (1921).
Five Open Champions and the Musselburgh Golf Story. George Colville. Colville Books
  1980.
Golf: A Royal and Ancient Game. Robert Clark. Mac Millan 1893 (2nd Edition).
Golf in the Making. Ian T. Henderson and David I. Stirk. Henderson and Stirk Ltd.
  (1979).
Golfiana Miscellanea. James Lindsay Stewart. Hamilton, Adam & Co. (1887).
Guinness Book of Golf Facts and Feats. Donald Steel. Guinness Superlatives Ltd. (1982).
In The Winds Eye History (History of N. Berwick G.C.). Alistair Beatson. Adamson
  (1980).
Irish Horse Racing. John Welcome. Gill and Macmillan (1982).
King Edward The Seventh. Sir Philip Magnus. John Murray (1964).
Muirfield and the Honourable Company. George Pottinger. Scottish Academic Press Ltd.
  (1972).
Prestwick Golf Club, A History and Some Records. James E. Shaw. Jackson Son & Co.
  (1938).
Reminiscences of Golf at St. Andrews Links. James Balfour. David Douglas (1887).
Royal Blackheath. Ian T. Henderson and David I Stirk. Henderson and Stirk Ltd. (1981).
Seventy Years Young. Elizabeth Countess of Fingal. Collins (1937).
The Chief (Life Story of Baden Powell). Eileen Wade. Wolfe Publishing Ltd. (1975).
The Chronicle of the Royal Burgess G.S. of Edinburgh — 1735 to 1935. J. Cameron
  Robbie. Morrison Gibb Ltd. (1936).
The Golf Book of East Lothian. Rev. John Kerr. T. & A. Constable (1896).
The Life of Tom Morris. W. W. Tulloch. T. Werner Laurie (1908).
The Montgomery Manuscripts. Rev. George Hill. Archer & Sons (1869).
The Story of the R. & A. J. B. Salmond. MacMillan & Co. Ltd. (1956).
The Troubles. Thames Futura (1980).

PRIVATE PUBLICATIONS:
Centenary Brochure Royal Belfast G.C. (1981).
Centenary Brochure Royal Dublin G.C. (1985).
Centenary Brochure The Army G.C. Aldershot (1983).
History of Royal Musselburgh G.C. 1774-1974. Robert Ironside (1974).
Ransomes, Sims & Jefferies 150th Anniversary Brochure(1982).
Rules & Records of the Officers Mess 72nd Regiment (Seaforth Highlanders). William
Blackwood. (1897).
Royal Cape G.C. Brochure. South African Championship 1985.

NEWSPAPERS:
Sport.
The Belfast Newsletter.
The Cork Examiner.
The Irish Field.
The Irish Independent.
The Irish Times.
The Field.
The Illustrated London News.
(Many local Irish newspaper accounts, as outlined in Appendix 1, were notified by Mr.
G. S. Glover and club secretaries of respective clubs).

PERIODICALS:
Irish Golf.
Irish Life.
The Irish Golfer.
Golf.
Golf Illustrated.

GOLF GUIDE BOOKS:
Irish Golfers Blue Book 1939. J. P. Rooney. Monument Press.
The Golfers and Sportsmans Holiday Guide to Ireland 1897. R. W. Grant. Simpkin,
Marshall, Hamilton, Kent & Co.
The Golfing Union of Ireland Yearbook 1927 to 1986.
The Irish Golfers Guide 1910.
The Irish Golfing Guide 1911, 1912, 1914, 1916.
Golfers Guide Vol. IV. W. H. White & Co. (1897).
The Golfing Annual, (Vol. I) 1887/88 to final edition (Vol. XXIII) 1909/10.

DIRECTORIES:
Burkes Landed Gentry (1937).
Burkes, The Landed Gentry of Ireland (1958).
Complete Peerage. N. Q. Doubleday and Lord. H. de Walden (1936).

Dictionary of National Biography. Oxford University Press.
Encyclopaedia Britannica.
Irish Tourist Directory 1937. Irish Wheelman Printing & Publishing.
Modern English Biography. Boase (1892).
Thoms Directory 1859, 1913, 1930, 1932, 1935, 1940, 1946.

MANUSCRIPTS:
NLI P 770 (16) Pamphlet − The Social State of Ireland 1858.
NLI MSS 11031 − Eglinton Correspondence.
PRO WO 17/1119 to 1122 − Strength Returns Queens Bays 1852 to 1859.
PRO WO 76/457 − Record of Service Maj. A. C. Bruce.
    NLI = National Library of Ireland (Dublin).
    PRO = Public Record Office, Kew, London.

MILITARY SOURCES:

Correspondence with the Regimental Secretaries of the following Regiments (present nomenclature shown in brackets where relevant):

The Blackwatch (Royal Highland) Regiment.

The Highland Light Infantry (The Royal Highland Fusiliers).

The Kings Own Borderers.

The Royal Scots.

The Royal Welch Fusiliers.

Seaforth Highlanders (Queens Own Highlanders).

The Queens Bays (1st The Queens Dragoon Guards).

13th Hussars (13/18 Royal Hussars).

The Army List Quarterly.

Early Irish Golf

GENERAL INDEX

NOTES

1. The General Index lists references to all material in the text of Chapters 1 to 10 and Appendixes 1 and 2.

2. Irish or other golf clubs mentioned in Chapters 1 to 10 are also referenced in the General Index.

3. The Special Index on pages 292 to 300 lists references to all Irish golf clubs, or courses, which are mentioned in Chapters 1 to 10 or Appendixes 1 and 2.

4. Numbers printed in **Bold Type** indicate that a significant entry on the subject material or club is carried on that page.

271 (see Royal Musselburgh G.C.).
Musselburgh Racecourse/Standhouse, 31, 38.

Naas (Co. Kildare) G.C., 103.
Naas, Lord, 22.
National Stud, Irish, 94.
Newbridge, Co. Kildare, 21.
Newcastle, Co. Down, **52, 53**, 61, 69, 110, 238, 239, 240.
Newtownards, 5, 6.
New York, U.S.A., 11, 13.
niblick brigade, 87.
Nolan, Sebastian, 151, 170, 171, 262.
North Berwick G.C., 13, 22, 25, 29, 54, 80, 169.
Northwest G.C., 71, 74, 106, 111, **221, 222**, 228.
Northwest Ladies G.C., 111, 112, 136, 221, 222.

O'Hare, Peter, 211.
O'Neill, Lord, 251.
Open, British (see British Open).
open competitions, 55, 56, 57, 74.
open competitions, ladies, **107, 108**.
Open, Irish Amateur (see Championships).
Ormonde, Marquis of, 183.
Oswald, John, of Dunnikier, 45.

Palmer, Arnold, 260.
Park, Mungo, 169, 229.
Park, Willie Jnr., 145, 181, 185, 261, 266.
Park, Willie Snr., 36.
Percy, J. W., 117.
Petrie, J., 242, 253.
Phoenix Park, 32, 43, 45, 46, 47, 48, 51, 71, 80.
Pickeman, W., 32, **75**, 141, 164, 188, 209, 214, 216, 226, 227, 250, 255.
Plantation of Ulster, Preface, 5, 6.
Plummer, R., 192, 197.
Poetry, 15, 76, 91, 118.
Portarlington, Lord, 225.
Portglenone Cup, 56, 244.
Portmarnock, **31, 32** (see Portmarnock G.C.).
Portrush, **50, 51,** 55, 56, 60, 67, 68, 73, 101 (see Royal Portrush G.C.).
Prestwick G.C., 1, 5, 6, 7, 22, 24, 26, 28, 31, 36, 38, 57.
Price, George, 86, 93.
Prince of Wales (see Edward VII, King).
prisoners of war, **88, 89**.
Professional Championships, Irish, 82, 83.
professional, travelling (see Fernie, G.).
professionals, Irish, **83, 84, 85**.
   See Barrett, J.; Brown, Anthony; Coburn, G.; Curley; Edmundson, J.; Hamill, H.;
      Kidd, H.; Larkin; McKenna, Jas.; McKenna, T. J.; McNamara, J.; McNamara, W.;

Early Irish Golf

SPECIAL INDEX − IRISH CLUBS

ACKNOWLEDGEMENTS

The author is indebted to many individuals for assistance rendered in the preparation of this book. An understanding wife and family were a heartwarming source of encouragement through six years of preparatory work. Without the keen interest of David Lalor, of Thomas Cook Travellers Cheques, this publication could not have been produced in its final form.

Sincere thanks are herewith acknowledged to Douglas Hewat (Captain, Royal Musselburgh G.C., 1983 to 1985) who provided invaluable assistance from the archives of that famous club. George Colville, D.C.M., was a prime source of information on the history of golf at Musselburgh; grateful thanks are extended to him for permission to reproduce photographs and material from his book *Five Open Champions*. R. A. L. (Bobby) Burnett, historian of the Royal and Ancient Golf Club, answered every request with patient efficiency; the archives of this most venerable club contains many items of great historical interest for the Irish golfer. Mr. R. A. Clement (Captain of Prestwick G.C. 1983) provided invaluable photographs and historical detail regarding the origins of that club. Mr. D. L. Pugson of Royal Cape G.C. (South Africa) provided material on Lt. General Sir Henry Torrens.

The author is indebted to Mr. G. S. (Gerry) Glover of Londonderry for all the warmhearted assistance rendered on Ulster golf. The following are also gratefully acknowledged for assistance rendered and permission granted to reproduce photographs and text from their respective club histories: Terence Templeton, Royal Belfast G.C.; Larry Gunning, Royal Dublin G.C.; Ian Bamford, Royal Portrush G.C.; Harry McCaw, Royal Co. Down G.C.; Tim Healy, Portmarnock G.C.

Many club secretaries kindly replied to questionnaires sent by the author; in many instances club brochures or reference material were forwarded. Lt. Col. Mick Tallon (Captain, Athlone G.C., 1986) was most helpful. The Golfing Union of Ireland gave every assistance and the author is indebted to Mr. Des Rea O'Kelly, Honorary Secretary, to Mr. Ivan Dickson, General Secretary, and especially to Mr. Bill Menton for their kind co-operation. All requests for information and access to their archives was provided by the Irish Ladies Golf Union and the author is indebted to Miss Pat Turvey, Secretary, and Mrs. Anne Tunney, Honorary Treasurer, for their assistance and continued interest in the project.

Many fruitful hours were spent in the National Library of Ireland, unfailingly the staff were courteous in answering all demands. The staff of the following institutions provided generous assistance: Public Record Office (Kew), London; National Army Museum, London; British Museum Newspaper Library, London; Linenhall Library, Belfast, and the Public Record Office, Belfast.

The reader will find much material on the military influence in the early years of Irish golf. Regimental Secretaries of the following regiments were specially helpful in providing details of service, photographs and extracts from unit histories: Major Donald Mack, Royal Highland Fusiliers (The Highland Light Infantry); Col. (Retd.) The Hon. W. D. Arbuthnott, M.B.E., The Blackwatch; Lt. Col. P. G. Woods, M.C., The Argyll and Sutherland Highlanders; Lt. Col. D. C. R. Ward, The Kings Own Scottish Borderers; Brigadier (Ret.) D. B. Riddel-Webster, O.B.E., The Cameronians (Scottish Rifles); Norman Holme, Assistant Curator, The Royal Welch Fusiliers; Mr. B. Thirkhill, Regimental Museum, Queens Dragoon Guards (Queens Bays) and, finally, Major (Retd.) E. J. S. Garbutt, 13/18 Royal Hussars.

The author is indebted to Mr. Dermot Gillece of *The Irish Times* who was instrumental in the discovery of Mrs. Christina Adams in July 1982, the grand-daughter of the founder of the first course on the Curragh in 1852. At the age of 89 years Mrs. Adams was a crucial link with the introduction of this favourite Scottish game to Ireland.

Ireland's foremost cartoonist, Martyn Turner, provided invaluable advice and assistance in the preparation of this book. Martyn is a keen member of the Curragh Golf Club and grateful thanks are herewith acknowledged for his witty and perceptive cartoons used in this publication. Without the wholehearted professional interest of Michael Dillon of Newbridge this book would not have seen the light of day in its final form. His advice and expertise are herewith acknowledged. Paul Ennis, a fellow member of the Curragh Golf Club, provided invaluable assistance with the design of the book cover and also with the colour separations. His help was most heartwarming.

Finally, the author thanks the following for their interest and support in this project; the Captain, Committee and members of the Curragh Golf Club; Mr. Seamus Leydon.

Early Irish Golf

POSTSCRIPT

The publication of this book was delayed for over twelve months due to the author's service with the United Nations Military Force in Lebanon. During this time the historian of the Island Golf Club had the good fortune to find an old notebook belonging to a close neighbour of the club. The material in this document provides key information on the founders first visit to the "Hills", the name given to the area by the local inhabitants of Donabate and Malahide.

The notebook relates: "In the Autumn of 1887 four gentlemen were ferried across the river from Malahide to 'The Island'. They were Mr. J. R. Blood, Mr. D. T. Moore, Mr. J. A. Law, Mr. J. R. Briscoe. They spent the afternoon looking over the place and decided it would make an ideal natural golf links. They got in touch with the landlord Mr. Charles Cobbe, grandfather of the present Mr. Tommy Cobbe and had a lease drawn up for I think 50 years at £60 per annum . . . . The formidable task of clearing the rough growth was begun in the early Spring of 1888. Mr. Blood and Mr. Moore came to see my father Michael Horish and asked if he would help with the work . . . ."

The writer, Mr. John Horish, gives further detail on the contemporary flora of the Island, the earliest shelter (a bell tent) and the first clubhouse which was a timber and galvanised iron structure.

The author is indebted to Mr. Bill Murphy and Mr. Wally Skelton of the Island Golf Club for notifying him of the discovery of this material. This club has made strenuous efforts to document its origins and subsequent history. It is sad that so many Irish golf clubs have lost their records, as can be seen from the entries in Appendix I. Hearsay and folklore are poor substitutes for honest endeavour in the local and National Library.

Irish club members will have found much hitherto undiscovered material on the origins of their club in this book. It is the author's earnest wish that some club members will take the initiative to delve further in their local newspaper archives, to document the memories of older members, to collect old and current photographs, to discover old scrapbooks and initiate new ones, to map the development of their course (or courses) and, apart from recording the results of their many club and interclub matches, to record the many humorous incidents which make this wonderful game so popular in Ireland.